CONTENTS

Introduction

There is no record in history of when man first started to bake, but we can assume his first effort was a flat bread cooked over or near a flame or on a hot rock. We do know from primitive picture writings that many ancient civilizations baked something described as honey cakes. Barley flour was much in use during these early periods, as well as eggs, dates, and honey. With these four ingredients, it is quite possible honey cakes were the first cookies.

Jumping forward to the early Europeans, we find every developing country has its particular cookie—or, in Germany the *kek*; in Holland, the *koekie*; in Italy, the *focaccina*; in Spain, the *galletas*, and across the Channel in England, the biscuit. One unusual fact stands out: The colder the climate, the greater the variety of cookies created.

England and Scotland, with their tradition of high tea, advanced the making of cookies to an art form. The British refer to their sweet treats as biscuits, and most of their biscuits are not-too-sweet, plain, small cookies. They may be eaten on their own but are usually served with tea or coffee.

In America, our cookie-baking traditions evolved from the early settlers. Our word *cookie*, in fact, comes from the Dutch, *koekie*. The British influence over this country in pre-revolutionary days turned what was a *koekie* into a "biscuit." Then in revolutionary times, our ancestors rejected most things British and called the biscuit a wafer.

Cherished European cookie recipes came to this country with millions of immigrants. Many of those treasured cookies were named for nationalities or national regions, such as Grenze Keks (Swiss Border Cookies). They were handed down from mother to daughter, from aunt to niece, from friend to friend. Thus a recipe that started out as Grenze Keks soon became known as Pricilla's Charms or Mrs. Smith's Favorite Cookies.

The number of different cookies is so large that we sometime forget they are just just combinations of flour, sugar, fat, and eggs. These four ingredients are the foundations of the cookie, although you can make cookies using just two of these items; for example, meringues are made from just egg whites and sugar. With the addition of chocolate, fruits, spices, and other flavorings, the possibilities for variation are endless.

In this book, I present the best from a collection of baking information developed over forty to fifty years. The recipes were accumulated by my father, also a baker, and myself. Some are original, and have never been made public before; and some are our versions and adaptations of classic recipes. Many of the recipes, especially those from other countries, date back to before 1900. And others were written on bits and pieces of paper and handed to us by friends, relatives, and even casual acquaintances. Ultimately, this is the definitive collection, in that, if you are looking for a cookie recipe, there is no need to look anywhere else.

In this collection, I have tried to put together recipes that represent all the most popular cookies. In cases where the recipes were similar or even identical, I had to disregard many so-called original cookie formulations. (With brownie recipes alone, in fact, fifty-three were exactly the same as others I had already selected—identical, that is, in all except name.) When recipes were almost identical—e.g., one uses a quarter teaspoon of salt, the other used no salt—I baked both and chose the one I liked best. But with recipes that were almost identical, but the basic flavoring was different, I chose to include all my favorites. Thus you will find several listings for brownies, for example, or for chocolate chip cookies. The basic cookie may be similar, but the flavoring enhancers or additives contribute sufficiently to the taste or texture to result in a different cookie.

This is not the collection for you if you are merely looking to impress your guests with fancy decoration. I don't tell you how to make a house out of cookie dough. Instead this cookbook is for those who just want to make good, simple cookies at home. It is for you and your family, cookies to eat and cookies to give as gifts. Nothing more! This collection is designed to be *used*—day after day, year after year.

INGREDIENTS FOR A BASIC COOKIE

The basic ingredients needed to make a simple cookie are flour, sugar, fat in one form or another, and, often, eggs. Baking powder and/or baking soda may be included, as may be salt. Proportions will vary from recipe to recipe and substitutions will be made; butter will be used in one recipe, vegetable shortening in another. Honey may be the sweetener rather than sugar. To change the taste and flavor of a basic cookie, we turn to the wide array of spices and other flavorings available. Here is a recipe for a basic cookie, which yields 4 to 5 dozen. Use this recipe later in the book when a basic cookie mixture is called for and embellish the flavor with additional ingredients.

DO EVERYTHING COOKIES
3 cups all-purpose flour
1 ½ cups granulated sugar
4 whole eggs
¾ teaspoon baking powder
¼ teaspoon salt

Flour, sugar, eggs, baking powder, and salt are there. But I omitted the shortening and added caraway seeds for a distinctive flavor. If you don't like the flavor of caraway seeds, you can add anise seeds, chocolate chips, or raisins, or add a liquid flavoring, such as vanilla or almond extract or liqueur. Finely chopped nuts could be added to the dough or sprinkled over the tops of the cookies. Add cocoa powder or powdered instant coffee to the dough—or sift cocoa or powered sugar over the tops of the cookies.

In this collection there are hundreds of similar simple recipes that can be adapted to make a cookie with the ever-so-specific taste you want. From the dozens and dozens of recipes in this book, you can go on to create hundreds more. With the recipes, knowledge, and information presented here, you will be able to give your family, your neighbors, and your friends any type of cookie they may desire.

UTENSILS

Baking pans For cookie baking, I would recommend that you have baking pans of the following sizes: 8-inch square, 9-inch square, 13 by 9-inch, 15 by 10-inch, 17 by 11-inch, 12 by 8-inch shallow baking pan. You will find that throughout the book the yields give a range. These numbers are based on whether you cut bar cookies into large or small bars.

Baking sheets/cookie sheets Have at least two baking sheets so you can be filling a sheet while the first is in the oven. If your oven is large enough to allow good heat circulation, you can bake two trays at once. The sheets should be bright and shiny, and they should fit in your oven leaving enough room all around the edges for heat to circulate between the baking sheets and the oven walls. Although some people argue that flat sheets, without lips or sides, result in more even baking, others believe that rimmed baking sheets are just as effective. (And just about all bakeries use rimmed baking sheets.)

Bowl scraper A rectangle of rubberized plastic, about the size of a 3 by 5-inch index card with one slightly rounded edge, is extremely handy in the kitchen.

Cookie cutters The variety of cookie cutters available is almost without end. Visit a few garage sales-you will probably find cookie cutters in all sizes and shapes: round, square, rectangular, octagonal, oblong, crescent, diamond, tree, flower, animal—I've even seen a dog bone shape. It's nice to have all sorts of styles, but I find a set of round cookie cutters to be particularly valuable. These sets come in round boxes, each containing six cutters of graduated sizes (or seven—if you would even use the box itself as a cutter). They range in size from 1/2 to 3 inches. Other collections, such as one of small animals, about the size of animal crackers, are fun to own, too.

Cookie molds Cookie molds used to be more popular, but specialty cookware stores often have a wide selection of large and small molds for gingerbread men, birds, flowers, and Santa Clauses. For the most part, the use of cookie molds has remained a European tradition. A springerle rolling pin is another utensil used to mold cookies. These pins, available in various designs and sizes, are rolled over rolled-out dough to imprint it and mark it into cookies. Actually, almost anything in your kitchen—or your house—can be used as a cookie mold. Be imaginative.

Cookie press/pastry bag A cookie press is an efficient way to deposit soft cookie dough directly onto baking sheets. There are a wide variety of tips available for pressing out cookies, and most cookie presses come with a set of eight to ten tips or plates for forming different shapes. Some bakers prefer to pipe out soft doughs using a pastry bag. The best pastry bags are made of canvas and coated on the inside with plastic; and large bags are much more practical than small ones. Some come with a set of tips and a coupling attachment, or you can buy these separately in good housewares shops.

Cooling racks These wire racks allow air to circulate around cookies as they cool, preventing them from getting soggy. You'll want at least two racks.

Flour sifter A sifter is handy for sifting powdered sugar or even brown sugar, as well as flour.

Large spoons Large wooden spoons are preferable to those made of plastic or metal; I like to keep at least three large spoons at hand.

Measuring cups Good measuring cups may be the most important purchase you make for the kitchen. If the measuring cups you use are inaccurate, you will never get good results in baking. You need both a set of dry measuring cups (I like to have at least two sets of these) and at least a 1-cup glass measure for liquids. Larger sizes can be handy to have. Do not use liquid measuring cups for dry ingredients, or vice-versa—the measurements will not be accurate.

Measuring spoons Measuring spoons can make the difference between success and failure of any baked product you make. Buy the best set you can afford.

Metal whisk Useful for combining dry ingredients, whipping egg whites, and stirring a cooked custard.

Mixing bowls Invest in a good set of mixing bowls, either ceramic or stainless steel. (Plastic tends to absorb odors and becomes difficult to clean.) Most professional bakers prefer stainless steel bowls: they don't rust, they are easy to clean, and they certainly don't break. A set of three to five different sizes is most practical.

Pastry blender A wire pastry blender is convenient but not a necessity; a fork or two knives can be used effectively for cutting the butter or another fat into flour.

Pastry Brush A fine-bristle pastry brush is an absolute must for spreading on egg washes, glazes, or melted butter. You can also purchase good quality 1/2-inch or 1-1/2 inch fine-bristle paintbrushes. Avoid using brushes with nylon bristles, as they will melt when used with hot liquids.

Rubber spatula Large rubber spatulas with wooden handles are useful for a multitude of kitchen tasks.

HINTS FOR COOKIE BAKING

1. Always read a recipe at least once before you attempt to make it.

2. Be sure to allow adequate time for the oven to preheat before you begin baking.

3. For the very delicate butter-type cookies, it is best to use butter to grease the cookie sheets.

4. When measuring liquids, read the measure at eye level.

5. An electric mixer will give cookies a more even texture than hand-beating.

6. To cream any mixture by hand, use the back of a large wooden spoon and beat until the mixture is soft and smooth.

7. Butter should always be creamed until it is light and fluffy before the sugar is beaten into it.

8. Unless otherwise stated in the recipe, all baking powder will be double-acting type.

9. Unless otherwise specified in the recipe, all of the ingredients should be at room temperature.

10. When separating eggs, do not break them over the ingredients you have already placed in the mixing bowl. Always crack them one at a time into a clean bowl.

11. Egg whites that are to be beaten should always be at room temperature.

12. When beating egg whites, make sure the bowl and beaters are immediately clean and free of any grease or oil. Copper and ceramic bowls are better than aluminum and plastic.

13. Roll a lemon back and forth on a countertop, pressing down with your hand; it will release more juice.

14. When measuring honey molasses, or corn syrup, lightly grease or oil the inside of the measuring cup first; the liquid will run out of the cup easily making the measurement more accurate.

15. To make chopping sticky dried fruit easier, heat the knife or food chopper blades before using them.

16. To keep fruits and nuts from settling to the bottom of baked goods, dredge them in flour before adding them to any mixture.

17. To clean utensils used for dough and other mixtures containing flour, use warm water, not hot.

18. When deep-frying cookies, do not overcrowd the deep fryer, or the cookies will absorb oil and be greasy.

19. Chilled dough is usually easier to handle when making rolled cookies.

20. When making rolled cookies, cut as many cookies as possible the first time the dough is rolled out; the dough dries out a little more every time it is rerolled.

21. Any smooth drop-cookie dough can be piped out using a pastry bag or cookie press.

22. If you are baking only one sheet of cookies at a time, place the rack in the center position. If you are baking two sheets at a time, remember that those on the rack closest to the heat have the greatest chance of browning or burning; rotate the baking sheets once or twice if necessary.

23. Use a wide spatula to transfer cookies from the baking sheets to wire racks to cool. Don't overlap the cookies, or they will stick to each other as they cool.

24. Let the baking sheets cool before reusing them.

25. Most cookie doughs and baked cookies can be stored in the freezer for 4 to 6 weeks. Double-wrap the dough or cookies and carefully label each package with the name of the cookie and date.

Abernathy Biscuits

ROLLED COOKIES

YIELD: 2 to 3 dozen
TOTAL TIME: 30 minutes

1. Preheat the oven to 375 degrees.

2. In a large bowl, combine the flour, sugar, and baking powder. Cut in the shortening until the mixture resembles coarse crumbs.

3. In another bowl, beat the eggs, milk, caraway seeds, and lemon zest until well blended. Blend into the dry ingredients until smooth. If the dough seems too stiff, add a little more milk 1 teaspoon at a time.

4. On a floured surface, roll out the dough ¼ inch thick. Using a 2-inch round cookie cutter, cut out cookies and place 1½ inches apart on ungreased baking sheets.

5. Bake for 7 to 10 minutes, until the edges are lightly browned. Transfer to wire racks to cool.

Baking notes: Sweet creams or a lemon sugar frosting can be drizzled over the tops of these cookies, or they can be served plain at teatime with jam or preserves. For variation, this dough can be rolled out to a thickness of ⅛ inch and used to make sandwich cookies. The filling can be melted chocolate or a thick lemon custard. (See Pantry for recipes.)

5½ cups all-purpose flour
1½ cups granulated sugar
1½ teaspoons baking powder
1½ cups vegetable shortening
3 large eggs
3 tablespoons milk, or more if needed
3 tablespoons caraway seeds
1½ teaspoons grated lemon zest

Afghans

FORMED COOKIES

YIELD: 3 to 4 dozen
TOTAL TIME: 30 minutes

1. Preheat the oven to 350 degrees.

2. Place the chopped dates in a small cup and cover with the boiling water for 10 to 15 minutes. Drain and discard the liquid.

3. Combine the flour, cocoa, and baking powder.

4. In a large bowl, cream the vegetable shortening and sugar until light and fluffy. Stir in the dates. Beat in the vanilla extract. Gradually blend in the dry ingredients. Fold in the cornflakes.

5. Break off walnut-sized pieces of the dough and roll into balls. Place 1½ inches apart on ungreased baking sheets.

6. Bake for 12 to 15 minutes, or until firm to the touch. Transfer to wire racks to cool.

Baking notes: The balls can be rolled in finely chopped nuts before baking. They can also be dredged in powdered sugar after baking, but these are quite sweet, so taste one before you decide to roll them in sugar.

⅓ cup pitted dates, chopped fine
½ cup boiling water, or more to cover dates
1 cup all-purpose flour
¼ cup unsweetened cocoa powder
1 teaspoon baking powder
¾ cup vegetable shortening
¼ cup granulated sugar
1 teaspoon vanilla extract
2 cups cornflakes

ALMOND BARS I

YIELD: *2 to 3 dozen*

TOTAL TIME: *35 minutes*

½ cup all-purpose flour
¼ teaspoon baking powder
2 large eggs, separated
Pinch of salt
1 cup packed light brown
*   sugar*
1 teaspoon vanilla extract
⅓ cup butter, at room
*   temperature*
1 cup almonds, ground
Powdered sugar for dusting

1. Preheat the oven to 350 degrees. Lightly grease and flour a 9-inch square baking pan.

2. Combine the flour and baking powder.

3. In a large bowl, beat the egg whites with the salt until foamy. Gradually beat in the brown sugar. Beat in the vanilla extract. Blend in the flour mixture.

4. In another bowl, beat the egg yolks and butter until well blended.

5. Gradually fold the butter mixture into the egg-white mixture. Fold in the almonds.

6. Press the dough evenly into the prepared pan. Bake for 20 to 25 minutes, or until the top is a golden brown. Cool in the pan on a wire rack.

7. Dust with powdered sugar and cut into large or small bars.

ALMOND BARS II

YIELD: *1 to 2 dozen*

TOTAL TIME: *30 minutes*

CRUST
1 large egg yolk
1 teaspoon vanilla extract
1 cup vegetable shortening
½ cup granulated sugar
½ cup packed light brown
*   sugar*
2 cups all-purpose flour

TOPPING
9 ounces milk chocolate,
*   chopped*
½ cup almonds, chopped

1. Preheat the oven to 350 degrees. Grease a 9-inch square baking pan.

2. To make the crust, in a medium bowl, beat the egg yolk until thick and light-colored. Beat in the vanilla extract.

3. In a large bowl, cream the vegetable shortening, granulated sugar, and brown sugar. Beat in the egg yolk. Gradually blend in the flour. The dough will be stiff.

4. Press the dough evenly into the prepared pan. Bake for 18 to 20 minutes, or until the top is golden brown.

5. Meanwhile, melt the chocolate in a double boiler over low heat, stirring until smooth. Remove from the heat.

6. Spread the melted chocolate over the top of the warm cookies. Sprinkle with the almonds. Cool in the pan on a rack before cutting into large or small bars.

Baking notes: The chocolate can be baking chocolate, chocolate chips, or a candy bar. For variation, use white chocolate. For a stronger almond taste, use almond extract in place of the vanilla extract.

Almond Bars III

BAR COOKIES

YIELD: 3 to 4 dozen
TOTAL TIME: 45 minutes

1. Preheat the oven to 375 degrees.

2. To make the crust, combine the flour, powdered sugar, coconut, and salt. Cut in the vegetable shortening until the mixture resembles coarse crumbs.

3. Spread the mixture evenly in an ungreased 13 by 9-inch baking pan. Bake for 12 minutes, until light-colored.

4. Meanwhile, make the topping: Prepare the frosting mix according to the package directions. Stir in the coconut, almonds, and almond extract.

5. Sprinkle the chocolate chips over the top of the warm cookies. Let sit for 1 to 2 minutes, or until melted, then spread the chocolate evenly over the cookies. Spread the frosting mixture over the chocolate.

6. Cool in the pan on a rack before cutting into large or small bars.

Baking notes: You can use all shredded or all flaked coconut, but the two types together give more varied texture to the cookies.

CRUST
1 cup all-purpose flour
½ cup powdered sugar
½ cup shredded coconut
¼ teaspoon salt
½ cup vegetable shortening

TOPPING
1 package white frosting mix
½ cup flaked coconut
½ cup almonds, chopped
½ teaspoon almond extract
½ cup (3 ounces) semisweet chocolate chips

Almond Bars IV

BAR COOKIES

YIELD: 2 dozen
TOTAL TIME: 50 minutes

1. Preheat the oven to 350 degrees. Grease a 13 by 9-inch baking pan.

2. To make the crust, combine the flour and baking powder.

3. In a large bowl, cream the butter and brown sugar. Blend in the dry ingredients. Fold in the chopped almonds.

4. Press the mixture evenly over the bottom of the prepared pan. Bake for 10 minutes.

5. Meanwhile, make the topping: In a large bowl, beat the eggs until foamy and light-colored. Beat in the corn syrup and almond extract. Blend in the brown sugar, flour, and salt.

6. Pour the topping mixture over the warm crust. Sprinkle the chopped almonds over the top.

7. Bake for 30 minutes longer, or until a toothpick inserted in the center comes out clean. Cool in the pan on a rack before cutting into large or small bars.

CRUST
1⅓ cups all-purpose flour
½ teaspoon baking powder
⅓ cup butter, at room temperature
½ cup packed light brown sugar
¼ cup almonds, chopped

TOPPING
2 large eggs
¾ cup light corn syrup
1½ teaspoons almond extract
¼ cup packed light brown sugar
3 tablespoons all-purpose flour
½ teaspoon salt
¾ cup almonds, ground

ALMOND BITS

FORMED COOKIES

YIELD: 6 dozen
TOTAL TIME: 30 minutes

2 cups all-purpose flour
1 teaspoon baking powder
¾ teaspoon ground
  cardamom
1 teaspoon ground
  cinnamon
½ teaspoon salt
½ cup vegetable shortening
½ cup granulated sugar
½ cup packed light brown
  sugar
1 large egg
1 teaspoon almond extract
60 whole blanched almonds

1. Preheat the oven to 350 degrees.

2. Combine the flour, baking powder, spices, and salt.

3. In a large bowl, cream the vegetable shortening and both sugars. Beat in the egg and vanilla extract. Gradually blend in the dry ingredients.

4. Divide the dough into 4 pieces. Roll each piece into a 15-inch-long rope. Cut each rope into 1-inch-long pieces.

5. Press an almond into each cookie, and place 1 inch apart on ungreased cookie sheets.

6. Bake for 12 to 14 minutes, until the edges are golden brown. Transfer to wire racks to cool.

ALMOND CAKES I

DROP COOKIES

YIELD: 4 to 5 dozen
TOTAL TIME: 30 minutes

2 cups all-purpose flour
½ teaspoon baking powder
1 cup vegetable shortening
½ cup granulated sugar
2 teaspoons ground ginger
½ teaspoon almond extract
About 60 whole blanched
  almonds

1. Preheat the oven to 350 degrees.

2. Combine the flour and baking powder.

3. In a large bowl, cream the vegetable shortening and sugar. Beat in the ginger and almond extract. Gradually blend in the dry ingredients.

4. Drop the dough by teaspoonfuls onto ungreased baking sheets. Flatten each cookie slightly with the back of a spoon dipped in flour. Press an almond into the center of each cookie.

5. Bake for 12 to 15 minutes, until the cookies are a nice golden brown. Transfer to wire racks to cool.

Baking notes: The ginger flavor will be more noticeable if the dough is refrigerated for 24 hours before baking. Melted almond bark or chocolate can be drizzled over the tops of the cooled cookies if desired.

ALMOND CAKES II

FORMED COOKIES

YIELD: 5 to 6 dozen
TOTAL TIME: 30 minutes

2 large eggs
1 cup granulated sugar
½ teaspoon vanilla extract
1 cup almonds, ground
1 cup all-purpose flour

1. Preheat the oven to 400 degrees. Lightly grease 2 baking sheets.

2. In a large bowl, beat the eggs until thick and light-colored. Beat in the sugar and vanilla extract. Beat in the almonds. Gradually blend in the flour.

3. Break off 1-inch pieces of dough and roll into balls. Place 2 inches apart on the prepared baking sheets.

4. Bake for 8 to 10 minutes, or until a light golden color. Transfer to wire racks to cool.

Baking notes: The balls of dough can be flattened and a half a glacé cherry or a nut pressed into each one before baking. Or, the cookies can be dipped in melted chocolate after they have cooled.

ALMOND CAKES III

ROLLED COOKIES

YIELD: 4 to 5 dozen
TOTAL TIME: 30 minutes

1. Preheat the oven to 350 degrees. Lightly grease 2 baking sheets.

2. Combine the flour and baking powder.

3. In a large bowl, beat the eggs until thick and light-colored. Beat in the brown sugar. Beat in the almonds. Gradually blend in the dry ingredients.

4. On a lightly floured surface, roll out the dough ¼ inch thick. Using cookie cutters, cut into shapes and place 1½ inches apart on the prepared baking sheets.

5. Bake for 10 to 12 minutes, until the edges are golden brown. Transfer to wire racks to cool.

3 cups all-purpose flour
1½ teaspoons baking powder
5 large eggs
1½ cups packed light brown sugar
1 cup almonds, ground

ALMOND-COFFEE DELIGHTS

BAR COOKIES

YIELD: 1 to 3 dozen
TOTAL TIME: 50 minutes

1. Preheat the oven to 350 degrees. Lightly grease a 9-inch square baking pan.

2. To make the crust, combine the butter, powdered sugar, egg yolks, coffee, and water in a large bowl and beat until smooth. Blend in the flour. The mixture should be crumbly. If necessary, add a little more flour.

3. Press the mixture evenly over the bottom of the prepared pan. Bake for 20 minutes.

4. Meanwhile, make the filling: Melt the chocolate chips in a double boiler over low heat, stirring until smooth. Let cool slightly.

5. In a large bowl, beat the egg whites with the salt until frothy. Gradually beat in the sugar and beat until stiff peaks form. Fold in the melted chocolate. Fold in the almonds.

6. Spread the filling over the hot crust. Sprinkle the chopped almonds over the top. Bake for 20 minutes longer, until topping is set. Cool in the pan on a rack before cutting into large or small bars.

CRUST
½ cup butter
3 tablespoons powdered sugar
2 large egg yolks
1 teaspoon instant coffee granules
1 tablespoon warm water
2 cups all-purpose flour, or more if needed

FILLING
½ cup (3 ounces) semisweet chocolate chips
2 large egg whites
Pinch of salt
¼ cup granulated sugar
¼ cup almonds, ground
¼ cup almonds, chopped

ALMOND COOKIES I REFRIGERATOR COOKIES

YIELD: *4 to 5 dozen*

TOTAL TIME: *35 minutes*

CHILLING TIME: *1 hour*

½ cup vegetable shortening
½ cup butter, at room
*   temperature*
2½ cups all-purpose flour
1¼ cups granulated sugar
½ teaspoon baking soda
¼ teaspoon salt
1 large egg
½ teaspoon almond extract
½ cup almonds, ground
¼ cup ground almonds
4 ounces semisweet
*   chocolate, chopped*

1. In a large bowl, cream the vegetable shortening and butter. Blend in 1 cup of the flour. Beat in the sugar, baking soda, and salt. Beat in the egg and almond extract. Gradually blend in the remaining 1½ cups flour and the ground almonds.

2. Roll the dough into a 1-inch-thick log. Roll the log in the ground almonds. Wrap in waxed paper and chill for 1 hour.

3. Preheat the oven to 350 degrees.

4. Cut the dough into ¼-inch-thick slices and place 1 inch apart on ungreased baking sheets.

5. Bake for 8 to 10 minutes, until the tops are very light golden brown. Transfer to wire racks to cool.

6. Melt the chocolate in a double boiler over low heat, stirring until smooth. Dip half of each cookie in the melted chocolate. Let cool on wire racks lined with waxed paper.

ALMOND COOKIES II BAR COOKIES

YIELD: *2 to 3 dozen*

TOTAL TIME: *60 minutes*

CRUST
1⅓ cups all-purpose flour
2 teaspoons baking powder
½ teaspoon salt
⅓ cup vegetable shortening
1 cup granulated sugar
2 large eggs
2 teaspoons almond extract
1 cup flaked coconut

TOPPING
1 tablespoon all-purpose
*   flour*
½ cup packed light brown
*   sugar*
1 large egg
¼ cup evaporated milk
½ cup almonds, chopped

1. Preheat the oven to 350 degrees. Lightly grease a 9-inch square baking pan.

2. To make the crust, combine the flour, baking powder and salt.

3. In a large bowl, cream the vegetable shortening and sugar. Beat in the eggs and almond extract. Gradually blend in the flour mixture. Fold in the coconut.

4. Press the mixture evenly over the bottom of the prepared pan.

5. To make the topping, combine all the ingredients in a medium bowl and beat until well blended. Spread the topping evenly over the prepared crust.

6. Bake for 35 to 40 minutes, until the topping has set. Let cool in the pan on a rack before cutting into large or small bars.

Almond Cookies III

FORMED COOKIES

YIELD: *2 to 3 dozen*
TOTAL TIME: *30 minutes*

*1 cup butter, at room
 temperature*
⅔ cup granulated sugar
3 large egg yolks
*½ cup almonds, ground
 fine*
½ teaspoon almond extract
*½ teaspoon fresh lemon
 juice*
2½ cups all-purpose flour

1. Preheat the oven to 400 degrees.

2. In a large bowl, cream the butter and sugar. Beat in the egg yolks. Beat in the almonds, then beat in the almond extract and lemon juice. Gradually blend in the flour.

3. Place the dough in a cookie press or a pastry bag fitted with a star tip. Press or pipe out the dough onto ungreased baking sheets, spacing the cookies about 1 inch apart.

4. Bake for 10 to 12 minutes, until lightly colored. Transfer to wire racks to cool.

Almond Cookies IV

REFRIGERATOR COOKIES

YIELD: *8 to 9 dozen*
TOTAL TIME: *30 minutes*
CHILLING TIME: *4 hours*

2 cups all-purpose flour
*¾ cup almonds, ground
 fine*
*½ teaspoon ground
 cinnamon*
½ teaspoon ground cloves
½ teaspoon ground nutmeg
½ cup vegetable shortening
½ cup granulated sugar
1 large egg
1 teaspoon almond extract
*½ teaspoon grated lemon
 zest*

1. Combine the flour, almonds, and spices.

2. In a large bowl, cream the vegetable shortening and sugar. Beat in the egg and almond extract. Beat in the lemon zest. Gradually blend in the dry ingredients.

3. Divide the dough into 4 pieces. Roll each piece into a log about 6-inches long. Wrap in waxed paper and chill in the refrigerator for at least 4 hours, or overnight.

4. Preheat the oven to 350 degrees. Lightly grease 2 baking sheets.

5. Cut the dough into 1¼-inch-thick slices and place 1 inch apart on the prepared baking sheets.

6. Bake for 6 to 8 minutes, or until the cookies are light golden brown. Transfer to wire racks to cool.

Almond-Cherry Cookies

ROLLED COOKIES

YIELD: *4 to 5 dozen*
TOTAL TIME: *30 minutes*

½ cup vegetable shortening
1 cup granulated sugar
1 large egg yolk
½ teaspoon lemon extract
½ teaspoon almond extract
*½ teaspoon grated orange
 zest*
1¼ cups all-purpose flour
*½ cup almonds, ground
 fine*
*25 to 30 glacé cherries,
 halved*

1. Preheat the oven to 350 degrees.

2. In a large bowl, cream the vegetable shortening and sugar. Beat in the egg yolk, almond extract, and lemon extract. Beat in the orange zest. Gradually blend in the flour.

3. On a floured surface, roll out the dough ¼ inch thick. Using cookie cutters, cut into shapes. Dredge the cookies in the ground almonds and place 1¼ inches apart on ungreased baking sheets.

4. Press a glacé cherry half into the center of each cookie.

5. Bake for 12 to 15 minutes, until the cookies are golden brown. Transfer to wire racks to cool.

Baking notes: For a different look, omit the ground almonds and sprinkle colored sugar crystals over the cookies as soon as they come from the oven.

YIELD: *2 to 3 dozen*

TOTAL TIME: *35 minutes*

1¼ cups all-purpose flour
½ teaspoon baking powder
¼ teaspoon salt
½ cup butter, at room temperature
½ cup powdered sugar
⅓ cup almonds, ground

ALMOND CRESCENTS

FORMED COOKIES

1. Preheat the oven to 350 degrees.

2. Combine the flour, baking powder, and salt.

3. In a large bowl, cream the butter and powdered sugar. Gradually stir in the flour mixture. If the dough is very stiff, add a little water ½ tablespoon at a time. Fold in the almonds.

4. Break off small pieces of dough and form into crescent shapes. Place 1-inch apart on ungreased baking sheets.

5. Bake for 8 to 12 minutes, until lightly colored. Transfer to wire racks to cool.

Baking notes: This dough may also be rolled out on a floured surface and cut into shapes with cookie cutters. Remember that a soft dough makes the most tender cookies, so don't use too much flour for rolling.

YIELD: *3 to 4 dozen*

TOTAL TIME: *30 minutes*

CHILLING TIME: *4 hours*

1¾ cups all-purpose flour
1 teaspoon cream of tartar
⅛ teaspoon salt
½ cup vegetable shortening
¾ cup granulated sugar
2 large eggs, separated
½ teaspoon almond extract
1½ teaspoons baking soda
1½ teaspoons warm water
2 tablespoons milk
¼ cup almonds, ground
Granulated sugar for sprinkling

ALMOND CRISPS I

REFRIGERATOR COOKIES

1. Combine the flour, cream of tartar, and salt.

2. In a large bowl, cream the vegetable shortening and sugar. Beat in the egg yolks and almond extract.

3. Dissolve the baking soda in the warm water and add to the egg yolk mixture, beating until smooth. Add the milk, beating until smooth. Gradually blend the dry ingredients. Fold in the almonds.

4. Roll the dough into a log about 2 inches in diameter. Wrap in waxed paper and chill for at least 4 hours.

5. Preheat the oven to 375 degrees.

6. Cut the dough into ⅛-inch-thick slices and place 2 inches apart on ungreased baking sheets.

7. In a medium bowl, beat the egg whites until stiff but not dry. Brush the cookies with the beaten whites and sprinkle with sugar.

8. Bake for 10 to 12 minutes, until lightly colored. Transfer to wire racks to cool.

Baking notes: For variation, roll the log of dough in additional ground almonds before chilling.

ALMOND CRISPS II

ROLLED COOKIES

YIELD: 4 to 5 dozen
TOTAL TIME: 35 minutes
CHILLING TIME: 24 hours

1. Combine the flour and baking powder.

2. In a large bowl, cream the vegetable shortening and sugar. Beat in the egg and rum. Stir in the almonds and lemon zest. Gradually blend in the dry ingredients.

3. Cover the dough and chill for at least 24 hours.

4. Preheat the oven to 325 degrees.

5. Divide the dough into 4 pieces. Work with one piece at a time, keeping the remaining dough refrigerated. On a lightly floured surface, roll out the dough ⅛ inch thick. Using cookie cutters, cut into shapes and place about 1¼ inches apart on ungreased baking sheets.

6. Combine the sugar and cinnamon for the topping and sprinkle over the cookies.

7. Bake for 10 to 12 minutes, until lightly colored. Transfer to wire racks to cool.

3 cups all-purpose flour
½ teaspoon baking powder
1 cup vegetable shortening
1 cup granulated sugar
1 large egg
2 tablespoons rum
½ cup almonds, ground
1 tablespoon grated lemon zest

TOPPING
¼ cup granulated sugar
½ teaspoon ground cinnamon

ALMOND CRISPS III

FORMED COOKIES

YIELD: 12 dozen
TOTAL TIME: 55 minutes

1. Preheat the oven to 350 degrees.

2. Combine the flour and baking powder.

3. In a large bowl, beat the oil, eggs, sugar, and almond extract until thick and light-colored. Gradually stir in the flour mixture and almonds.

4. Divide the dough into 6 pieces. Shape each piece into a loaf about 12 inches long and 1 inch wide, and place on ungreased baking sheets.

5. Bake for 30 minutes. Transfer the loaves to a cutting board and slice on the diagonal, ½ inch thick.

6. Lay the slices on the baking sheets and bake for 15 minutes longer, or until dry. Transfer to wire racks to cool.

4 cups all-purpose flour
2 teaspoons baking powder
1 cup vegetable oil
4 large eggs
1 cup granulated sugar
1 teaspoon almond extract
1 cup almonds, ground

ALMOND CROSTATA

BAR COOKIES

YIELD: 3 to 4 dozen
TOTAL TIME: 60 minutes

CRUST
2½ cups all-purpose flour
2 teaspoons baking powder
¼ cup butter, at room
*   temperature*
¾ cup granulated sugar
2 large eggs
2 tablespoons vegetable
*   shortening*
2 teaspoons rum

FILLING
5 ounces semisweet
*   chocolate, chopped*
2 large eggs
5 tablespoons granulated
*   sugar*
2 teaspoons almond extract
2 cups slivered almonds
1 cup walnuts, chopped
5 tablespoons Amaretto

1. Preheat the oven to 350 degrees. Lightly grease a 13 by 9-inch baking pan.

2. To make the crust, combine the flour and baking powder.

3. In a large bowl, cream the butter and sugar. Beat in the eggs. Beat in the vegetable shortening and rum. Gradually blend in the flour mixture.

4. Divide the dough into 2 pieces, one twice as large as the other. On a floured surface, roll out the larger piece to a 13 by 9-inch rectangle. Fit the dough into the prepared pan.

5. To make the filling, melt the chocolate in a double boiler over low heat, stirring until smooth. Remove from the heat.

6. In a large bowl, lightly beat the eggs. Beat in the sugar. Beat in the melted chocolate and almond extract. Stir in the nuts.

7. Spread the filling evenly over the prepared crust.

8. Roll out the remaining dough to a ¼-inch-thick rectangle. Cut into ½-inch-wide strips and arrange in a lattice pattern over the filling.

9. Bake for 25 to 35 minutes, or until a the lattice strips are golden brown. Sprinkle the Amaretto over the hot cookies. Let cool slightly in the pan on a rack before cutting into large or small bars.

ALMOND DREAMS

DROP COOKIES

YIELD: 3 to 4 dozen
TOTAL TIME: 45 minutes

3½ cups granulated sugar
2 cups almonds, ground
5 large egg whites
1 teaspoon almond extract

1. Preheat the oven to 275 degrees. Line 2 baking sheets with parchment paper.

2. Combine the sugar and ground almonds.

3. In a large bowl, beat the egg whites until stiff but not dry. Fold in the almond extract. Gradually fold in the almond mixture.

4. Drop by teaspoonful 2 inches apart onto the prepared baking sheets.

5. Bake for 25 to 30 minutes, until just starting to color. Transfer to wire racks to cool.

Baking notes: Be sure to beat the egg whites to stiff peaks. Do not use waxed paper to line the baking sheets, or the cookies may stick to the paper.

ALMOND-FLAVORED CRUNCHY COOKIES

DROP COOKIES

YIELD: 2 to 4 dozen
TOTAL TIME: 30 minutes

1. Preheat the oven to 350 degrees. Grease 2 baking sheets.

2. Combine the oats, almonds, and flour.

3. In a large bowl, beat the oil and sugar until smooth.

4. Beat the eggs into the oil mixture, then beat in the evaporated milk and almond extract. Blend in the dry ingredients.

5. Drop by teaspoonfuls 2 inches apart onto the prepared baking sheets. Flatten each cookie with the back of a spoon dipped in flour.

6. Bake for 7 to 10 minutes, until golden brown. Transfer to wire racks to cool.

2½ cups (15 ounces) rolled oats
2 cups almonds, ground
½ cup whole wheat flour
1 cup canola oil
1 cup raw sugar
2 large eggs, beaten
¼ cup evaporated milk
1½ teaspoons almond extract

ALMOND-FRUIT COOKIES

DROP COOKIES

YIELD: 1 to 2 dozen
TOTAL TIME: 35 minutes

1. Preheat the oven to 350 degrees. Grease 2 baking sheets.

2. Combine the oats, all-purpose flour, and soy flour.

3. In a large bowl, beat the oil and brown sugar until smooth. Beat in the eggs, milk, and salt. Gradually blend in the oat mixture. Stir in the apricots.

4. Drop the dough by tablespoonfuls 1½ inches apart onto the prepared baking sheets. Flatten each cookie with the bottom of a glass dipped in soy flour.

5. Bake for 10 to 12 minutes, until golden brown. Transfer to wire racks to cool.

Baking notes: Soy flour can be found in natural food stores and the natural food sections of large supermarkets.

3 cups rolled oats
1 cup all-purpose flour
1 cup soy flour
1 cup canola oil
1 cup packed dark brown sugar
2 large eggs
¼ cup skim milk
¼ teaspoon salt
1 cup dried apricots, chopped fine

ALMOND-FRUIT WREATHS

FORMED COOKIES

YIELD: 2 dozen
TOTAL TIME: 35 minutes

1. Preheat the oven to 325 degrees.

2. In a large bowl, cream the vegetable shortening and brown sugar. Beat in the egg yolks and almond extract. Gradually blend in the flour. Fold in the almonds and candied fruit.

3. Pinch off walnut-sized pieces of dough and roll into pencil-thin ropes. Form the ropes into rings on ungreased baking sheets, placing them 1¼ inches apart, and pinch the ends together.

4. In a medium bowl, beat the egg white and corn syrup until smooth. Brush the rings with the mixture and place a glacé cherry half on each ring at the point where the ends meet.

5. Bake for 18 to 20 minutes, or until the cookies are lightly colored. Transfer to wire racks to cool.

Baking notes: For an even more festive variation, shape the cookies as directed and bake without the cherries. After the cookies have cooled, frost with a white icing and place the cherries on top.

1 cup vegetable shortening
¾ cup packed light brown sugar
2 large egg yolks
1 teaspoon almond extract
2½ cups all-purpose flour
¾ cup slivered almonds
½ cup dried candied fruit, chopped fine
1 large egg white
1 tablespoon light corn syrup
6 to 12 glacé cherries halved

ALMOND HEALTH COOKIES

DROP COOKIES

YIELD: 3 to 4 dozen
TOTAL TIME: 40 minutes

1½ cups (9 ounces) rolled oats
1 cup whole wheat flour
¼ cup nonfat dry milk
¼ cup wheat germ
¼ teaspoon baking powder
½ teaspoon ground cinnamon
½ teaspoon salt
¾ cup vegetable shortening
1¼ cups raw sugar
1 large egg
¼ cup frozen lemon juice concentrate, thawed
1 cup sliced almonds
½ cup golden raisins

1. Preheat the oven to 350 degrees.

2. Combine the oats, flour, dry milk, wheat germ, baking powder, cinnamon, and salt.

3. In a large bowl, cream the vegetable shortening and sugar. Beat in the egg and lemon juice concentrate. Gradually blend in the oat mixture. Fold in the almonds and raisins.

4. Drop the batter by spoonfuls 1½ inches apart onto ungreased baking sheets. Flatten each cookie with the back of a spoon dipped in flour.

5. Bake for 25 to 30 minutes, until the cookies are golden brown. Transfer to wire racks to cool.

Baking notes: If you like, sprinkle the cookies with sesame seeds before you flatten them.

ALMOND MACAROONS

FORMED COOKIES

YIELD: 3 to 4 dozen
TOTAL TIME: 30 minutes
STANDING TIME: 8 hours

1 cup almond paste
¾ cup granulated sugar
1 teaspoon grated lemon zest
3 large egg whites
½ cup powdered sugar

1. Line 2 baking sheets with parchment paper.

2. Crumble the almond paste into a medium bowl. Add the granulated sugar and lemon zest and beat until smooth. Add the egg whites and beat until a soft dough is formed.

3. Place the dough in a pastry bag fitted with a large pliant tip. Pipe out 1-inch mounds onto the prepared baking sheets, spacing the cookies about 1½ inches apart.

4. Sift the powdered sugar over the cookies, coating them heavily. Let stand for at least 8 and up to 24 hours, until the cookies form a crust.

5. Preheat the oven to 350 degrees.

6. Bake for 12 to 15 minutes, until firm to the touch. Spread a large kitchen towel on the countertop and slide the cookies, still on the parchment paper, onto the towel. Let cool before removing the cookies from the paper.

Baking notes: Don't use waxed paper or the cookies may stick or tear apart when you remove them; brown wrapping paper may be used instead of parchment.

ALMOND PRETZELS

FORMED COOKIES

YIELD: 3 to 4 dozen
TOTAL TIME: 45 minutes

1. Preheat the oven to 375 degrees.

2. In a large bowl, cream the vegetable shortening and sugar. Beat in the eggs and egg yolks. Blend in the flour and ground almonds.

3. Break off small pieces of dough and roll each piece into a rope. Form ropes into pretzel shapes and place 1 inch apart on ungreased baking sheets.

4. Brush the cookies with the beaten egg white and sprinkle with the chopped almonds.

5. Bake for 10 to 12 minutes, or until golden brown. Transfer to wire racks to cool.

Baking notes: For decoration, drizzle colored icing over the pretzels, or dip them in melted chocolate when cool. The ropes can also be folded in half and twisted into braids, or they can be formed into circles.

1 cup vegetable shortening
1 cup granulated sugar
2 large eggs
2 large egg yolks
2 cups all-purpose flour
½ cup almonds, ground
1 large egg white, beaten
3 tablespoons chopped
   almonds

ALMOND ROCA COOKIES

BAR COOKIES

YIELD: 1 to 2 dozen
TOTAL TIME: 35 minutes

1. Preheat the oven to 350 degrees. Grease a 15 by 10-inch baking pan.

2. In a large bowl, cream the vegetable shortening and sugar. Beat in the egg yolk and almond extract. Blend in the flour.

3. Spread the dough evenly in the prepared pan. Bake for 18 to 20 minutes, until lightly colored.

4. Meanwhile, melt the chocolate in a double boiler over low heat, stirring until smooth. Remove from the heat.

5. Spread the melted chocolate over the top of the warm cookies. Sprinkle with the almonds. Let cool in the pan on a rack before cutting into large or small bars.

Baking notes: Do not use melted candy bars; use only baker's-style milk chocolate.

1 cup vegetable shortening
½ cup granulated sugar
1 large egg yolk
1 teaspoon almond extract
2 cups all-purpose flour
10 ounces milk chocolate
   (see Baking notes),
   chopped
½ cup almonds, sliced

ALMOND SHORTBREAD

BAR COOKIES

YIELD: 4 to 6 dozen
TOTAL TIME: 40 minutes

1. Preheat the oven to 350 degrees.

2. In a large bowl, cream the butter and powdered sugar. Blend in the flour and almonds. If the dough seems too dry, beat in a little water, ½ teaspoon at a time, until smooth.

3. Spread the dough evenly in an ungreased 9-inch square baking pan. Prick all over with a fork. Using the back of a knife, score the dough into large or small bars.

4. Bake for 28 to 30 minutes until very lightly colored. Let cool in the pan on a rack before cutting into bars.

Baking notes: This dough will keep for up to 2 weeks in the refrigerator or several months in the freezer. Half a teaspoon of almond extract can be substituted for the ground almonds. This recipe is a variation of classic Scotch shortbread; to obtain the traditional texture, substitute rice flour for half of the all-purpose flour.

½ cup butter, at room
   temperature
½ cup powdered sugar
2 cups all-purpose flour
½ cup almonds, ground

ALMOND SQUARES I

YIELD: 1 to 2 dozen
TOTAL TIME: 50 minutes

CRUST
1 cup all-purpose flour
¼ teaspoon salt
¼ cup vegetable shortening

FILLING
2 large eggs
¾ cup granulated sugar
1 teaspoon almond extract
2 tablespoons all-purpose
  flour
¼ teaspoon salt
2 cups shredded coconut
1 cup slivered almonds
Granulated sugar for
  sprinkling

1. Preheat the oven to 350 degrees. Grease a 9-inch square baking pan.

2. To make the crust, combine the flour and salt in a medium bowl. Cut in the shortening until the mixture resembles coarse crumbs.

3. Press the mixture evenly over the bottom of the prepared pan. Bake for 15 minutes.

4. Meanwhile, make the filling: Combine the eggs and sugar in a large bowl and beat until thick and light-colored. Beat in the almond extract. Stir in the flour and salt. Fold in the coconut and almonds.

5. Spread the filling over the warm crust. Sprinkle lightly with sugar. Bake for 15 minutes longer, until the filling is set and it is lightly browned.

6. Let cool in the pan on a rack before cutting into large or small bars.

ALMOND SQUARES II

YIELD: 1 to 2 dozen
TOTAL TIME: 60 minutes

1 cup vegetable shortening
1 cup granulated sugar
1 large egg, separated
½ teaspoon almond extract
¼ teaspoon salt
2 cups all-purpose flour
1½ cups sliced almonds

1. Preheat the oven to 325 degrees.

2. In a large bowl, cream the vegetable shortening and sugar. Beat in the egg yolk and almond extract. Beat in the salt. Gradually blend in the flour. The dough will be stiff.

3. Spread the dough evenly in an ungreased 9-inch baking pan.

4. In a medium bowl, beat the egg white until stiff but not dry. Spread evenly over the cookie dough. Sprinkle with the almonds.

5. Bake for 40 minutes, until the top is lightly colored. Let cool in the pan on a rack before cutting into large or small bars.

Baking notes: For variation, spread your favorite fruit preserves over the unbaked crust, then spread the beaten egg white over the fruit. Bake for 30 to 35 minutes.

ALMOND STRIPS I

BAR COOKIES

YIELD: *6 dozen*
TOTAL TIME: *40 minutes*

1. Preheat the oven to 350 degrees.

2. To make the crust, combine the flour and salt.

3. In a large bowl, cream the vegetable shortening and sugar. Beat in the egg and almond extract. Blend in the flour mixture.

4. Spread the dough evenly over the bottom of an ungreased 13 by 9-inch baking pan.

5. To make the filling, beat the egg white in a medium bowl until frothy. Beat in the sugar and cinnamon until the whites hold stiff peaks. Fold in the almonds.

6. Spread the almond mixture evenly over the dough. Bake for 25 to 30 minutes, until the top is a golden color.

7. While the cookies are still warm, cut into 1½ by 1-inch strips. Transfer to wire racks to cool.

CRUST
2 cups all-purpose flour
¼ teaspoon salt
1 cup vegetable shortening
1 cup granulated sugar
1 large egg yolk
1 teaspoon almond extract

FILLING
1 large egg white
2 tablespoons granulated sugar
¼ teaspoon ground cinnamon
¼ cup almonds, ground

ALMOND STRIPS II

ROLLED COOKIES

YIELD: *3 to 4 dozen*
TOTAL TIME: *35 minutes*
CHILLING TIME: *4 hours*

1. Combine the flour, ginger, and salt.

2. In a large bowl, cream the butter and brown sugar. Beat in the molasses.

3. Dissolve the baking soda in the hot water and add to the molasses mixture, beating until smooth. Gradually blend in the dry ingredients. Stir in the almonds. Cover and chill for at least 4 hours.

4. Preheat the oven to 350 degrees. Grease 2 baking sheets.

5. On a floured surface, roll out the dough ¼ inch thick. Cut into 3 by 1-inch strips and place 1 inch apart on the prepared baking sheets.

6. Bake for 10 to 12 minutes, until lightly colored. Transfer to wire racks to cool.

Baking notes: See Hint 14 in Pantry for an easy way to measure molasses.

3 cups all-purpose flour
1 teaspoon ground ginger
1 teaspoon salt
½ cup butter, at room temperature
½ cup packed dark brown sugar
½ cup molasses
1 teaspoon baking soda
¼ cup hot water
1½ cups almonds, chopped

ALMOND TEA COOKIES

ROLLED COOKIES

YIELD: *2 to 3 dozen*
TOTAL TIME: *35 minutes*

1. Preheat the oven to 350 degrees. Grease 2 baking sheets.

2. In a large bowl, cream the butter and sugar until light and fluffy. Beat in the almonds and salt. Beat in the almond extract. Gradually blend in the flour.

3. On a floured surface, roll out the dough ½ inch thick. Cut into 2 by ½-inch strips and place 1¼ inches apart on the prepared baking sheets.

4. Bake for 15 to 20 minutes, until golden brown.

5. Dust the warm cookies with powdered sugar. Transfer to wire racks to cool.

7 tablespoons butter, at room temperature
½ cup granulated sugar
¾ cup almonds, ground fine
Pinch of salt
1 teaspoon almond extract
3 cups all-purpose flour
Powdered sugar for dusting

ALMOND TULIP PASTRY CUPS

DROP COOKIES

YIELD: 2 to 3 dozen
TOTAL TIME: 60 minutes

¼ cup vegetable shortening
½ cup powdered sugar
2 large egg whites
¾ teaspoon Amaretto
¼ cup all-purpose flour
⅓ cup almonds,
    ground fine

1. Preheat the oven to 425 degrees.

2. In a large bowl, cream the vegetable shortening and powdered sugar. Add the egg whites and Amaretto, beating until very smooth. Gradually blend in the flour. Fold in the almonds.

3. Drop 1½ teaspoonfuls of the batter 5 inches apart onto ungreased baking sheets. With the back of a spoon, spread into 4- to 5-inch rounds.

4. Bake for 5 to 6 minutes, or until the edges are lightly browned. Using a spatula, remove the cookies from the sheets and place each cookie over an upside-down cup or glass. (If they become too firm to shape, return briefly to the oven.) Let cool completely before removing.

Baking notes: These are very easy to overbake; watch them closely. The cups can be used to hold fresh fruit, custards, or mousses.

ALMOND WAFER ROLLS

DROP COOKIES

YIELD: 1 to 3 dozen
TOTAL TIME: 60 minutes
CHILLING TIME: 2 hours

½ cup almonds, ground
    fine
1 tablespoon milk, plus
    more if necessary
1 cup granulated sugar
4 large egg whites
Pinch of salt
Powdered sugar for
    sprinkling

1. Combine the almonds and milk in a blender and blend to a smooth paste. Transfer to a bowl and add the sugar. Stir in enough additional milk so the mixture is the consistency of corn syrup.

2. In a large bowl, beat the egg whites with the salt until stiff but not dry. Gradually fold about 2 tablespoons of the egg whites into the almond mixture. Then fold the mixture back into the egg whites.

3. Heat a griddle. Drop the batter by tablespoonfuls onto the hot griddle and cook, turning once, until golden brown on both sides.

4. While the cookies are still hot, roll each one up into a cylinder. Transfer to wire racks, sprinkle with powdered sugar, and let cool.

AMBROSIA BARS

BAR COOKIES

YIELD: 2 to 3 dozen
TOTAL TIME: 35 minutes

2 cups all-purpose flour
½ teaspoon baking powder
½ teaspoon baking soda
¼ teaspoon salt
¾ cup vegetable shortening
1 cup packed light brown
    sugar
1 large egg
¼ cup fresh orange juice
1 tablespoon grated orange
    zest
1 cup (6 ounces)
    butterscotch chips
1 cup shredded coconut

1. Preheat the oven to 350 degrees. Grease a 13 by 9-inch baking pan.

2. Combine the flour, baking powder, baking soda, and salt.

3. In a large bowl, cream the vegetable shortening and brown sugar. Beat in the egg, orange juice, and zest. Gradually blend in the dry ingredients. Fold in the butterscotch chips and coconut.

4. Spread the batter evenly in the prepared pan.

5. Bake for 25 to 30 minutes, or until the top is a golden brown. Cool in the pan on a rack before cutting into large or small squares.

American Oatmeal Crisps

DROP COOKIES

YIELD: 2 to 3 dozen
TOTAL TIME: 30 minutes

1. Preheat the oven to 350 degrees.

2. Combine the flour, baking powder, baking soda, and salt.

3. In a large bowl, cream the vegetable shortening and both sugars. Beat in the eggs. Beat in the milk and almond extract. Gradually blend in the dry ingredients. Fold in the oats and chips.

4. Drop the dough by teaspoonfuls about 1½ inches apart onto ungreased baking sheets.

5. Bake for 10 to 12 minutes, until golden brown. Transfer to wire racks to cool.

Baking notes: The baking chips can be semisweet, milk chocolate, white chocolate, peanut butter or butterscotch. For a cookie the children will love, omit the baking chips and press 4 or 5 M & M's into the top of each cookie.

1¼ cups all-purpose flour
½ teaspoon baking powder
½ teaspoon baking soda
½ teaspoon salt
1 cup vegetable shortening
¼ cup granulated sugar
1 cup packed light brown sugar
2 large eggs
¼ cup milk
1 teaspoon almond extract
3 cups (18 ounces) rolled oats
1 cup (6 ounces) baking chips (see Baking notes)

American Shortbread

ROLLED COOKIES

YIELD: 8 dozen
TOTAL TIME: 30 minutes

1. Preheat the oven to 400 degrees.

2. In a large bowl, cream the butter and sugar until light and fluffy.

3. In another bowl, beat the eggs until thick and light-colored. Beat the eggs into the butter mixture. Stir in the caraway seeds. Gradually blend in the flour.

4. On a floured surface, roll out the dough ¼ inch thick. Cut into 1-inch squares and place 1 inch apart on ungreased baking sheets.

5. Bake for 12 to 15 minutes, until lightly colored. Transfer to wire racks to cool

Baking notes: For variation, substitute anise seeds for the caraway seeds. For variety, cut half of the cookies into squares and half into rounds with a cookie cutter.

2 cups (1 pound) butter, at room temperature
1¾ cups granulated sugar
6 large eggs
1 tablespoon caraway seeds
8 cups all-purpose flour

Anise Cookies I

DROP COOKIES

YIELD: 2 to 3 dozen
TOTAL TIME: 30 minutes
CHILLING TIME: 8 hours

1. Combine the flour, baking powder, and salt.

2. In a large bowl, beat the eggs until foamy. Beat in the sugar and anise extract. Gradually blend in the dry ingredients. Cover and chill for at least 8 hours, or overnight.

3. Preheat the oven to 325 degrees. Grease 2 baking sheets.

4. Drop the dough by spoonfuls 1½ inches apart onto the prepared baking sheets.

5. Bake for 10 to 12 minutes, until lightly colored. Transfer to wire racks to cool.

Baking notes: For a more subtle flavor, substitute 2 teaspoons of anise seeds for the anise extract.

2¼ cups all-purpose flour
½ teaspoon baking powder
¼ teaspoon salt
2 large eggs
1½ cups granulated sugar
2 teaspoons anise extract

YIELD: 3 to 4 dozen
TOTAL TIME: 35 minutes
CHILLING TIME: 8 hours

2 cups all-purpose flour
¼ teaspoon baking powder
⅛ teaspoon salt
½ cup vegetable shortening
¾ cups granulated sugar
1 large egg
¼ teaspoon baking soda
1 tablespoon warm water
¼ cup molasses
2 teaspoons anise seeds

ANISE COOKIES II

ROLLED COOKIES

1. Combine the flour, baking powder, and salt.

2. In a large bowl, cream the vegetable shortening and sugar. Beat in the egg.

3. Dissolve the baking soda in the warm water and add to the egg mixture, beating until smooth. Beat in the molasses. Fold in the anise seeds. Gradually blend in the dry ingredients. Cover and chill for 8 hours.

4. Preheat the oven to 350 degrees. Grease 2 baking sheets.

5. On a floured surface, roll out the dough ¼ inch thick. Using cookie cutters, cut into shapes and place 1¼ inches apart on the prepared baking sheets.

6. Bake for 6 to 8 minutes, until the edges are golden brown. Transfer to wire racks to cool.

Baking notes: For variation, cut out round cookies and place on the baking sheets. Press your thumb into the center of each one and put a bit of jam or preserves in the depression.

YIELD: 2 to 3 dozen
TOTAL TIME: 35 minutes
CHILLLING TIME: 2 hours

2 cups all-purpose flour
1½ teaspoons baking powder
1¼ teaspoons baking soda
¼ teaspoon salt
2 large eggs
½ cup granulated sugar
1 teaspoon anise extract
1¼ teaspoons anise seeds

ANISEED BISCUITS

FORMED COOKIES

1. Combine the flour, baking powder, baking soda, and salt.

2. In a large bowl, beat the eggs and sugar until thick and light-colored. Beat in the anise extract and anise seeds. Gradually blend in the dry ingredients. Cover and chill for 2 hours.

3. Preheat the oven to 350 degrees. Grease a baking sheet.

4. Form the dough into two 12-inch-long logs and place side-by-side on the prepared baking sheet. Bake for 8 to 10 minutes, or until firm to the touch.

5. Transfer the logs to the cutting board and slice each log diagonally into ½-inch-thick slices. Lay the slices on ungreased baking sheet and bake for 10 minutes longer, until dry. Transfer to wire racks to cool.

6. When cool, drizzle with Vanilla Icing (see Pantry).

APPLE BARS I

BAR COOKIES

1. Preheat the oven to 350 degrees.

2. Combine the flour, baking powder, baking soda, ginger, and nutmeg.

3. In a large bowl, cream the vegetable shortening and sugar. Beat in the eggs. Gradually blend in the dry ingredients. Fold in the apples.

4. Spread the dough evenly in an ungreased 9-inch square baking pan.

5. Combine the cinnamon and sugar for the topping. Sprinkle evenly over the dough.

6. Bake for 25 to 30 minutes, or until firm to the touch. Let cool in the pan on a rack before cutting into large or small bars.

Baking notes: Add ½ cup raisins and/or ½ cup chopped nuts to the dough if desired. Drizzle white icing over the top as soon as the bars are baked. (See Pantry.)

YIELD: 1 to 2 dozen
TOTAL TIME: 50 minutes

¾ cup all-purpose flour
½ teaspoon baking powder
¼ teaspoon baking soda
½ teaspoon ground ginger
¼ teaspoon ground nutmeg
⅓ cup vegetable shortening
¾ cup granulated sugar
2 large eggs
1 cup diced, peeled apples

TOPPING
1½ teaspoons granulated sugar
½ teaspoon ground cinnamon

APPLE BARS II

BAR COOKIES

1. Preheat the oven to 350 degrees.

2. To make the crust, combine the vegetable shortening, flour, and sugar in a bowl. Spread the mixture evenly over the bottom of an ungreased 9-inch square baking pan.

3. Bake for 15 minutes.

4. Meanwhile, make the filling: Combine the flour, baking powder, and salt.

5. In a large bowl, beat the eggs and brown sugar together until thick. Beat in the brandy. Gradually blend in the dry ingredients. Fold in the apples and walnuts.

6. Spread the filling over the hot crust. Bake for 30 minutes longer, or until the filling is set. Cool in the pan on a rack before cutting into large or small bars.

YIELD: 3 to 4 dozen
TOTAL TIME: 55 minutes

CRUST
½ cup vegetable shortening
1 cup all-purpose flour
¼ cup granulated sugar

FILLING
⅓ cup all-purpose flour
½ teaspoon baking powder
¼ teaspoon salt
2 large eggs
1 cup packed light brown sugar
⅓ cup brandy
3 large apples, peeled, cored, and diced
½ cup walnuts, chopped

Apple-Bran Cookies

DROP COOKIES

YIELD: 4 to 5 dozen

TOTAL TIME: 35 minutes

3 medium apples, peeled, cored, and diced
½ cup bran cereal
½ cup fresh lemon juice
1½ cups all-purpose flour
1 teaspoon baking powder
¾ teaspoon ground cinnamon
½ teaspoon salt
½ cup vegetable shortening
½ cup granulated sugar
½ cup packed light brown sugar
1 large egg
1 teaspoon vanilla extract
⅓ cup walnuts, chopped

1. Preheat the oven to 375 degrees. Grease 2 baking sheets.

2. Place the apples in a medium bowl and add boiling water to cover. Set aside.

3. Combine the bran cereal and lemon juice in a small bowl. Combine the flour, baking powder, cinnamon, and salt.

4. In a large bowl, cream the vegetable shortening and both sugars. Beat in the egg and vanilla extract. Gradually blend in the dry ingredients. Fold in the bran cereal and walnuts.

5. Drain the apples and return them to the bowl. Mash with a fork and stir into the dough.

6. Drop the dough by spoonfuls 1½ inches apart onto the prepared baking sheets.

7. Bake for 10 to 12 minutes, until lightly colored. Transfer to wire racks to cool.

Baking notes: Raisins may be added if desired. For variation, use almonds or hazelnuts in place of walnuts

Apple Butter-Oatmeal Bars

BAR COOKIES

YIELD: 2 to 3 dozen

TOTAL TIME: 30 minutes

⅔ cup all-purpose flour
½ teaspoon baking powder
¼ teaspoon salt
½ cup vegetable shortening
½ cup apple butter
½ cup packed dark brown sugar
1 large egg
½ teaspoon baking soda
1 tablespoon warm water
1 cup (6 ounces) rolled oats
1 cup flaked coconut (optional)

1. Preheat the oven to 350 degrees. Grease a 13 by 9-inch baking pan.

2. Combine the flour, baking powder and salt.

3. In a large bowl, cream the vegetable shortening, apple butter, and brown sugar. Beat in the egg.

4. Dissolve the baking soda in the warm water and add to the creamed mixture, beating until smooth. Gradually blend in the dry ingredients. Fold in the oats coconut.

5. Spread the mixture evenly in the prepared pan.

6. Bake for 15 to 20 minutes, or until lightly colored. Cool in the pan on a rack before cutting into large or small bars.

Baking notes: If you like chocolate, add chocolate chips to the dough and drizzle melted chocolate over the top of the cooled cookies.

APPLE-COCONUT DREAMS

DROP COOKIES

YIELD: *4 to 5 dozen*
TOTAL TIME: *30 minutes*

1. Preheat the oven to 375 degrees. Grease 2 baking sheets.

2. Combine the flour, baking powder, cinnamon, and salt.

3. In a large bowl, cream the vegetable shortening and both sugars. Beat in the egg and vanilla extract.

4. Dissolve the baking soda in the warm water and add to the egg mixture, beating until smooth. Gradually blend in the dry ingredients. Fold in the coconut, oats, and apples.

5. Drop the dough by spoonfuls 1½ inches apart onto the prepared baking sheets.

6. Bake for 10 to 12 minutes, or until golden brown. Transfer to wire racks to cool.

1 cup all-purpose flour
½ teaspoon baking powder
1 teaspoon ground cinnamon
½ teaspoon salt
½ cup vegetable shortening
½ cup packed light brown sugar
½ cup granulated sugar
1 large egg
1 teaspoon vanilla extract
½ teaspoon baking soda
1 teaspoon warm water
2 cups flaked coconut
½ cup (3 ounces) rolled oats
½ cup diced, peeled apples

APPLE DROPS

DROP COOKIES

YIELD: *4 dozen*
TOTAL TIME: *30 minutes*

1. Preheat the oven to 375 degrees. Grease 2 baking sheets.

2. In a large bowl, combine the flour, baking powder, baking soda, and spices. Cut in the vegetable shortening until mixture to resembles fine crumbs.

3. In a medium bowl, beat the eggs until thick and light-colored. Beat in the apple juice concentrate. Add the dry mixture and blend to make a smooth dough.

4. Drop the dough by spoonfuls 1½-inches apart onto the prepared baking sheets.

5. Bake for 6 to 8 minutes, or until golden brown. Transfer to wire racks to cool.

2 cups all-purpose flour
½ teaspoon baking powder
¼ teaspoon baking soda
½ teaspoon ground cinnamon
¼ teaspoon ground cloves
¼ teaspoon ground nutmeg
½ cup vegetable shortening
4 large eggs
¾ cup frozen apple juice concentrate, thawed

APPLE-OATMEAL COOKIES

BAR COOKIES

YIELD: *1 to 2 dozen*
TOTAL TIME: *50 minutes*

1. Preheat the oven to 350 degrees. Grease an 8-inch square baking pan.

2. In a large bowl, cream the vegetable shortening and brown sugar.

3. Dissolve the baking soda in the warm water and add to the creamed mixture, beating until smooth.

4. In another bowl, combine the eggs, vanilla extract, cinnamon, and salt. Fold in the apples. Stir into the creamed mixture. Gradually blend in the flour. Fold in the walnuts and oats.

5. Spread the mixture evenly in the prepared pan.

6. Bake for 30 to 35 minutes, until a toothpick comes out clean. Cool in the pan on a rack before cutting into large or small bars.

½ cup vegetable shortening
1 cup packed light brown sugar
½ teaspoon baking soda
1 tablespoon warm water
2 large eggs
1 teaspoon vanilla extract
1 teaspoon ground cinnamon
¼ teaspoon salt
½ cup diced, peeled apples (about 1 apple)
1½ cups all-purpose flour
1 cup walnuts, ground
½ cup (3 ounces) rolled oats

APPLE-RAISIN DROPS

DROP COOKIES

YIELD: 3 to 4 dozen

TOTAL TIME: 35 minutes

2 cups all-purpose flour
1 teaspoon baking powder
1 teaspoon ground cinnamon
½ teaspoon ground nutmeg
¼ teaspoon ground cloves
½ teaspoon salt
½ cup vegetable shortening
1 cup packed light brown
    sugar
2 large eggs
¼ cup milk
1½ cups diced, peeled apples
1 cup golden raisins
½ cup walnuts, chopped

1. Preheat the oven to 350 degrees. Grease 2 baking sheets.

2. Combine the flour, baking powder, spices, and salt.

3. In a large bowl, cream the vegetable shortening and brown sugar. Beat in the eggs and milk. Gradually blend in the dry ingredients. Fold in the apples, raisins and walnuts.

4. Drop the dough by spoonfuls 1½ inches apart onto the prepared baking sheets.

5. Bake for 12 to 14 minutes, or until lightly colored. Transfer to wire racks to cool.

APPLESAUCE BROWNIES

BAR COOKIES

YIELD: 1 to 2 dozen

TOTAL TIME: 40 minutes

2 ounces semisweet
    chocolate, chopped
1 cup all-purpose flour
1 teaspoon baking powder
½ teaspoon ground
    cinnamon
¼ teaspoon salt
½ cup vegetable shortening
1¼ cups granulated sugar
2 large eggs
1 teaspoon vanilla extract
½ cup unsweetened
    applesauce, at room
    temperature
½ cup walnuts, chopped

1. Preheat the oven to 350 degrees. Grease a 13 by 9-inch baking pan.

2. Melt the chocolate in a double boiler over low heat, stirring until smooth. Let cool.

3. Combine the flour, baking powder, cinnamon, and salt.

4. In a large bowl, cream the vegetable shortening and sugar. Beat in the eggs one at a time.

5. In a medium bowl, combine the applesauce, melted chocolate, and vanilla extract. Add to the egg mixture, beating until smooth. Gradually blend in the dry ingredients. Fold in the nuts.

6. Spread the mixture evenly in the prepared pan.

7. Bake for 20 to 25 minutes, or until a toothpick inserted in the center comes out clean. Cool in the pan on a rack before cutting into large or small bars.

APPLESAUCE DATE BARS

BAR COOKIES

YIELD: 2 to 3 dozen

TOTAL TIME: 45 minutes

2 cups all-purpose flour
1 teaspoon ground cinnamon
½ teaspoon ground
    cardamom
Pinch of salt
¾ cup vegetable shortening
1 cup granulated sugar
2 teaspoons baking soda
1 tablespoon warm water
2 large eggs
2 cups unsweetened
    applesauce
1 cup pitted dates, chopped
1 cup walnuts, chopped

1. Preheat the oven to 350 degrees. Grease a 13 by 9-inch baking pan.

2. Combine the flour, cinnamon, cardamom, and salt.

3. In a large bowl, cream the vegetable shortening and sugar.

4. Dissolve the baking soda in the warm water and add to the creamed mixture, beating until smooth. Beat in the eggs. Beat in the applesauce. Gradually blend in the dry ingredients. Fold in the dates and walnuts.

5. Spread the mixture evenly in the prepared pan.

6. Bake for 25 to 30 minutes, or until golden brown on top. Cool in the pan on a rack before cutting into large or small bars.

APPLESAUCE-NUT-RAISIN COOKIES

DROP COOKIES

1. Combine the raisins and enough brandy to cover in a small bowl. Set aside to plump for 1 hour.

2. Preheat the oven to 350 degrees. Grease 2 baking sheets.

3. Drain the raisins and return to the bowl. Add the walnuts. Combine the flour, spices, and salt.

4. In a large bowl, cream the vegetable shortening and sugar. Beat in the egg.

5. In a small bowl, dissolve the baking soda in the warm water. Stir in the applesauce. Add to the egg mixture, beating until smooth. Gradually blend in the dry ingredients. Fold in the raisins and walnuts.

6. Drop the dough by spoonfuls 1½ inches apart onto the prepared baking sheets

7. Bake for 12 to 15 minutes, until lightly colored. Transfer to wire racks to cool.

Baking notes: For a decorative touch, drizzle vanilla icing (see Pantry) over the baked cookies.

YIELD: 2 to 3 dozen
TOTAL TIME: 35 minutes

1 cup raisins
About ⅓ cup brandy
1 cup walnuts, chopped
2 cups all-purpose flour
1 teaspoon ground
*   cinnamon*
½ teaspoon ground nutmeg
¼ teaspoon ground cloves
½ teaspoon salt
½ cup vegetable shortening
1 cup granulated sugar
1 large egg
1 teaspoon baking soda
1 tablespoon warm water
1 cup unsweetened
*   applesauce*

APPLE STRIPS

BAR COOKIES

1. To make the crust, combine the flour and sugar in a bowl. Cut in the vegetable shortening until the mixture resembles coarse crumbs. Stir in the sour cream and lemon zest.

2. Divide the dough in half. Wrap in waxed paper and let chill for 2 hours.

3. Preheat the oven to 325 degrees.

4. On a lightly floured surface, roll out half of the dough to a 9-inch square. Fit the dough into an ungreased 9-inch square baking pan.

5. To make filling, layer the apples evenly over the crust. Sprinkle the sugar and the raisins on top.

6. Roll out the remaining dough to a 9-inch square. Cut into 1-inch-wide strips and arrange in a lattice pattern over the filling. Brush the lattice strips with the beaten egg yolk.

7. Bake for 18 to 20 minutes, or until the crust is golden brown. Sprinkle powdered sugar over the warm cookies, and cut into 2 by 1-inch strips.

Baking notes: Shredded coconut may be added to the crust for a different flavor and texture.

YIELD: 3 to 4 dozen
TOTAL TIME: 45 minutes
CHILLING TIME: 2 hours

CRUST
2 cups all-purpose flour
¼ cup granulated sugar
¾ cup vegetable shortening
3 tablespoons sour cream
½ teaspoon grated lemon
*   zest*

FILLING
5 medium apples, peeled,
*   cored and sliced thin*
½ cup granulated sugar
1 tablespoon raisins
1 large egg yolk, beaten
Powdered sugar for
*   sprinkling*

APRICOT BARS I

YIELD: 2 to 3 dozen
TOTAL TIME: 45 minutes

1¾ cups all-purpose flour
½ cup almonds, ground
    fine
½ teaspoon salt
¾ cup vegetable shortening
¾ cup powdered sugar
½ teaspoon almond extract

FILLING
One 12-ounce jar apricot
    preserves
½ cup glacé cherries, diced
1½ teaspoons brandy

1. Preheat the oven to 350 degrees.

2. Combine the flour, almonds, and salt.

3. In a large bowl, cream the vegetable shortening and powdered sugar. Beat in the almond extract. Gradually blend in the dry ingredients.

4. Set aside 1 cup of the almond mixture for the topping. Spread the remaining mixture evenly over the bottom of an ungreased 13 by 9-inch baking pan.

5. To make the filling, combine the apricot preserves, cherries, and brandy in a small bowl, and stir until blended. Spread the filling evenly over the almond mixture. Crumble the reserved almond mixture over the filling.

6. Bake for 30 to 35 minutes, until the edges are brown. Cut into bars while still warm, and cool in the pan on a rack.

APRICOT BARS II

BAR COOKIES

YIELD: 2 to 3 dozen
TOTAL TIME: 75 minutes

FILLING
⅔ cup dried apricots
⅓ cup all-purpose flour
½ teaspoon baking powder
¼ teaspoon salt
½ cup walnuts, chopped
1½ cups packed light
    brown sugar
2 large eggs
½ teaspoon vanilla extract

CRUST
1 cup all-purpose flour
¼ cup granulated sugar
½ cup vegetable shortening
Powdered sugar for
    sprinkling

1. Preheat the oven to 350 degrees. Lightly grease an 8-inch square baking pan.

2. Combine the apricots and ⅓ cup water in a small saucepan. Cover and bring to a boil over medium heat. Cook for 15 minutes, or until soft. Drain and let cool, then chop fine. Set aside.

3. To make the crust, combine the flour and sugar in a bowl. Cut in the vegetable shortening until the mixture resembles coarse crumbs.

4. Press the mixture evenly into the bottom of the prepared pan. Bake for 25 minutes.

5. Meanwhile, make the filling: Combine the flour, baking powder, and salt. Add the walnuts and apricots.

6. In a medium bowl, beat the brown sugar, eggs, and vanilla extract together until thick. Gradually blend in the dry ingredients.

7. Spread the apricot mixture evenly over the warm crust. Bake for 25 minutes longer, until filling is set.

8. Cool in the pan on a rack before cutting into large or small bars. Sprinkle with powdered sugar.

APRICOT-CHERRY BARS

BAR COOKIES

YIELD: 2 to 3 dozen
TOTAL TIME: 40 minutes

¼ cup vegetable shortening
¼ cup packed light brown
    sugar
2 large eggs
¼ cup warm water
1 package yellow cake mix
1 cup dried apricots, diced
½ cup maraschino cherries,
    drained and chopped
Powdered sugar for
    sprinkling

1. Preheat the oven to 350 degrees. Grease a 15½ by 10½-inch baking pan.

2. In a large bowl, cream the vegetable shortening and brown sugar. Beat in the eggs and warm water. Beat in half the cake mix. Stir in the apricots and cherries.

3. Spread the mixture evenly in the prepared pan. Sprinkle the remaining mix over the top.

4. Bake for 20 to 25 minutes until firm to the touch.

5. Cool in the pan on a rack. Sprinkle with powdered sugar and cut into bars.

Apricot Crescents

ROLLED COOKIES

YIELD: 3 dozen
TOTAL TIME: 40 minutes
CHILLING TIME: 4 hours

2 cups all-purpose flour
1 teaspoon granulated
   sugar
Pinch of salt
1 cup vegetable shortening
1 cup sour cream
1 large egg
½ cup apricot preserves
½ cup walnuts, chopped
Powdered sugar for dusting

1. Combine the flour, sugar, and salt in a bowl. Cut in the vegetable shortening until the mixture resembles coarse crumbs. With a fork stir in the sour cream and egg until a stiff dough forms. Cover and chill for at least 4 hours, or overnight.

2. Preheat the oven to 350 degrees. Grease 2 baking sheets.

3. Divide the dough into 3 pieces. On a floured surface, roll out each piece to an 11-inch round. Spread one-third of the apricot preserves evenly over each round, and sprinkle each round with one-third of the walnuts.

4. Cut each round into 12 wedges. Starting at the wide end, roll up each wedge. Place seam side down on the prepared baking sheets, placing the cookies about 1 inch apart and curving the ends to form crescent shapes.

5. Bake for 25 to 30 minutes, until lightly colored. Dust the warm cookies with powdered sugar and transfer to wire racks to cool.

Apricot-Filled Cookies

BAR COOKIES

YIELD: 2 to 3 dozen
TOTAL TIME: 55 minutes

FILLING
½ cup dried apricots
½ cup granulated sugar
½ cup pecans, ground

CRUST
1 cup all-purpose flour
1 cup (6 ounces) rolled oats
⅔ cup packed light brown
   sugar
¼ teaspoon salt
½ teaspoon vegetable
   shortening

1. Preheat the oven to 350 degrees. Grease an 8-inch square baking pan.

2. To make the filling, place the apricots in a bowl and add boiling water to cover. Let soak for 15 minutes.

3. Drain the apricots and dice very fine. Place in a bowl, add the sugar and pecans, and toss to mix.

4. To make the crust, combine the flour, oats, baking powder, brown sugar, and salt in a bowl. Cut in the vegetable shortening until the mixture resembles coarse crumbs.

5. Spread two-thirds of the crust mixture evenly over the bottom of the prepared pan. Spread the apricot filling over the crust. Sprinkle the remaining crust mixture over the filling, and press down lightly.

6. Bake for 20 to 35 minutes, until firm to the touch. Cool in the pan on a rack before cutting into large or small bars.

APRICOT SQUARES

BAR COOKIES

YIELD: 2 to 3 dozen
TOTAL TIME: 45 minutes

2 cups all-purpose flour
¼ teaspoon salt
¾ cup vegetable shortening
1 cup granulated sugar
1 large egg
¼ teaspoon salt
1 teaspoon vanilla extract
1½ cups shredded coconut
½ cup walnuts, chopped
One 10-ounce jar apricot
preserves

1. Preheat the oven to 350 degrees.

2. Combine the flour and salt.

3. In a large bowl, cream the vegetable shortening and sugar. Beat in the egg and vanilla extract. Gradually blend in the dry ingredients. Fold in the coconut and walnuts.

4. Press three-quarters of the mixture evenly into the bottom of an ungreased 13 by 9-inch baking pan. Spread the apricot preserves over the mixture. Crumble the remaining coconut mixture over the preserves.

5. Bake for 25 to 30 minutes, until firm to the touch and lightly browned. Cool in the pan on a rack before cutting into large or small bars.

APRICOT STRIPS

BAR COOKIES

YIELD: 3 to 4 dozen
TOTAL TIME: 40 minutes
SOAKING TIME: 30 minutes
CHILLING TIME: 2 hours

CRUST
2 cups all-purpose flour
¼ cup granulated sugar
¾ cup vegetable shortening
3 tablespoons sour cream
½ teaspoon grated lemon
zest

FILLING
1½ cups dried apricots,
sliced
½ cup granulated sugar
1 tablespoon raisins
1 large egg yolk, beaten
Powdered sugar for
sprinkling

1. To make the crust, combine the flour and sugar in a bowl. Cut in the vegetable shortening until the mixture resembles coarse crumbs. Stir in the sour cream and lemon zest until a stiff dough forms.

2. Divide the dough in half. Wrap in waxed paper and chill for 2 hours.

3. Place the apricots in a small bowl and add boiling water to cover. Let soak for 30 minutes.

4. Preheat the oven to 325 degrees. Grease a 9-inch square baking pan.

5. On a floured surface, roll out half the dough to a 9-inch square. Fit the dough into the prepared pan.

6. Drain the apricots well. Layer the apricots on the crust and sprinkle with the sugar. Sprinkle the raisins on top.

7. Roll out the remaining dough to a 9-inch square. Cut into 1-inch-wide strips and arrange in a lattice pattern on top of the apricot filling. Brush the lattice strips with the beaten egg yolk.

8. Bake for 18 to 20 minutes, until firm to the touch and crust is golden.

9. Dust the warm cookies with powdered sugar, and cut into strips.

Apricot-Walnut Bars

BAR COOKIES

YIELD: *2 to 3 dozen*
TOTAL TIME: *70 minutes*

1. Preheat the oven to 325 degrees.

2. Place the apricots in a small saucepan and add just enough water to cover. Bring to a boil, reduce the heat, and simmer for 10 minutes, or until soft. Drain and let cool.

3. To make the crust, combine the flour and sugar in a medium bowl. Cut in the vegetable shrotening until the mixture resembles coarse crumbs.

4. Press the mixture evenly into the bottom of an ungreased 9-inch square baking pan. Bake for 25 minutes.

5. Meanwhile, make the filling: Combine the flour, baking powder, and salt.

6. In a large bowl, beat the eggs and brown sugar until thick. Beat in the vanilla extract. Gradually blend in the dry ingredients. Fold in the apricots and walnuts.

7. Spread the filling evenly over the warm crust. Bake for 35 minutes longer, until the filling is set.

8. Cool in the pan on a rack before cutting into bars.

FILLING
¾ cup dried apricots, diced
⅓ cup all-purpose flour
½ teaspoon baking powder
¼ teaspoon salt
2 large eggs
1 cup packed light brown sugar
½ teaspoon vanilla extract
½ cup walnuts, chopped

CRUST
1 cup all-purpose flour
¼ cup granulated sugar
½ cup vegetable shortening

Aunt Lizzie's Cookies

DROP COOKIES

YIELD: *5 to 6 dozen*
TOTAL TIME: *30 minutes*

1. Preheat the oven to 325 degrees. Grease 2 baking sheets.

2. Combine the flour and baking powder.

3. In a large bowl, cream the vegetable shortening and sugar until light and fluffy.

4. In another bowl, beat the eggs until thick and light-colored. Beat the eggs into the shortening mixture. Beat in the vanilla extract.

5. Dissolve the baking soda in the hot water and add to the egg mixture, beating until smooth. Gradually blend in the dry ingredients. Fold in the walnuts and raisins.

6. Drop the dough by spoonfuls 1½ inches apart onto the prepared baking sheets.

7. Bake for 10 to 12 minutes, until lightly colored. Transfer to wire racks to cool.

3 cups all-purpose flour
1 teaspoon baking powder
1 cup vegetable shortening
1½ cups granulated sugar
3 large eggs
1 teaspoon vanilla extract
1 teaspoon baking soda
2 tablespoons hot water
1 cup walnuts, chopped
1 cup raisins

Austrian Walnut Crescents

FORMED COOKIES

YIELD: *4 to 6 dozen*
TOTAL TIME: *40 minutes*
CHILLING TIME: *4 hours*

1. In a large bowl, cream the vegetable shortening and sugar. Beat in the vanilla extract. Gradually blend in the flour and nuts. Cover and chill for at least 4 hours.

2. Preheat the oven to 325 degrees.

3. Break off small pieces of the dough and form into crescent shapes, curving the ends. Place 1 inch apart on ungreased baking sheets.

4. Bake for 15 to 20 minutes, until the edges are a light brown. Transfer to wire racks to cool slightly.

5. Roll the warm cookies in powdered sugar to coat. Let cool on the racks.

Baking notes: To make hazelnut crescents, an elegant variation, substitute hazelnut extract for the vanilla extract and chopped hazelnuts for the walnuts.

1 cup vegetable shortening
⅔ cup granulated sugar
2 teaspoons vanilla extract
2½ cups all-purpose flour
¼ cup walnuts, chopped
Powdered sugar for rolling

BACKPACKERS' BARS

YIELD: *1 to 3 dozen*

TOTAL TIME: *45 minutes*

CRUST

½ cup vegetable shortening
¾ cup packed light brown sugar
¾ cup all-purpose flour
½ cup (3 ounces) rolled oats
¼ cup toasted wheat germ
1 tablespoon grated orange zest

FILLING

2 large eggs
¼ cup packed light brown sugar
½ cup shredded coconut
⅔ cup slivered almonds

1. Preheat the oven to 350 degrees.

2. To make the crust, cream the vegetable shortening and brown sugar in a large bowl. Blend in the flour, oats, wheat germ, orange zest. The mixture will be dry.

3. Press the crust mixture evenly over the bottom of an ungreased 8-inch square baking pan.

4. To make the filling, combine the eggs and brown sugar in a medium bowl and beat until well blended. Stir in the coconut.

5. Spread the filling over the crust. Sprinkle the almonds over the top.

6. Bake for 30 to 35 minutes, until firm to the touch. Cool in the pan on a rack before cutting into large or small bars.

Baking notes: To enhance the flavor of these bars, add ¼ teaspoon almond extract to the filling. Raisins may also be added if desired.

BAKED CHEESECAKE BARS

YIELD: *1 to 3 dozen*

TOTAL TIME: *50 minutes*

CRUST

⅓ cup vegetable shortening
⅓ cup packed light brown sugar
1 cup all-purpose flour
½ cup walnuts, chopped

FILLING

7 ounces cream cheese, at room temperature
¼ cup granulated sugar
1 large egg
2 tablespoons milk
1 tablespoon fresh lemon juice
½ teaspoon vanilla extract

1. Preheat the oven to 350 degrees.

2. To make the crust, cream the vegetable shortening and brown sugar in a large bowl. Gradually blend in the flour. Stir in the walnuts. The mixture will be crumbly.

3. Reserve 1 cup of the crust mixture, and press the remaining mixture evenly into the bottom of an 8-inch square baking pan. Bake for 15 minutes.

4. Meanwhile, make the filling: In a large bowl, beat the cream cheese and sugar. Beat in the egg, milk, lemon juice, and vanilla extract until well blended.

5. Spread the filling over the warm crust. Sprinkle with the reserved crust mixture. Bake for 25 minutes longer, or until firm to the touch.

6. Cool in the pan on a rack before cutting into large or small bars.

Baking notes: For variation, substitute almonds for the walnuts and almond extract for the vanilla extract.

BAKLAVA

BAR COOKIES

1. Preheat the oven to 450 degrees.

2. Melt the butter in a small saucepan.

3. Pour 2 tablespoons of the butter into the bottom of a 13 by 9-inch baking pan. Layer 3 sheets of phyllo dough in the pan, trimming them to fit. Sprinkle about 2 tablespoons of the pecans over the phyllo. Top with 3 more sheets of phyllo and sprinkle with pecans. Continue layering until the pan is three-quarters full. (Do not sprinkle nuts over the top sheet.)

4. Using a sharp knife, score the phyllo to form diamonds. Press a clove into the pointed ends of each diamond. Gradually pour the remaining melted butter over the pastry.

5. Bake for 45 to 50 minutes, until the phyllo is golden brown.

6. Meanwhile, combine the sugar, water, and cinnamon stick in a medium saucepan and bring to a boil, stirring until the sugar dissolves. Lower the heat and simmer for 10 minutes. Add the honey and simmer for 2 minutes longer. Remove from the heat and remove and discard the cinnamon stick.

7. Pour the honey mixture over the hot baklava. Cool in the pan on a rack before cutting into diamonds.

Baking notes: You must use unsalted (sweet) butter for this recipe.

YIELD: 1 to 4 dozen
TOTAL TIME: 75 minutes

1 pound unsalted butter
½ pound phyllo dough, thawed if frozen
2 cups pecans, chopped
1 to 2 tablespoons whole cloves
⅓ cup granulated sugar
3 cups water
1 cinnamon stick
1 cup honey

BANANA-BRAN COOKIES

DROP COOKIES

1. Preheat the oven to 375 degrees.

2. Combine the flour, bran flakes, baking powder, baking soda, and salt.

3. In a large bowl, cream the vegetable shortening and sugar. Beat in the egg and bananas. Beat in the spices. Gradually blend in the dry ingredients. Fold in the nuts.

4. Drop the dough by spoonfuls 1½ inches apart onto ungreased baking sheets.

5. Bake for 10 to 12 minutes, until golden brown. Transfer to wire racks to cool.

Baking notes: For even more flavor, add ⅓ cup semisweet chocolate chips to the dough. If you live in the Northeast, you may be familiar with a product called English Spice; ¾ teaspoon English Spice can replace the cinnamon, allspice, and cloves in this recipe.

YIELD: 1 to 2 dozen
TOTAL TIME: 35 minutes

¾ cup all-purpose flour
1 cup bran flakes
½ teaspoon baking powder
¼ teaspoon baking soda
¼ teaspoon salt
⅓ cup vegetable shortening
⅓ cup granulated sugar
1 large egg
½ cup mashed bananas
½ teaspoon ground cinnamon
⅛ teaspoon ground allspice
⅛ teaspoon ground cloves
¼ cup walnuts, chopped fine

BANANA-CHIP BARS

BAR COOKIES

YIELD: 1 to 2 dozen

TOTAL TIME: 40 minutes

2 cups all-purpose flour
2 teaspoons baking powder
½ teaspoon salt
¾ cup vegetable shortening
1 cup granulated sugar
¼ cup packed light brown
 sugar
1 large egg
1 teaspoon vanilla extract
1 cup mashed bananas
1 cup (6 ounces) semisweet
 chocolate chips

1. Preheat the oven to 350 degrees. Grease a 13 by 9-inch baking pan.

2. Combine the flour, baking powder, and salt.

3. In a large bowl, cream the vegetable shortening and both sugars. Beat in the egg and vanilla extract. Beat in the bananas. Gradually blend in the dry ingredients. Fold in the chocolate chips.

4. Spread the mixture evenly in the prepared pan.

5. Bake for 25 to 30 minutes, until golden brown on top. Cool in the pan on a rack before cutting into large or small bars.

Baking notes: A packaged banana cream frosting goes very well with these bars.

BANANA-COCONUT BARS

BAR COOKIES

YIELD: 2 to 3 dozen

TOTAL TIME: 30 minutes

1¾ cups all-purpose flour
2 teaspoons baking powder
1 teaspoon baking soda
⅓ cup vegetable shortening
2 to 3 medium bananas,
 mashed
1 large egg
½ cup milk
¼ teaspoon fresh lemon
 juice
1½ cups flaked coconut

1. Preheat the oven to 350 degrees. Grease a 13 by 9-inch baking pan.

2. Combine the flour, baking powder, and baking soda.

3. In a large bowl, beat the vegetable shortening and bananas until smooth. Beat in the egg, milk, and lemon juice. Gradually blend in the dry ingredients. Fold in 1 cup of the coconut.

4. Spread the mixture evenly in the prepared pan. Sprinkle the remaining ½ cup coconut over the top.

5. Bake for 15 to 20 minutes, until the top is lightly colored, and a toothpick inserted into the center comes out clean. Cool in the pan on a rack before cutting into large or small bars.

BANANA DROPS

DROP COOKIES

YIELD: 3 to 4 dozen

TOTAL TIME: 35 minutes

1½ cups all-purpose flour
1 cup granulated sugar
½ teaspoon baking soda
¾ teaspoon ground
 cinnamon
¼ teaspoon ground nutmeg
1 teaspoon salt
¾ cup vegetable shortening
1 large egg
2 to 3 large bananas,
 mashed
1¾ cups (10 ½ ounces)
 rolled oats
2 cups (12 ounces)
 semisweet chocolate chips

1. Preheat the oven to 400 degrees.

2. Sift the flour, sugar, baking soda, cinnamon, nutmeg, and salt into a large bowl. Cut in the vegetable shortening. Stir in the egg and bananas until smooth. Fold in the oats and chocolate chips.

3. Drop the dough by spoonfuls 1½ inches apart onto ungreased baking sheets.

4. Bake for 12 to 15 minutes, until lightly colored. Transfer to wire racks to cool.

Baking notes: Raisins may be added to the dough. The chips can be of any type: semisweet or milk chocolate, butterscotch, or peanut butter.

Banana-Nut Drops

DROP COOKIES

1. Preheat the oven to 350 degrees. Grease 2 baking sheets.

2. Combine the flour, baking powder, and salt.

3. In a large bowl, cream the vegetable shortening and sugar. Beat in the eggs, vanilla extract, and lemon extract. Beat in the bananas and ground walnuts. Gradually blend in the dry ingredients.

4. Drop the dough by spoonfuls 1½ inches apart onto the prepared baking sheets.

5. Bake for 12 to 15 minutes, until lightly colored. Transfer to wire racks to cool.

YIELD: *3 to 4 dozen*
TOTAL TIME: *35 minutes*

2¼ cups all-purpose flour
2 teaspoons baking powder
½ teaspoon salt
⅓ cup vegetable shortening
1 cup granulated sugar
2 large eggs
½ teaspoon vanilla extract
¼ teaspoon lemon extract
2 to 3 large bananas, mashed
½ cup walnuts, ground fine

Banana-Oatmeal Cookies

DROP COOKIES

1. Preheat the oven to 400 degrees.

2. Combine the flour, baking soda, cinnamon, nutmeg, and salt.

3. In a large bowl, cream the vegetable shortening and sugar. Beat in the egg and bananas. Gradually blend in the dry ingredients. Fold in the oats and almonds.

4. Drop the dough by spoonfuls 1½ inches apart onto ungreased baking sheets.

5. Bake for 12 to 15 minutes, until lightly colored. Transfer to wire racks to cool.

YIELD: *3 to 5 dozen*
TOTAL TIME: *30 minutes*

1½ cups all-purpose flour
½ teaspoon baking soda
¾ teaspoon ground cinnamon
¼ teaspoon ground nutmeg
¼ teaspoon salt
¾ cup vegetable shortening
1 cup granulated sugar
1 large egg
2 to 3 large bananas, mashed
1¾ cups (10 ½ ounces) rolled oats
½ cup almonds, choppe

Bannocks

ROLLED COOKIES

1. Preheat the oven to 350 degrees.

2. Combine the rolled oats, flour, sugar, baking powder, and salt in a bowl. Using your fingertips, work in the vegetable shortening until the mixture resembles coarse crumbs. Add just enough water to form the mixture into a smooth dough.

3. On a floured surface, roll out the dough ½ inch thick. Using a butter plate as a guide, cut out 6-inch circles and place 1 inch apart on ungreased baking sheets.

4. Bake for 18 to 20 minutes, until the Bannocks are slightly colored and firm to the touch. Transfer to wire racks to cool.

Baking notes: This is a very old Scottish recipe. Bannocks are usually served with jam or jelly.

YIELD: *4 to 6*
TOTAL TIME: *35 minutes*

1¼ cups rolled oats
¾ cup all-purpose flour
1 tablespoon granulated sugar
1 tablespoon baking powder
½ teaspoon salt
5 tablespoons vegetable shortening
2 to 3 tablespoons water, or more as needed

Basic Bars

YIELD: 1 to 2 dozen
TOTAL TIME: 35 minutes

1 cup all-purpose flour
1 cup almonds, ground fine
1 teaspoon baking powder
3 large eggs, separated
1 cup granulated sugar
1 large egg white
⅛ teaspoon salt

1. Preheat the oven to 350 degrees. Grease a 13 by 9-inch baking pan.

2. Combine the flour, almonds, and baking powder.

3. In a large bowl, beat the egg yolks and sugar until thick and light-colored. Gradually blend in the dry ingredients.

4. In another bowl, beat the egg whites with the salt until stiff but not dry. Fold the beaten whites into the egg yolk mixture.

5. Spread the mixture evenly in the prepared pan.

6. Bake for 20 to 25 minutes, until the cookies form a crust and are lightly colored on top. Cool in the pan on a rack before cutting.

Basic Brownie Mix

YIELD: 14 cups
TOTAL TIME: 40 minutes

3 cups all-purpose flour
2 cups unsweetened cocoa powder
1 tablespoon baking powder
2 teaspoons salt
3½ cups vegetable shortening (see Baking notes)
5 cups granulated sugar

1. Combine the flour, cocoa powder, baking powder, and salt.

2. In a large bowl, cream the vegetable shortening and sugar. Gradually blend in the dry ingredients. Store in an airtight container until ready to use.

3. Preheat the oven to 350 degrees. Grease a 9-inch baking pan.

4. To make the cookies: add 2 beaten eggs and 1 teaspoon vanilla extract to 2¾ cups of the Basic Brownie Mix. Beat thoroughly.

5. Spread the mixture evenly in a prepared baking pan.

6. Bake for 25 to 30 minutes, or until a toothpick inserted in the cookie is removed clean. Cool in the pan on a rack before cutting into large or small bars.

Baking notes: This mix will make enough to make 5 recipes. The vegetable shortening must be of the type that does not need refrigeration.

Basic Drop Cookies

YIELD: 3 to 4 dozen
TOTAL TIME: 30 minutes

1½ cups all-purpose flour
1½ teaspoons baking powder
¼ teaspoon salt
6 tablespoons vegetable shortening
¾ cup granulated sugar
1 large egg
2 tablespoons milk
½ teaspoon vanilla extract

1. Preheat the oven to 375 degrees. Grease 2 baking sheets.

2. Combine the flour, baking powder, and salt.

3. In a large bowl, cream the vegetable shortening and sugar. Beat in the egg. Beat in the milk and vanilla extract. Gradually blend in the dry ingredients.

4. Drop the dough by spoonfuls 1½ inches apart onto the prepared baking sheets.

5. Bake for 10 to 12 minutes, until the edges start to color. Transfer to wire racks to cool

Baking notes: This basic recipe is the starting point for endless variations: Add nuts, raisins, coconut, chocolate chips, peanut butter, peanut butter chips, and/or candied citrus peel. Add cinnamon and/or nutmeg, or spices, as you like.

BASIC FILLED COOKIES

ROLLED COOKIES

YIELD: 5 to 6 dozen
TOTAL TIME: 40 minutes

1. Preheat the oven to 400 degrees. Grease 2 baking sheets.

2. Combine the flour and salt.

3. In a large bowl, cream the vegetable shortening and sugar. Beat in the eggs and vanilla extract.

4. Dissolve the baking soda in the warm water and add to the egg mixture, beating until smooth. Beat in the sour cream. Gradually blend in the dry ingredients.

5. On a floured surface, roll out the dough ¼ inch thick. Using a round cookie cutter, cut out an even number of cookies.

6. Place ½ teaspoonful of the filling in the center of half the cookies, and top each one with another cookie. Pinch the edges to seal and place 1½ inches apart on the prepared baking sheets.

7. Bake for 10 to 12 minutes, until golden brown in color. Transfer to wire racks to cool.

Baking notes: You can cut out these cookies in almost any shape you like; just be sure to have equal numbers of matching "tops" and "bottoms." If you make round cookies, you can cut out holes in the center of the tops before baking so the filling will show through.

4¾ cups all-purpose flour
¼ teaspoon salt
¾ cup vegetable shortening
1½ cups granulated sugar
2 large eggs
2 teaspoons vanilla extract
½ teaspoon baking soda
1 tablespoon warm water
¾ cup sour cream
1½ cups filling, such as jams or preserves

BASIC FUDGE BROWNIES

BAR COOKIES

YIELD: 1 to 2 dozen
TOTAL TIME: 30 minutes

1. Preheat the oven to 350 degrees. Grease a 9-inch square baking pan.

2. Combine the vegetable shortening and cocoa in the top of a double boiler and heat over low heat, stirring occasionally, until the shortening is melted.

3. Remove from the heat and stir in the sugar. Stir in the eggs and vanilla extract until well blended. Stir in the flour.

4. Spread the mixture evenly in the prepared pan.

5. Bake for 18 to 20 minutes, until a toothpick inserted in the center comes out clean. Cool in the pan on a rack before cutting into large or small bars.

Baking notes: When cool, these can be spread with chocolate glaze and sprinkled with chopped walnuts before being cut into bars.

½ cup plus 2 tablespoons vegetable shortening
2 tablespoons unsweetened cocoa powder
1 cup granulated sugar
2 large eggs
1 teaspoon vanilla extract
½ cup all-purpose flour

BEAUMONT INN COOKIES

DROP COOKIES

YIELD: *2 to 3 dozen*
TOTAL TIME: *30 minutes*

2½ cups all-purpose flour
1 teaspoon baking powder
2 tablespoons butter, at
*   room temperature*
1 cup granulated sugar
1 large egg
½ cup milk

1. Preheat the oven to 425 degrees. Grease 2 baking sheets.

2. Combine the flour and baking powder.

3. In a large bowl, cream the butter and sugar. Beat in the egg and milk. Gradually blend in the dry ingredients.

4. Drop the dough by spoonfuls 1½ inches apart onto the prepared baking sheets.

5. Bake for 12 to 15 minutes, until golden brown. Transfer to wire racks to cool.

Baking notes: The Beaumont Inn is located in Harrodsburg, Kentucky. These cookies can be decorated with raisins, slivered nuts, or glacé cherries before baking.

BENNE (SESAME SEED) ICEBOX COOKIES

REFRIGERATOR COOKIES

YIELD: *3 to 4 dozen*
TOTAL TIME: *30 minutes*
CHILLING TIME: *8 hours*

2 cups all-purpose flour
¼ teaspoon salt
½ cup butter, at room
*   temperature*
1 cup granulated sugar
1 large egg
¼ cup milk
7½ tablespoons sesame
*   seeds, toasted*

1. Combine the flour and salt.

2. In a large bowl, cream the butter and sugar. Beat in the egg and milk. Gradually blend in the dry ingredients. Fold in the sesame seeds.

3. Form the dough into a 1-inch-thick log. Wrap in waxed paper and chill for at least 8 hours.

4. Preheat the oven to 375 degrees. Grease 2 baking sheets.

5. Slice the log into ¼-inch-thick slices and place 1½ inches apart on the prepared baking sheets.

6. Bake for 10 to 12 minutes, until lightly colored. Transfer to wire racks to cool.

BIENENSTICH

BAR COOKIES

YIELD: *5 to 7 dozen*
TOTAL TIME: *75 minutes*

TOPPING
½ cup vegetable shortening
¼ cup granulated sugar
2 tablespoons honey
2 tablespoons milk
2 tablespoons almond extract
1 cup almonds, ground fine

CRUST
1¾ cups all-purpose flour
2 teaspoons baking powder
¼ teaspoon salt
½ cup vegetable shortening
½ cup granulated sugar
1 large egg
1 teaspoon vanilla extract

1. Preheat the oven to 350 degrees.

2. To make the topping, combine all the ingredients in a medium saucepan and bring to a rolling boil. Stir to dissolve the sugar. Remove from the heat and let cool.

3. To make the crust, combine the flour, baking powder, and salt.

4. In a large bowl, cream the vegetable shortening and sugar. Beat in the egg and vanilla extract. Gradually blend in the dry ingredients.

5. Press the mixture evenly into the bottom of 13 by 9-inch baking pan. Pour the topping mixture over the crust.

6. Bake for 55 to 60 minutes, until the top is lightly colored. Cool in the pan on a wire rack before cutting into bars.

BIG ORANGE BARS

BAR COOKIES

1. Preheat the oven to 350 degrees. Grease a 13 by 9-inch baking pan.

2. To make the crust, combine the flour and powdered sugar in a bowl. Cut in the butter until the mixture resembles coarse crumbs. Blend in the cream.

3. Press the mixture evenly into the bottom of the prepared pan. Bake for 20 minutes.

4. Meanwhile, make the topping: In a large bowl, beat the eggs until thick and light-colored. Beat in the powdered sugar. Beat in the orange juice and lemon juice. Fold in the orange zest.

5. Pour the topping mixture over the warm crust. Bake for 25 to 30 minutes longer, until the topping is set.

6. Cool in the pan on a rack before cutting into large or small bars.

Baking notes: These can be garnished with thin slices of sweet oranges.

YIELD: 1 to 3 dozen
TOTAL TIME: 60 minutes

CRUST
1 cup all-purpose flour
½ cup powdered sugar
6 tablespoons butter, at room temperature
1 tablespoon heavy cream

TOPPING
4 large eggs
1¼ cups powdered sugar
6 tablespoons fresh orange juice
2 tablespoons fresh lemon juice
3 tablespoons grated orange zest

BILLY GOATS

DROP COOKIES

1. Preheat the oven to 350 degrees. Grease 2 baking sheets.

2. Combine the flour, baking powder, allspice, and salt.

3. In a large bowl, cream the vegetable shortening and sugar. Beat in the eggs one at a time. Beat in the vanilla extract.

4. Dissolve the baking soda in the warm water and add to the egg mixture, beating until smooth. Beat in the sour cream. Gradually blend in the dry ingredients. Fold in the dates and walnuts.

5. Drop the dough by spoonfuls 1½ inches apart onto the prepared baking sheets.

6. Bake for 12 to 15 minutes, until golden. Transfer to wire racks to cool.

Baking notes: Raisins may be substituted for the dates; plump them in warm water before using. For a slightly different flavor, ground nutmeg may be used in place of the allspice.

YIELD: 5 to 6 dozen
TOTAL TIME: 30 minutes

4 cups all-purpose flour
1 tablespoon plus 1 teaspoon baking powder
1 teaspoon ground allspice
1 cup walnuts, chopped
½ teaspoon salt
1 cup vegetable shortening
2 cups granulated sugar
4 large eggs
1 teaspoon vanilla extract
1 teaspoon baking soda
1 tablespoon warm water
1 cup sour cream
1½ cups dates, pitted and chopped

Bird's Nest Cookies

FORMED COOKIES

YIELD: *3 to 4 dozen*

TOTAL TIME: *35 minutes*

2 cups all-purpose flour
¼ teaspoon salt
1 cup vegetable shortening
½ cup granulated sugar
1 large egg, separated
1 large egg yolk
1½ teaspoons vanilla
*   extract*
1 cup walnuts, chopped
Chocolate kisses for garnish

1. Preheat the oven to 375 degrees.

2. Combine the flour and salt.

3. In a large bowl, cream the vegetable shortening and sugar. Beat in the egg yolks and vanilla extract. Gradually blend in the dry ingredients.

4. In a shallow bowl, beat the egg white until frothy. Spread the walnuts on waxed paper.

5. Break off 1-inch pieces of dough and roll into balls. Dip the balls in the egg white to coat, then roll in the walnuts and place 1 inch apart on ungreased baking sheets.

6. With your finger, make a small depression in the center of each cookie. Bake for 12 to 15 minutes, until lightly colored.

7. Press an upside-down chocolate kiss into the center of each hot cookie, and transfer to wire racks to cool.

Biscotti

FORMED COOKIES

YIELD: *4 dozen*

TOTAL TIME: *45 minutes*

1½ cups whole wheat flour
1 cup toasted hazelnuts,
*   grated*
2 teaspoons baking powder
½ cup butter, at room
*   temperature*
6 tablespoons honey
2 large eggs

1. Preheat the oven to 350 degrees. Grease a baking sheet.

2. Combine the flour, hazelnuts, and baking powder.

3. In a large bowl, beat the butter and honey until smooth. Beat in the eggs one at a time, beating well after each addition. Gradually blend in the dry ingredients.

4. Divide the dough in half. On the prepared baking sheet, form each half into a log about 12 inches long and 2 inches wide, spacing them about 2 inches apart.

5. Bake for 14 to 16 minutes, until golden brown. Transfer the logs to the cutting board and cut on the diagonal into ½-inch-thick slices. Lay the slices on ungreased baking sheets and bake for 10 to 12 minutes longer, until dry.

6. Transfer to wire racks to cool. Store in a tightly sealed container and let age for a few days before serving.

Bittersweet Brownies

BAR COOKIES

YIELD: *1 to 3 dozen*

TOTAL TIME: *35 minutes*

2 ounces unsweetened
*   chocolate, chopped*
½ cup all-purpose flour
1 teaspoon baking soda
¼ teaspoon salt
½ cup vegetable shortening
¾ cup granulated sugar
2 large eggs
1 teaspoon vanilla extract
1½ cups pecans, chopped

1. Preheat the oven to 350 degrees. Grease a 9-inch square baking pan.

2. Melt the chocolate in a double boiler over low heat, stirring until smooth. Remove from the heat.

3. Combine the flour, baking powder, and salt.

4. In a large bowl, cream the vegetable shortening and sugar. Beat in the eggs and vanilla extract. Beat in the melted chocolate. Gradually blend in the dry ingredients. Stir in the pecans.

5. Spread the mixture evenly in the prepared pan.

6. Bake for 20 to 25 minutes, until a toothpick inserted in the center comes out clean. Cool in the pan on a rack.

7. Frost with chocolate frosting and cut into large or small bars.

BLACKBERRY COOKIES

DROP COOKIES

1. Combine the flour, baking powder, and salt.

2. In a large bowl, cream the vegetable shortening and sugar. Beat in the egg and milk. Beat in the lemon zest. Gradually blend in the dry ingredients. Fold in the blackberry puree. Cover and chill for at least 4 hours.

3. Preheat the oven to 375 degrees.

4. Drop the dough by spoonfuls 1½ inches apart onto ungreased baking sheets.

5. Bake for 12 to 15 minutes, until lightly colored. Transfer to wire racks to cool.

Baking notes: You can make these with fresh blackberries instead of the puree. Rinse and thoroughly dry fresh berries. Add the berries to the flour mixture, tossing them gently to coat thoroughly.

YIELD: 4 to 5 dozen
TOTAL TIME: 30 minutes
CHILLING TIME: 4 hours

2 cups all-purpose flour
2 teaspoons baking powder
½ teaspoon salt
½ cup vegetable shortening
1 cup granulated sugar
1 large egg
¼ cup milk
1½ teaspoons grated lemon
  zest
1 cup blackberry puree,
  unstrained

BLACKBERRY MERINGUE BARS

BAR COOKIES

1. Preheat the oven to 350 degrees.

2. To make the crust, in a large bowl, cream the vegetable shortening and sugar. Beat in the egg yolks. Gradually blend in the flour.

3. Spread the mixture evenly in the bottom of an ungreased 13 by 9-inch baking pan. Bake for 15 minutes.

4. Meanwhile, make the topping: In a medium bowl, beat the egg whites into stiff peaks. Beat in the sugar. Fold in the nuts.

5. Spread the blackberry puree over the warm crust. Sprinkle with the coconut. Spread the meringue evenly over the top.

6. Bake for 20 to 25 minutes longer, until the topping is set. Cool in the pan on a rack before cutting into large or small bars.

Baking notes: The blackberry puree can be fresh, canned, frozen, preserved, or a compote. If you do not have fresh coconut available, packaged flaked coconut can be used.

YIELD: 3 to 4 dozen
TOTAL TIME: 45 minutes

CRUST
¾ cup vegetable shortening
¼ cup granulated sugar
2 large egg yolks
1½ cups all-purpose flour

TOPPING
2 large egg whites
½ cup granulated sugar
1 cup almonds, chopped
1 cup blackberry puree,
  unstrained
1 cup shaved fresh coconut
  (see Baking notes)

Black Walnut Refrigerator Cookies

YIELD: 8 to 9 dozen
TOTAL TIME: 30 minutes
CHILLING TIME: 24 hours

2⅔ cups all-purpose flour
2 teaspoons baking powder
¼ teaspoon salt
¾ cup butter, at room
    temperature
1½ cups packed light
    brown sugar
2 large eggs
1 teaspoon vanilla extract
1½ cups black walnuts,
    chopped

1. Combine the flour, baking powder, and salt.

2. In a large bowl, cream the butter and brown sugar. Beat in the eggs and vanilla extract. Gradually blend in the dry ingredients. Fold in the walnuts. Cover and refrigerate just until firm enough to shape, about 30 minutes.

3. Divide the dough into 3 pieces. Form each piece into a log about 8 inches long. Wrap in waxed paper and chill for at least 24 hours.

4. Preheat the oven to 375 degrees. Grease 2 baking sheets.

5. Slice the logs into ¼-inch-thick slices and place 1 inch apart on the prepared baking sheets.

6. Bake for 8 to 10 minutes, until lightly colored. Transfer to wire racks to cool.

Blitzkuchen

YIELD: 1 to 2 dozen
TOTAL TIME: 45 minutes

CRUST
1 cup vegetable shortening
1 cup granulated sugar
2 large eggs, separated
3 cups flour
½ teaspoon salt

TOPPING
2 large egg whites
½ cup almonds, ground
    fine
¾ teaspoon ground
    cinnamon
¼ teaspoon granulated
    sugar

1. Preheat the oven to 350 degrees.

2. To make the crust, cream the vegetable shortening and sugar in a large bowl. Combine flour and salt and add to mixture. Beat in the egg yolks.

3. In another bowl, beat the egg whites until they hold stiff peaks. Fold the egg whites into the egg yolk mixture.

4. Press the mixture evenly into the bottom of an ungreased 8-inch square baking pan.

5. To make the topping: In a medium bowl, beat the egg whites until stiff but not dry. Fold in the ground almonds, then fold in the cinnamon and sugar.

6. Spread the topping evenly over the prepared crust.

7. Bake for 25 to 30 minutes, until firm to the touch. Cool in the pan on a rack before cutting into large or small bars.

BLOND BROWNIES

BAR COOKIES

1. Preheat the oven to 375 degrees.

2. In a large bowl, cream the butter and brown sugar. Beat in the eggs and almond extract. Gradually blend in the flour and baking powder. Stir in the almonds and chocolate chips.

3. Spread the batter evenly in an ungreased 13 by 9-inch baking pan.

4. Bake for 15 to 20 minutes, until a toothpick inserted in the center comes out clean. Cut into large or small bars while still warm and cool in the pan on a rack.

YIELD: 1 to 2 dozen
TOTAL TIME: 30 minutes

½ cup butter, at room
*   temperature*
2 cups packed light brown
*   sugar*
4 large eggs
2 teaspoons almond extract
2½ cups all-purpose flour
2 teaspoons baking powder
1½ cups almonds, chopped
1½ cups (9 ounces)
*   semisweet chocolate chips*

BLUEBERRY BARS

BAR COOKIES

1. Preheat the oven to 350 degrees. Lightly grease a 9-inch square baking pan.

2. To make the crust, combine the flour and baking powder.

3. In a large bowl, cream the vegetable shortening and sugar. Beat in the egg and almond extract. Beat in the milk. Gradually blend in the dry ingredients.

4. Spread the mixture evenly in the prepared baking pan.

5. Sprinkle the blueberries over the crust in the pan.

6. To make the topping, in a medium bowl, beat the eggs and cream cheese until smooth. Beat in the powdered sugar and almond extract. Spread this mixture over the blueberries.

7. Bake for 55 to 60 minutes, or until firm to the touch. Cool in the pan on a wire rack before cutting into large or small bars.

YIELD: 1 to 2 dozen
TOTAL TIME: 1 hour and 10
minutes

CRUST
1 cup all-purpose flour
1¼ teaspoons baking powder
½ cup vegetable shortening
¾ cup granulated sugar
1 large egg
¾ teaspoon almond extract
⅓ cup milk
1½ cups fresh blueberries,
*   cleaned*

TOPPING
2 large eggs
8 ounces cream cheese, at
*   room temperature*
⅓ cup powdered sugar
1 teaspoon almond extract

BLUEBERRY COOKIES

DROP COOKIES

1. Combine the flour, baking powder, and salt.

2. In a large bowl, cream the vegetable shortening and sugar. Beat in the egg. Beat in the milk, almond extract, and lemon zest. Gradually blend in the dry ingredients. Fold in the blueberries.

3. Cover and chill for at least 4 hours.

4. Preheat the oven to 375 degrees.

5. Drop the dough by spoonfuls about 1 inch apart onto ungreased baking sheets.

6. Bake for 12 to 15 minutes, until lightly colored. Transfer to wire racks to cool

Baking notes: Canned or frozen blueberries can be used, but fresh give the best results.

YIELD: 4 to 5 dozen
TOTAL TIME: 30 minutes
CHILLING TIME: 4 hours

2 cups all-purpose flour
2 teaspoons baking powder
½ teaspoon salt
½ cup vegetable shortening
1 cup granulated sugar
1 large egg
¼ cup milk
1 teaspoon almond extract
1½ teaspoons grated lemon
*   zest*
1 cup blueberries

BLUSHING COOKIES

YIELD: 2 to 3 dozen
TOTAL TIME: 30 minutes

2 cups all-purpose flour
1 cup walnuts, chopped fine
¼ teaspoon ground
   cinnamon
½ cup vegetable shortening
¾ cup powdered sugar
Red jimmies for sprinkling

1. Preheat the oven to 400 degrees.

2. Combine the flour, walnuts, and cinnamon.

3. In a large bowl, cream the vegetable shortening and powdered sugar until light and fluffy. Gradually blend in the dry ingredients.

4. On a floured surface, roll out the dough ¼ inch thick. Using cookie cutter, cut into shapes and place on ungreased baking sheets. Sprinkle the red jimmies over the tops of the cookies.

5. Bake for 8 to 10 minutes, until lightly colored. Transfer to wire racks to cool.

BONBONS

YIELD: 3 dozen
TOTAL TIME: 40 minutes

1½ cups all-purpose flour
½ teaspoon salt
½ cup vegetable shortening
½ cups powdered sugar
2 tablespoons heavy cream
2 teaspoons vanilla extract
36 candied glacé cherries

1. Preheat the oven to 350 degrees.

2. Combine the flour and salt.

3. In a large bowl, cream the vegetable shortening and powdered sugar. Beat in the cream and vanilla extract. Gradually blend in the dry ingredients.

4. Break off pieces of dough and flatten each one on a floured surface into a round about 3 to 4 inches in diameter. Place a candied cherry in the center of each round and wrap the dough up around the cherry. Pinch to seal. Place 1 inch apart on ungreased baking sheets.

5. Bake for 8 to 10 minutes, until the dough is set (see Baking notes). Transfer to wire racks to cool.

Baking notes: It is important not to overbake these cookies; bake only until the dough is set. Do not let it color at all. To decorate, dip the top of each ball into sugar icing or melted chocolate. To completely coat the cookies with chocolate, place the cookies one at a time on a bamboo skewer and dip in melted chocolate. Hold the skewer at an angle so cookie does not slip off it.

BORDER COOKIES

ROLLED COOKIES

1. Line 2 baking sheets with parchment paper.

2. In a large bowl, start beating the egg whites and gradually add the powdered sugar, then beat to very stiff peaks. Beat for about 5 minutes.

3. Measure out ⅓ cup of the mixture and set aside. Fold the hazelnuts, lemon zest, and ground cinnamon into the remaining mixture.

4. Line a work surface with parchment paper and sprinkle liberally with powdered sugar. Roll out the dough to ¼ inch thick. Sprinkle the dough with powdered sugar and cut with a 2-inch star cutter. Sprinkle each star with powdered sugar and place on the prepared baking sheets. Place a ⅛ dessert teaspoon of strawberry preserves in the center of each star and place a dab of the reserved egg mixture on the strawberry preserves. Set aside for 1½ hours.

5. Preheat the oven to 375 degrees.

6. Bake for 7 to 10 minutes, until firm to the touch. Cool on the baking sheets on wire racks before removing from the parchment paper.

YIELD: 2 to 4 dozen
TOTAL TIME: 40 minutes
SITTING TIME: 90 minutes

⅓ cup large egg whites (3 to 4)
1 cup powdered sugar
2 cups hazelnuts, ground
1 teaspoon grated lemon zest
¾ cup ground cinnamon
Powdered sugar for rolling
Strawberry preserves

BOURBON BALLS

FORMED COOKIES

1. Combine the vanilla wafers and walnuts.

2. Melt the chocolate chips in a double boiler over low heat, stirring until smooth. Stir in the sugar and corn syrup. Remove from the heat and stir in the bourbon. Add the vanilla wafer mixture all at once and blend to form a thick dough.

3. Break off pieces of dough and form into balls. Roll each ball in powdered sugar. Store in an airtight container until ready to serve.

Baking notes: Almost any type of whiskey can be substituted for the bourbon. Obviously, these cookies are not for children.

YIELD: 3 to 5 dozen
TOTAL TIME: 30 minutes

2½ cups crushed vanilla wafers
1 cup walnuts, ground fine
¾ cup (4½ ounces) semisweet chocolate chips
½ cup granulated sugar
2 tablespoons corn syrup
½ cup bourbon
Powdered sugar for rolling

BOURBON CHEWS

DROP COOKIES

1. Preheat the oven to 325 degrees. Lightly grease 2 baking sheets.

2. Combine the flour, ginger, and salt together.

3. In a small saucepan combine the molasses and vegetable shortening and heat over low heat, stirring until smooth. Remove from the heat and add the bourbon. Beat in the brown sugar. Gradually blend in the dry ingredients. Fold in the walnuts.

4. Drop the dough by spoonfuls onto the prepared baking sheets.

5. Bake for 10 to 12 minutes, until lightly colored. Transfer to wire racks to cool.

YIELD: 3 to 4 dozen
TOTAL TIME: 30 minutes

1 cup all-purpose flour
1 teaspoon ground ginger
½ teaspoon salt
½ cup molasses
¼ cup vegetable shortening
2 tablespoons bourbon
½ cup packed light brown sugar
¼ cup walnuts, chopped

B

Bow Cookies

ROLLED COOKIES

YIELD: *4 to 5 dozen*
TOTAL TIME: *30 minutes*

3 large eggs
3 tablespoons granulated
    sugar
¼ teaspoon salt
1 tablespoon vanilla extract
3 cups all-purpose flour
Vegetable oil for deep-frying
Powdered sugar for
    sprinkling

1. In a large bowl, beat the eggs until thick and light-colored. Beat in the sugar and salt. Beat in the vanilla extract. Gradually blend in the flour.

2. On a floured surface, roll out the dough ⅛ inch thick. Cut into strips 6 inches by 1½ inches. Make a ¾-inch-long slit down the center of each strip and pull one end of the strip through the slit to form a bow tie.

3. In a deep-fryer or deep heavy pot, heat the oil to 375 degrees. Fry the cookies, in batches, until golden brown. Drain on a wire rack lined with paper towels, then sprinkle with powdered sugar.

Baking notes: Colored sugar crystals can be used to create colored bows for the holidays. For a distinctive look, use a pastry wheel to cut the strips.

Boysenberry Meringue Bars

BAR COOKIES

YIELD: *1 to 4 dozen*
TOTAL TIME: *30 minutes*

CRUST
¾ cup vegetable shortening
¼ cup granulated sugar
2 large eggs yolks
1½ cups all-purpose flour

TOPPING
2 large egg whites
¾ cup granulated sugar
1 cup hazelnuts, chopped
1 cup shredded coconut
1 cup boysenberry puree

1. Preheat the oven to 350 degrees.

2. To make the crust, cream the vegetable shortening and sugar in a large bowl. Beat in the egg yolks. Gradually blend in the flour to make a crumbly dough.

3. Spread the dough evenly over the bottom of a 13 by 9-inch baking pan. Bake for 15 minutes.

4. Meanwhile, make the topping: In a large bowl, beat the egg whites until foamy. Gradually beat in the sugar. Beat to stiff peaks. Fold in the hazelnuts and coconut.

5. Spread the boysenberry puree over the warm crust. Spread the meringue evenly over the puree. Bake for 20 to 25 minutes longer, or until the topping is firm.

6. Cool in the pan on a wire rack before cutting into large or small bars.

Brandied Breakfast Cookies

DROP COOKIES

YIELD: *4 to 5 dozen*
TOTAL TIME: *30 minutes*

1½ cups all-purpose flour
1½ teaspoons baking soda
¼ teaspoon salt
2 cups cornflakes, crushed
½ cup vegetable shortening
1 cup packed light brown
    sugar
2 large eggs
¼ cup strong brewed coffee
1 teaspoon brandy

1. Preheat the oven to 400 degrees. Lightly grease 2 baking sheets.

2. Combine the flour, baking soda, and salt. Spread the crushed cornflakes on a large plate.

3. In a large bowl, cream the vegetable shortening and brown sugar. Beat in the eggs one at a time, beating well after each addition. Beat in the coffee and brandy. Gradually blend in the dry ingredients.

4. Drop the dough by spoonfuls, a few at a time, onto the cornflakes. Roll each one in the cornflakes until well coated and place 1½ inches apart on the prepared baking sheets.

5. Bake for 10 to 12 minutes, until golden. Transfer to wire racks to cool.

Brandy Cones

DROP COOKIES

YIELD: 5 to 6 dozen
TOTAL TIME: 30 minutes

1 cup all-purpose flour
½ teaspoon ground ginger
½ teaspoon ground nutmeg
6 tablespoons vegetable
  shortening
½ cup packed light brown
  sugar
¼ cup molasses
1 tablespoon brandy

1. Preheat the oven to 350 degrees.

2. Combine the flour, ginger, and nutmeg.

3. In a large bowl cream the vegetable shortening and brown sugar. Beat in the molasses and brandy. Gradually blend in the dry ingredients.

4. Drop the dough by spoonfuls 2 inches apart onto ungreased baking sheets.

5. Bake for 5 to 6 minutes, or until lightly colored. As soon as the cookies cool enough so you can handle them, lift them one at a time from the baking sheet and roll up around a metal cone. If cookies harden before you are able to form them, re-heat them for 30 second in a hot oven. Cool on wire racks before using.

Baking notes: You need metal cone forms to shape the cookies; they are available in cookware shops. These cones can be filled with many types of dessert topping or ice cream. If you use ice cream, place the cones in the freezer for at least 30 minutes before you fill them.

Bratislavian Thins

ROLLED COOKIES

YIELD: 1 to 2 dozen
TOTAL TIME: 30 minutes
CHILLING TIME: 1 hour

2 cups all-purpose flour
1 teaspoon baking powder
½ cup vegetable shortening
1 cup granulated sugar
1 large egg
1 tablespoon heavy cream
2 tablespoons poppy seeds

TOPPING
1 tablespoon granulated
  sugar
½ teaspoon ground
  cinnamon

1. Combine the flour and baking powder.

2. In a large bowl, cream the vegetable shortening and sugar. Beat in the egg and heavy cream. Gradually blend in the dry ingredients.

3. Divide the dough in half. Knead the poppy seeds into half the dough. Wrap the dough in waxed paper and chill for at least 1 hour.

4. Preheat the oven to 400 degrees.

5. On a floured surface, roll out the poppy seed dough as thin as possible. Using a knife or a pastry wheel, cut the dough into 2 by 1-inch rectangles and place ½ inch apart on ungreased baking sheets. Combine the sugar and cinnamon for the topping and sprinkle over the cookies. Roll out the remaining dough and, using a 2-inch round cookie cutter, cut into circles.

6. Bake for 10 to 12 minutes, until lightly colored. Transfer to wire racks to cool.

B

YIELD: *3 to 4 dozen*

TOTAL TIME: *30 minutes*

CHILLING TIME: *4 days*

4 cups all-purpose flour
1 teaspoon baking soda
1 teaspoon ground cinnamon
1 teaspoon ground cloves
½ teaspoon salt
⅔ cup honey
1 cup sugar
½ cup butter
1 large egg
⅓ cup warm water
⅔ cup hazelnuts, chopped
½ cup candied citron,
*   chopped*

BRAUNE LEBKÜCHEN

ROLLED COOKIES

1. Combine the flour, baking soda, cinnamon, cloves, and salt.

2. Combine the honey, sugar, and butter in a saucepan and bring to a boil. Cook for 5 minutes. Remove from the heat and let cool slightly.

3. Beat the egg and water into the honey mixture. Gradually blend in the dry ingredients. Stir in the nuts and candied citron.

4. Form into a ball and wrap in waxed paper and chill for 4 days.

5. Preheat the oven to 350 degrees. Grease 2 baking sheets.

6. On a floured surface, roll out the dough to a thickness of ¼ inch. Using cookie cutters, cut into shapes and place 1½ inches apart on the prepared baking sheets.

7. Bake for 15 to 18 minutes, or until lightly colored. Transfer to wire racks to cool.

Baking notes: By tradition, these cookie are iced with colored sugar icing.

YIELD: *1 to 2 dozen*

TOTAL TIME: *40 minutes*

CRUST
½ cup vegetable shortening
1 cup all-purpose flour
¼ teaspoon salt

TOPPING
2 large eggs
¾ cup packed light brown
*   sugar*
1½ cups brazil nuts,
*   ground fine*
¼ teaspoon salt
½ cup flaked coconut
1 teaspoon vanilla extract
2 tablespoons all-purpose
*   flour*
Frosting to decorate

BRAZIL-NUT BARS

BAR COOKIES

1. Preheat the oven to 375 degrees. Lightly grease a 9-inch square baking pan.

2. To make the crust, cream the vegetable shortening in a large bowl. Blend in the flour and salt.

3. Press the mixture evenly into the bottom of the prepared baking pan. Bake for 15 minutes.

4. Meanwhile make the topping: In a large bowl, beat the eggs and brown sugar together until thick. Beat in the brazil nuts and salt. Beat in the coconut, vanilla extract, and flour.

5. Spread this mixture evenly over the warm crust. Bake for 15 minutes longer, until firm to the touch.

6. Cool in the pan on a rack and top with frosting before cutting into large or small bars. (See Pantry).

Brazil-Nut Cookies I

DROP COOKIES

YIELD: *2 to 3 dozen*
TOTAL TIME: *30 minutes*
CHILLING TIME: *4 hours*

1. Combine the flour and salt.

2. In a large bowl, cream the vegetable shortening and sugar. Beat in the egg. Beat in the vanilla extract. Gradually blend in the dry ingredients. Fold in the sliced nuts. Cover and chill for at least 4 hours.

3. Preheat the oven to 375 degrees. Lightly grease 2 baking sheets.

4. Drop the dough by tablespoonfuls 1½ inches apart onto the prepared baking sheets. Press a whole brazil nut into each cookie.

5. Bake for 10 to 12 minutes, until golden brown. Transfer to wire racks to cool.

1¾ cups all-purpose flour
½ teaspoon salt
1 cup vegetable shortening
1 cup granulated sugar
1 large egg
1 teaspoon vanilla extract
1 cup brazil nuts, sliced thin
About 1½ cups whole brazil nuts

Brazil-Nut Cookies II

DROP COOKIES

YIELD: *5 dozen*
TOTAL TIME: *30 minutes*

1. Preheat the oven to 400 degrees.

2. Combine the flour, brazil nuts, and salt.

3. In a large bowl, cream the vegetable shortening and sugar. Beat in the egg yolks and orange juice. Beat in the lemon zest. Gradually blend in the dry ingredients.

4. Drop the dough by spoonfuls 1½ inches apart onto ungreased baking sheets.

5. Bake for 10 to 12 minutes, until lightly colored. Sprinkle with powdered sugar and transfer to wire racks to cool.

1 cup all-purpose flour
¼ cup brazil nuts, chopped fine
¼ teaspoon salt
½ cup vegetable shortening
⅓ cup granulated sugar
2 large egg yolks
3 tablespoons fresh orange juice
½ teaspoon grated lemon zest
Powdered sugar for sprinkling

Brazil-Nut Strips

ROLLED COOKIES

YIELD: *3 to 4 dozen*
TOTAL TIME: *35 minutes*
CHILLING TIME: *4 hours*

1. Combine the flour, spices, and salt.

2. In a large bowl, cream the butter and brown sugar. Beat in the molasses.

3. Dissolve the baking soda in the hot water and beat into the molasses mixture. Gradually blend in the dry ingredients. Fold in the nuts. Cover and chill for at least 4 hours.

4. Preheat the oven to 350 degrees. Lightly grease 2 baking sheets.

5. On a floured surface, roll out the dough to a thickness of ¼ inch. With a sharp knife or a pastry wheel, cut into 3 by 1-inch strips. Place 1 inch apart on the prepared baking sheets.

6. Bake for 10 to 12 minutes, until lightly colored. Transfer to wire racks to cool.

3 cups all-purpose flour
1 teaspoon ground ginger
¼ teaspoon ground nutmeg
½ teaspoon salt
½ cup butter, at room temperature
½ cup packed dark brown sugar
½ cup molasses
1 teaspoon baking soda
¼ cup hot water
1¾ cups brazil nuts, chopped fine

BROWN-EYED SUSANS

FORMED COOKIES

YIELD: *4 to 5 dozen*
TOTAL TIME: *30 minutes*
CHILLING TIME: *1 hour*

1¾ cups all-purpose flour
¼ teaspoon salt
¾ cup vegetable shortening
½ cup granulated sugar
1 large egg
1 teaspoon vanilla extract
7 ounces milk chocolate,
 chopped

1. Combine the flour and salt.

2. In a large bowl, cream the vegetable shortening and sugar. Beat in the egg. Beat in the vanilla extract. Gradually blend in the dry ingredients. Cover and chill for 1 hour.

3. Preheat the oven to 400 degrees.

4. Melt the milk chocolate in the top half of a double boiler over a low heat, stirring until smooth. Remove from the heat; keep warm over hot water.

5. Break off small pieces of the dough and roll into balls. Place 1½ inches apart on ungreased baking sheets. Press your finger into the center of each ball to make a slight indentation.

6. Bake for 8 to 10 minutes, until lightly colored. Spoon a little of the melted milk chocolate into the center of each hot cookie and transfer to wire racks to cool.

Baking notes: This dough can be frozen for up to a month. You can also shape the dough into balls and freeze until ready to bake; let stand for two hours at room temperature. Then bake according to the instructions above.

BROWNIES I

BAR COOKIES

YIELD: *1 to 2 dozen*
TOTAL TIME: *50 minutes*

4 ounces unsweetened
 chocolate, chopped
¾ cup vegetable shortening
2 cups granulated sugar
1 teaspoon vanilla extract
3 large eggs
1 cup all-purpose flour
1 cup walnuts, chopped fine

1. Preheat the oven to 350 degrees. Lightly grease a 13 by 9-inch baking pan.

2. In a large saucepan, melt the unsweetened chocolate and vegetable shortening over low heat, stirring until smooth. Remove from the heat and beat in the sugar and vanilla extract. Beat in the eggs. Gradually blend in the flour. Fold in the walnuts. Spread the batter evenly in the prepared baking pan.

3. Bake for 35 to 40 minutes, until a toothpick inserted into the center comes out clean. Cool in the pan on a wire rack before cutting into large or small bars.

Brownies II

BAR COOKIES

YIELD: *1 to 2 dozen*
TOTAL TIME: *35 minutes*

1. Preheat the oven to 350 degrees. Lightly grease a 9-inch square baking pan.

2. In a medium bowl, beat the eggs until thick and light-colored. Beat in the sugar.

3. Melt the vegetable shortening, bittersweet chocolate, semisweet chocolate, and vanilla extract in the top of a double boiler over low heat, stirring until smooth. Remove from the heat and add the egg mixture in a thin steady stream, beating constantly. Gradually blend in the flour. Fold in the almonds and marshmallows. Spread the batter evenly in the prepared baking pan.

4. Bake for 25 to 30 minutes, until a toothpick inserted in the center comes out clean. Cut into large or small squares while still warm and cool in the pan on a wire rack.

Baking notes: For variation, substitute white chocolate chips for the marshmallows.

2 large eggs
1 cup granulated sugar
½ cup vegetable shortening
2 ounces bittersweet chocolate, chopped
½ cup semisweet chocolate chips
½ teaspoon vanilla extract
1 cup all-purpose flour
½ cup almonds, chopped
1 cup miniature marshmallows

Brownies III

BAR COOKIES

YIELD: *1 to 2 dozen*
TOTAL TIME: *35 minutes*

1. Preheat the oven to 350 degrees.

2. In a large bowl, cream the granulated sugar and vegetable shortening. Beat in the eggs and chocolate syrup. Gradually blend in the flour.

3. Spread the batter evenly in an ungreased 9-inch square baking pan. Bake for 25 to 30 minutes, until a toothpick inserted in the center comes out clean.

4. Meanwhile, prepare the topping: In a saucepan, bring the milk to a boil, and boil for 1 minute. Remove from the heat and add the chocolate chips and walnuts. Let cool.

5. Spread the topping over the brownies. Cool in the pan on a wire rack before cutting into large or small bars.

Baking notes: Shredded coconut can be sprinkled over the still-warm topping.

1 cup granulated sugar
1 cup vegetable shortening
4 large eggs
1 cup chocolate syrup
1 cup all-purpose flour

TOPPING
⅓ cup milk
½ cup semisweet chocolate chips
½ cup walnuts, chopped

Brownies (Sugarless)

BAR COOKIES

YIELD: 1 to 2 dozen
TOTAL TIME: 30 minutes

2 ounces unsweetened
   chocolate, chopped
¾ cup all-purpose flour
1 teaspoon baking powder
½ cup unsalted butter, at
   room temperature
3 tablespoons nonnutritive
   sweetener (see Baking
   notes)
2 large eggs
½ teaspoon vanilla extract
½ cup walnuts, chopped
   fine

1. Preheat the oven to 350 degrees. Lightly grease an 8-inch square baking pan.

2. Melt the chocolate in a double boiler over low heat, stirring until smooth. Remove from the heat.

3. Combine the flour and baking powder.

4. In a large bowl, cream the butter and sweetener. Beat in the melted chocolate. Beat in the eggs and vanilla. Gradually blend in the dry ingredients. Fold in the walnuts. Spread the batter evenly in the prepared baking pan.

5. Bake for 25 to 30 minutes, until firm to the touch. Cool in the pan on a wire rack before cutting into large or small squares.

Baking notes: Although created for diabetics, these brownies will appeal to anyone on a sugar-restricted diet. There are several nonnutritive sweeteners on the market.

Brown Moravian

ROLLED COOKIES

YIELD: 2 to 3 dozen
TOTAL TIME: 30 minutes
CHILLING TIME: 2 hours

4 cups all-purpose flour
¼ teaspoon baking soda
1 teaspoon ground cinnamon
½ teaspoon ground cloves
¼ teaspoon ground ginger
¼ teaspoon salt
1 cup vegetable shortening
1 cup packed light brown
   sugar
1½ cups molasses, warmed
½ teaspoon red wine
   vinegar

1. Combine the flour, baking soda, spices, and salt.

2. In a large bowl, cream the vegetable shortening and brown sugar. Beat in the molasses and vinegar. Gradually blend in the dry ingredients. Cover and chill for at least 2 hours.

3. Preheat the oven to 350 degrees.

4. On a floured surface, roll out the dough to a thickness of ¼ inch. Using cookie cutters, cut into shapes and place the cookies 1½ inches apart on ungreased baking sheets.

5. Bake for 10 to 12 minutes, until firm to the touch. Transfer to wire racks to cool.

Brown Sugar Christmas Cookies

ROLLED COOKIES

YIELD: 4 to 5 dozen
TOTAL TIME: 30 minutes
CHILLING TIME: 2 hours

2½ cups all-purpose flour
¼ teaspoon salt
½ cup dark corn syrup
½ cup molasses
¼ cup vegetable shortening
½ cup packed light brown
   sugar
½ teaspoon baking soda
1½ teaspoons ground ginger
1½ teaspoons ground
   cinnamon
¼ teaspoon ground cloves

1. Combine the flour and salt.

2. In a double boiler, combine the corn syrup, molasses, and vegetable shortening and heat. Stir until well blended. Remove from the heat, and beat in the brown sugar, baking soda, and spices. Gradually blend in the flour mixture.

3. Wrap the dough in waxed paper and chill for at least 2 hours.

4. Preheat the oven to 375 degrees. Lightly grease 2 baking sheets.

5. On a floured surface, roll out the dough ¼ inch thick. Using cookie cutters, cut into shapes and place 1½ inches apart on the prepared baking sheets.

6. Bake for 7 to 10 minutes, until lightly colored. Transfer to wire racks to cool.

Brown Sugar Cookies

ROLLED COOKIES

YIELD: 3 to 5 dozen
TOTAL TIME: 30 minutes
CHILLING TIME: 4 hours

1. Combine the flour, baking powder, and salt.

2. In a large bowl, cream the butter and brown sugar. Beat in the egg. Beat in the heavy cream and vanilla extract. Gradually blend in the dry ingredients. The dough will be stiff. If it seems too dry, add a little water, ½ teaspoon at a time. Cover and chill for 4 hours.

3. Preheat the oven to 375 degrees.

4. On a floured surface, roll out the dough to a thickness of ⅛ inch. With cookie cutters, cut into shapes and place 1½ inches apart on ungreased baking sheets.

5. Bake for 8 to 10 minutes, until lightly browned around the edges. Transfer to wire racks to cool.

Baking Notes: Store these cookies in an airtight container.

2 cups all-purpose flour
1½ teaspoons baking
    powder
¼ teaspoon salt
½ cup butter, at room
    temperature
½ cup packed light brown
    sugar
1 large egg
1 tablespoon heavy cream
1½ teaspoons vanilla
    extract

Brown Sugar Refrigerator Cookies

REFRIGERATOR COOKIES

YIELD: 8 to 9 dozen
TOTAL TIME: 30 minutes
CHILLING TIME: 8 hours

1. Combine the flour, baking soda, and salt.

2. In a large bowl, cream the vegetable shortening and brown sugar. Beat in the eggs. Beat in the vanilla. Gradually blend in the dry ingredients. Fold in the walnuts.

3. Divide the dough in thirds. Form each piece into a log 8 about inches long. Wrap in waxed paper and chill for 8 hours or overnight.

4. Preheat the oven to 375 degrees.

5. Slice the log into ¼-inch-thick-slices and place 1 inch apart on ungreased baking sheets.

6. Bake for 7 to 10 minutes, until lightly colored. Transfer to wire racks to cool.

3½ cups all-purpose flour
½ teaspoon baking soda
½ teaspoon salt
1 cup vegetable shortening
2 cups packed light brown
    sugar
3 large eggs
1 teaspoon vanilla extract
½ cup walnuts, chopped

Brown Sugar Sand Tarts

ROLLED COOKIES

YIELD: 3 to 5 dozen
TOTAL TIME: 30 minutes
CHILLING TIME: 2 hours

1. Combine the flour, baking powder, and salt.

2. In a large bowl, cream the butter and brown sugar. Beat in the egg. Beat in the vanilla extract. Gradually blend in the dry ingredients. Cover and chill for 2 hours.

3. Preheat the oven to 375 degrees. Lightly grease 2 baking sheets.

4. On a floured surface, roll out the dough to a thickness of ⅛ inch. With cookie cutters, cut into shapes and place 1 inch apart on the prepared baking sheets. Sprinkle with brown sugar and lightly press the sugar into the cookie.

5. Bake for 8 to 10 minutes, until firm to the touch. Transfer to wire racks to cool.

¾ cup all-purpose flour
¼ teaspoon baking powder
¼ teaspoon salt
¼ cup butter, at room
    temperature
⅓ cup packed light brown
    sugar
1 large egg
½ teaspoon vanilla extract
Light brown sugar for
    sprinkling

Brown Sugar Spritz Cookies   FORMED COOKIES

YIELD: *4 to 6 dozen*
TOTAL TIME: *30 minutes*

2¼ cups all-purpose flour
¼ cup hazelnuts, ground fine
¼ teaspoon salt
1 cup butter, at room temperature
⅓ cup packed light brown sugar
¼ cup granulated sugar
1 large egg yolk
½ teaspoon hazelnut extract

1. Preheat the oven to 350 degrees.

2. Combine the flour, hazelnuts, and salt.

3. In a large bowl, cream the butter and both sugars. Beat in the egg yolk. Beat in the hazelnut extract. Gradually blend in the dry ingredients.

4. Place the dough in a cookie press or a pastry bag with a ribbon tip. Press or pipe 2½-inch-long strips onto ungreased baking sheets, spacing the cookies 1 inch apart.

5. Bake for 8 to 10 minutes, until lightly browned. Transfer to wire racks to cool.

Baking notes: This recipe must be made with butter; do not substitute vegetable shortening. To decorate, dip one end of each cookie in melted semisweet chocolate.

Bulgarian Cookies   FORMED COOKIES

YIELD: *4 to 6 dozen*
TOTAL TIME: *30 minutes*
CHILLING TIME: *24 hours*

2⅓ cups all-purpose flour
1 cup hazelnuts, ground fine
¾ teaspoon baking soda
½ teaspoon ground cloves
¼ teaspoon salt
⅔ cup vegetable shortening
¾ cup granulated sugar
½ cup plain yogurt
2 teaspoons orange extract
Powdered sugar for rolling

1. Combine the flour, hazelnuts, baking soda, cloves, and salt.

2. In a large bowl, cream the vegetable shortening and sugar. Beat in the yogurt and orange extract. Gradually blend in the dry ingredients. Cover and chill 24 hours.

3. Preheat the oven to 350 degrees. Lightly grease 2 baking sheets.

4. Break off walnut-sized pieces of dough and roll into balls. Place 1 inch apart on the prepared baking sheets.

5. Bake for 15 to 20 minutes, until lightly browned. Roll in powdered sugar and transfer to wire racks to cool.

6. After the balls have cooled, roll them again in powdered sugar.

Butterballs   FORMED COOKIES

YIELD: *3 to 4 dozen*
TOTAL TIME: *30 minutes*

1 cup butter, at room temperature
½ cup powdered sugar
2 cups all-purpose flour
1½ cups shredded coconut
Powdered sugar for rolling

1. Preheat the oven to 350 degrees.

2. In a large bowl, cream the butter and powdered sugar. Gradually blend in the flour. Fold in the coconut.

3. Break off walnut-sized pieces of dough and roll into balls. Roll in powdered sugar and place 1 inch apart on ungreased baking sheets.

4. Bake for 18 to 20 minutes, until lightly colored. Roll in powdered sugar again and transfer to wire racks to cool.

BUTTER COOKIES I

ROLLED COOKIES

YIELD: 2 to 3 dozen
TOTAL TIME: 30 minutes
CHILLING TIME: 12 hours

1. In a large bowl, cream the butter and sugar. Beat in the egg yolk. Beat in the almond extract. Gradually blend in the flour. Cover and chill for 12 hours.

2. Preheat the oven to 350 degrees.

3. On a floured surface, roll out the dough to a thickness of ¼ inch. Using a 2-inch round cookie cutter, cut into circles. Using a ½-inch round cookie cutter, cut out the centers of one half of the cookies. Place the cookies 1½ inches apart on ungreased baking sheets. Brush the cut-out cookies with beaten egg white and sprinkle the ground almonds over the top.

4. Bake for 8 to 10 minutes, until lightly colored. Transfer to wire racks to cool.

5. Spread a layer of jam or preserves over the plain cookies and top with the cut-out cookies.

Baking notes: Jelly does not usually make a good filling for cookies because it is too thin. Use any small cookie cutter to make the center cut-out: angels, dogs, cats, Santa's, etc.

1 cup butter, at room
    temperature
½ cup granulated sugar
1 large egg yolk
½ teaspoon almond extract
2⅓ cups all-purpose flour
½ cup almonds, ground
    fine
1 large egg white, lightly
    beaten
Jam or preserves for filling

BUTTER COOKIES II

FORMED COOKIES

YIELD: 4 to 5 dozen
TOTAL TIME: 30 minutes

1. Preheat the oven to 350 degrees. Lightly grease 2 baking sheets.

2. Combine the flour and salt.

3. In a large bowl, cream the butter and sugar. Beat in the egg. Beat in the orange juice and almond extract. Gradually blend in the dry ingredients.

4. Place the dough in a cookie press or a pastry bag fitted with a large star tip. Press or pipe out cookies 1½ inches apart on the prepared baking sheets.

5. Bake for 7 to 10 minutes, until lightly colored. Transfer to wire racks to a cool.

2 cups all-purpose flour
½ teaspoon salt
¾ cup butter, at room
    temperature
½ cup granulated sugar
1 large egg
2 tablespoons fresh orange
    juice
½ teaspoon almond extract

BUTTER COOKIES III

ROLLED COOKIES

YIELD: 4 to 5 dozen
TOTAL TIME: 30 minutes

1. Preheat the oven to 350 degrees.

2. Combine the flour, spices, and salt.

3. In a large bowl, cream the butter and sugar. Beat in the eggs one at a time. Beat in the lemon zest. Gradually blend in the dry ingredients.

4. On a floured surface, roll out the dough ¼ inch thick. Using cookie cutters, cut into shapes and place 1½ inches apart on ungreased baking sheets.

5. Bake for 12 to 15 minutes, until lightly colored. Transfer to wire racks to cool.

4 cups all-purpose flour
1 teaspoon ground
    cinnamon
1 teaspoon ground ginger
¼ teaspoon salt
1 cup butter, at room
    temperature
1½ cups packed light
    brown sugar
2 large eggs
1 tablespoon grated lemon
    zest

BUTTER CRISPS

YIELD: 3 to 4 dozen
TOTAL TIME: 30 minutes

2½ cups rolled oats
2 teaspoons baking powder
½ teaspoon salt
2 tablespoons butter, at
  room temperature
1 cup granulated sugar
2 large eggs
1 teaspoon almond extract

1. Preheat the oven to 375 degrees. Lightly grease 2 baking sheets.

2. Combine the oats, baking powder, and salt.

3. In a large bowl, cream the butter and sugar. Beat in the eggs. Beat in the almond extract. Gradually blend in the dry ingredients.

4. Drop the dough by spoonfuls 1½ inches apart onto the prepared baking sheets.

5. Bake for 10 to 12 minutes, until lightly browned. Transfer to wire racks to cool.

BUTTERMILK BROWNIES

YIELD: 1 to 2 dozen
TOTAL TIME: 30 minutes

2 cups all-purpose flour
1¾ cups granulated sugar
¼ cup packed light brown
  sugar
½ teaspoon salt
1 cup vegetable shortening
⅓ cup unsweetened cocoa
  powder
1 cup water
1 teaspoon baking soda
1 tablespoon warm water
2 large eggs
½ cup buttermilk
1 teaspoon vanilla extract

1. Preheat the oven to 375 degrees. Lightly grease a 13 by 9-inch baking pan.

2. Combine the flour, both sugars, and salt.

3. In a large saucepan, combine the vegetable shortening, cocoa powder, and the 1 cup water, stir until smooth and bring to a boil over high heat. Remove from the heat.

4. Dissolve the baking soda in the warm water and beat into the cocoa mixture. Beat in the eggs. Beat in the buttermilk and vanilla extract. Gradually blend in the dry ingredients. Pour the batter into the prepared baking pan.

5. Bake for 18 to 20 minutes, or until a toothpick inserted in the center comes out clean. Cool in the pan on a wire rack before cutting into large or small bars.

BUTTERNUT DROPS

YIELD: 4 to 6 dozen
TOTAL TIME: 30 minutes
CHILLING TIME: 4 hours

½ cup vegetable shortening
¼ cup granulated sugar
1 large egg
1 teaspoon vanilla extract
1 tablespoon fresh lemon
  juice
2 tablespoons grated orange
  zest
1 tablespoon grated lemon
  zest
1 cup all-purpose flour
1 egg white
½ cup brazil nuts, chopped
Candied cherries for garnish

1. In a large bowl, cream the vegetable shortening and sugar. Beat in the egg. Beat in the vanilla extract and lemon juice. Beat in the orange and lemon zest. Gradually blend in the flour. Cover and chill for 4 hours.

2. Preheat the oven to 350 degrees.

3. In a small bowl, beat the egg white until stiff but not dry. Spread the chopped nuts on a plate.

4. Break off small pieces of dough and form into balls. Roll each ball in the beaten egg white, then in the brazil nuts, and place 1½ inches apart on ungreased baking sheets. Press a candied cherry into the center of each ball.

5. Bake for 12 to 15 minutes, or until golden brown. Transfer to wire racks to cool.

BUTTERNUTS

1. Preheat the oven to 325 degrees.

2. Combine the flour, almonds, salt.

3. In a large bowl, cream the vegetable shortening and powdered sugar. Gradually blend in the dry ingredients. Fold in the crushed candy.

4. Break off small pieces of the dough and roll into balls. Place the balls 1½ inches apart on ungreased baking sheets. Dip the bottom of a glass in granulated sugar and flatten each cookie.

5. Bake for 12 to 15 minutes, or until lightly colored. Transfer to wire racks to cool.

Baking notes: If you like, place a pecan half in the center of each cookie before baking.

YIELD: 7 to 8 dozen
TOTAL TIME: 30 minutes

1½ cups all-purpose flour
1 cup almonds, ground fine
¼ teaspoon salt
¾ cup vegetable shortening
½ cup powdered sugar
1 cup hard butterscotch
   candies, crushed
Granulated sugar

BUTTER PECAN DROP COOKIES

1. Combine the flour and salt.

2. In a large bowl, cream the butter and brown sugar. Beat in the egg. Gradually blend in the dry ingredients. Cover and chill for at least 1 hour.

3. Preheat the oven to 375 degrees.

4. Break off walnut-sized pieces of dough and roll into balls. Place 1½ inches apart on ungreased baking sheets. Flatten the balls with the bottom of a glass dipped in flour and press a pecan into the center of each cookie.

5. Bake for 10 to 12 minutes, until lightly colored. Transfer to wire racks to cool.

YIELD: 3 to 4 dozen
TOTAL TIME: 30 minutes
CHILLING TIME: 1 hour

2 cups all-purpose flour
½ teaspoon salt
1 cup butter, at room
   temperature
⅔ cup packed light brown
   sugar
1 large egg
About 1½ cups pecan
   halves

BUTTERSCOTCH BARS

1. Preheat the oven to 350 degrees. Lightly grease a 9-inch square baking pan.

2. Combine the flour, baking powder, salt, and almonds.

3. In a large bowl, cream the vegetable oil and brown sugar. Beat in the eggs. Beat in the vanilla extract. Gradually blend in the dry ingredients. Stir in the coconut. Spread the batter evenly in the prepared baking pan.

4. To make the topping, cream the vegetable shortening and brown sugar in a small bowl. Beat in the corn syrup, cream, and vanilla extract. Spread the topping over the batter.

5. Bake for 25 to 30 minutes, until a toothpick inserted in the center comes out clean. Cool in the pan on a wire rack before cutting into large or small bars.

YIELD: 2 to 3 dozen
TOTAL TIME: 45 minutes

1⅓ cups all-purpose flour
2 teaspoons baking powder
1 teaspoon salt
1 cup almonds, ground
½ cup vegetable oil
2 cups packed light brown
   sugar
2 large eggs
1 teaspoon vanilla extract
1 cup flaked coconut

TOPPING
2 tablespoons vegetable
   shortening
¾ cup packed light brown
   sugar
¼ cup light corn syrup
3 tablespoons heavy cream
1 teaspoon vanilla extract

BUTTERSCOTCH BROWNIES   **BAR COOKIES**

YIELD: 1 to 2 dozen
TOTAL TIME: 35 minutes

⅔ cup all-purpose flour
½ cup walnuts, ground
  fine
1 teaspoon baking powder
¼ teaspoon salt
¼ cup vegetable shortening
1 cup packed light brown
  sugar
1 large egg
1 teaspoon vanilla extract

1. Preheat the oven to 350 degrees. Lightly grease an 8-inch square baking pan.

2. Combine the flour, walnuts, baking powder, and salt.

3. In a large bowl, cream the vegetable shortening and sugar. Beat in the egg. Beat in the vanilla extract. Gradually blend in the dry ingredients. Spread the dough evenly in the prepared baking pan.

4. Bake for 20 to 25 minutes, or until a toothpick inserted in the center comes out clean. Cut into large or small bars and cool in the pan on a wire rack.

BUTTERSCOTCH CHEESECAKE BARS   **BAR COOKIES**

YIELD: 1 to 2 dozen
TOTAL TIME: 30 minutes

CRUST
¾ cup butterscotch chips
⅓ cup butter, at room
  temperature
2 cups graham cracker
  crumbs
1 cup walnuts, ground fine

FILLING
8 ounces cream cheese, at
  room temperature
One 14-ounce can
  sweetened condensed
  milk
1 large egg
1 teaspoon vanilla extract

1. Preheat the oven to 350 degrees. Lightly grease a 13 by 9-inch baking pan.

2. To make the crust, melt the butterscotch chips and butter in a medium saucepan, stirring until smooth. Remove from the heat and blend in the graham cracker crumbs and walnuts. Spread half of this mixture evenly into the bottom of the prepared baking pan.

3. To make the filling, beat the cream cheese and condensed milk together in a small bowl. Beat in the egg and vanilla extract. Pour this mixture over the crust.

4. Spread the remaining crust mixture over the filling.

5. Bake for 25 to 30 minutes, until a knife inserted into the center comes out clean. Cool in the pan on a wire rack before cutting into large or small bars.

BUTTERSCOTCH CHEWS   **BAR COOKIES**

YIELD: 1 to 2 dozen
TOTAL TIME: 35 minutes

2 cups all-purpose flour
2 teaspoons baking powder
¼ teaspoon salt
½ cup vegetable shortening
2 cups packed light brown
  sugar
2 large eggs
½ teaspoon vanilla extract
1⅓ cups sliced almonds

1. Preheat the oven to 350 degrees. Lightly grease a 9-inch square baking pan.

2. Combine the flour, baking powder, and salt.

3. In a large bowl, cream the vegetable shortening and sugar. Beat in the eggs. Beat in the vanilla extract. Gradually blend in the dry ingredients.

4. Spread the mixture evenly in the prepared baking pan. Sprinkle the almonds over the top and press down gently.

5. Bake for 20 to 25 minutes, until firm to the touch. Cool in the pan on a wire rack before cutting into large or small bars.

Butterscotch Cookies

DROP COOKIES

YIELD: 3 to 5 dozen
TOTAL TIME: 30 minutes

1. Preheat the oven to 350 degrees. Lightly grease 2 baking sheets.

2. Combine the flour, baking soda, and salt.

3. In a large bowl, cream the vegetable shortening and brown sugar. Beat in the eggs. Gradually blend in the dry ingredients. Fold in the oats and almonds. Fold in the butterscotch chips.

4. Drop the dough by spoonfuls 2 inches apart onto the prepared baking sheets.

5. Bake for 10 to 12 minutes, until lightly browned. Transfer to wire racks to cool.

2 cups all-purpose flour
½ teaspoon baking soda
½ teaspoon salt
¾ cup vegetable shortening
1 cup packed light brown
　sugar
2 large eggs
1 cup (6 ounces) rolled oats
½ cup almonds, chopped
1 cup (6 ounces)
　butterscotch chips

Butterscotch Drops

DROP COOKIES

YIELD: 2 to 3 dozen
TOTAL TIME: 30 minutes

1. Line 2 baking sheets with waxed paper.

2. Combine the butterscotch chips and peanut butter in the top of a double boiler and heat over medium heat, stirring, until the butterscotch chips are melted and the mixture is smooth. Remove from the heat, add the cornflakes and stir until well coated.

3. Drop by spoonfuls onto the prepared baking sheets and chill until set.

Baking notes: Almost any type of sweet-ened cereal can be used in this recipe.

1 cup (6 ounces)
　butterscotch chips
½ cup peanut butter
3 cups cornflakes (see
　Baking notes)

Butterscotch-Oatmeal Cookies

DROP COOKIES

YIELD: 3 to 4 dozen
TOTAL TIME: 30 minutes

1. Preheat the oven to 375 degrees. Lightly grease 2 baking sheets.

2. Combine the flour and baking soda.

3. In a large bowl, cream the vegetable shortening and the two sugars. Beat in the eggs. Beat in the vanilla extract. Gradually blend in the dry ingredients. Fold in the rolled oats and walnuts. Fold in the butterscotch chips.

4. Drop the dough by spoonfuls 1½ inches apart onto the prepared baking sheets.

5. Bake for 10 to 12 minutes, until lightly col-ored. Transfer to wire racks to cool.

Baking notes: For an unusual variation, use crushed butterscotch candy in place of the but-terscotch chips.

1½ cups all-purpose flour
1 teaspoon baking soda
1 cup vegetable shortening
¾ cup packed light brown
　sugar
¾ cup granulated sugar
2 large eggs
1 teaspoon vanilla extract
2 cups (12 ounces) rolled
　oats
½ cup walnuts, chopped
2 cups (12 ounces)
　butterscotch chips

BUTTERSCOTCH REFRIGERATOR COOKIES

YIELD: 2 to 3 dozen

TOTAL TIME: 30 minutes

CHILLING TIME: 8 hours

1 cup all-purpose flour
1 package butterscotch
    pudding mix
½ teaspoon baking powder
¼ teaspoon salt
¼ cup butter, at room
    temperature
2 tablespoons light brown
    sugar
1 large egg
¼ teaspoon vanilla extract

1. Combine the flour, butterscotch pudding mix, baking powder and salt.

2. In a large bowl, cream the butter and brown sugar. Beat in the egg. Beat in the vanilla extract. Gradually blend in the dry ingredients.

3. Form the dough into a log 2 inches in diameter. Wrap in waxed paper and chill for 8 hours or overnight.

4. Preheat the oven to 375 degrees. Lightly grease 2 baking sheets.

5. Slice the log into ⅛-inch-thick slices and place 1 inch apart on the prepared baking sheets.

6. Bake for 8 to 10 minutes, until firm. Transfer to wire racks to cool.

BUTTERSCOTCH SQUARES

YIELD: 1 to 2 dozen

TOTAL TIME: 40 minutes

1¼ cups all-purpose flour
1 teaspoon baking powder
¼ teaspoon salt
½ cup vegetable shortening
½ cup peanut butter
1½ cups packed light
    brown sugar
2 large eggs
1 teaspoon vanilla extract

1. Preheat the oven to 350 degrees. Lightly grease a 9-inch square baking pan.

2. Combine the flour, baking powder, and salt.

3. In medium saucepan, combine the vegetable shortening, peanut butter, and brown sugar and heat over medium heat, stirring, until the shortening melts and the sugar dissolves. Remove from the heat and let cool slightly.

4. Beat the eggs into the peanut butter mixture. Beat in the vanilla extract. Gradually blend in the dry ingredients.

5. Spread the mixture evenly in the prepared baking pan.

6. Bake for 25 to 30 minutes, or until a toothpick inserted in the center comes out clean. Cool in the pan on a wire rack before cutting into large or small bars.

Butterscotch-Wheat Germ Cookies **DROP COOKIES**

1. Preheat the oven to 375 degrees. Lightly grease 2 baking sheets.

2. Combine the two flours, the wheat germ, baking soda, cinnamon, and salt.

3. In a large bowl, cream the vegetable shortening and brown sugar. Beat in the egg and almond extract. Gradually blend in the dry ingredients. If the mixture seems a little dry, add a little water 1 teaspoon at a time. Fold in the oats.

4. Drop the dough by spoonfuls 1½ inches apart onto the prepared baking sheets.

5. Bake for 7 to 9 minutes, until lightly colored. Transfer to wire racks to cool.

YIELD: 6 to 7 dozen
TOTAL TIME: 30 minutes

¾ cup all-purpose flour
¾ cup whole wheat flour
1 cup wheat germ
1 teaspoon baking soda
1 teaspoon ground
 cinnamon
½ teaspoon salt
1 cup vegetable shortening
1⅓ cup packed dark brown
 sugar
1 large egg
1 teaspoon almond extract
2 cups rolled oats

Buttery Caraway Cakes **ROLLED COOKIES**

1. Combine the flour, baking soda, and mace.

2. In a large bowl, cream the butter and sugar. Beat in the eggs. Beat in the sherry. Gradually blend in the dry ingredients. Fold in the caraway seeds. Cover and chill for 2 to 4 hours, until firm enough to roll.

3. Preheat the oven to 350 degrees. Lightly grease 2 baking sheets.

4. On a floured surface, roll out the dough to a thickness of ¼ inch. Using cookie cutters, cut into shapes and place 1½ inches apart on the prepared baking sheets.

5. Bake for 10 to 12 minutes, until lightly colored. Transfer to wire racks to cool.

Baking notes: These make very good Christmas cookies. For variation, anise seeds can be substituted for the caraway seeds. Other sweet wines can be used in place of the sherry.

YIELD: 3 to 4 dozen
TOTAL TIME: 30 minutes
CHILLING TIME: 2 to 4 hours

3 cups all-purpose flour
½ teaspoon baking soda
¾ teaspoon ground mace
1½ cups butter, at room
 temperature
3 cups powdered sugar
4 large eggs
¼ cup sherry
½ teaspoon caraway seeds

CALLA LILIES

DROP COOKIES

YIELD: 2 to 3 dozen
TOTAL TIME: 30 minutes

1 cup all-purpose flour
1 teaspoon baking powder
⅛ teaspoon salt
3 large egg whites
¾ cup granulated sugar
1 teaspoon vanilla extract

FILLING
½ cup heavy cream
2 tablespoons granulated
   sugar

1. Preheat the oven to 400 degrees. Lightly grease 2 baking sheets.

2. Combine the flour, baking powder, and salt.

3. In a large bowl, beat the egg whites until stiff but not dry. Beat in the sugar and vanilla extract. Gradually fold in the dry ingredients. Beat for 2 minutes.

4. Drop the dough by spoonfuls onto the prepared baking sheets.

5. Bake for 8 to 10 minutes, until golden. While the cookies are still hot, roll each one into a cone shape and place seam side down on wire racks to cool.

6. To prepare the filling, in a small bowl beat the heavy cream with the sugar until it holds soft peaks. Just before serving, fill the cones with the whipped cream

Baking notes: For variation, add diced fresh fruit to the whipped cream before filling the cones.

CANDY GUMDROP COOKIES

FORMED COOKIES

YIELD: 2 to 3 dozen
TOTAL TIME: 30 minutes

2 cups all-purpose flour
1 teaspoon baking soda
1 teaspoon salt
1 cup vegetable shortening
1 cup granulated sugar
1 cup packed light brown
   sugar
2 large eggs
1 teaspoon vanilla extract
2 cups (12 ounces) rolled
   oats
1 cup shredded coconut
1 cup gumdrops, diced
Powdered sugar for rolling

1. Preheat the oven to 350 degrees. Lightly grease 2 baking sheets.

2. Combine the flour, baking soda and salt.

3. In a large bowl, cream the vegetable shortening and two sugars. Beat in the eggs one at a time. Beat in the vanilla extract. Gradually blend in the dry ingredients. Fold in the oats, coconut, and gumdrops.

4. Pinch off small pieces of the dough and form into balls. Place 1 inch apart on the prepared baking sheets.

5. Bake for 10 to 12 minutes, until firm to the touch. Transfer to wire racks to cool.

6. When the cookies are cool, roll them in powdered sugar.

Baking notes: For flat cookies, place the balls 1½ inches apart on the baking sheets and flatten them with the bottom of a glass dipped in flour.

CARAMEL BARS

BAR COOKIES

YIELD: 1 to 2 dozen
TOTAL TIME: 45 minutes

One 14-ounce package
   caramels (light or dark)
⅔ cup evaporated milk
¾ cup vegetable shortening
1 package German
   chocolate cake mix
1 cup peanuts, chopped
1 cup (6 ounces) semisweet
   chocolate chips

1. Preheat the oven to 350 degrees. Lightly grease a 9-inch square baking pan.

2. In the top of a double boiler, melt the caramel candy with ⅓ cup of the evaporated milk, stirring until smooth. Remove from the heat.

3. In a large bowl, combine the vegetable shortening and cake mix and beat until smooth. Beat in the milk and stir in the peanuts. The mixture will be crumbly.

4. Press half of the cake mixture into the prepared baking pan. Bake for 8 minutes.

5. Sprinkle the chocolate chips over the warm dough. Spread the caramel mixture over the chocolate chips and spread the remaining cake mixture over the caramel layer.

6. Bake for 18 to 20 minutes longer, until firm to the touch. Cool in the pan on a wire rack before cutting into large or small bars.

CAROB DROP COOKIES

DROP COOKIES

YIELD: 3 to 4 dozen
TOTAL TIME: 35 minutes

1. Line 2 baking sheets with waxed paper.

2. In the top of a double boiler, melt the carob chips, stirring until smooth. Blend in the oats, almonds, and coconut.

3. Drop the mixture by spoonfuls 1 inch apart onto the prepared baking sheets.

4. Chill until the cookies are firm.

1 cup carob chips
1 cup rolled oats
1 cup almonds, chopped
    fine
1 cup unsweetened flaked
    coconut

CARROT COOKIES

DROP COOKIES

YIELD: 4 to 6 dozen
TOTAL TIME: 30 minutes

1. Preheat the oven to 400 degrees. Lightly grease 2 baking sheets.

2. Combine the flour, almonds, baking powder, baking soda, spices, and salt.

3. In a large bowl, cream the vegetable shortening and brown sugar. Beat in the eggs. Beat in the buttermilk and almond extract. Beat in the carrots. Gradually blend in the dry ingredients. Fold in the oats.

4. Drop the dough by spoonfuls 1½ inches apart onto the prepared baking sheets.

5. Bake for 12 to 15 minutes, until lightly browned. Transfer to wire racks to cool.

2 cups all-purpose flour
½ cup almonds, ground
    fine
1 teaspoon baking powder
½ teaspoon baking soda
1 teaspoon ground
    cinnamon
¼ teaspoon ground nutmeg
¼ teaspoon ground cloves
¼ teaspoon salt
⅔ cup vegetable shortening
1 cup packed light brown
    sugar
2 large eggs
½ cup buttermilk
1 teaspoon almond extract
1 cup carrots, grated
1 cup (6 ounces) rolled oats

CARROT-MOLASSES COOKIES

DROP COOKIES

YIELD: 3 to 4 dozen
TOTAL TIME: 30 minutes

1. Preheat the oven to 350 degrees. Lightly grease 2 baking sheets.

2. Combine the two flours, optional yeast, and spices.

3. In a saucepan, heat the molasses and canola oil until warm. Remove from the heat and beat in the carrots. Gradually blend in the dry ingredients. If the dough seems dry, stir in a little water 1 teaspoon at a time. Fold in the pecans and dates.

4. Drop by the dough by spoonfuls 1½ inches apart onto the prepared baking sheets.

5. Bake for 12 to 15 minutes, until golden brown. Transfer to wire racks to cool.

1½ cups all-purpose flour
½ cup soy flour
2 tablespoons active dry
    yeast (optional)
½ teaspoon ground
    cinnamon
½ teaspoon ground nutmeg
½ cup molasses
2 tablespoons canola oil
½ cup mashed, cooked
    carrots (about 1 to 2
    carrots)
1 cup pecans, chopped
½ cup dates, pitted and
    chopped

CASHEW BARS

BAR COOKIES

YIELD: 2 to 3 dozen
TOTAL TIME: 30 minutes

2 cups all-purpose flour
1 cup cashews, ground fine
2 teaspoons baking powder
1 teaspoon baking soda
1 teaspoon ground nutmeg
½ cup vegetable shortening
3 large eggs
½ cup mashed bananas
½ cup cashews, chopped

1. Preheat the oven to 350 degrees. Lightly grease a 13 by 9-inch baking pan.

2. Combine the flour, ground cashews, baking powder, baking soda, and nutmeg.

3. In a large bowl, beat the vegetable shortening and eggs together. Beat in the bananas. Gradually blend in the dry ingredients.

4. Spread the mixture evenly in the prepared baking pan. Sprinkle the chopped cashews over the batter and press down gently.

5. Bake for 18 to 20 minutes, or until a toothpick inserted in the center comes out clean. Cool in the pan on a wire rack before cutting into large or small bars.

CASHEW-CARAMEL COOKIES

BAR COOKIES

YIELD: 1 to 2 dozen
TOTAL TIME: 35 minutes

¾ cup all-purpose flour
½ teaspoon baking powder
¼ teaspoon salt
2 large eggs
½ cup granulated sugar
2 tablespoons light brown
    sugar
½ cup cashews, chopped

TOPPING
2 tablespoons butter
1 tablespoon evaporated
    milk
2 tablespoons light brown
    sugar
½ cup cashews, chopped

1. Preheat the oven to 350 degrees. Lightly grease a 9-inch square baking pan.

2. Combine the flour, baking powder, and salt.

3. In a large bowl, beat the eggs, and both sugars together until thick. Add the cashews. Gradually blend in the dry ingredients.

4. Spread the dough evenly in the prepared baking pan. Bake for 25 minutes.

5. Meanwhile, make the topping in a saucepan: Combine all the ingredients and cook, stirring, until smooth. Remove from the heat.

6. Preheat the boiler.

7. Spread the topping over the warm cookies and place under the broiler for 1 minute, or until the topping starts to bubble. Cut into large or small bars while still warm, and cool in the pan on a rack.

CASHEW COOKIES

DROP COOKIES

YIELD: 3 to 5 dozen
TOTAL TIME: 30 minutes

⅓ cup all-purpose flour
⅓ cup rice flour
2 cups cashews, ground fine
¼ teaspoon baking soda
4 large eggs
1 tablespoon rum
Chopped cashews for
    topping

1. Preheat the oven to 350 degrees. Lightly grease 2 baking sheets.

2. Combine the two flours, the ground cashews, and baking soda.

3. In a large bowl, beat the eggs until light and foamy. Beat in the rum. Gradually blend in the dry ingredients.

4. Drop the cookies by spoonfuls 1½ inches apart onto the prepared baking sheets and sprinkle chopped cashews on top of the cookies.

5. Bake for 5 to 8 minutes, until lightly colored. Transfer to wire racks to cool.

CASHEW GRANOLA BARS

BAR COOKIES

YIELD: *3 to 4 dozen*
TOTAL TIME: *45 minutes*

1. Preheat the oven to 350 degrees. Lightly grease a 13 by 9-inch baking pan.

2. In a large bowl, combine the oats, coconut, wheat germ, raisins, sunflower seeds, sesame seeds, and allspice.

3. In a medium saucepan, combine the honey, oil, water, and vanilla extract and heat until warm.

4. Pour over the dry ingredients and blend thoroughly. Spread the mixture evenly in the prepared baking pan.

5. Bake for 30 to 40 minutes, until firm and no longer sticking. Cut into large or small bars while still warm, and cool in the pan on a wire rack.

6 cups(36 ounces) rolled oats
1 cup shredded coconuts
1 cup wheat germ
1 cup golden raisins
½ cup sunflower seeds, shelled
¼ cup sesame seeds, toasted
1 teaspoon ground allspice
1 cup honey
¾ cup canola oil
⅓ cup water
1½ teaspoons vanilla extract

CEREAL REFRIGERATOR COOKIES

REFRIGERATOR COOKIES

YIELD: *4 to 5 dozen*
TOTAL TIME: *30 minutes*
CHILLING TIME: *4 hours*

1. Combine the flour, baking powder, and salt.

2. In a large bowl, cream the vegetable shortening and brown sugar. Beat in the eggs. Gradually blend in the dry ingredients. Fold in the two cereals.

3. Form the dough into a log 2 inches in diameter. Wrap in waxed paper and chill for 4 hours.

4. Preheat the oven to 375 degrees.

5. Cut the log into ¼-inch-thick slices and place 1 inch apart on ungreased baking sheets.

6. Bake for 12 to 15 minutes, until lightly colored. Transfer to wire racks to cool.

3 cups all-purpose flour
2 teaspoons baking powder
¼ teaspoon salt
1 cup vegetable shortening
2 cups packed light brown sugar
2 large eggs
1 cup All-Bran
1 cup Grape Nuts

CHEDDAR DREAMS

ROLLED COOKIES

YIELD: *5 to 6 dozen*
TOTAL TIME: *45 minutes*

1. Preheat the oven to 400 degrees.

2. Combine the flour, paprika, salt, and cayenne pepper.

3. In a large bowl, cream the butter. Beat in the dry ingredients. Blend in the Cheddar cheese.

4. On a floured surface, roll out the dough to a thickness of ⅛ inch. With cookie cutters, cut into shapes and place 1 inch apart on ungreased baking sheets.

5. Bake for 4 to 6 minutes, until lightly colored. Sprinkle with optional granulated sugar and transfer to wire racks to cool.

Baking notes: You can substitute Swiss cheese or Colby for the Cheddar. For a different flavor, use onion powder in place of the cayenne pepper.

2 cups all-purpose flour
1 teaspoon paprika
½ teaspoon salt
¼ teaspoon cayenne pepper
¾ cup butter, at room temperature
1½ cups grated Cheddar cheese
Granulated sugar for sprinkling (optional)

CHEESECAKE COOKIES

BAR COOKIES

YIELD: 1 to 3 dozen
TOTAL TIME: 40 minutes

CRUST
½ cup canola oil
¼ cup powdered sugar
24 gingersnaps, crushed

FILLING
1 pound cream cheese, at
* room temperature*
½ cup granulated sugar
2 large eggs
1 tablespoon fresh lemon
* juice*
1 tablespoon marsala
1 tablespoon honey
¼ teaspoon ground allspice

1. Preheat the oven to 375 degrees.

2. To make the crust, beat the canola oil and powdered sugar together in a large bowl. Gradually work in the crushed gingersnaps.

3. Press the mixture evenly into an ungreased 9-inch square baking pan.

4. Bake for about 6 minutes.

5. Meanwhile, make the filling: In a large bowl, beat the cream cheese and sugar until creamy. Beat in the eggs. Beat in the lemon juice, marsala, honey, and allspice.

6. Spread the filling over the hot crust. Bake for 12 to 15 minutes longer, until set. Cool in the pan on a wire rack before cutting into large or small bars.

Baking notes: For dessert, serve cut into large bars with sliced strawberries and whipped cream.

CHERRY-ALMOND KOLACKY

ROLLED COOKIES

YIELD: 3 to 4 dozen
TOTAL TIME: 35 minutes
CHILLING TIME: 4 hours

⅔ cup butter, at room
* temperature*
¼ cup rice flour
½ teaspoon Amaretto
1 tablespoon plus 1
* teaspoon orange liqueur*
10 ounces cream cheese, at
* room temperature*
2 cups all-purpose flour
Approximately 1 cup glacé
* cherries, cut in half*

1. In a large bowl, beat the butter and rice flour until smooth. Beat in the Amaretto and 1 teaspoon of the orange liqueur. Beat in the cream cheese. Gradually blend in the all-purpose flour. Cover and chill for 4 hours.

2. Meanwhile, combine the cherries, 1 cup warm water, and the remaining 1 tablespoon orange liqueur in a small bowl. Set aside and let plump for at least 1 hour.

3. Preheat the oven to 350 degrees.

4. Drain the cherries, discarding the liquid.

5. On a floured surface, roll out the dough to a thickness of ¼ inch. Using a 2- to 2½-inch round cookie cutter, cut into rounds and place 1 inch apart on ungreased baking sheets. Press a cherry half into the center of each cookie.

6. Bake for 10 to 15 minutes, until the edges are lighly colored. Transfer to wire racks to cool.

Baking notes: Use a combination of both red and green cherries if you like.

CHERRY CRESCENTS

ROLLED COOKIES

YIELD: 2 to 3 dozen
TOTAL TIME: 40 minutes
CHILLING TIME: 4 hours

1. In a large bowl, combine the flour, sugar, and salt. Cut in the vegetable shortening.

2. In a medium bowl, beat the sour cream and the egg until well-blended. Blend into the flour mixture. Divide the dough into 3 pieces, wrap in waxed paper and chill for 4 hours.

3. Preheat the oven to 350 degrees. Lightly grease 2 baking sheets.

4. On a floured surface, roll out one piece of dough into an 11-inch round. Brush the dough with one-third of the cherry preserves and sprinkle with one-third of the almonds. Cut the round into 8 wedges. Starting at the wide end, roll up each piece, curve the ends to form crescents, and place, seam side down, 1½ inches apart on the prepared baking sheets. Repeat with the remaining dough.

5. Bake for 18 to 20 minutes, until lightly colored. Dust with powdered sugar and transfer to wire racks to cool.

2 cups all-purpose flour
1 tablespoon granulated sugar
¼ teaspoon salt
1 cup vegetable shortening
1 cup sour cream
1 large egg

TOPPING
½ cup cherry preserves
½ cup almonds, chopped
Powdered sugar for dusting

CHERRY-NUT CLOVERS

FORMED COOKIES

YIELD: 2 to 3 dozen
TOTAL TIME: 40 minutes
CHILLING TIME: 4 hours

1. In a large bowl, beat the egg yolks and sugar together until thick and light. Stir in the almonds.

2. In a medium bowl, beat the egg whites until stiff but not dry. Fold the whites into the yolks. Cover and chill for 4 hours.

3. Preheat the oven to 300 degrees. Line 2 baking sheets with parchment paper.

4. Dust your hands with powdered sugar. Pinching off pieces about the size of an olive, roll into balls. Place the balls in groups of 3, touching each other, 1 inch apart on the prepared baking sheets. Press a half-cherry, round side up, into the center of each threesome.

5. Bake for 28 to 30 minutes, or until the edges start to color. Transfer to wire racks to cool.

Baking notes: If the dough seems thin, add more powdered sugar a tablespoonful at a time.

3 large eggs, separated
1½ cups powdered sugar
2 cups almonds, chopped
1 cup glacé cherries, cut in half
Powdered sugar for dusting

CHERRY SQUARES

YIELD: 2 to 3 dozen
TOTAL TIME: 45 minutes

2 cups all-purpose flour
¼ teaspoon salt
¾ cup vegetable shortening
1 cup granulated sugar
1 large egg
1 teaspoon vanilla extract
1½ cups shredded coconut
One 10-ounce jar cherry
preserves

1. Preheat the oven to 350 degrees. Lightly grease a 13 by 9-inch baking pan.

2. Combine the flour and salt.

3. In a large bowl, cream the vegetable shortening and sugar. Beat in the egg. Beat in the vanilla extract. Gradually blend in the dry ingredients. Fold in the coconut.

4. Press three-quarters of the dough evenly into the prepared baking pan. Spread the cherry preserves over the dough. Crumble the remaining dough over the preserves.

5. Bake for 25 to 30 minutes, until firm and lightly colored on top. Cool in the pan on a wire rack before cutting into large or small bars.

CHERRY STRIPS

YIELD: 3 to 5 dozen
TOTAL TIME: 35 minutes
CHILLING TIME: 2 hours

CRUST
2 cups all-purpose flour
¼ cup granulated sugar
1½ tablespoons grated
lemon zest
¾ cup vegetable shortening
3 tablespoons sour cream
½ teaspoon almond extract

FILLING
1½ cups canned cherries,
pitted & sliced
1 tablespoon raisins
¼ cup granulated sugar
1 large egg yolk, beaten
Powdered sugar for dusting

1. To make the crust, combine the flour, sugar, and lemon zest in a large bowl. Cut in the vegetable shortening. Stir in the sour cream and almond extract.

2. Divide the dough in half. Wrap in waxed paper and set aside at room temperature for 2 hours.

3. Drain the cherries and reserve for at least one hour.

4. Preheat the oven to 325 degrees. Lightly grease a 9-inch square baking pan.

5. On a floured surface, roll out half the dough to a 9-inch square. Fit it into the prepared baking pan. Layer the sliced cherries over the dough. Sprinkle the raisins and then the sugar over the top.

6. Roll out the remaining dough to a 9-inch square. Cut into 1-inch strips. Arrange the strips over filling in a lattice pattern. Brush the strips with the egg yolk.

7. Bake for 18 to 20 minutes, until the lattice strips start to color. Dust the top with powdered sugar and cool in the pan on a wire rack before cutting into large or small strips.

Baking notes: Shredded coconut is a good addition to these bars.

CHEWY PECAN BARS

BAR COOKIES

1. Preheat the oven to 300 degrees.

2. Combine the flour, baking powder, cinnamon, and salt.

3. In a large bowl, cream the vegetable shortening and sugar. Beat in the large egg yolks. Gradually blend in the dry ingredients. Spread the dough evenly into a 13 by 9-inch baking pan.

4. To make the topping, beat the large egg whites in a medium bowl, until stiff and frothy. Fold in the powdered sugar. Spread the topping over the dough. Sprinkle the chopped pecans over the top.

5. Bake for 40 to 45 minutes, or until the topping is lightly colored. Cool in the pan on a wire rack before cutting into large or small bars.

YIELD: 1 to 2 dozen
TOTAL TIME: 60 minutes

1 cup all-purpose flour
½ teaspoon baking powder
1 tablespoon ground
 cinnamon
¼ teaspoon salt
1 cup vegetable shortening
1 cup granulated sugar
2 large egg yolks

TOPPING
2 large egg whites
1½ teaspoons powdered
 sugar
1 cup pecans, chopped

CHOCOLATE BONBONS

DROP COOKIES

1. Preheat the oven to 350 degrees. Lightly grease 2 baking sheets.

2. Combine the flour and salt.

3. In a large bowl, cream the butter and sugar. Beat in the egg. Beat in the milk and vanilla extract. Stir in the cocoa powder. Gradually blend in the dry ingredients.

4. Drop the dough by spoonfuls 1 inch apart onto the prepared baking sheets.

5. Bake for 10 to 12 minutes, until lightly colored. Roll the warm cookies in the ground walnuts before transferring to wire racks to cool.

Baking notes (Alternate method): 1. Combine all the ingredients except the walnuts in the top of a double boiler and cook over high heat, stirring for 15 minutes, or until the mixture is very stiff. 2. Drop by spoonfuls onto wax paper-lined baking sheets. Sprinkle with half the chopped nuts. 3. Let cool slightly, then roll in the remaining chopped nuts.

YIELD: 3 to 5 dozen
TOTAL TIME: 40 minutes

½ cup all-purpose flour
¼ teaspoon salt
2 tablespoons butter, at
 room temperature
½ cup granulated sugar
1 large egg
2 tablespoons evaporated
 milk
1 teaspoon vanilla extract
⅓ cup unsweetened cocoa
 powder
 1¼ cups walnuts,
 ground fine

CHOCOLATE CHIP BAR COOKIES

BAR COOKIES

YIELD: *2 to 3 dozen*
TOTAL TIME: *45 minutes*

2 cups all-purpose flour
1 teaspoon baking powder
¼ teaspoon baking soda
¼ teaspoon salt
1 cup vegetable shortening
1½ cups packed light
    brown sugar
2 large eggs
2 tablespoons milk
1 teaspoon vanilla extract
1 cup (6 ounces) semisweet
    chocolate chips

1. Preheat the oven to 350 degrees. Lightly grease a 9-inch square baking pan.

2. Combine the flour, baking powder, baking soda, and salt.

3. In a large bowl, cream the vegetable shortening and brown sugar. Beat in the eggs. Beat in the milk and vanilla extract. Gradually blend in the dry ingredients. Fold in the chocolate chips.

4. Spread the dough evenly in the prepared baking pan.

5. Bake for 25 to 30 minutes, or until golden brown on top. Cool in the pan on a wire rack before cutting into large or small bars.

Baking notes: For an unusual variation, substitute white crème de menthe for the vanilla extract.

CHOCOLATE CHIP COOKIES

DROP COOKIES

YIELD: *6 to 7 dozen*
TOTAL TIME: *30 minutes*

2¼ cups all-purpose flour
1 teaspoon baking soda
1 package vanilla-flavored
    instant pudding
1 cup vegetable shortening
¼ cup granulated sugar
¾ cup packed light brown
    sugar
2 large eggs
1 teaspoon vanilla extract
1½ cups (9 ounces)
    semisweet chocolate chips
1 cup walnuts, chopped fine

1. Preheat the oven to 375 degrees.

2. Combine the flour, baking soda, and vanilla pudding

3. In a large bowl, cream the vegetable shortening and the two sugars. Beat in the eggs. Beat in the vanilla extract. Gradually blend in the dry ingredients. Fold in the chocolate chips and walnuts.

4. Drop the dough by spoonfuls 1½ inches apart onto ungreased baking sheets.

5. Bake for 8 to 10 minutes, until lightly colored. Transfer to wire racks to cool.

Baking notes: For chocolate chocolate chip cookies, use a chocolate instant pudding in place of the vanilla pudding.

CHOCOLATE CHIP NUT BARS

BAR COOKIES

YIELD: *2 to 3 dozen*
TOTAL TIME: *45 minutes*

½ cup all-purpose flour
½ teaspoon baking powder
¼ teaspoon salt
1 large egg
½ cup granulated sugar
1 teaspoon butter, melted
2 teaspoons hot water
⅔ cup walnuts, chopped
    fine
½ cup almonds, chopped
    fine
1 cup (6 ounces) semisweet
    chocolate chips

1. Preheat the oven to 325 degrees. Lightly grease an 8-inch square baking pan.

2. Combine the flour, baking powder, and salt.

3. In a large bowl, beat the egg until thick and light-colored. Beat in the sugar. Beat in the butter and and hot water. Beat in the nuts. Gradually blend in the dry ingredients. Fold in the chocolate chips.

4. Spread the batter evenly into the prepared baking pan. Bake for 25 to 30 minutes, or until lightly colored on top. Cool in the pan on a wire rack before cutting into large or small bars.

Chocolate Chip Peanut Logs

FORMED COOKIES

YIELD: 2 to 3 dozen
TOTAL TIME: 30 minutes

1. Lightly grease a 9-inch square baking pan.

2. Melt the chocolate chips with the peanut butter in a saucepan over a low heat, stirring until smooth. Blend in the optional peanuts. Gradually blend in the krispies, stirring until well coated.

3. Spread the mixture out evenly in the prepared pan. Let cool in the pan on a wire rack until the mixture hardens slightly.

4. Cut into 2 by 1-inch bars. Roll each bar between your hands to form logs. Wrap individually in waxed paper and store tightly covered.

Baking notes: This is a great cookie for children to make with your help. Let them form the logs.

1 cup (6 ounces) semisweet chocolate chips
½ cup peanut butter
½ cup peanuts, chopped (optional)
4 cups cocoa krispies

Chocolate Chip Squares

BAR COOKIES

YIELD: 3 to 5 dozen
TOTAL TIME: 30 minutes

1. Preheat the oven to 350 degrees. Lightly grease a 13 by 9-inch baking pan.

2. Combine the flour, baking soda, and salt.

3. In a large bowl, beat the canola oil and the two sugars. Beat in the egg. Beat in the crème de menthe. Gradually blend in the dry ingredients. Fold in the chocolate chips.

4. Spread the dough evenly in the prepared pan. Bake for 15 to 20 minutes, until the top is golden brown.

5. For the topping, spread the chocolate chips over the hot cookies. With a spatula, spread the melted chocolate chips evenly over the top. Cool in the pan on a wire rack before cutting into large or small bars.

CRUST
2¼ cups all-purpose flour
1 teaspoon baking soda
½ teaspoon salt
1 cup canola oil
½ cup granulated sugar
¾ cup packed light brown sugar
1 large egg
2½ teaspoons white crème de menthe
1⅓ cups (8 ounces) semisweet chocolate chips

TOPPING
½ cup (3 ounces) semisweet chocolate chips

Chocolate-Coconut Bars

BAR COOKIES

YIELD: 1 to 2 dozen
TOTAL TIME: 40 minutes

1. Preheat the oven to 350 degrees. Grease a 9-inch square baking pan.

2. In a large bowl, combine all the ingredients, stirring until well blended. Press the mixture evenly into the prepared baking pan.

3. Bake for 30 minutes until set. Cool in the pan on a wire rack before cutting into large or small bars.

1½ cups crushed graham crackers
One 14-ounce can sweetened condensed milk
1½ cups flaked coconut
½ cup semisweet chocolate chips

Chocolate-Coconut Tea Strips

BAR COOKIES

YIELD: 3 to 4 dozen
TOTAL TIME: 35 minutes

1½ cups all-purpose flour
1½ teaspoons baking
　powder
¼ teaspoon salt
6 tablespoons butter, at
　room temperature
¾ cup plus 2 tablespoons
　granulated sugar
1 large egg
2 tablespoons milk
½ teaspoon vanilla extract
1 ounce bittersweet
　chocolate, chopped
1 teaspoon grated orange
　zest
¼ cup pecans, chopped
⅔ cup shredded coconut

1. Preheat the oven to 375 degrees. Lightly grease two 8-inch square baking pans.

2. Combine the flour, baking powder, and salt.

3. In a large bowl, cream the butter and sugar. Beat in the egg. Beat in the milk and vanilla extract. Gradually blend in the dry ingredients. Divide the dough in half and transfer half to another bowl.

4. Melt the chocolate in a double boiler over low heat, stirring until smooth. Remove from the heat and work into half the dough.

5. On a floured surface, roll out the chocolate dough to an 8-inch square. Fit it into one of the prepared baking pans and sprinkle with 1 tablespoon of the sugar and half the orange zest.

6. Bake 10 to 15 minutes, until firm to the touch. Cool in the pan on a wire rack before cutting into 2 by 1-inch strips.

7. Meanwhile, blend the pecans and coconut into the remaining dough. Roll out the dough, fit it into the second baking pan, and sprinkle with the remaining 1 tablespoon of sugar and remaining orange zest.

8. Bake as directed, cool, and cut into strips.

Chocolate Cookies

ROLLED COOKIES

YIELD: 4 to 5 dozen
TOTAL TIME: 40 minutes

1½ cups all-purpose flour
½ cup unsweetened cocoa
　powder
1½ teaspoons baking
　powder
¼ teaspoon salt
½ cup butter, at room
　temperature
1 cup packed light brown
　sugar
1 large egg
½ cup milk
1 tablespoon heavy cream
1 teaspoon vanilla extract
¾ cup walnuts, chopped
Granulated sugar for
　sprinkling

1. Preheat the oven to 400 degrees.

2. Combine the flour, cocoa, baking powder, and salt.

3. In a large bowl, cream the butter and brown sugar. Beat in the egg. Beat in the milk, cream, and vanilla extract. Gradually blend in the dry ingredients. Fold in the walnuts.

4. On a floured surface, roll out the dough to a thickness of ¼ inch. Using a 1½-inch round cookie cutter, cut into circles and place 1½ inches apart on ungreased baking sheets.

5. Bake for 10 to 12 minutes, or until firm to the touch. Sprinkle the warm cookies with granulated sugar and transfer to wire racks to cool.

Chocolate Crinkles

FORMED COOKIES

YIELD: *3 to 4 dozen*
TOTAL TIME: *30 minutes*

1. Preheat the oven to 350 degrees. Lightly grease 2 baking sheets.

2. Combine the flour and baking powder.

3. Melt the chocolate in a double boiler over low heat, stirring until smooth. Remove from the heat.

4. In a large bowl, beat the canola oil and sugar until well blended. Beat in the eggs one at a time, beating well after each addition. Beat in the chocolate. Beat in the milk and vanilla extract. Gradually blend in the dry ingredients.

5. Pinch off walnut-sized pieces of dough and roll into balls. Roll in powdered sugar and place 1½ inches apart on the prepared baking sheets.

6. Bake for 12 to 15 minutes, or until firm to the touch. Roll in powdered sugar while still warm and transfer to wire racks to cool.

2 cups all-purpose flour
2 teaspoons baking powder
3 ounces semisweet chocolate, chopped
½ cup canola oil
1½ cups granulated sugar
2 large eggs
¼ cup milk
1 teaspoon vanilla extract
Powdered sugar for rolling

Chocolate Delight Bars

BAR COOKIES

YIELD: *1 to 2 dozen*
TOTAL TIME: *40 minutes*

1. Preheat the oven to 350 degrees. Lightly grease a 9-inch square baking pan.

2. In a large bowl, combine the butter, powdered sugar, egg yolks, coffee crystals, and water and beat until well blended. Gradually blend in the flour. The mixture will be crumbly.

3. Press the mixture evenly into the bottom of the prepared baking pan. Bake for 20 minutes.

4. Meanwhile, melt the chocolate in the top of a double boiler, stirring until smooth. Remove from the heat.

5. In a medium bowl, beat the egg whites until foamy. Gradually beat in the sugar and beat until the whites hold stiff peaks. In a steady stream, beat in the melted chocolate. Fold in the ground almonds.

6. Spread the topping over the warm crust. Sprinkle with the chopped almonds and bake for 20 minutes longer, until set.

CRUST
½ cup butter, at room temperature
3 tablespoons powdered sugar
2 large egg yolks
1 teaspoon instant coffee crystals
1 tablespoon warm water
2 cups all-purpose flour

TOPPING
½ cup semisweet chocolate chips
2 large egg whites
¼ cup granulated sugar
¼ cup almonds, ground fine
¼ cup almonds, chopped

Chocolate Drop Cookies

DROP COOKIES

YIELD: 3 to 4 dozen

TOTAL TIME: 30 minutes

½ cup butter
3 ounces unsweetened chocolate, chopped
1 large egg, beaten
¼ cup water
1 teaspoon almond extract
2 cups Basic Cookie Mix (see Ingredients for a Basic Cookie, page vii)

1. Preheat the oven to 350 degrees. Lightly grease 2 baking sheets.

2. Melt the butter and chocolate in the top of a double boiler over low heat, stirring until smooth. Remove from the heat and beat in the egg. Beat in the water and almond extract. Gradually blend in the cookie mix.

3. Drop the dough by spoonfuls 1½ inches apart onto the prepared baking sheets.

4. Bake for 10 to 12 minutes, until firm to the touch. Transfer to wire racks to cool.

Chocolate-Filled Pinwheels

REFRIGERATOR COOKIES

YIELD: 4 to 5 dozen

TOTAL TIME: 45 minutes

CHILLING TIME: 2 hours and overnight

2 cups all-purpose flour
1 teaspoon baking powder
½ teaspoon salt
¾ cup vegetable shortening
1 cup granulated sugar
1 large egg
1 tablespoon vanilla extract

FILLING

1 cup (6 ounces) semisweet chocolate chips
2 tablespoons butter
1 cup walnuts, ground fine
½ tablespoon vanilla extract

1. Combine the flour, baking powder, and salt.

2. Cream the vegetable shortening and sugar in a large bowl. Beat in the egg. Beat in the vanilla extract. Gradually blend in the dry ingredients. Measure out ⅔ cup of the dough and set aside. Cover the remaining dough and chill for 2 hours.

3. To make the filling, melt the chocolate and butter in the top of a double boiler over low heat, strring until smooth. Remove from the heat and stir in the walnuts and vanilla extract. Blend in the reserved dough.

4. On a floured surface, roll out the chilled dough to a 16 by 12-inch rectangle. Spread the chocolate mixture over the dough to within ¼ inch of the edges. Starting on a long side, roll the dough up jelly-roll fashion. Pinch the seam to seal. Cut in half to make two 8-inch logs. Wrap in waxed paper and chill overnight.

5. Preheat the oven to 350 degrees.

6. Slice the logs into ¼-inch-thick slices and place 1½ inches apart on ungreased baking sheets.

7. Bake for 10 to 12 minutes, until lightly colored. Transfer to wire racks to cool.

Baking notes: To decorate, drizzle melted white or dark chocolate over the top of the cooled cookie.

Chocolate Jumbo Cookies

DROP COOKIES

YIELD: *2 to 4 dozen*
TOTAL TIME: *30 minutes*

1. Preheat the oven to 350 degrees. Lightly grease 2 baking sheets.

2. Combine the flour, cocoa powder, baking soda, and salt.

3. In a large bowl, cream the vegetable shortening and sugar. Beat in the egg. Beat in the water and vanilla extract. Gradually blend in the dry ingredients. Fold in the oats and chocolate chips.

4. Drop the dough by tablespoonfuls 2 inches apart onto the prepared baking sheets.

5. Bake for 12 to 15 minutes, until lightly colored. Transfer to wire racks to cool.

1 cup all-purpose flour
6 tablespoons unsweetened
* cocoa powder*
½ teaspoon baking soda
½ teaspoon salt
1½ cups vegetable shortening
1½ cups granulated sugar
1 large egg
¼ cup water
1 teaspoon vanilla extract
3 cups (18 ounces) rolled
* oats*
¾ cup (4 ounces) semisweet
* chocolate chips*

Chocolate-Lemon Dessert Cookies

DROP COOKIES

YIELD: *3 to 4 dozen*
TOTAL TIME: *45 minutes*

1. Preheat the oven to 350 degrees. Lightly grease 2 baking sheets.

2. In a saucepan, stir the lemon dessert, cold water, and chocolate over low heat until smooth. Stir in the condensed milk. Cook for 3 minutes, stirring constantly. Remove from the heat and stir in the coconut. Stir in the vanilla extract.

3. Drop the dough by spoonfuls onto the prepared baking sheets.

4. Bake for 10 to 12 minutes, until lightly colored and firm to the touch. Transfer to wire racks to cool.

2 tablespoons packaged
* lemon dessert*
3 tablespoons cold water
1 ounce semisweet
* chocolate, grated*
One 14-ounce can
* sweetened condensed*
* milk*
1½ cups shredded coconut
1 teaspoon vanilla extract

Chocolate Oatmeal Bars

BAR COOKIES

YIELD: *3 to 4 dozen*
TOTAL TIME: *45 minutes*

1. Preheat the oven to 350 degrees.

2. To make the crust, combine the flour, baking soda, and salt.

3. In a large bowl, cream the vegetable shortening and brown sugar. Beat in the eggs and vanilla. Gradually blend in the dry ingredients. Fold in the rolled oats.

4. Press two-thirds of the crust mixture evenly into an ungreased 13 by 9-inch baking pan.

5. To prepare the filling, melt the chocolate chips and butter in a double boiler over low heat, stirring until smooth. Remove from the heat and stir in the condensed milk and vanilla extract. Fold in the nuts.

6. Spread the filling evenly over the crust in the baking pan. Press the remaining crust mixture on top of the filling.

7. Bake for 25 to 30 minutes, until firm to the touch. Cool in the pan on a wire rack before cutting into large or small bars.

CRUST
2½ cups all-purpose flour
1 teaspoon baking soda
1 teaspoon salt
1 cup vegetable shortening
2 cups packed light brown
* sugar*
2 large eggs
2 teaspoons vanilla extract
3 cups (18 ounces) rolled oats

FILLING
2 cups (12 ounces)
* semisweet chocolate chips*
2 tablespoons butter
One 14-ounce can sweetened
* condensed milk*
2 teaspoons vanilla extract
1 cup walnuts, chopped

Chocolate Oatmeal Cookies

FORMED COOKIES

YIELD: 3 to 4 dozen
TOTAL TIME: 30 minutes

*2 ounces bittersweet
chocolate, chopped
1 cup all-purpose flour
½ teaspoon baking soda
½ cup vegetable shortening
1 cup granulated sugar
1 large egg
1½ teaspoons Amaretto
1 cup (6 ounces) rolled oats
½ cup pecans, chopped
Granulated sugar*

1. Preheat the oven to 350 degrees. Lightly grease 2 baking sheets.

2. Melt the chocolate in a double boiler over low heat, stirring until smooth. Remove from the heat.

3. Combine the flour and baking soda.

4. In a large bowl, cream the vegetable shortening and sugar. Beat in the egg. Beat in the Amaretto. Stir in the melted chocolate. Gradually blend in the dry ingredients. Fold in the oats and pecans.

5. Pinch off walnut-sized pieces of dough and roll into balls. Place 1½ inches apart on the prepared baking sheets. Flatten the balls with the bottom of a glass dipped in sugar.

6. Bake for 10 to 12 minutes, until lightly colored. Transfer to wire racks to cool.

Chocolate Pudding Brownies

BAR COOKIES

YIELD: 1 to 2 dozen
TOTAL TIME: 45 minutes

*½ cup all-purpose flour
One 4-ounce package
chocolate pudding mix
½ teaspoon baking powder
¼ teaspoon salt
6 tablespoons vegetable
shortening
⅔ cup granulated sugar
2 large eggs
¼ cup milk
1 teaspoon vanilla extract
½ cup walnuts, chopped
Powdered sugar for
sprinkling*

1. Preheat the oven to 350 degrees. Lightly grease a 9-inch square baking pan.

2. Combine the flour, chocolate pudding mix, baking powder, and salt.

3. In a large bowl, cream the vegetable shortening and sugar. Beat in the eggs. Beat in the milk and vanilla extract. Gradually blend in the dry ingredients. Fold in the walnuts. Spread the mixture evenly in the prepared baking pan.

4. Bake for 25 to 30 minutes, until a toothpick inserted in the center comes out clean. Cool in the pan on a wire rack.

5. Place a paper doily on top of the cooled cookies and sprinkle with powdered sugar. Remove the doily and cut into large or small bars.

Chocolate Refrigerator Cookies

REFRIGERATOR COOKIES

YIELD: 7 to 8 dozen
TOTAL TIME: 40 minutes
CHILLING TIME: 4 hours

*3 ounces bittersweet
chocolate, chopped
3 cups all-purpose flour
1 tablespoon baking powder
½ teaspoon salt
1 cup vegetable shortening
1 cup granulated sugar
1 large egg
2 teaspoons crème de cacao*

1. Melt the chocolate in a double boiler over low heat, stirring until smooth. Remove from the heat.

2. Combine the flour, baking powder, and salt.

3. In a large bowl, cream the vegetable shortening and sugar. Beat in the egg. Beat in the melted chocolate and crème de cacao. Gradually blend in the dry ingredients.

4. Divide the dough in half. Form each piece into a log 2 inches in diameter. Wrap in waxed paper and chill for 4 hours.

5. Preheat the oven to 350 degrees.

6. Cut the logs into ⅛-inch-thick slices. Place 1 inch apart on ungreased baking sheets.

7. Bake for 10 to 12 minutes, until firm to the touch and dry. Transfer to wire racks to cool.

CHOCOLATE RUM BALLS

FORMED COOKIES

1. In a large bowl, combine the crushed cookies, powdered sugar, and walnuts.

2. In a small saucepan, heat the light corn syrup and rum until warm. Add the dry ingredients and blend thoroughly.

3. Pinch off walnut-sized pieces of dough and roll into balls. Roll in powdered sugar and place on wire racks.

4. Let sit for 1 hour.

5. Roll the balls in powdered sugar a second time. Store in an airtight container.

YIELD: 2 to 3 dozen
TOTAL TIME: 30 minutes
SITTING TIME: 1 hour

1½ cups crushed chocolate
    wafer cookies
½ cup powdered sugar
½ cup walnuts, ground
    fine
¼ cup light corn syrup
3 tablespoons rum
Powdered sugar for rolling

CHOCOLATE SANDWICHES

ROLLED COOKIES

1. Preheat the oven to 400 degrees. Lightly grease 2 baking sheets.

2. Combine the flour, walnuts, and salt.

3. In a large bowl, cream the vegetable shortening and sugar. Beat in the vanilla. Gradually blend in the dry ingredients.

4. On a floured surface, roll out the dough to a thickness of ⅛ inch. Using a 2-inch fluted round cookie cutter, cut the dough into rounds and place 1 inch apart on the prepared baking sheets.

5. Bake for 8 to 10 minutes, until firm to the touch. Transfer to wire racks to cool.

6. Melt the chocolate in a double boiler over low heat, stirring until smooth. Spread a thin layer of chocolate on the bottom half of the cookies and top with the remaining cookies to form sandwich cookies.

YIELD: 3 to 4 dozen
TOTAL TIME: 45 minutes

1¼ cups all-purpose flour
1 cup walnuts, ground fine
½ teaspoon salt
⅔ cup vegetable shortening
1 cup granulated sugar
1 teaspoon vanilla extract
¾ cup (4½ ounces)
    semisweet chocolate chips

CHOCOLATE SPICE DROPS

DROP COOKIES

1. Preheat the oven to 350 degrees.

2. Melt the chocolate in a double boiler over low heat, stirring until smooth. Remove from the heat.

3. Combine the flour, walnuts, baking soda, and spices.

4. In a large bowl, cream the butter and sugar. Beat in the eggs one at a time, beating vigorously after each addition. Beat in the sour cream and melted chocolate. Gradually blend in the dry ingredients. Fold in the raisins.

5. Drop the dough by spoonfuls 1½ inches apart onto ungreased baking sheets.

6. Bake for 18 to 20 minutes, until firm. Transfer to wire racks to cool.

YIELD: 6 to 7 dozen
TOTAL TIME: 30 minutes

2 ounces bittersweet
    chocolate, chopped
3 cups all-purpose flour
1 cup walnuts, ground fine
1 teaspoon baking soda
1 teaspoon ground cinnamon
1 teaspoon ground allspice
½ teaspoon ground cloves
½ cup butter, at room
    temperature
1½ cups granulated sugar
2 large eggs
⅔ cup sour cream
1 cup raisins

CHOCOLATE SQUARES

BAR COOKIES

YIELD: 1 to 3 dozen
TOTAL TIME: 30 minutes

*2 ounces semisweet
    chocolate, chopped*
1½ cups all-purpose flour
½ teaspoon baking soda
¼ teaspoon salt
½ cup vegetable shortening
*1 cup packed light brown
    sugar*
1 large egg
1 teaspoon vanilla extract
½ cup shredded coconut
½ cup walnuts, chopped

1. Preheat the oven to 350 degrees. Lightly grease a 13 by 9-inch baking pan.

2. Melt the chocolate in a double boiler over low heat, stirring until smooth. Remove from the heat.

3. Combine the flour, baking soda, and salt.

4. In a large bowl, cream the vegetable shortening and brown sugar. Beat in the egg. Beat in the melted chocolate and vanilla extract. Gradually blend in the dry ingredients.

5. Spread the batter evenly in the prepared baking pan. Sprinkle the coconut and walnuts over the top.

6. Bake for 10 to 12 minutes, until firm to the touch. Cool in the pan on a wire rack before cutting into large or small bars.

CHRISTMAS BELLS

ROLLED COOKIES

YIELD: 3 to 4 dozen
TOTAL TIME: 30 minutes
CHILLING TIME: 8 hours

2 cups all-purpose flour
½ teaspoon baking powder
*¼ teaspoon ground
    cinnamon*
½ cup vegetable shortening
1¾ cups powdered sugar
2 large eggs
1 teaspoon fresh lemon juice
Vanilla Icing (see Pantry)

1. Combine the flour, baking powder, and cinnamon.

2. In a large bowl, cream the vegetable shortening and powdered sugar. Beat in the eggs one at a time, beating vigorously after each addition. Beat in the lemon juice. Gradually blend in the dry ingredients. Cover and chill for 8 hours.

3. Preheat the oven to 350 degrees. Lightly grease 2 baking sheets.

4. On a floured surface, roll out the dough to a thickness of ⅛ inch. Using a bell-shaped cookie cutter, cut out cookies and place 1½ inches apart on the prepared baking sheets.

5. Bake for 8 to 10 minutes, until firm to the touch. Transfer to wire racks to cool.

6. Decorate the cookies with the icing (see Baking notes).

Baking notes: There are many different ways to decorate these cookies. You can frost them with the vanilla frosting and then pipe lines of colored icing across the bells. Or press small candies or colored sprinkles into the white icing. Or don't ice them at all—simply sprinkle the cookies with colored sugar crystals or powdered sugar.

CHRISTMAS COOKIES I

FORMED COOKIES

YIELD: 5 to 6 dozen
TOTAL TIME: 30 minutes
CHILLLING TIME: 8 hours

1. Combine the flour, baking soda, and salt.

2. In a large bowl, cream the vegetable shortening and sugar. Beat in the egg. Beat in the vinegar and rum. Gradually blend in the dry ingredients. Fold in the coconut, candied citrus peel, and glacé cherries. Cover and chill for 8 hours or overnight.

3. Preheat the oven to 350 degrees. Lightly grease 2 baking sheets.

4. Working with one quarter of the dough at a time, pinch off walnut-sized pieces of dough and roll into balls. Place 2 inches apart on the prepared baking sheets. Flatten each ball with the bottom of a glass dipped in flour, then brush the cookies with the beaten egg white and sprinkle with the slivered almonds.

5. Bake for 8 to 10 minutes, until lightly colored. Transfer to wire racks to cool.

2 cups all-purpose flour
1 teaspoon baking soda
¼ teaspoon salt
½ cup vegetable shortening
⅔ cup packed light brown sugar
1 large egg
¼ cup cider vinegar
1½ teaspoons rum
½ cup flaked coconut
½ cup candied citrus peel, chopped fine
½ cup red and green glacé cherries
1 large egg white, beaten
¼ cup slivered almonds for the topping

CHRISTMAS COOKIES II

ROLLED COOKIES

YIELD: 4 to 5 dozen
TOTAL TIME: 40 minutes
CHILLING TIME: 4 hours

1. Combine the flour, milk, and spices.

2. In a large saucepan, heat the molasses and canola oil until warm. Remove from the heat and gradually blend into the dry ingredients. The dough will be stiff. Wrap the dough in waxed paper and chill for 4 hours.

3. Preheat the oven to 375 degrees. Lightly grease 2 baking sheets.

4. On a floured surface, roll out the dough to a thickness of ¼-inch. Using cookie cutters, cut into shapes and place 1½ inches apart on the prepared baking sheets. Sprinkle colored sugar crystals over the cookies.

5. Bake for 6 to 8 minutes, until lightly colored. Transfer to wire racks to cool.

Baking notes: These cookies should be stored in airtight containers for at least 2 weeks to age before serving. They keep very well.

4½ cups unbleached all-purpose flour
1 cup nonfat dry milk
¾ teaspoon ground ginger
¾ teaspoon ground cinnamon
¼ teaspoon ground mace
¼ teaspoon ground allspice
¼ teaspoon ground nutmeg
¼ teaspoon ground cloves
1 cup molasses
½ cup canola oil
Colored sugar crystals for sprinkling

CHRISTMAS EVE COOKIES

YIELD: *2 to 4 dozen*
TOTAL TIME: *30 minutes*

2½ cups whole wheat flour
1½ tablespoons brewer's yeast
¾ cup nonfat dry milk
1 teaspoon salt
1 tablespoon honey
¼ cup water

FORMED COOKIES

1. Preheat the oven to 400 degrees. Lightly grease 2 baking sheets.

2. Combine the flour, yeast, dry milk, and salt.

3. In a saucepan, warm the honey and water. Remove from the heat. Gradually blend in the dry ingredients. Form the dough into a log ½ inch square. Cut the log into ½ inch strips and cut the strips into ½ inch cubes. Place the cubes 1 inch apart on the prepared baking sheets.

4. Bake for 8 to 10 minutes, until lightly colored. Transfer to wire racks to cool.

CHRISTMAS WREATHS I

YIELD: *3 to 4 dozen*
TOTAL TIME: *30 minutes*

1 cup vegetable shortening
½ cup granulated sugar
1 large egg
1 teaspoon vanilla extract
2½ tablespoons all-purpose flour
1⅓ cups almonds, ground fine
¼ cup maple syrup
Red and green glacé cherries, halved

FORMED COOKIES

1. Preheat the oven to 350 degrees. Lightly grease 2 baking sheets.

2. In a large bowl, cream the vegetable shortening and sugar. Beat in the egg and vanilla extract. Gradually blend in the flour. Transfer one-third of the dough to a medium ball.

3. Fill a cookie press or a pastry bag fitted with a small star tip with the remaining dough and press or pipe out small rings onto the prepared baking sheets, spacing them 1 inch apart.

4. Add the almonds and maple syrup to the reserved cookie dough and blend well. Place ¼ to ½ teaspoon of this filling in the center of each ring, and place a half cherry at the point where the ends of each ring join.

5. Bake for 10 to 12 minutes, until lightly colored. Transfer to wire racks to cool.

CHRISTMAS WREATHS II

YIELD: *2 dozen*
TOTAL TIME: *30 minutes*
CHILLING TIME: *1 hour*

6 tablespoons vegetable shortening
32 marshmallows
½ teaspoon vanilla extract
½ teaspoon almond extract
½ teaspoon green food coloring
4 cups cornflakes
Red cinnamon candies for decoration

FORMED COOKIES

1. Line 2 baking sheets with waxed paper.

2. In a double boiler, melt the vegetable shortening and marshmallows over low heat, stirring until smooth. Remove from the heat and beat in the vanilla extract, almond extract, and food coloring. Gradually blend in the cornflakes.

3. Return the double boiler to the heat. Lightly oil your hands to make working with the mixture easier.

4. Drop the mixture by tablespoonfuls 1½ inches apart onto the prepared baking sheets. With your fingers, form each mound into a wreath. Sprinkle with a few red cinnamon candies. Let cool for 15 minutes, then chill for 1 hour to firm.

Baking notes: These are great cookies to make with your kids. Prepare the cornflake mixture and let the children form the wreaths.

CHUNKY CHOCOLATE BROWNIES

BAR COOKIES

YIELD: 1 to 2 dozen
TOTAL TIME: 30 minutes

1. Preheat the oven to 350 degrees. Lightly grease a 9-inch square baking pan.

2. In the top of a double boiler, melt the vegetable shortening with the cocoa powder, stirring until smooth. Remove from the heat and beat in the sugar. Beat in the eggs and vanilla extract. Gradually blend in the flour. Fold in the milk and white chocolate chunks. Spread the mixture evenly in the prepared baking pan.

3. Bake for 18 to 20 minutes until firm to the touch.

4. Spread the chocolate glaze over the top. Cut into large or small bars, then place a walnut in the center of each. Cool in the pan on a wire rack.

½ cup plus 2 tablespoons vegetable shortening
¼ cup unsweetened cocoa powder
1 cup granulated sugar
2 large eggs
1 teaspoon vanilla extract
⅔ cup all-purpose flour
2½ ounces milk chocolate, cut into small chunks
2½ ounces white chocolate, cut into small chunks
¾ cup chocolate glaze
12 to 24 walnut halves for decoration

CINNAMON BALLS

FORMED COOKIES

YIELD: 3 to 4 dozen
TOTAL TIME: 30 minutes

1. Preheat the oven to 350 degrees. Lightly grease 2 baking sheets.

2. Combine the flour, baking powder, and salt.

3. In a large bowl, cream the vegetable shortening and sugar. Beat in the eggs and vanilla extract. Gradually blend in the dry ingredients.

4. Combine the sugar and cinnamon in a shallow dish.

5. Pinch off 1-inch pieces of dough and roll into balls. Roll in the cinnamon sugar and place 1½ inches apart on the prepared baking sheets.

6. Bake for 10 to 14 minutes, until lightly colored. Transfer to wire racks to cool.

3 cups all-purpose flour
2 teaspoons baking powder
¼ teaspoon salt
1 cup vegetable shortening
1⅓ cups granulated sugar
2 large eggs
1 teaspoon vanilla extract

Cinnamon Sugar
3 tablespoons granulated sugar
2 teaspoons ground cinnamon

CINNAMON-CREAM MOLASSES COOKIES ROLLED COOKIES

YIELD: *3 to 4 dozen*

TOTAL TIME: *40 minutes*

4½ cups all-purpose flour
1 teaspoon baking soda
2 teaspoons ground ginger
1 teaspoon salt
¾ cup vegetable shortening
¾ cup granulated sugar
1 large egg
1 cup molasses, warmed

FILLING
1 tablespoon butter, at
  room temperature
1 cup powdered sugar
½ teaspoon ground
  cinnamon
1 tablespoon boiling water

1. Preheat the oven to 350 degrees. Lightly grease 2 baking sheets.

2. Combine the flour, baking soda, ginger, and salt.

3. In a large bowl, cream the vegetable shortening and sugar. Beat in the egg. Beat in the molasses. Gradually blend in the dry ingredients.

4. On a floured surface, roll out the dough to a thickness of ⅛ inch. Using a 2-inch round cookie cutter, cut out an even numbers of cookies. Using a 1-inch fancy cookie cutter, cut out the centers of half the rounds. Place the rounds 1½ inches apart on the prepared baking sheets.

5. Bake for 10 to 12 minutes, until lightly colored. Transfer to wire racks to cool.

6. To make the filling, cream the butter and sugar together in a medium bowl. Beat in the cinnamon. Beat in the boiling water.

7. To assemble the sandwiches, spread ½ teaspoon of the filling across the bottom of each plain cookie. Top with the cut-out cookies and press together gently.

CINNAMON CRISPS FORMED COOKIES

YIELD: *3 to 4 dozen*

TOTAL TIME: *30 minutes*

1¼ cups all-purpose flour
1 teaspoon baking soda
¼ teaspoon salt
½ cup vegetable shortening
1 cup granulated sugar
1 large egg
1 teaspoon almond extract
½ cup almonds, chopped
  fine
2 teaspoons ground
  cinnamon

1. Preheat the oven to 375 degrees. Lightly grease 2 baking sheets.

2. Combine the flour, baking soda, and salt.

3. In a large bowl, cream the vegetable shortening and sugar. Beat in the egg. Beat in the almond extract. Gradually blend in the dry ingredients.

4. Combine the almonds and cinnamon in a shallow dish.

5. Pinch off walnut-sized pieces of dough and roll into balls. Roll in the almond mixture and place 1½ inches apart on the prepared baking sheets.

6. Bake for 10 to 12 minutes, until lightly colored. Transfer to wire racks to cool.

CINNAMON-GINGER WAFERS   **FORMED COOKIES**

YIELD: 3 to 5 dozen
TOTAL TIME: 30 minutes
CHILLING TIME: 4 hours

1. Combine the flour, baking powder, and spices.

2. In a double boiler, heat the molasses and sugar, stirring until the sugar is dissolved. Remove from the heat and beat in the egg yolk. Gradually blend in the dry ingredients. Transfer to a bowl, cover, and refrigerate for 4 hours.

3. Preheat the oven to 400 degrees. Lightly grease 2 baking sheets.

4. Dust your hands with flour. Pinch off ½-inch pieces of dough and roll into balls. Place 1 inch apart on the prepared baking sheets. With the back of a spoon dipped in flour, flatten each cookie into a wafer-thin round.

5. Bake for 3 to 4 minutes, just until the edges begin to color. Carefully transfer to wire racks to cool.

Baking notes: The secret of making these cookies is in the handling. They burn easily, so watch carefully. And they are so thin that they break easily after they are baked.

2 cups all-purpose flour
¼ teaspoon baking powder
1¼ teaspoons ground ginger
1¼ teaspoons ground cinnamon
6 tablespoons molasses
⅓ cup granulated sugar
1 large egg yolk

CITRUS BARS   **BAR COOKIES**

YIELD: 2 to 3 dozen
TOTAL TIME: 45 minutes

1. Preheat the oven to 350 degrees. Lightly grease a 13 by 9-inch baking pan.

2. Combine the flour, baking powder, baking soda, and spices.

3. In a large bowl, beat the vegetable shortening, eggs, grapefruit juice, and orange extract. Gradually blend in the dry ingredients. Fold in the cranberries and walnuts.

4. Spread the mixture evenly in the prepared baking pan. Sprinkle the coconut and pineapple over the top.

5. Bake for 20 to 25 minutes, until firm to the touch. Cool in the pan on a wire rack before cutting into large or small bars.

2½ cups all-purpose flour
2 teaspoons baking powder
1 teaspoon baking soda
½ teaspoon ground cinnamon
¼ teaspoon ground cloves
¼ cup vegetable shortening
2 large eggs
1½ cups grapefruit juice
1 teaspoon orange extract
1 cup cranberries, chopped
1 cup walnuts, chopped

TOPPING
¾ cup flaked coconut
¾ cup crushed pineapple, drained

Cocoa Brownies

BAR COOKIES

YIELD: *2 to 3 dozen*
TOTAL TIME: *45 minutes*

½ cup all-purpose flour
½ cup unsweetened cocoa powder
1 teaspoon baking powder
Pinch of salt
3 large eggs
1¼ cups packed light brown sugar
1 teaspoon vanilla extract
1 cup walnuts, chopped

1. Preheat the oven to 325 degrees. Lightly grease a 9-inch square baking pan.

2. Combine the flour, cocoa, baking powder, and salt.

3. In a large bowl, beat the eggs and brown sugar together until thick. Beat in the vanilla extract. Gradually blend in the dry ingredients.

4. Spread the mixture evenly into the prepared baking pan. Sprinkle the walnuts over the top.

5. Bake for 20 to 25 minutes, until a toothpick inserted in the center comes out clean. Cool in the pan on a wire rack before cutting into large or small bars.

Cocoa Drop Cookies

DROP COOKIES

YIELD: *4 to 5 dozen*
TOTAL TIME: *40 minutes*

2 cups all-purpose flour
2 teaspoons baking powder
¼ teaspoon salt
6 tablespoons butter, at room temperature
1 cup granulated sugar
3 tablespoons unsweetened cocoa powder
3 large eggs
1 tablespoon milk
2 teaspoons vanilla extract
Walnut halves for decoration

1. Preheat the oven to 375 degrees. Lightly grease 2 baking sheets.

2. Combine the flour, baking powder, and salt.

3. In a large bowl, cream the butter and sugar. Beat in the cocoa. Beat in the eggs, milk, and vanilla extract.

4. Drop the dough by spoonfuls 1½ inches apart onto the prepared baking sheets. Press a walnut half into the center of each cookie.

5. Bake for 10 to 12 minutes, until firm to the touch. Transfer to wire racks to cool.

Coconut Balls I

DROP COOKIES

YIELD: *2 to 3 dozen*
TOTAL TIME: *30 minutes*

2 cups grated fresh (or packaged) coconut
3 tablespoons marsala
3 tablespoons Amaretto
2 large egg whites
Powdered sugar

1. Preheat the oven to 350 degrees. Generously grease 2 baking sheets.

2. In a medium bowl, combine the coconut, marsala and Amaretto.

3. In a large bowl, beat the egg whites until they hold stiff peaks. Fold in the coconut mixture.

4. Using a spoon dipped in powdered sugar, drop the dough by spoonfuls 1½ inches apart onto the prepared baking sheets.

5. Bake for 18 to 20 minutes, until lightly colored. Transfer to wire racks to cool

Coconut Balls II

FORMED COOKIES

YIELD: 5 to 6 dozen
TOTAL TIME: 30 minutes
CHILLING TIME: 4 hours

1. In a large bowl, blend together the sugar, mashed potatoes, coconut, and Amaretto. Cover and chill for 4 hours.

2. In the top of a double boiler, combine all the topping ingredients and heat, stirring, until butter melts and mixture is smooth. Remove from the heat.

3. Line 2 baking sheets with waxed paper.

4. Pinch off large walnut-sized pieces of the coconut mixture. Dip in the topping and place on the prepared baking sheets. Chill in the refrigerator for at least 2 hours.

Baking notes: The mashed potatoes in this recipe are used to form a paste base, similar to using flour and eggs as binding components.

2 cups powdered sugar
¾ cup mashed potatoes
4 cups shredded coconut
1 tablespoon Amaretto

TOPPING
*1 package chocolate frosting
    mix*
3 tablespoons water
2 tablespoons butter
2 tablespoons corn syrup

Coconut Bars

BAR COOKIES

YIELD: 1 to 2 dozen
TOTAL TIME: 30 minutes

1. Preheat the oven to 350 degrees. Lightly grease a 13 by 9-inch baking pan.

2. Combine the flour and baking soda.

3. In a large bowl, cream the vegetable shortening and brown sugar. Beat in the applesauce and vanilla extract. Fold in the flaked coconut.

4. Spread the dough evenly in the prepared baking pan. Sprinkle the shredded coconut on top.

5. Bake for 18 to 20 minutes, until the top is lightly colored. Cool in the pan on a wire rack before cutting into large or small bars.

Baking notes: For an added touch, drizzle Vanilla Frosting over the top before cutting into bars (see Pantry).

2 cups all-purpose flour
1½ teaspoons baking soda
¾ cup vegetable shortening
*½ cup packed light brown
    sugar*
*1 cup unsweetened
    applesauce*
½ teaspoon vanilla extract
2 cups flaked coconut
½ cup shredded coconut

COCONUT BUTTERBALLS

FORMED COOKIES

2 cups all-purpose flour
½ teaspoon salt
1 cup butter, at room
    temperature
½ cup powdered sugar
2 teaspoons vanilla extract
1 cup flaked coconut
Powdered sugar for rolling

1. Combine the flour and salt.

2. In a large bowl, cream the butter and powdered sugar. Beat in the vanilla extract. Gradually blend in the dry ingredients. Fold in the coconut. Cover and chill for 4 hours.

3. Preheat the oven to 350 degrees.

4. Pinch off walnut-sized pieces of dough and roll into balls. Place each ball 1 inch apart on ungreased baking sheets.

5. Bake for 10 to 12 minutes, until lightly colored. Transfer to wire racks to cool.

6. Just before serving, roll the balls in powdered sugar.

YIELD: 1 to 2 dozen
TOTAL TIME: 55 minutes

CRUST
½ cup vegetable shortening
½ cup powdered sugar
1 cup all-purpose flour

TOPPING
One 14-ounce can
    sweetened condensed
    milk
1 cup (6 ounces)
    butterscotch chips
1 cup flaked coconut
1 teaspoon vanilla extract

COCONUT-CARAMEL BARS

BAR COOKIES

1. Preheat the oven to 350 degrees. Lightly grease a 9-inch square baking pan.

2. To make the crust, cream the vegetable shortening and powdered sugar in a medium bowl. Gradually work in the flour. Press the mixture evenly into the prepared baking pan.

3. Bake for 14 minutes.

4. Meanwhile, make the topping: In a large bowl, combine the condensed milk, butterscotch chips, coconut, and vanilla extract and stir until well blended.

5. Pour the topping mixture over the hot crust. Bake for 25 to 30 minutes longer, until a toothpick inserted in the center comes out clean. Cool in the pan on a wire rack before cutting into large or small bars.

YIELD: 1 to 2 dozen
TOTAL TIME: 35 minutes

2 cups all-purpose flour
1 teaspoon baking powder
½ teaspoon salt
⅔ cup vegetable shortening
2 cups packed light brown
    sugar
3 large eggs
1 teaspoon vanilla extract
1½ cups (9 ounces)
    semisweet chocolate chips
¾ cup walnuts, chopped
½ cup shredded coconut

COCONUT CHEWIES

BAR COOKIES

1. Preheat the oven to 350 degrees. Lightly grease a 9-inch square baking pan.

2. Combine the flour, baking powder, and salt.

3. In a large bowl, cream the vegetable shortening and brown sugar. Beat in the eggs. Beat in the vanilla extract. Gradually blend in the dry ingredients. Fold in the chocolate chips, walnuts, and coconut. Spread the mixture evenly in the prepared baking pan.

4. Bake for 20 to 25 minutes, until firm to the touch. Cool in the pan on a wire rack before cutting into large or small bars.

Coconut Chews

BAR COOKIES

YIELD: 2 to 3 dozen
TOTAL TIME: 45 minutes

1. Preheat the oven to 375 degrees. Lightly grease a 13 by 9-inch baking pan.

2. To make the crust, cream the vegetable shortening and sugar in a medium bowl. Gradually blend in the flour. Press the mixture evenly into the bottom of the prepared baking pan.

3. Bake for 15 minutes.

4. Meanwhile, prepare the topping: In a large bowl, beat the eggs with the almonds and coconut.

5. Spread the topping over the hot crust and bake for 20 minutes longer, until set. Cool in the pan on a wire rack before cutting into large or small bars.

CRUST
¾ teaspoon vegetable shortening
3 tablespoons granulated sugar
1½ cups whole wheat flour

TOPPING
2 large eggs
1 cup almonds, chopped
1 cup flaked coconut

Coconut Cookies

REFRIGERATOR COOKIES

YIELD: 5 to 6 dozen
TOTAL TIME: 45 minutes
CHILLING TIME: 8 hours

1. Combine the flour and baking soda.

2. In a large bowl, cream the vegetable shortening and sugar. Beat in the egg and almond extract. Fold in 2 cups of the coconut. Gradually blend in the dry ingredients.

3. Divide the dough into thirds. Form each piece into logs 1½ inches in diameter. Roll the logs in the remaining 1½ cups coconut, pressing gently so it adheres. Wrap in waxed paper and chill for 8 hours or overnight.

4. Preheat the oven to 350 degrees.

5. In a small bowl, beat the egg yolk and milk together for an egg glaze.

6. Cut the logs into ¼-inch-thick slices and place 1 inch apart on ungreased baking sheets. Brush the cookies with the egg glaze and press an almond into the center of each cookie.

7. Bake for 12 to 15 minutes, until lightly colored. Transfer to wire racks to cool.

2 cups all-purpose flour
½ teaspoon baking soda
1 cup vegetable shortening
1 cup granulated sugar
1 large egg
½ teaspoon almond extract
3½ cups shredded coconut
1 large egg yolk
1 tablespoon milk
About 1 cup whole blanched almonds

Coconut-Cornflake Cookies

DROP COOKIES

YIELD: 3 to 4 dozen
TOTAL TIME: 35 minutes

1. Preheat the oven to 350 degrees. Grease 2 baking sheets.

2. Combine the flour, baking powder, baking soda, and salt.

3. In a large bowl, cream the vegetable shortening and brown sugar. Beat in the egg, milk, and vanilla. Gradually blend in the dry ingredients. Fold in the cornflakes and coconut.

4. Drop the dough by spoonfuls 2 inches apart onto the prepared baking sheets.

5. Bake for 12 to 15 minutes, until lightly colored. Transfer to wire racks to cool.

1½ cups all-purpose flour
1 teaspoon baking powder
¼ teaspoon baking soda
¼ teaspoon salt
½ cup vegetable shortening
1 cup packed light brown sugar
1 large egg
⅓ cup milk
1½ teaspoon vanilla extract
1½ cups cornflakes
1 cup shredded coconut

COCONUT DREAMS

FORMED COOKIES

YIELD: 2 to 4 dozen
TOTAL TIME: 45 minutes

1 cup all-purpose flour
⅓ cup granulated sugar
¾ teaspoon baking powder
2 ounces semisweet
*   chocolate, coarsely*
*   chopped*
¼ cup vegetable shortening
1½ cups flaked coconut

1. Preheat the oven to 350 degrees.

2. Combine the flour, sugar, and baking powder.

3. In a double boiler, melt the chocolate and vegetable shortening over low heat, stirring until smooth. Remove from the heat. Blend in the dry ingredients. Fold in the coconut.

4. Pinch off walnut-sized pieces of dough and roll into balls. Place 1 inch apart on ungreased baking sheets.

5. Bake for 20 to 30 minutes, until firm to the touch. Transfer to wire racks to cool.

COCONUT DROP COOKIES I

DROP COOKIES

YIELD: 3 to 4 dozen
TOTAL TIME: 30 minutes

2 cups all-purpose flour
2 teaspoons baking powder
⅔ cup vegetable shortening
1 cup packed light brown
*   sugar*
2 large eggs
2 tablespoons milk
1 teaspoon almond extract
2 cups flaked coconut

1. Preheat the oven to 350 degrees. Lightly grease 2 baking sheets.

2. Combine the flour and baking powder.

3. In a large bowl, combine the vegetable shortening, brown sugar, eggs, milk, and almond extract and beat until smooth. Gradually blend in the dry ingredients. Fold in the coconut.

4. Drop the dough by spoonfuls 1½ inches apart onto the prepared baking sheets.

5. Bake for 12 to 15 minutes, until lightly colored. Transfer to wire racks to cool.

COCONUT DROP COOKIES II

DROP COOKIES

YIELD: 2 to 4 dozen
TOTAL TIME: 30 minutes

1½ cups flaked coconut
One 14-ounce can
*   sweetened condensed*
*   milk*
1 teaspoon vanilla extract
⅛ teaspoon salt

1. Preheat the oven to 250 degrees. Lightly grease 2 baking sheets.

2. In a large bowl, combine all of the ingredients and stir until well blended.

3. Drop the dough by spoonfuls 1 inch apart onto the prepared baking sheets.

4. Bake for 20 to 25 minutes, or until firm to the touch and dry. Transfer to wire racks to cool. (If the cookies fall apart when you remove them from the baking sheet, return to the oven and bake for a few minutes longer.)

Coconut Gems

DROP COOKIES

YIELD: 4 to 6 dozen
TOTAL TIME: 60 minutes

1. Line 2 baking sheets with parchment paper.

2. In a large bowl, beat the egg whites until they hold stiff picks. Blend in the sugar. Fold in the lemon juice and almond extract. Fold in the coconut.

3. Drop the dough by spoonfuls 1 inch apart onto the prepared baking sheets. Set aside for 30 minutes at room temperature.

4. Preheat the oven to 250 degrees.

5. Just before baking, pinch the cookies so they come to a point, like a pyramid shape.

6. Bake for 35 to 40 minutes, until lightly colored. Transfer to wire racks to cool.

Baking notes: If all the cookies don't fit on 2 baking sheets, place on additional sheets of parchment (cut to fit pans) to dry.

4 large egg whites
2 cups granulated sugar
½ teaspoon fresh lemon
  juice
¼ teaspoon almond extract
1½ cups shredded coconut

Coconut Homesteads

DROP COOKIES

YIELD: 3 to 4 dozen
TOTAL TIME: 30 minutes

1. Preheat the oven to 375 degrees. Lightly grease 2 baking sheets.

2. Combine the flour, oats, baking powder, baking soda, and salt. Combine the coconut and apples in a medium bowl and toss to mix.

3. In a large bowl, cream the butter and the two sugars. Beat in the egg. Beat in the almond extract. Gradually blend in the dry ingredients. Fold in the apples and coconut.

4. Drop the dough by spoonfuls 1½ inches apart onto the prepared baking sheets.

5. Bake for 8 to 10 minutes, until lightly colored. Transfer to wire racks to cool.

1 cup all-purpose flour
½ cup (3 ounces) rolled
  oats
½ teaspoon baking powder
½ teaspoon baking soda
½ teaspoon salt
2 cups flaked coconut
1 cup finely chopped apples
  (2 apples)
½ cup butter, at room
  temperature
½ cup granulated sugar
½ cup packed light brown
  sugar
1 large egg
1 teaspoon almond extract

Coconut-Jam Squares

BAR COOKIES

YIELD: 2 to 3 dozen
TOTAL TIME: 60 minutes

1. Preheat the oven to 425 degrees. Lightly grease a 9-inch square baking pan.

2. To make the crust, combine the flour and salt in a large bowl. Cut in the vegetable shortening until the mixture resembles coarse crumbs. Press the mixture evenly into the bottom of the prepared baking pan, and sprinkle the water over the top.

3. Bake for 20 minutes.

4. Meanwhile, make the topping: In a large bowl, beat the eggs and sugar until thick and light-colored. Gently fold in the coconut.

5. Spread the raspberry preserves over the warm baked crust. Spread the filling over the preserves.

6. Reduce the oven temperature to 375 degrees and bake for 20 to 25 minutes longer, or until firm to the touch. Cool in the pan on a wire rack before cutting into large or small bars.

CRUST
1¼ cups all-purpose flour
¼ teaspoon salt
½ cup vegetable shortening
3 tablespoons ice water

FILLING
2 large eggs
½ cup powdered sugar
2⅔ cup flaked coconut
⅓ cup raspberry preserves

COCONUT KISSES

DROP COOKIES

YIELD: 2 to 3 dozen
TOTAL TIME: 55 minutes

4 large egg whites
¼ teaspoon cream of tartar
¼ teaspoon salt
1 cup granulated sugar
¼ teaspoon almond extract
1½ cups flaked coconut

1. Preheat the oven to 250 degrees. Line 2 baking sheets with parchment paper.

2. In a large bowl, beat the egg whites until foamy. Beat in the cream of tartar and salt. Beat in the sugar a tablespoon at a time. Beat in the almond extract and beat until the whites hold stiff peaks. Gently fold in the coconut.

3. Drop the mixture by spoonfuls 1½ inches apart onto the prepared baking sheets.

4. Bake for 35 to 45 minutes, until firm to the touch. Transfer to wire racks to cool.

Baking notes: For crisper kisses, when the cookies are done, turn the oven off and let the cookies cool completely in the oven.

COCONUT MACAROONS

DROP COOKIES

YIELD: 2 to 3 dozen
TOTAL TIME: 40 minutes

½ cup shredded coconut
2 teaspoons cornstarch
⅛ teaspoon salt
3 large egg whites
1 cup granulated sugar
1 teaspoon vanilla extract

1. Preheat the oven to 275 degrees. Line 2 baking sheets with parchment paper.

2. Combine the coconut, cornstarch, and salt in a medium bowl and toss to mix.

3. In a large bowl, beat the egg whites until stiff but not dry. Fold in the sugar and vanilla extract. Gradually fold in the coconut mixture.

4. Drop the dough by spoonfuls 1½ inches apart onto the prepared baking sheets.

5. Bake for 28 to 30 minutes, until lightly colored. Transfer to wire racks to cool.

COCONUT MACAROONS DELUXE

FORMED COOKIES

YIELD: 5 to 6 dozen
TOTAL TIME: 50 minutes

2½ cups shredded coconut
1 cup granulated sugar
1 tablespoon cornstarch
6 large egg whites
¼ teaspoon almond extract
About 1½ cups candied
    cherries, halved

1. Preheat the oven to 350 degrees. Line 2 baking sheets with parchment paper.

2. Combine the coconut, sugar, and cornstarch in a medium bowl and toss to mix.

3. Combine the egg whites and almond extract in the top of a double boiler. Add the coconut mixture and cook, stirring for about 20 minutes until thickened (a candy thermometer will register about 148 degrees). Remove from the heat and let cool for 5 minutes.

4. Place the mixture in a cookie press or a pastry bag fitted with a large star tip and press or pipe out rounds 1½ inches apart onto the prepared baking sheets. Press a half-cherry into the center of each cookie.

5. Bake for 18 to 20 minutes, or until lightly colored. Transfer to wire racks to cool.

COCONUT-OATMEAL COOKIES

DROP COOKIES

1. Preheat the oven to 350 degrees. Lightly grease 2 baking sheets.

2. Combine the flour, baking powder, baking soda, and salt.

3. In a large bowl, beat the vegetable shortening, granulated sugar, brown sugar, egg, and Amaretto. Gradually blend in the dry ingredients. Fold in the oatmeal, coconut, almonds. The dough will be stiff.

4. Pinch off large walnut-sized pieces of dough and roll into balls. Place 3 inches apart on the prepared baking sheets.

5. Bake for 10 to 12 minutes, until lightly colored. Transfer to wire racks to cool.

Baking notes: Be sure to leave ample space between the cookies on the baking sheets. They spread more than most cookies.

YIELD: 5 to 6 dozen
TOTAL TIME: 35 minutes.

¾ cup all-purpose flour
½ teaspoon baking powder
½ teaspoon baking soda
½ teaspoon salt
¼ cup vegetable shortening
½ cup granulated sugar
½ cup packed light brown
  sugar
1 large egg
1 tablespoon Amaretto
1 cup (6 ounces) rolled oats
1 cup shredded coconut
½ cup almonds, chopped

COCONUT-PINEAPPLE SQUARES

BAR COOKIES

1. Preheat the oven to 350 degrees. Lightly grease a 13 by 9-inch baking pan.

2. Combine the flour, baking powder, baking soda, and cinnamon.

3. In a large bowl, beat the vegetable shortening, eggs, and pineapple juice. Gradually blend in the dry ingredients. Fold in the flaked coconut and pineapple.

4. Spread the mixture evenly in the prepared baking pan.

5. Bake for 15 minutes. Sprinkle the shredded coconut over the top and bake for 10 to 15 minutes longer, until coconut is lightly colored. Cool in the pan on a wire rack before cutting into large or small bars.

YIELD: 1 to 3 dozen
TOTAL TIME: 30 minutes

2½ cups all-purpose flour
2 teaspoons baking powder
1 teaspoon baking soda
1 teaspoon ground
  cinnamon
½ cup vegetable shortening
3 large eggs
1 cup pineapple juice
2 cups flaked coconut
One 20-ounce can crushed
  pineapple, drained
½ cup shredded coconut

COCONUT SANDWICHES

ROLLED COOKIES

1. In a large bowl, cream the vegetable shortening and sugar. Beat in the egg yolk. Beat in the vanilla extract. Gradually blend in the flour. Fold in the coconut. Cover and chill for 2 hours.

2. Preheat the oven to 350 degrees. Lightly grease 2 baking sheets.

3. On a floured surface, roll out the dough to a thickness of ¼ inch. Using a 1½-inch round cookie cutter, cut out an even number of cookies and place 1 inch apart on the prepared baking sheets.

4. Bake for 8 to 10 minutes, or until lightly colored. Transfer to wire racks to cool.

5. To sandwich the cookies, spread a thin layer of the filling over the bottom of half the cookies. Place the remaining cookies on top and press together gently.

YIELD: 2 to 3 dozen
TOTAL TIME: 30 minutes
CHILLING TIME: 2 hours

¾ cup vegetable shortening
½ cup granulated sugar
1 large egg yolk
½ teaspoon vanilla extract
2 cups all-purpose flour
1⅓ cups flaked coconut
¾ to 1 cup Butter Cream
  Filling (see Pantry)

COCONUT SUGAR COOKIES

ROLLED COOKIES

YIELD: *5 to 6 dozen*
TOTAL TIME: *30 minutes*
CHILLING TIME: *2 hours*

3¾ cups all-purpose flour
1¼ cups coconut, ground fine
1½ teaspoons baking powder
½ teaspoon salt
1 cup vegetable shortening
1½ cups granulated sugar
2 large eggs
1 teaspoon coconut extract
Granulated sugar for sprinkling

1. Combine the flour, coconut, baking powder, and salt.

2. In a large bowl, cream the vegetable shortening and sugar. Beat in the eggs one at a time. Beat in the coconut extract. Gradually blend in the dry ingredients. Cover and chill for 2 hours.

3. Preheat the oven to 375 degrees. Lightly grease 2 baking sheets.

4. On a floured surface, roll out the dough to a thickness of ⅛ inch. Using a 2-inch round cookie cutter, cut into rounds and place 1½ inches apart on the prepared baking sheets. Lightly brush the cookies with water and sprinkle with granulated sugar.

5. Bake for 8 to 10 minutes, until lightly colored. Transfer to wire racks to cool.

Baking notes: The secret of these cookies is to grind the coconut as fine as possible. You can also form this dough into a log 2 inches in diameter, wrap in waxed paper, and chill for 4 hours. Slice into ¼-inch-thick slices and bake as directed.

COFFEE COOKIES

ROLLED COOKIES

YIELD: *6 to 7 dozen*
TOTAL TIME: *30 minutes*
CHILLING TIME: *3 hours*

5 cups all-purpose flour
1 tablespoon baking soda
2 teaspoons ground ginger
1 teaspoon salt
1 cup vegetable shortening
2 cups granulated sugar
1 large egg
1 cup molasses
2 tablespoons brewed coffee
½ teaspoon vanilla extract

1. Combine the flour, baking soda, ginger, and salt.

2. In a large bowl, cream the vegetable shortening and sugar. Beat in the egg. Beat in the molasses, coffee, and vanilla extract. Gradually blend in the dry ingredients. Cover and chill for 3 hours.

3. Preheat the oven to 350 degrees. Lightly grease 2 baking sheets.

4. On a floured surface, roll out the dough to a thickness of ⅜ inch. Using cookie cutters, cut into shapes and place the cookies 1½ inches apart on the prepared baking sheets.

5. Bake for 12 to 15 minutes, until lightly colored. Transfer to wire racks to cool.

COFFEE-FLAVORED BROWNIES   **BAR COOKIES**

YIELD: 1 to 2 dozen
TOTAL TIME: 35 minutes

1. Preheat the oven to 375 degrees. Lightly grease an 8-inch square baking pan.

2. Combine the flour, baking powder, coffee crystals, and salt.

3. In the top of a double boiler, melt the chocolate and shortening over low heat, stirring until smooth. Remove from the heat.

4. In a large bowl, beat the eggs until thick and light-colored. Gradually beat in the chocolate mixture and vanilla extract. Beat in the sugar. Gradually blend in the dry ingredients. Stir in the walnuts.

5. Spread the batter evenly in the prepared baking pans.

6. Bake for 20 to 25 minutes, until a toothpick inserted in the center comes out clean. Cool in the pan on a wire rack before cutting into large or small bars.

¾ cup all-purpose flour
½ teaspoon baking powder
2 tablespoons instant coffee crystals
¼ teaspoon salt
2 ounces unsweetened chocolate, chopped
⅓ cup vegetable shortening
2 large eggs
1 teaspoon vanilla extract
1 cup granulated sugar
½ cup walnuts, chopped

COFFEE KISSES   **DROP COOKIES**

YIELD: 2 to 3 dozen
TOTAL TIME: 60 minutes

1. Preheat the oven to 250 degrees. Line 2 baking sheets with parchment paper.

2. In a cup, dissolve the coffee powder in the boiling water. Let cool.

3. In a large bowl, beat the egg whites until foamy. Beat in the cream of tartar and salt. Beat in the sugar 1 tablespoon at a time. Beat in the crème de cacao and beat until the whites form stiff peaks. Fold in the coffee.

4. Drop the dough by spoonfuls 1 inch apart onto the prepared baking sheets.

5. Bake for 35 to 40 minutes, until firm to the touch. Cool completely on the baking sheets on wire racks.

1 tablespoon plus 1 teaspoon instant coffee powder
1 tablespoon boiling water
4 large egg whites
¼ teaspoon cream of tartar
¼ teaspoon salt
1 cups granulated sugar
1 teaspoon crème de cacao

COFFEE SQUARES   **BAR COOKIES**

YIELD: 2 to 3 dozen
TOTAL TIME: 35 minutes

1. Preheat the oven to 350 degrees. Lightly grease a 13 by 9-inch baking pan.

2. Combine the flour, baking powder, baking soda, cardamom, and salt.

3. Combine milk and coffee crystals in a saucepan and heat, stirring, until the coffee dissolves. Remove from the heat.

4. In a large bowl, cream the vegetable shortening and both sugars. Beat in the egg. Beat in the coffee. Gradually blend in the dry ingredients. Fold in the almonds.

5. Spread the dough evenly in the prepared baking pan.

6. Bake for 18 to 20 minutes, until a toothpick inserted in the center comes out clean. Cool in the pan on a wire rack.

7. Frost the cooled cookies with the icing and cut into large or small bars.

1½ cups all-purpose flour
1 teaspoon baking powder
¼ teaspoon baking soda
½ teaspoon ground cardamom
¼ teaspoon salt
½ cup milk
2 teaspoons instant coffee crystals
¼ cup vegetable shortening
1 cup granulated sugar
1 cup powdered sugar
1 large egg
1 cup almonds, chopped
1 recipe for Vanilla Icing (see Pantry)

COOKIE-BRITTLE COOKIES

YIELD: 2 to 4 dozen
TOTAL TIME: 35 minutes

2 cups all-purpose flour
½ teaspoon salt
1 cup vegetable shortening
1 cup granulated sugar
½ teaspoon vanilla extract
1 cup (6 ounces) semisweet
    chocolate chips
1 cup peanuts, unsalted

1. Preheat the oven to 350 degrees. Lightly grease a 15 by 10-inch baking pan.

2. Combine the flour and salt.

3. In a large bowl, cream the vegetable shortening and sugar. Beat in the vanilla extract. Gradually blend in the dry ingredients. Fold in the chocolate chips.

4. Spread the dough evenly in the prepared baking pan (it will make a very thin layer). Sprinkle the peanuts over the top and press them gently into the dough.

5. Bake for 20 to 25 minutes, until the top is lightly colored. Cool in the pan on a wire rack before breaking into large or small pieces.

Baking notes: The secret of this cookie is that it should be very thin.

COOKIE FACES

YIELD: 2 to 3 dozen
TOTAL TIME: 35 minutes

3½ cups all-purpose flour
2 teaspoons baking powder
1 teaspoon ground cinnamon
1 teaspoon salt
1⅓ cups vegetable
    shortening
¾ cup granulated sugar
¾ cup packed light brown
    sugar
2 large eggs
2 teaspoons vanilla extract
Popsicle sticks

1. Preheat the oven to 350 degrees. Lightly grease 2 baking sheets.

2. Combine the flour, baking powder, cinnamon, and salt.

3. In a large bowl, cream the vegetable shortening and the two sugars. Beat in the eggs one at a time. Beat in the vanilla extract. Gradually blend in the dry ingredients.

4. On a floured surface, roll out the dough to a thickness of ⅜ inch. Using cookie cutter, cut into 3- or 4-inch rounds or ovals. Use the scraps of dough to make the cookie faces (see Baking notes). Place 1 inch apart on the prepared baking sheets. Insert a popsicle stick into each cookie.

5. Bake for 12 to 15 minutes, until firm to the touch. Transfer to wire racks to cool.

Baking notes: These are cookies to make with kids. To create the faces, pinch the center of each dough circle or oval to form the nose. Make an indentation on either side of the nose for the eyes. Roll small bits of dough into very thin ropes for the eyebrows, eyes, and lips. Roll out another small piece of dough and cut into ears. (The dough used for the eyebrows, eyes, and lips can be colored using food coloring.)

COOKIE PIZZA

FORMED COOKIES

1. Preheat the oven to 350 degrees. Lightly grease a 14 to 15-inch pizza pan.

2. Combine the flour, baking powder, baking soda, and salt.

3. In a large bowl, cream the vegetable shortening and brown sugar. Beat in the egg and vanilla. Gradually blend in the dry ingredients. Fold in the oats and coconut.

4. Press the dough evenly into the prepared pan. Sprinkle the chocolate chips and walnuts evenly over the top.

5. Bake for 12 to 15 minutes, until lightly colored. Sprinkle the M&Ms over the hot cookies. Cool in the pan on a wire rack for a few minutes before cutting into wedges.

YIELD: 4 dozen
TOTAL TIME: 30 minutes

CRUST
¾ cup all-purpose flour
½ teaspoon baking powder
½ teaspoon baking soda
Pinch of salt
½ cup vegetable shortening
¾ cup packed light brown sugar
1 large egg
1 teaspoon vanilla extract
1 cup (6 ounces) rolled oats
½ cup flaked coconut

TOPPING
1 cup (6 ounces) semisweet chocolate chips
1 cup walnuts, chopped
½ cup M&Ms

COOKIE SANDWICHES

ROLLED COOKIES

1. Preheat the oven to 350 degrees.

2. Combine the flour, baking soda, and salt.

3. In a large bowl, cream the vegetable shortening and powdered sugar. Beat in the milk and vanilla and almond extracts. Gradually blend in the dry ingredients.

4. On a floured surface, roll out the dough to a thickness of ¼ inch. Using a 1½-inch round cookie cutter, cut out an even number of cookies. Using a small star or diamond cookie cutter, cut out the centers of half of the cookies. Place the cookies 1 inch apart on ungreased baking sheets.

5. Bake for 12 to 15 minutes, until lightly colored. Transfer to wire racks to cool.

6. Spread a thin layer of filling over the bottom of each solid cookie, top with a cut-out cookie, and gently press together.

YIELD: 1 to 3 dozen
TOTAL TIME: 30 minutes

2½ cups all-purpose flour
¼ teaspoon baking soda
½ teaspoon salt
1 cup vegetable shortening
½ cup powdered sugar
2 tablespoons evaporated milk
1 teaspoon vanilla extract
1 teaspoon almond extract
About 1 cup jam, preserves, or softened cream cheese

CORNFLAKE COOKIES

DROP COOKIES

YIELD: 5 to 6 dozen
TOTAL TIME: 30 minutes

2 cups all-purpose flour
½ teaspoon baking powder
½ teaspoon baking soda
½ teaspoon salt
1 cup vegetable shortening
1 cup granulated sugar
1 cup packed light brown sugar
2 large eggs
½ teaspoon vanilla extract
1 cup cornflakes
1 cup (6 ounces) rolled oats
1 cup shredded coconut
½ cup walnuts, chopped

1. Preheat the oven to 350 degrees.

2. Combine the flour, baking powder, baking soda, and salt.

3. In a large bowl, cream the vegetable shortening and two sugars. Beat in the eggs. Beat in the vanilla extract. Gradually blend in the dry ingredients. Stir in the cornflakes, oats, coconut, and walnuts. The dough will be stiff, so knead it together.

4. Drop the dough by spoonfuls 1½ inches apart onto ungreased baking sheets.

5. Bake for 10 to 12 minutes, until lightly colored. Transfer to wire racks to cool.

CRACKLE BROWNIES

BAR COOKIES

YIELD: 1 to 2 dozen
TOTAL TIME: 45 minutes

1 cup (6 ounces) semisweet chocolate chips
1 cup all-purpose flour
½ teaspoon baking powder
⅓ cup vegetable shortening
¾ cup granulated sugar
2 large eggs
1 teaspoon vanilla extract
¾ cup rice krispies

TOPPING
½ cup (3 ounces) semisweet chocolate chips
¼ cup rice krispies

1. Preheat the oven to 350 degrees. Lightly grease an 8-inch square baking pan.

2. Melt the chocolate chips in a double boiler over low heat, stirring until smooth. Remove from the heat.

3. Combine the flour and baking powder.

4. In a large bowl, cream the vegetable shortening and sugar. Beat in the eggs and vanilla extract. Beat in the melted chocolate. Gradually blend in the dry ingredients. Fold in the rice krispies. Spread the mixture evenly in the prepared baking pan.

5. Bake for 20 to 25 minutes, until a toothpick inserted in the center comes out clean.

6. For the topping, sprinkle the chocolate chips over the top of the warm brownies. Let sit for 1 to 2 minutes, until the chocolate melts, then spread the chocolate evenly over the brownies. Sprinkle the rice krispies over the top. Cool in the pan on a wire rack before cutting into large or small bars.

CRANBERRY COOKIES

REFRIGERATOR COOKIES

YIELD: 3 to 4 dozen
TOTAL TIME: 45 minutes
CHILLING TIME: 8 hours

1½ cups all-purpose flour
½ teaspoon baking powder
¼ teaspoon salt
½ cup vegetable shortening
¾ cup powdered sugar
3 tablespoons milk
1 teaspoon Amaretto
¾ cup cranberries, fresh or dried, chopped fine (see Baking notes)
½ cup flaked coconut

1. Combine the flour, baking powder, and salt.

2. In a large bowl, cream the vegetable shortening and powdered sugar. Beat in the milk and Amaretto. Gradually blend in the dry ingredients. Fold in the cranberries.

3. Divide the dough in half. Form each half into a log 1½ inches in diameter. Roll in coconut. Wrap in waxed paper and chill for 8 hours.

4. Preheat the oven to 375 degrees.

5. Cut the logs into ¼-inch-thick slices and place each slice 1 inch apart on ungreased baking sheets.

6. Bake for 12 to 15 minutes, until lightly colored. Transfer to wire racks to cool.

Baking notes: If using dried cranberries, cover cranberries with boiling water and plump for 10 minutes before chopping.

CRANBERRY ORANGE BARS

BAR COOKIES

YIELD: 1 to 2 dozen
TOTAL TIME: 45 minutes

1½ cups all-purpose flour
1 teaspoon baking powder
½ teaspoon salt
6 tablespoons vegetable shortening
¾ cup granulated sugar
2 large eggs
1 cup cranberries, chopped fine
¾ cup orange marmalade

TOPPING
2 tablespoons butter, at room temperature
1 cup powdered sugar
¼ cup pecans, ground fine
1 tablespoon milk
2 tablespoons diced cranberries

1. Preheat the oven to 350 degrees. Lightly grease a 13 by 9-inch baking pan.

2. Combine the flour, baking powder, and salt.

3. In a large bowl, cream the vegetable shortening and sugar. Beat in the eggs. Beat in the cranberries and marmalade. Gradually blend in the dry ingredients. Spread the dough evenly into the prepared baking pan.

4. Bake for 25 to 30 minutes, until firm to the touch.

5. Meanwhile, make the topping: In a medium bowl, cream the butter and powdered sugar. Beat in the pecans. Beat in the milk.

6. Spread the topping evenly over the hot cookies. Sprinkle the diced cranberries on top. Cool in the pan on a wire rack before cutting into large or small bars.

Baking notes: Refrigerate these bars once they have cooled. Serve them with whipped cream.

Cream Cheese Brownies   BAR COOKIES

YIELD: 2 to 3 dozen

TOTAL TIME: 50 minutes

½ cup all-purpose flour
½ teaspoon baking powder
¼ teaspoon salt
⅓ cup semisweet chocolate
*   chips*
5 tablespoons vegetable
*   shortening*
1 cup granulated sugar
3 ounces cream cheese, at
*   room temperature*
3 large eggs
2 teaspoons vanilla extract
½ teaspoon almond extract
½ cup almonds, chopped

1. Preheat the oven to 350 degrees. Lightly grease a 9-inch square baking pan.

2. Combine the flour, baking powder, and salt.

3. In the top of a double boiler, melt the chocolate chips and vegetable shortening, stirring until smooth. Transfer to a large bowl.

4. Add the sugar to the chocolate mixture and beat until smooth. Beat in the cream cheese. Beat in the eggs, beating well after each addition. Beat in the vanilla and almond extracts. Gradually blend in the dry ingredients. Fold in the almonds. Scrape the batter into the prepared baking pan.

5. Bake for 35 to 40 minutes, until a toothpick inserted in the center comes out clean. Cool in the pan on a wire rack before cutting into large or small bars.

Cream Cheese Refrigerator Cookies   REFRIGERATOR COOKIES

YIELD: 2 to 3 dozen

TOTAL TIME: 30 minutes.

CHILLING TIME: 4 hours

1 cup all-purpose flour
3 tablespoons poppy seeds
¼ teaspoon salt
4 ounces cream cheese, at
*   room temperature*
⅓ cup canola oil
¼ cup honey, warmed

1. Combine the flour, poppy seeds, and salt.

2. In a large bowl, beat the cream cheese, oil, and honey until well blended and smooth. Gradually blend in the dry ingredients. Shape the dough into a log 2½ inches in diameter. Wrap in waxed paper and chill for 4 hours.

3. Preheat the oven to 400 degrees. Lightly grease 2 baking sheets.

4. Cut the log into ¼-inch-thick slices and place 1 inch apart on the prepared baking sheets.

5. Bake for 6 to 8 minutes, or until lightly browned. Transfer to wire racks to cool.

CREAM CHEESE TASTIES

ROLLED COOKIES

YIELD: *3½ dozen*
TOTAL TIME: *40 minutes*
CHILLING TIME: *8 hours*

2 cups all-purpose flour
¼ teaspoon salt
1 cup vegetable shortening
8 ounces cream cheese, at room temperature
½ cup powdered sugar
About ¼ cup raspberry preserves
Powdered sugar for sprinkling

1. Combine the flour and salt.

2. In a large bowl, beat the vegetable shortening, cream cheese, and powdered sugar until smooth. Gradually blend in the dry ingredients. Divide the dough in half. Wrap each half in waxed paper and chill for 8 hours.

3. Preheat the oven to 375 degrees.

4. On a floured surface, roll out one-half of the dough to a rectangle approximately 10 inches by 11½ inches. Trim the edges of the dough and cut lengthwise into 4 strips. Cut each strip into 5 squares. Place ¼ teaspoon raspberry preserves in the center of each square and fold the dough over to form a triangle. Press the edges together to seal and place 1 inch apart on ungreased baking sheets. Repeat with the other half of the dough.

5. Bake for 10 to 12 minutes, until lightly colored. Sprinkle with powdered sugar and transfer to wire racks to cool.

Baking notes: Use fluted pastry cutter to cut the dough into decorative shapes if you like.

CRÈME DE MENTHE BROWNIES

BAR COOKIES

YIELD: *1 to 2 dozen*
TOTAL TIME: *40 minutes*
CHILLING TIME: *1 hour*

½ cup plus 2 tablespoons vegetable shortening
¼ cup unsweetened cocoa powder
1 cup granulated sugar
2 large eggs
½ teaspoon crème de menthe
⅔ cup all-purpose flour
Green crème de menthe icing (see Pantry)
Walnut halves

1. Preheat the oven to 350 degrees. Lightly grease a 9-inch square baking pan.

2. Melt the vegetable shortening in a large saucepan. Beat in the cocoa powder. Remove from the heat and beat in the sugar. Beat in the eggs and crème de menthe. Gradually blend in the flour. Spread the batter evenly in the prepared baking pan.

3. Bake for 18 to 20 minutes, until a toothpick inserted into the center comes out clean. Cool in the pan on a wire rack.

4. Spread the icing over the top of the brownies and cut into large or small bars. Place a walnut half in the center of each brownie. Chill for about at least 1 hour before removing from the pan.

C

CRISP LEMON COOKIES

ROLLED COOKIES

YIELD: *7 to 10 dozen*
TOTAL TIME: *35 minutes*
CHILLING TIME: *4 hours*

4 cups all-purpose flour
1 teaspoon baking powder
1 cup butter, at room temperature
2 cups granulated sugar
2 large eggs
1 teaspoon lemon extract
Granulated sugar for spinkling

1. Combine the flour and baking powder.

2. In a large bowl, cream the butter and sugar. Beat in the eggs. Beat in the lemon extract. Gradually blend in the dry ingredients. Cover and chill for 4 hours.

3. Preheat the oven to 375 degrees. Lightly grease 2 baking sheets.

4. On a floured surface, roll the dough out to a thickness of ⅛ inch. Using cookie cutters, cut into shapes and place 1 inch apart on the prepared baking sheets. Sprinkle the cookies with granulated sugar.

5. Bake for 10 to 12 minutes, until lightly colored. Transfer to wire racks to cool.

Baking notes: For a different look, sprinkle some of the cookies with colored crystals.

CRISP SUGAR COOKIES

FORMED COOKIES

YIELD: *5 to 6 dozen*
TOTAL TIME: *30 minutes*
CHILLING TIME: *8 hours*

5 cups all-purpose flour
1 tablespoon plus 1 teaspoon cream of tartar
2 teaspoons baking soda
1 teaspoon salt
2 cups vegetable shortening
2 cups granulated sugar
4 large eggs
2 teaspoons vanilla extract
Granulated sugar

1. Combine the flour, cream of tartar, baking soda, and salt.

2. In a large bowl, cream the vegetable shortening and sugar. Beat in the eggs. Beat in the vanilla extract. Gradually blend in the dry ingredients. Cover and chill for 8 hours or overnight.

3. Preheat the oven to 375 degrees. Lightly grease 2 baking sheets.

4. Pinch off walnut-sized pieces of dough and roll into balls. Place the balls 1½ inches apart on the prepared baking sheets. Dip the bottom of a glass in water and then in granulated sugar, and press to flatten each ball to a thickness of ¼ inch.

5. Bake for 8 to 10 minutes, until lightly colored. Transfer to wire racks to cool.

CRUNCHY BUTTERSCOTCH COOKIES

DROP COOKIES

YIELD: *3 to 4 dozen*
TOTAL TIME: *30 minutes*

2 cups all-purpose flour
1 teaspoon baking soda
1 teaspoon salt
1 cup vegetable shortening
½ cup granulated sugar
1 cup packed light brown sugar
2 large eggs
2 tablespoons milk
1 teaspoon vanilla extract
1 cup hard butterscotch candies, crushed

1. Preheat the oven to 375 degrees.

2. Combine the flour, baking soda, and salt.

3. In a large bowl, cream the vegetable shortening and two sugars. Beat in the eggs. Beat in the milk and vanilla extract. Gradually blend in the dry ingredients. Fold in the candies.

4. Drop the dough by spoonfuls 1½ inches apart onto ungreased baking sheets.

5. Bake for 10 to 12 minutes, until lightly colored. Transfer to wire racks to cool.

Baking notes: You can also use this dough to make formed cookies: Chill the dough for at least 4 hours. Pull off walnut-sized chunks of dough and roll them into balls. Place the balls 1½ inches apart on ungreased baking sheets and bake as directed.

CRUNCHY CHOCOLATE BARS

BAR COOKIES

YIELD: *1 to 2 dozen*
TOTAL TIME: *30 minutes*

2 cups (12 ounces) semisweet chocolate chips
¾ cup chunky peanut butter
3 cups Cheerios

1. Grease an 8-inch square baking pan.

2. In the top of a double boiler, melt the chocolate chips with the peanut butter, stirring until smooth. Remove from the heat and gradually blend in the cereal.

3. Spread the dough evenly in the prepared baking pan. Refrigerate until thoroughly chilled, then cut into large or small bars.

CURRANT BARS

BAR COOKIES

YIELD: *2 to 4 dozen*
TOTAL TIME: *35 minutes*

3 cups all-purpose flour
½ teaspoon baking soda
½ teaspoon ground cinnamon
¼ teaspoon ground cloves
½ teaspoon salt
1 cup vegetable shortening
¾ cup granulated sugar
¾ cup packed light brown sugar
2 large eggs, slightly beaten
⅓ cup orange juice
1 cup currants
1 cup flaked coconut

TOPPING
¾ cup powdered sugar
1 tablespoon plus 1 teaspoon fresh orange juice
1 teaspoon finely shredded orange zest

1. Preheat the oven to 350 degrees. Lightly grease 2 baking sheets.

2. Combine the flour, baking soda, spices, and salt.

3. Melt the vegetable shortening in a large saucepan. Remove from the heat and beat in the two sugars. Beat in the eggs one at a time. Beat in the orange juice. Gradually blend in the dry ingredients. Fold in the currants and coconut. Spread the mixture evenly in the prepared baking pan.

4. Bake for 20 to 25 minutes, until light colored on top.

5. Meanwhile, in a small bowl combine all of the ingredients for the topping and stir until smooth.

6. Spread the topping over the warm cookies. Cool in the pan on a wire rack before cutting into large or small bars.

CZECHOSLOVAKIAN COOKIES

ROLLED COOKIES

YIELD: *4 to 6 dozen*
TOTAL TIME: *30 minutes*
CHILLING TIME: *4 hours*

1 cup vegetable shortening
1 cup granulated sugar
2 large eggs
1 teaspoon vanilla extract
2½ cups all-purpose flour
1 cup hazelnuts, chopped fine
About ¼ cup strawberry jam

1. In a large bowl, cream the vegetable shortening and sugar. Beat in the eggs. Beat in the vanilla. Gradually blend in the flour. Blend in the hazelnuts. Cover and chill for 4 hours.

2. Preheat the oven to 325 degrees.

3. On a floured surface, roll out the dough to a thickness of ¼ inch. Using cookie cutters, cut into shapes and place 1 inch apart on ungreased baking sheets. Place ¼ teaspoon of strawberry jam in the center of each cookie.

4. Bake for 8 to 12 minutes, until lightly colored. Transfer to wire racks to cool.

Baking notes: This is a very basic recipe that lends itself to many variations; substitute your favorite nuts for the hazelnuts and use a variety of fruit jams and preserves to fill the centers of the cookies.

DATE BALLS

FORMED COOKIES

YIELD: *4 to 5 dozen*
TOTAL TIME: *30 minutes*

1¼ cups all-purpose flour
Pinch of salt
½ cup vegetable shortening
⅓ cup powdered sugar
1 tablespoon water
1 teaspoon vanilla extract
⅔ cup dates, pitted and chopped
½ cup walnuts, chopped
Powdered sugar for rolling

1. Preheat the oven to 300 degrees.

2. Combine the flour and salt.

3. In a large bowl, cream the vegetable shortening and powdered sugar. Beat in the water and vanilla extract. Gradually blend in the dry ingredients. Fold in the dates and walnuts.

4. Pinch off 1-inch pieces of dough and roll into balls. Place 1 inch apart on the ungreased baking sheets.

5. Bake for 18 to 20 minutes, or just until the cookies start to color slightly. Roll in powdered sugar and transfer to wire racks to cool.

DATE BARS

BAR COOKIES

YIELD: *2 to 3 dozen*
TOTAL TIME: *45 minutes*

1 cup whole wheat flour
½ cup soy flour
¼ teaspoon salt
2 large eggs, separated
1 cup packed light brown sugar
¼ cup boiling water
1 teaspoon vanilla extract
1 cup dates, pitted and chopped
1 cup walnuts, chopped

1. Preheat the oven to 350 degrees. Lightly grease a 13 by 9-inch baking pan.

2. Combine the flour, soy flour, and salt.

3. In a large bowl, beat the egg yolks until thick and light-colored. Beat in the brown sugar and water. Beat in the vanilla extract. Gradually blend in the dry ingredients. Fold in the dates and walnuts.

4. In a large bowl, beat the egg whites until stiff but not dry. Fold the whites into the date mixture. Spread the batter evenly in the prepared baking pan.

5. Bake for 30 to 35 minutes, until lightly colored on top. Cool in the pan on a wire rack before cutting into large or small bars.

DATE BROWNIES

BAR COOKIES

YIELD: *1 to 3 dozen*
TOTAL TIME: *35 minutes*

½ cup all-purpose flour
¼ teaspoon baking powder
¼ teaspoon salt
2 ounces bittersweet chocolate, chopped
½ cup vegetable shortening
1 cup granulated sugar
2 large eggs
1 teaspoon vanilla extract
1 cup walnuts, chopped
⅔ cup dates, pitted and chopped

1. Preheat the oven to 325 degrees. Lightly grease a 9-inch square baking pan.

2. Combine the flour, baking powder, and salt.

3. In the top of a double boiler, melt the chocolate and vegetable shortening, stirring until smooth. Remove from the heat and beat in the sugar. Beat in the eggs one at a time. Beat in the vanilla extract. Gradually blend in the dry ingredients. Stir in the walnuts and dates. Spread the mixture evenly in the prepared baking pan.

4. Bake for 20 to 25 minutes, or until a toothpick inserted in the center comes out clean. Cool in the pan on a wire rack before cutting into large or small bars.

DATE DROPS

DROP COOKIES

YIELD: 1 to 2 dozen
TOTAL TIME: 40 minutes

1. Preheat the oven to 400 degrees. Lightly grease 2 baking sheets.

2. Combine the flour, baking powder, baking soda, and salt.

3. In a large bowl, cream the vegetable shortening and brown sugar. Beat in the egg and sour cream. Gradually blend in the dry ingredients. Fold in the dates.

4. Drop the dough by spoonfuls 1½ inches apart onto the prepared baking sheets. Press a walnut into the center of each cookie.

5. Bake for 8 to 10 minutes, until lightly colored. Transfer to wire racks to cool.

6. Fill a pastry bag fitted with a small plain tip with the icing and pipe a ring of icing around each walnut.

Baking notes: In an old version of this recipe, whole pitted dates are stuffed with walnut halves and placed on baking sheets, then the dough is dropped on top of the dates.

1¼ cups all-purpose flour
½ teaspoon baking powder
½ teaspoon baking soda
¼ teaspoon salt
¼ cup vegetable shortening
¾ cup packed light brown sugar
1 large egg
½ cup sour cream
1 pound dates, pitted and chopped
About ½ cup walnuts
Vanilla Icing (see Pantry)

DATE-GRANOLA SQUARES

BAR COOKIES

YIELD: 1 to 3 dozen
TOTAL TIME: 35 minutes

1. Preheat the oven to 350 degrees. Lightly grease a 13 by 9-inch baking pan.

2. Combine the flour, baking powder, baking soda, spices, and salt.

3. In a large bowl, beat the canola oil and eggs together. Beat in the pear juice. Gradually blend in the dry ingredients. Stir in the granola and dates. Spread the mixture evenly in the prepared baking pan.

4. To make the topping, combine the dates and granola in a small bowl and toss to mix. Sprinkle evenly over the top of the granola mixture.

5. Bake for 25 to 30 minutes, until firm to the touch. Cool in the pan on a wire rack before cutting into large or small bars.

Baking notes: If you wish to make your own granola, combine equal amounts of rolled oats, chopped nuts, flaked coconut, sesame seeds, chopped sunflower seeds, and chopped dried fruit, such as banana chips and/or raisins.

2½ cups all purpose flour
2 teaspoons baking powder
½ teaspoon baking soda
1 teaspoon ground cinnamon
½ teaspoon ground nutmeg
¼ teaspoon ground ginger
¼ teaspoon salt
½ cup canola oil
2 large eggs
1½ cups pear juice
1 cup unsweetened granola (see Baking notes)
1 cup dates, pitted & chopped
topping
½ cup dates, pitted and chopped very fine
½ cup unsweetened granola

DATE-NUT FINGERS

FORMED COOKIES

YIELD: 4 to 5 dozen
TOTAL TIME: 50 minutes

1¼ cups toasted rice cereal
1 cup dates, pitted and
    chopped fine
1 cup pecans, chopped
½ cup butter
¼ cup granulated sugar
¼ cup packed light brown
    sugar
1 large egg
1 cup shredded coconut

1. Combine the cereal, dates, and pecans in a large bowl.

2. Combine the butter and two sugars in the top of a double boiler and cook over low heat, stirring, until the butter melts and the sugar dissolves. Beat in the egg and cook for 20 minutes, stirring occasionally, until very thick. Do not allow the mixture to boil.

3. Pour the hot sugar mixture over the date mixture and stir to coat well. Let cool slightly.

4. Pinch off pieces of dough and form into 2 by 1-inch strips. Roll the strips in the shredded coconut and let cool.

DATE PINWHEELS

ROLLED COOKIES

YIELD: 4 to 5 dozen
TOTAL TIME: 45 minutes
CHILLING TIME: Crust: 4
hours Roll: 24 hours

2⅓ cups all-purpose flour
½ teaspoon baking powder
¼ teaspoon baking soda
¼ teaspoon ground
    cinnamon
¼ teaspoon salt
½ cup vegetable shortening
1 cup packed light brown
    sugar
2 large eggs
½ teaspoon vanilla extract

FILLING
1½ cups dates, pitted and
    chopped fine
⅓ cup water
⅓ cup granulated sugar
½ cup walnuts, ground
    fine
½ teaspoon vanilla extract

1. Combine the flour, baking powder, baking soda, cinnamon, and salt.

2. In a large bowl, cream the vegetable shortening and brown sugar. Beat in the eggs. Beat in the vanilla extract. Gradually blend in the dry ingredients. Cover and chill for 4 hours.

3. To make the filling, combine the dates, water, and sugar in a saucepan and bring to a boil. Reduce the heat and cook, stirring, until very thick. Remove from the heat and stir in the walnuts and vanilla.

4. On a floured surface, roll out the dough to a 1/4-inch-thick rectangle. Spread the date filling evenly over the dough, leaving a 1/4-inch border all around the edges. Starting on a long side, roll up the dough jelly-roll fashion and pinch the seam to seal. Cut the roll in half, wrap in waxed paper, and chill for 24 hours.

5. Preheat the oven to 350 degrees. Lightly grease 2 baking sheets.

6. Cut the rolls into 1/4-inch-thick slices and place 1 inch apart on the prepared baking sheets.

7. Bake for 8 to 10 minutes, until lightly colored. Transfer to wire racks to cool.

DATE SQUARES

BAR COOKIES

YIELD: 1 to 2 dozen
TOTAL TIME: 50 minutes

1. Preheat the oven to 400 degrees. Lightly grease a 9-inch square baking pan.

2. To make the filling, combine the dates, orange juice, and water in a saucepan and bring to a boil. Cook, stirring, for 15 minutes or until very thick. Remove from the heat.

3. To make the crust, combine the flour, baking soda, and salt.

4. In a large bowl, cream the vegetable shortening and brown sugar. Beat in the almond extract. Gradually blend in the dry ingredients. Stir in the oats and pecans.

5. Press half of the crust mixture into the prepared baking pan. Spread the date filling over the top of the crust. Spread the remaining crust mixture over the filling and press lightly.

6. Bake for 20 to 25 minutes, until lightly colored on top. Cool in the pan on a wire rack before cutting into large or small bars.

FILLING
2 cups dates, pitted and
*   chopped*
½ cup fresh orange juice
¼ cup water

CRUST
1½ cups all-purpose flour
¾ teaspoon baking soda
¼ teaspoon salt
¾ cup vegetable shortening
⅔ cup packed light brown
*   sugar*
⅛ teaspoon almond extract
1¼ cups oats
½ cup pecans, chopped

DECORATIVE COOKIES

ROLLED COOKIES

YIELD: 4 to 5 dozen
TOTAL TIME: 50 minutes

1. Preheat the oven to 375 degrees. Lightly grease 2 baking sheets.

2. Combine the flour, baking powder, and salt.

3. In a large bowl, cream the vegetable shortening and sugar. Beat in the eggs. Beat in the vanilla extract. Gradually blend in the dry ingredients.

4. On a floured surface, roll out the dough to a thickness of ¼ inch. Using cookie cutters, cut into shapes and place 1½ inches apart on the prepared baking sheets.

5. Bake for 8 to 10 minutes, or until lightly colored. Transfer to wire racks to cool.

Baking notes: These cookies are sweeter than most rolled cookies. To decorate them, spread a frosting over them or pipe designs onto them (see Icings and Frostings, in Pantry).

3¾ cups all purpose flour
1½ teaspoons baking
*   powder*
1 teaspoon salt
1 cup vegetable shortening
2 cups granulated sugar
2 large eggs
2 teaspoons vanilla extract

DELICIOUS FUDGE BROWNIES

BAR COOKIES

YIELD: 1 to 2 dozen
TOTAL TIME: 45 minutes

1⅓ cups all-purpose flour
¾ cup unsweetened cocoa powder
¼ teaspoon salt
⅔ cup vegetable oil
2 cups granulated sugar
2 large eggs
1 teaspoon vanilla extract
½ cup walnuts, chopped

1. Preheat the oven to 350 degrees. Lightly grease a 13 by 9-inch baking pan.

2. Combine the flour, cocoa powder, and salt.

3. In a large bowl, beat the vegetable oil and sugar. Beat in the eggs one at a time. Beat in the vanilla extract. Gradually blend in the dry ingredients. Fold in the walnuts. Spread the mixture evenly in the prepared baking pan.

4. Bake for 25 to 30 minutes, or until a toothpick inserted in the center comes out clean. Cool in the pan on a wire rack before cutting into large or small bars.

Baking notes: For a more decorative appearance, sprinkle the walnuts on top of the batter before baking.

DESERT MYSTERIES

ROLLED COOKIES

YIELD: 2 to 3 dozen
TOTAL TIME: 40 minutes

FILLING
1 tablespoon vegetable shortening
1 cup packed light brown sugar
1 large egg
1 teaspoon vanilla extract
¼ cup walnuts, chopped
1 cup dates, pitted and chopped

CRUST
1 cup vegetable shortening
2 cups packed light brown sugar
4 large eggs
4 cups whole wheat flour

1. Preheat the oven to 350 degrees. Lightly grease 2 baking sheets.

2. To make the filling, cream the vegetable shortening and brown sugar in a medium bowl. Beat in the egg and vanilla extract. Stir in the walnuts and dates.

3. To make the crust, cream the vegetable shortening and brown sugar in a large bowl. Beat in the eggs. Gradually blend in the flour.

4. On a floured surface, roll out the dough into a 15 by 15-inch square to a thickness of ¼ inch. Using a knife, cut into 3-inch squares. Drop a teaspoonful of the filling into the center of each square. Working quickly, bring up the 4 corners of each square over the filling and pinch together to form a little bag. Place 1 inch apart on the prepared baking sheet.

5. Bake for 12 to 15 minutes, until lightly colored. Transfer to wire racks to cool.

DOUBLE PEANUT-FLAVORED COOKIES

FORMED COOKIES

YIELD: 5 to 6 dozen
TOTAL TIME: 30 minutes

2¼ cups all-purpose flour
2 teaspoons baking soda
1 cup vegetable shortening
1 cup granulated sugar
1 cup packed light brown sugar
1 cup peanut butter
2 large eggs
1 teaspoon vanilla extract
1 cup unsalted peanuts, chopped

1. Preheat the oven to 350 degrees.

2. Combine the flour and baking soda.

3. In a large bowl, cream the vegetable shortening and two sugars. Beat in the peanut butter. Beat in the eggs and vanilla extract. Gradually blend in the dry ingredients. Fold in the peanuts.

4. Pinch off walnut-sized pieces of dough and roll into small balls. Place each 1½ inches apart on ungreased baking sheets and flatten each ball with the bottom of a glass dipped in flour.

5. Bake for 8 to 10 minutes, until lightly colored. Transfer to wire racks to cool.

DREAMS END

FORMED COOKIES

YIELD: 3 to 4 dozen
TOTAL TIME: 30 minutes

2½ cups all-purpose flour
½ teaspoon baking soda
½ teaspoon cream of tartar
1 cup butter, at room temperature
1 cup powdered sugar
2 teaspoons raspberry brandy

1. Preheat the oven to 325 degrees. Lightly grease 2 baking sheets.

2. Combine the flour, baking soda, and cream of tartar.

3. In a large bowl, cream the butter and powdered sugar. Beat in the brandy. Gradually blend in the dry ingredients. The dough will be very stiff; if it seems too dry, add water a teaspoonful at a time.

4. Pinch off pieces of the dough about the size of large olives and roll into balls. Place 1 inch apart on the prepared baking sheets.

5. Bake for 8 to 10 minutes, or until lightly colored. Transfer to wire racks to cool.

DUTCH-CRUNCH APPLESAUCE BARS

BAR COOKIES

YIELD: 1 to 2 dozen
TOTAL TIME: 40 minutes

2 cups all-purpose flour
1 teaspoon baking soda
1 teaspoon ground cinnamon
½ teaspoon ground nutmeg
¼ teaspoon salt
1 cup granulated sugar
1 cup unsweetened
    applesauce
1 teaspoon vanilla extract
½ cup walnuts, chopped

TOPPING
2 tablespoons butter, at
    room temperature
¼ cup granulated sugar
⅔ cup crushed breakfast
    cereal (such as
    cornflakes)

1. Preheat the oven to 350 degrees. Lightly grease a 13 by 9-inch baking pan.

2. Combine the flour, baking soda, spices, and salt.

3. In a large bowl, beat the sugar, applesauce, and vanilla extract. Gradually blend in the dry ingredients. Stir in the walnuts. Spread the mixture evenly in the prepared baking pan.

4. To make the topping, cream the butter and sugar in a small bowl. Gradually blend in the cereal. Spread this over the dough.

5. Bake for 20 to 30 minutes, until lightly browned on top. Cool in the pan on a wire rack before cutting into large or small bars.

DUTCH SOUR CREAM COOKIES

REFRIGERATOR COOKIES

YIELD: 3 to 4 dozen
TOTAL TIME: 40 minutes
CHILLING TIME: 8 hours

3 cups all-purpose flour
¼ teaspoon baking soda
½ cup vegetable shortening
1 cup granulated sugar
1 large egg
½ teaspoon vanilla extract
½ teaspoon lemon extract
¼ cup sour cream

1. Combine the flour and baking soda.

2. In a large bowl, cream the vegetable shortening and sugar. Beat in the egg, vanilla and lemon extracts. Beat in the sour cream. Gradually blend in the dry ingredients.

3. Shape the dough into a log 2 inches in diameter. Wrap in waxed paper and chill for 8 hours.

4. Preheat the oven to 375 degrees. Lightly grease 2 baking sheets.

5. Cut the log into ¼-inch-thick slices, and place 1 inch apart on the prepared baking sheets.

6. Bake for 10 to 12 minutes, until lightly colored. Transfer to wire racks to cool.

DUTCH SPICE COOKIES

ROLLED COOKIES

1. Combine the flour, almonds, baking powder, spices, and salt.

2. In a large bowl, cream the shortening and brown sugar. Beat in the milk. Gradually blend in the dry ingredients. Fold in the citrus peel.

3. Transfer the dough to a floured surface and knead until smooth. Wrap in waxed paper and chill for 8 hours.

4. Preheat the oven to 350 degrees. Lightly grease 2 baking sheets.

5. On a floured surface, roll out the dough to a thickness of ¼ inch. Using cookie cutters, cut into shapes and place 1 inch apart on the prepared baking sheets.

6. Bake for 18 to 20 minutes, until firm to the touch. Transfer to wire racks to cool.

Baking notes: This dough may also be used with a speculaas mold to form cookies.

YIELD: 4 to 5 dozen
TOTAL TIME: 30 minutes
CHILLING TIME: 8 hours

1 cup all-purpose flour
3 tablespoons almonds, ground
¼ teaspoon baking powder
½ teaspoon ground cinnamon
¼ teaspoon ground cloves
¼ teaspoon ground ginger
¼ teaspoon ground nutmeg
¼ teaspoon salt
5 tablespoons vegetable shortening
⅓ cup packed light brown sugar
1 tablespoon milk
2 tablespoons chopped candied citrus peel

DUTCH TEA CAKES

BAR COOKIES

1. Preheat the oven to 300 degrees. Lightly grease a 9-inch square baking pan.

2. In a large bowl, combine the flour, brown sugar, baking powder, spices, and candied peel. Gradually stir in the milk and molasses. Spread the dough evenly in the prepared baking pan.

3. Bake for 1½ to 2 hours, or until firm and the top looks dry. Place a paper doily on top of the hot cookies and sprinkle with sugar. Let cool on a rack before cutting into large or small bars.

YIELD: 3 to 4 dozen
TOTAL TIME: 2 hours

4 cups all-purpose flour
1 cup packed light brown sugar
1 teaspoon baking powder
1 teaspoon ground cinnamon
½ teaspoon ground cloves
1 cup candied citrus peel, chopped fine
1 cup milk
1 cup molasses
Powdered sugar for sprinkling

EASY BUTTERSCOTCH DROP COOKIES

DROP COOKIES

YIELD: 3 to 4 dozen
TOTAL TIME: 30 minutes

2 cups all-purpose flour
2 teaspoons baking powder
½ teaspoon salt
⅔ cup canola oil
1 cup packed dark brown sugar
2 large eggs
2 teaspoons vanilla extract
1 teaspoon sugar
½ teaspoon cinnamon

1. Preheat the oven to 350 degrees.

2. Combine the flour, baking powder, and salt.

3. In a large bowl, beat the oil and brown sugar. Beat in the eggs one at a time. Beat in the vanilla extract. Gradually blend in the dry ingredients.

4. Combine sugar and cinnamon in a small bowl.

5. Drop the dough by spoonfuls 1½ inches apart onto ungreased baking sheets. Flatten each cookie with the bottom of a glass dipped in canola oil and then in the cinnamon sugar.

6. Bake for 12 to 15 minutes, until lightly colored. Transfer to wire racks to cool.

EASY FUDGE COOKIES

REFRIGERATOR COOKIES

YIELD: 6 to 7 dozen
TOTAL TIME: 35 minutes
CHILLING TIME: 8 hours

2 ounces semisweet chocolate, chopped
4⅓ cups all-purpose flour
1 teaspoon baking powder
½ teaspoon baking soda
¼ teaspoon salt
1 cup vegetable shortening
1 cup packed light brown sugar
1 cup granulated sugar
2 large eggs
⅓ cup milk
1 teaspoon vanilla extract
½ cup walnuts, chopped (optional)

1. Melt the chocolate in a double boiler over low heat, stirring until smooth. Remove from the heat.

2. Combine the flour, baking powder, baking soda, and salt.

3. In a large bowl, cream the vegetable shortening and two sugars. Beat in the eggs one at a time. Beat in the milk and vanilla extract. Beat in the melted chocolate. Gradually blend in the dry ingredients. Fold in the walnuts.

4. Divide the dough in half. Form each half into a 2-inch-thick logs. Wrap in waxed paper and chill for 8 hours or overnight.

5. Preheat the oven to 375 degrees.

6. Cut the logs into ⅛-inch-thick slices and place 1 inch apart on ungreased baking sheets.

7. Bake for 12 to 15 minutes, until lightly colored. Transfer to wire racks to cool.

ENGLISH SNAPS

ROLLED COOKIES

YIELD: 5 to 6 dozen
TOTAL TIME: 30 minutes

1. Preheat the oven to 350 degrees. Lightly grease 2 baking sheets.

2. Combine the flour, baking soda, and spices.

3. In a large bowl, cream the vegetable shortening and sugar. Beat in the egg. Beat in the corn syrup and cider vinegar. Gradually blend in the dry ingredients.

4. On a floured surface, roll out the dough to a thickness of ¼ inch. Using a 1½-inch round cookie cutter, cut the dough into rounds and place 1½ inches apart on the prepared baking sheets.

3 cups all-purpose flour
1½ teaspoons baking soda
1 teaspoon ground
    cinnamon
¼ teaspoon ground allspice
¼ teaspoon ground cloves
1 cup vegetable shortening
1 cup granulated sugar
1 large egg
¾ cup corn syrup
1½ teaspoons cider vinegar

5. Bake for 8 to 12 minutes, until firm to the touch. Transfer to wire racks to cool.

Baking notes: The vinegar adds a great very faintly sour taste that really enhances these cookies. You may want to try a teaspoon or so as flavoring in other spice recipes.

ENGLISH TEA BISCUITS

ROLLED COOKIES

YIELD: 3 to 4 dozen
TOTAL TIME: 30 minutes

1. Preheat the oven to 350 degrees. Lightly grease 2 baking sheets.

2. Combine the flour, baking soda, and nutmeg.

3. In a large bowl, cream the vegetable shortening and sugar. Beat in the eggs one at a time. Beat in the cream. Gradually blend in the dry ingredients.

4. On a floured surface, roll out the dough to a thickness of ⅛ inch. Using a 1½- to 2-inch round cookie cutter, cut into rounds and place 1 inch apart on the prepared baking sheets.

4¼ cups all-purpose flour
¼ teaspoon baking soda
¼ teaspoon ground nutmeg
½ cup vegetable shortening
1½ cups granulated sugar
2 large eggs
½ cup heavy cream

5. Bake for 12 to 15 minutes, until lightly colored. Transfer to wire racks to cool.

Baking notes: Other spices, such as cinnamon, cloves, or allspice, can be substituted for the nutmeg. If you use ground cloves, reduce the amount by half.

ENGLISH TOFFEE BARS

BAR COOKIES

YIELD: 1 to 2 dozen
TOTAL TIME: 75 minutes

1. Preheat the oven to 275 degrees. Lightly grease a 9-inch square baking pan.

2. Combine the flour and cinnamon.

3. In a large bowl, cream the vegetable shortening and brown sugar. Beat in the egg yolk. Gradually blend in the dry ingredients. Fold in the walnuts. Spread the mixture evenly in the prepared baking pan.

2 cups all-purpose flour
1 teaspoon ground
    cinnamon
1 cup vegetable shortening
1 cup packed light brown
    sugar
1 large egg yolk
1 cup black or regular
    walnuts, chopped

4. Bake for 55 to 60 minutes, until firm to the touch. Cool in the pan on a wire rack before cutting into large or small bars.

FENNEL COOKIES

FORMED COOKIES

YIELD: 5 to 6 dozen
TOTAL TIME: 30 minutes

2½ cups all-purpose flour
½ teaspoon baking powder
1 teaspoon fennel seeds
1 cup vegetable shortening
½ cup granulated sugar
1 large egg
1 teaspoon vanilla extract

1. Preheat the oven to 350 degrees.

2. Combine the flour, baking powder, and fennel seeds.

3. In a large bowl, cream the vegetable shortening and sugar. Beat in the egg. Beat in the vanilla extract. Gradually blend in the dry ingredients

4. Place dough in a cookie press or a pastry bag fitted with a large star tip and press or pipe out the dough in small mounds onto ungreased baking sheets, spacing them 1 inch apart.

5. Bake for 10 to 12 minutes, until lightly colored. Transfer to wire racks to cool.

FIG DROPS

DROP COOKIES

YIELD: 4 to 5 dozen
TOTAL TIME: 30 minutes

1 cup canola oil
1½ cups packed dark
   brown sugar
3 large eggs
1 tablespoon water
1 teaspoon vanilla extract
1½ cups whole wheat flour
1 cup soy flour
2 cups ripe figs, chopped
   fine
1 cup walnuts, chopped
   fine (optional)

1. Preheat the oven to 350 degrees. Lightly grease 2 baking sheets

2. In a large bowl, beat the oil and brown sugar. Beat in the eggs one at a time. Beat in the water and vanilla extract. Gradually blend in the two flours. Fold in the figs and the optional walnuts.

3. Drop the dough by spoonfuls 1½ inches apart onto the prepared baking sheets.

4. Bake for 10 to 12 minutes, until lightly colored. Transfer to wire racks to cool.

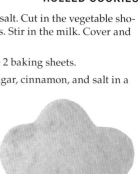

FILLED CHEESE COOKIES

ROLLED COOKIES

YIELD: 3 to 5 dozen
TOTAL TIME: 30 minutes
CHILLING TIME: 2 hours

2 cups all-purpose flour
2 cups Cheddar cheese,
   grated fine
½ teaspoon salt
½ cup vegetable shortening
¼ cup milk

FILLING
¾ cup raspberry jam
2 tablespoons light brown
   sugar
2 teaspoons ground
   cinnamon
¼ teaspoon salt
1½ cups walnuts, chopped
   fine

1. In a large bowl, combine the flour, cheese, and salt. Cut in the vegetable shortening until the mixture resembles coarse crumbs. Stir in the milk. Cover and chill in the refrigerator for at least 2 hours.

2. Preheat the oven to 400 degrees. Lightly grease 2 baking sheets.

3. To make the filling, combine the jam, brown sugar, cinnamon, and salt in a small bowl and stir to blend. Stir in the walnuts.

4. On a floured surface, roll out the dough to a thickness of ⅛ inch. Using a 1½-inch round cookie cutter, cut out an even number of cookies. Place a spoonful of the filling in the center of half the cookie. Place the remaining cookies on top and seal the edges. Place 1 inch apart on the prepared baking sheets.

5. Bake for 12 to 15 minutes, until lightly colored. Transfer to wire racks to cool

Finnish Bridal Cookies

ROLLED COOKIES

YIELD: *3 to 4 dozen*
TOTAL TIME: *30 minutes*

1 cup vegetable shortening
½ cup Vanilla Sugar (see Pantry)
¾ cup all-purpose flour
1 large egg white
About ¼ cup jam or preserves of your choice for filling

1. Preheat the oven to 375 degrees. Lightly grease 2 baking sheets.

2. In a large bowl, cream the vegetable shortening and vanilla sugar. Gradually blend in the flour.

3. In a small bowl, beat the egg white until stiff but not dry. Fold the egg white into the dough.

4. On a floured surface, roll the dough out to a thickness of ¼ inch. Using a 1½-inch round cookie cutter, cut out an even number of rounds and place 1 inch apart on the prepared baking sheets.

5. Bake for 8 to 10 minutes, until lightly colored. Transfer to wire racks to cool.

6. To assemble, spread ½ teaspoon of the jam or preserves over the bottom of half the cookies, top with the remaining cookies and gently press together.

Finnish Coffee Strips

ROLLED COOKIES

YIELD: *5 to 6 dozen*
TOTAL TIME: *35 minutes*
CHILLING TIME: *1 hour*

2½ cups unbleached flour
3 tablespoons bitter almonds, grated fine
Pinch of salt
1 cup butter, at room temperature
2 tablespoons granulated sugar
1 large egg, beaten
½ cup almonds, chopped fine

1. Combine the flour, grated almonds, and salt.

2. In a large bowl, cream the butter and sugar. Gradually blend in the dry ingredients. Cover and chill in for 1 hour.

3. Preheat the oven to 375 degrees. Lightly grease 2 baking sheets.

4. On a floured surface, roll out the dough to a thickness of ¾ inch. Using a sharp knife or a pastry wheel, cut the dough into strips 2 inches long. Brush with the beaten egg, and dredge in the chopped almonds, and place 1½ inches apart on the prepared baking sheets.

5. Bake for 8 to 10 minutes, until lightly colored. Tansfer to wire racks to cool.

Baking notes: Bitter almonds can be found in specialty stores, but if you can't find them substitute hazelnuts.

F

YIELD: 2 to 4 dozen
TOTAL TIME: 30 minutes

¾ cup almonds, ground fine
¼ cup all-purpose flour
¼ cup butter
⅓ cup granulated sugar
5 tablespoons heavy cream
½ cup grated orange zest

TOPPING
4 ounces semisweet chocolate, chopped
3 tablespoons butter

FLORENTINES

DROP COOKIES

1. Preheat the oven to 375 degrees. Lightly grease and flour 2 baking sheets.

2. Combine the almonds and flour.

3. Combine the butter, sugar, and cream in a saucepan and bring to a boil. Remove from the heat and gradually blend in the dry ingredients. Stir in the orange zest. The mixture will be very thin.

4. Drop the batter by tablespoonfuls 3 inches apart onto the prepared baking sheets. With the back of a spoon dipped in flour, spread the batter into 2- inch rounds.

5. Bake for 12 to 15 minutes, until the edges start to brown (the centers may still look bubbly). Cool on the baking sheets on wire racks.

6. For the topping, melt the chocolate and butter in the top of a double boiler, stirring until smooth. Remove from the heat.

7. Place the cooled cookies upside down on the wire racks. Using a pastry brush, paint a thin layer of the melted chocolate over the bottom of each one. Let cool until the chocolate sets.

YIELD: 3 to 4 dozen
TOTAL TIME: 70 minutes

2 cups granulated sugar
1 cup water
6 large egg whites
¼ teaspoon cream of tartar
¼ teaspoon salt
1 teaspoon vanilla extract

FRENCH MERINGUE COOKIES

DROP COOKIES

1. Preheat the oven to 250 degrees. Line 2 baking sheets with parchment paper.

2. Combine the sugar and water in a heavy saucepan and bring to a boil, stirring to dissolve the sugar. Brush down the sides of the pan with a pastry brush and boil until the syrup registers 238 degrees on a candy thermometer. Immediately remove from the heat.

3. Meanwhile, in a large bowl beat the egg whites until frothy. Beat in the cream of tartar and salt.

4. Slowly pour the sugar syrup, into the egg whites, beating constantly. Beat in the vanilla extract and beat until the mixture is cool.

5. Place the dough in a pastry bag fitted with a star tip and pipe out mounds 1 inch apart onto the prepared baking sheets (or drop the batter by spoonfuls onto the sheets).

6. Bake for 40 to 45 minutes, until lightly colored. Cool on the baking sheets on wire racks.

Baking notes: Finely ground almonds may be sprinkled over the meringues before baking.

Fresh Plum Bars

BAR COOKIES

1. Preheat the oven to 350 degrees. Lightly grease a 9-inch square baking pan.

2. To make the crust, combine the flour and salt.

3. In a large bowl, cream the vegetable shortening and sugar. Beat in the egg yolk. Gradually blend in the dry ingredients. Spread the dough evenly in the prepared baking pan.

4. Arrange the sliced plums on top of the dough. Sprinkle the powdered sugar over the plums. Bake for 15 minutes.

5. Meanwhile, make the filling: In a large bowl, combine the cream cheese, sour cream, eggs, powdered sugar, lemon zest, almond extract, and spices and beat until smooth.

6. Spread the topping evenly over the hot crust. Bake for 30 to 35 minutes longer, or until firm to the touch. Cool in the pan on a wire rack before cutting into large or small bars, then refrigerate until ready to serve.

Baking notes: These bars should be served well chilled, with a dab of whipped cream on top.

YIELD: 1 to 3 dozen
TOTAL TIME: 55 minutes

CRUST
1½ cups all-purpose flour
¼ teaspoon salt
½ cup vegetable shortening
¼ cup granulated sugar
1 large egg yolk
4 cups pitted plums, sliced
½ cup powdered sugar

FILLING
8 ounces cream cheese, at room temperature
¾ cup sour cream
3 large eggs
¾ cup powdered sugar
½ teaspoon grated lemon zest
1 teaspoon almond extract
1 teaspoon ground cinnamon
¼ teaspoon ground cloves

Frosted Chocolate Drops

DROP COOKIES

1. Preheat the oven to 375 degrees. Lightly grease 2 baking sheets.

2. Combine the flour, baking soda, and salt.

3. In the top of a double boiler, melt the chocolate and vegetable shortening, stirring until smooth. Remove from the heat and beat in the sugar. Beat in the egg. Beat in the milk and vanilla extract. Gradually blend in the dry ingredients. Fold in the chopped walnuts.

4. Drop the dough by spoonfuls 1½ inches apart onto the prepared baking sheets.

5. Bake for 12 to 15 minutes, until firm to the touch. Transfer to wire racks to cool.

6. Frost the cookies with the chocolate icing.

YIELD: 3 to 4 dozen
TOTAL TIME: 30 minutes

1¾ cups all-purpose flour
½ teaspoon baking soda
½ teaspoon salt
2 ounces unsweetened chocolate, chopped
½ cup vegetable shortening
¾ cups granulated sugar
1 large egg
½ cup evaporated milk
1 teaspoon vanilla extract
½ cup walnuts, chopped
Chocolate Icing (see Pantry)

F

FROSTED GINGER CREAMS

BAR COOKIES

YIELD: 8 to 9 dozen
TOTAL TIME: 30 minutes

3½ cups all-purpose flour
2 teaspoons baking soda
1 teaspoon ground ginger
1 teaspoon ground
*   cinnamon*
½ teaspoon salt
1 cup vegetable shortening
½ cup granulated sugar
2 large egg yolks
1 cup molasses, warmed
½ cup milk
1 cup raisins
White Sugar Icing (see
*   Pantry)*

1. Preheat the oven to 350 degrees. Lightly grease a 15 by 10-inch baking pan.

2. Combine the flour, baking soda, ginger, cinnamon, and salt.

3. In a large bowl, cream the vegetable shortening and sugar. Beat in the egg yolks. Beat in the molasses and milk. Gradually blend in the dry ingredients. Fold in the raisins. Spread the mixture evenly in the prepared baking pan.

4. Bake for 12 to 15 minutes, until lightly colored. Cool in the pan on a wire rack.

5. Frost the cookies with the sugar glaze and cut into 2 by 1½-inch bars.

FRUIT BARS

BAR COOKIES

YIELD: 1 to 4 dozen
TOTAL TIME: 45 minutes
CHILLING TIME: 8 hours

3 cups all-purpose flour
1 teaspoon baking soda
½ teaspoon ground
*   cinnamon*
¼ teaspoon ground nutmeg
¼ teaspoon ground cloves
¼ teaspoon ground ginger
½ teaspoon salt
¾ cup vegetable shortening
1 cup granulated sugar
¼ cup white port
1 cup evaporated milk
½ cup finely chopped
*   candied citron*
¼ cup finely chopped
*   candied pineapple*
¼ cup finely chopped
*   candied cherries*
¼ cup finely chopped
*   candied orange peel*
1 tablespoon grated lemon
*   zest*
½ cup walnuts, chopped

1. Combine the flour, baking soda, spices, and salt.

2. In a large bowl, cream the vegetable shortening and sugar. Beat in the port. Beat in the milk. Gradually blend in the dry ingredients. Fold in the candied fruit and lemon zest. Stir in the walnuts. Cover and chill for 8 hours or overnight.

3. Preheat the oven to 350 degrees.

4. Spread the dough evenly in an ungreased 13 by 9-inch baking pan. Bake for 25 to 30 minutes, until golden on top.

5. Cool in the pan on a wire rack before cutting into large or small bars.

Baking notes: These are good frosted with Rum Buttercream (see Pantry). Store these bars tightly covered.

FRUITCAKE COOKIES

BAR COOKIES

YIELD: 1 to 3 dozen
TOTAL TIME: 45 minutes

1. Preheat the oven to 350 degrees. Lightly grease a 9-inch square baking pan.

2. Combine the flour and baking powder.

3. In a large bowl, cream the vegetable shortening and sugar. Beat in the eggs. Beat in the orange juice. Gradually blend in the dry ingredients. Fold in the candied fruit, raisins, the optional dates, and walnuts. Spread the dough evenly into the prepared baking pan.

4. Bake for 30 to 35 minutes, until lightly colored on top. Cool in the pan on a wire rack before cutting into large or small bars.

Baking notes: These bars are like miniature holiday fruitcakes. Add a little ground cinnamon or ground nutmeg, or both, just to emphasize the fruitcake flavor.

1 cup all-purpose flour
½ teaspoon baking powder
6 tablespoons vegetable shortening
½ cup granulated sugar
2 large eggs
¼ cup fresh orange juice
1 cup mixed candied fruit
1 cup raisins
½ cup dates, pitted and chopped (optional)
½ cup walnuts, chopped

FRUIT CHEWIES

BAR COOKIES

YIELD: 1 to 3 dozen
TOTAL TIME: 40 minutes

1. To make the filling, combine the apricots, dates, water, and lemon juice in a blender and blend to a puree. Transfer to a bowl and refrigerate until cold.

2. Preheat the oven to 350 degrees. Lightly grease a 13 by 9-inch baking pan.

3. Combine the flour, baking soda, and salt.

4. In a large bowl, cream the vegetable shortening and brown sugar. Beat in the molasses and vanilla extract. Gradually blend in the dry ingredients. Fold in the oats.

5. Press half of the dough evenly into the bottom of the prepared baking pan, packing it down.

6. Spread the chilled filling over the dough, leaving a ½-inch border all around the edges. Spread the remaining dough evenly on top of the fruit.

7. Bake for 20 to 25 minutes, until lightly colored on top. Cool in the pan on a wire rack before cutting into large or small bars.

FILLING
1¾ cups dried apricots, chopped
1 cup dates, pitted and chopped
1¾ cups water
¼ teaspoon fresh lemon juice
2 cups all-purpose flour
1 teaspoon baking soda
¼ teaspoon salt
¾ cup vegetable shortening
¾ cup packed dark brown sugar
¼ cup molasses
1 teaspoon vanilla extract
2 cup (12 ounces) rolled oats

FRUIT COOKIES

DROP COOKIES

YIELD: 5 to 6 dozen
TOTAL TIME: 30 minutes

2 cups all-purpose flour
1 teaspoon baking powder
½ teaspoon baking soda
2 teaspoons ground allspice
¼ teaspoon salt
1 cup granulated sugar
⅓ cup vegetable oil
2 large eggs
2 cups raisins
⅓ cup almonds, chopped

1. Preheat the oven to 375 degrees. Lightly grease 2 baking sheets.

2. Combine the flour, baking powder, baking soda, allspice, and salt.

3. In a large bowl, beat the sugar and vegetable oil. Beat in the eggs. Gradually blend in the dry ingredients. Stir in the raisins and almonds.

4. Drop the dough by spoonfuls 1½ inches apart onto the prepared baking sheets.

5. Bake for 10 to 12 minutes, until lightly colored and firm to the touch. Transfer to wire racks to cool.

FRUIT DREAMS

ROLLED COOKIES

YIELD: 3 to 4 dozen
TOTAL TIME: 35 minutes
CHILLING TIME: 8 hours

1¾ cups all-purpose flour
½ teaspoon ground
　cinnamon
½ cup vegetable shortening
½ cup granulated sugar
1 large egg
½ teaspoon vanilla extract
1 cup heavy cream

1. Combine the flour and cinnamon.

2. In a large bowl, cream the vegetable shortening and sugar. Beat in the egg. Beat in the vanilla extract and heavy cream. Gradually blend in the dry ingredients. Cover and chill for 8 hours or overnight.

3. Preheat the oven to 375 degrees.

4. On a floured surface, roll out the dough to a thickness of ¼ inch. Using a 3-inch round cookie cutter, cut out an even number of rounds and place 1 inch apart on ungreased baking sheets.

5. Bake for 12 to 15 minutes, until lightly colored. Transfer to wire racks to cool.

6. In a small bowl, whip the cream until it holds stiff peaks.

7. To assemble, spread a thin layer of whipped cream over the bottom of one cookie, place another cookie on top and gently press together. Repeat with the remaining cookies and cream.

FRUIT DROPS

DROP COOKIES

YIELD: 2 to 3 dozen
TOTAL TIME: 30 minutes

1 cup cornflakes, crushed
2 cups shredded coconut
½ teaspoon salt
1 cup sweetened condensed
　milk
1 cup dates, pitted and
　chopped fine
1 cup pitted prunes,
　chopped fine
1 cup figs, chopped fine
1 cup golden raisins,
　chopped fine
1 cup currants

1. Preheat the oven to 350 degrees. Lightly grease 2 baking sheets.

2. In a large bowl, combine the cornflakes, coconut, and salt. Stir in the condensed milk. Stir in all the fruit and blend thoroughly.

3. Drop the mixture by spoonfuls 1 inch apart onto the prepared baking sheets.

4. Bake for 12 to 15 minutes, until golden colored. Transfer to wire racks to cool.

Baking notes: If you like, drizzle melted chocolate or vanilla icing over the top of the cooled cookies.

Fruit-Filled Oatcakes

BAR COOKIES

YIELD: *1 to 3 dozen*
TOTAL TIME: *45 minutes*

1. Preheat the oven to 350 degrees. Lightly grease a 13 by 9-inch baking pan.

2. Cream the flour, rolled oats, baking soda, and salt.

3. In a large bowl, cream the vegetable shortening and brown sugar. Gradually blend in the dry ingredients.

4. Spread half of the dough evenly into the prepared pan. Spread the fruit filling over the dough and press the remaining dough over the top of the fruit.

5. Bake for 20 to 25 minutes, until lightly colored on top. Cool in the pan on a wire rack before cutting into large or small bars.

Baking notes: You can dress up these bars with a drizzle of white or lemon frosting (see Pantry).

1½ cups all-purpose flour
1½ cups rolled oats
½ teaspoon baking soda
½ teaspoon salt
½ cup vegetable shortening
1 cup packed light brown sugar
Fruit filling (your choice of jam or preserves)

Fruit Meringue Bars

BAR COOKIES

YIELD: *1 to 4 dozen*
TOTAL TIME: *45 minutes*

1. Preheat the oven to 350 degrees. Lightly grease a 13 by 9-inch baking pan.

2. To make the crust, cream the vegetable shortening and sugar in a medium bowl. Beat in the egg yolks. Gradually blend in the flour. Press the dough evenly into the prepared baking pan.

3. Bake for 15 minutes.

4. Meanwhile, make the topping: In a medium bowl, beat the egg whites until foamy. Fold in the sugar and almonds.

5. Spread the raspberry puree over the hot crust. Sprinkle the coconut over the puree. Spread the topping over the coconut.

6. Bake for 20 to 25 minutes longer until the topping is set and lightly colored. Cool in a pan on a wire rack before cutting into large or small bars.

Baking notes: To make raspberry puree, place drained, frozen raspberries in a blender and puree.

CRUST
¾ cup vegetable shortening
¼ cup granulated sugar
2 large egg yolks
1½ cups all-purpose flour

TOPPING
2 large egg whites, beaten
½ cup granulated sugar
1 cup almonds, chopped

FILLING
1 cup raspberry puree (see Baking notes)
1 cup flaked coconut

Fruit Squares

YIELD: *1 to 3 dozen*
TOTAL TIME: *45 minutes*

1 cup all-purpose flour
1 teaspoon baking powder
½ teaspoon salt
2 large eggs
1 cup packed light brown sugar
2 teaspoons vanilla extract
1 cup mixed candied fruit, chopped fine
1 cup raisins, chopped

1. Preheat the oven to 350 degrees.

2. Combine the flour, baking powder, and salt.

3. In a large bowl, beat the eggs with the brown sugar until thick and light-colored. Beat in the vanilla extract. Gradually blend in the dry ingredients. Stir in the candied fruit and raisins. Spread the dough evenly in an ungreased 8-inch square baking pan.

4. Bake for 30 to 35 minutes, until lightly colored on top. Cool in the pan on a wire rack before cutting into large or small bars.

Baking notes: Lemon Sugar Icing goes very well with these bars (see Pantry).

Fudge Brownies

YIELD: *1 to 2 dozen*
TOTAL TIME: *45 minutes*

¾ cup all-purpose flour
½ teaspoon baking powder
½ teaspoon salt
6 ounces bittersweet chocolate, chopped
⅓ cup vegetable shortening
1 cup granulated sugar
2 large eggs
½ cup walnuts, chopped

1. Preheat the oven to 350 degrees. Lightly grease a 9-inch square baking pan.

2. Combine the flour, baking powder, and salt.

3. In the top of a double boiler, melt the chocolate and vegetable shortening, stirring until smooth. Remove from the heat and beat in the sugar. Beat in the eggs one at a time. Gradually blend in the dry ingredients. Fold in the walnuts.

4. Spread the batter evenly in the prepared pan.

5. Bake for 30 to 35 minutes, until a toothpick inserted in the center comes out clean. Cool in the pan on a wire rack before cutting into large or small bars.

Baking notes: Frost before cutting into bars if you like (see Pantry).

Fudgies

YIELD: *4 to 6 dozen*
TOTAL TIME: *30 minutes*

2 cups all-purpose flour
½ cup unsweetened cocoa powder
½ teaspoon baking soda
¼ teaspoon salt
¼ cup vegetable shortening
½ cup granulated sugar
1 large egg
½ cup buttermilk
½ cup molasses
1 teaspoon vanilla extract
¾ cup walnuts, chopped

1. Preheat the oven to 350 degrees. Lightly grease 2 baking sheets.

2. Combine the flour, cocoa powder, baking soda, and salt.

3. In a large bowl, cream the vegetable shortening and sugar. Beat in the egg. Beat in the buttermilk and molasses. Beat in the vanilla extract. Gradually blend in the dry ingredients. Fold in the walnuts.

4. Drop the dough by spoonfuls 1½ inches apart onto the prepared baking sheets.

5. Bake for 12 to 15 minutes, until firm to the touch. Transfer to wire racks to cool.

Baking notes: Sour milk can be used in place of the buttermilk.

German Almond Wafers

FORMED COOKIES

YIELD: 2 to 3 dozen
TOTAL TIME: 30 minutes
CHILLING TIME: 4 hours

1. Combine the flour and baking powder.

2. In a large bowl, cream the vegetable shortening and sugar. Beat in the egg. Beat in the vanilla extract. Gradually blend in the dry ingredients. Cover and chill for 4 hours.

3. To prepare the topping, combine the cream and sugar in a saucepan. Remove from the heat and add the almonds.

4. Preheat the oven to 350 degrees. Lightly grease 2 baking sheets.

5. Pinch off walnut-sized pieces of dough and roll into balls. Place 1½ inches apart on the prepared baking sheets. Using the bottom of a glass dipped in flour, flatten each ball to a thickness of ¼ inch. Spread a teaspoon of the topping over each cookie.

6. Bake for 10 to 14 minutes, until lightly colored. Transfer to wire racks to cool.

1⅔ cups all-purpose flour
2 teaspoons baking powder
½ cup vegetable shortening
1 cup granulated sugar
1 large egg
1 teaspoon vanilla extract

TOPPING
⅔ cup heavy cream
2 teaspoons granulated sugar
1 cup sliced almonds

German Brownies

BAR COOKIES

YIELD: 1 to 2 dozen
TOTAL TIME: 45 minutes

1. Preheat the oven to 350 degrees. Lightly grease a 9-inch square baking pan.

2. Combine the flour, walnuts, baking powder, and salt.

3. In the top of a double boiler, melt 3 tablespoons of the vegetable shortening and the chocolate, stirring until smooth. Remove from the heat and beat in the remaining 2 tablespoons shortening and the cream cheese. Beat in the sugar. Beat in the eggs and almond extract. Gradually blend in the dry ingredients. Spread the batter evenly in the prepared baking pan.

4. Bake for 12 to 15 minutes, or until a toothpick inserted in the center comes out clean. Cool in the pan on a wire rack before cutting into large or small bars.

Baking notes: Frost these with chocolate icing to make them even more indulgent.

½ cup all-purpose flour
½ cup walnuts, ground
½ teaspoon baking powder
¼ teaspoon salt
5 tablespoons vegetable shortening
4 tablespoons semisweet chocolate
3 ounces cream cheese, at room temperature
1 cup granulated sugar
3 large eggs
½ teaspoon almond extract

G

German Christmas Cookies

ROLLED COOKIES

YIELD: 4 to 5 dozen
TOTAL TIME: 35 minutes

2 cups all-purpose flour
Pinch of pimento powder
Pinch of ground coriander
Pinch of ground anise
Pinch of salt
1 cup vegetable shortening
1 cup granulated sugar
2 large eggs
1 teaspoon fresh lemon juice
2 tablespoons grated lemon zest

1. Preheat the oven to 350 degrees.

2. Combine the flour, pimento powder, coriander, anise, and salt.

3. In a large bowl, cream the vegetable shortening and sugar. Beat in the eggs one at a time. Beat in the lemon juice and lemon zest. Gradually blend in the dry ingredients.

4. On a floured surface, roll out the dough out to a thickness of ¼ inch. Using cookie cutters, cut into shapes and place 1 inch apart on ungreased baking sheets.

5. Bake for 12 to 15 minutes, until lightly colored. Transfer to wire racks to cool.

Baking notes: Ice and decorate the cookies if desired.

German Honey Cookies

BAR COOKIES

YIELD: 5 to 7 dozen
TOTAL TIME: 75 minutes

CRUST
1¾ cups all-purpose flour
¼ cup granulated sugar
1 cup almonds, ground fine
2 teaspoons baking powder
¼ teaspoon salt
½ cup vegetable shortening

TOPPING
½ cup vegetable shortening
½ cup granulated sugar
1 large egg
2 tablespoons honey
2 tablespoons milk
1 teaspoon vanilla extract
2 tablespoons almond extract

1. Preheat the oven to 350 degrees.

2. To make the crust, combine the flour, sugar, almonds, baking powder, and salt in a large bowl. Cut inthe vegetable shortening until the mixture resembles coarse crumbs. Press the mixture evenly into an ungreased 9-inch square baking pan.

3. To make the topping, combine the vegetable shortening, sugar, egg, honey, and milk in a saucepan and bring to a boil. Remove from the heat and stir in the almond and vanilla extracts. Let cool slightly.

4. Pour the topping over the crust. Bake for 55 to 60 minutes, until lightly colored on top and firm to the touch. Cool in the pan on a wire rack before cutting into large or small bars.

Baking notes: Older versions of this recipe call for buttermilk in place of the whole milk. Others use hazelnuts instead of almonds and schnapps instead of almond extract. These are traditionally cut into squares or triangles.

German Molasses Cookies

BAR COOKIES

YIELD: 2 to 3 dozen
TOTAL TIME: 40 minutes

1. Preheat the oven to 350 degrees. Lightly grease a 13 by 9-inch baking pan.

2. Combine the flour, baking powder, and spices.

3. In a large bowl, cream the butter and powdered sugar. Beat in the molasses. Gradually blend in the dry ingredients. Fold in the walnuts and candied peel. Spread the dough evenly in the prepared baking pan.

4. Bake for 20 to 25 minutes, until lightly colored. Cool in the pan on a wire rack.

5. Frost the cooled cookies with the buttercream and cut into large or small bars.

3¾ cups all-purpose flour
1 teaspoon baking powder
1 teaspoon ground cinnamon
½ teaspoon ground cloves
½ teaspoon ground cardamom
¼ teaspoon ground ginger
3 tablespoons butter, at room temperature
1 cup powdered sugar
1½ cups dark molasses, warmed
½ cup walnuts, chopped fine
½ cup candied citrus peel, chopped
Rum Buttercream (see Pantry)

German Spice Cookies

ROLLED COOKIES

YIELD: 2 to 4 dozen
TOTAL TIME: 35 minutes
CHILLING TIME: 8 hours

1. Combine the flour, walnuts, baking powder, and spices.

2. In a large bowl, cream the vegetable shortening with the sugar until light and fluffy. Beat in the egg. Gradually blend in the dry ingredients. Cover and chill for 8 hours.

3. Preheat the oven to 350 degrees.

4. On a floured surface, roll out the dough to a thickness of ¼ inch. Using a 2-inch round cookie cutter, cut into rounds and place 1½ inches apart on ungreased baking sheets.

5. Bake for 15 to 18 minutes, until lightly colored. Transfer to wire racks to cool.

Baking notes: If desired, drizzle melted chocolate over the cooled cookies.

4 cups all-purpose flour
2 cups walnuts, ground
2 teaspoons baking powder
¼ teaspoon paprika
¼ teaspoon freshly ground black pepper
¼ teaspoon ground ginger
¼ teaspoon ground cloves
¼ teaspoon ground coriander
¼ teaspoon anise seeds
1½ cups vegetable shortening
1 cup granulated sugar
1 large egg

GINGER BARS

YIELD: 1 to 4 dozen
TOTAL TIME: 35 minutes

1½ cups all-purpose flour
½ teaspoon ground cinnamon
½ teaspoon ground ginger
½ teaspoon ground nutmeg
½ teaspoon salt
½ teaspoon baking soda
½ cup hot water
½ cup butter, at room temperature
½ cup packed light brown sugar
2 large eggs
½ cup molasses
Vanilla Icing (see Pantry)

1. Preheat the oven to 350 degrees. Lightly grease a 13 by 9-inch baking pan.

2. Combine the flour, spices, and salt.

3. In a small bowl, dissolve the baking soda in the hot water. Stir in the molasses.

4. In a large bowl, cream the butter and brown sugar. Beat in the eggs. Beat in the molasses mixture. Gradually blend in the dry ingredients. Spread the dough evenly in the prepared baking pan.

5. Bake for 18 to 20 minutes, or until a toothpick inserted in the center comes out clean.

6. Frost the warm cookies with icing. Let cool before cutting into large or smalls.

GINGERBREAD COOKIES

YIELD: 8 to 10 dozen
TOTAL TIME: 35 minutes
CHILLING TIME: 24 hours

6½ cups all-purpose flour
1 teaspoon ground ginger
1 teaspoon ground cinnamon
¼ teaspoon ground cloves
2 teaspoons salt
1 cup vegetable shortening
1 cup packed light brown sugar
2 teaspoons baking soda
½ teaspoon warm water
1½ cups molasses

1. Combine the flour, spices, and salt.

2. In a large bowl, cream the vegetable shortening and brown sugar.

3. Dissolve the baking soda in the warm water and add to the creamed mixture, beating until smooth. Beat in the molasses. Gradually blend in the dry ingredients. Cover and chill for 24 hours.

4. Preheat the oven to 350 degrees. Lightly grease 2 baking sheets.

5. On a floured surface, roll out the dough to a thickness of ¼ inch. Using a 1¾-inch round cookie cutter, cut out cookies and place 1½ inches apart on the prepared baking sheets.

6. Bake for 10 to 12 minutes, until dry-looking and firm to the touch. Transfer to wire racks to cool.

Baking notes: This dough can be used for making gingerbread houses or gingerbread men (see Pantry); it can also be pressed into large cookie molds and baked.

Gingerbread Men

ROLLED COOKIES

YIELD: *3 to 5 dozen*
TOTAL TIME: *35 minutes*
CHILLING TIME: *24 hours*

1. Combine the flour, spices, and salt.

2. In a large bowl, cream the vegetable shortening and sugar. Beat in the egg. Beat in the molasses.

3. Dissolve the baking soda in the warm water and add the molasses to the mixture, beating until smooth. Gradually blend in the dry ingredients. Cover and chill for 24 hours.

4. Preheat the oven to 350 degrees. Lightly grease 2 baking sheets.

5. On a floured surface, roll out the dough to a thickness of ¼ inch. Using cookie cutters, cut out gingerbread men and place 1½ inches apart on the prepared baking sheets. Use raisins to make eyes, noses, and 2 to 3 buttons on the belly.

6. Bake for 10 to 12 minutes, until dry-looking and firm to the touch. Transfer to wire racks to cool.

Baking notes: You can make these cookies a little thicker if you like, and decorate the cooled cookies using Vanilla Frosting (see Pantry).

3½ cups all-purpose flour
1½ teaspoons ground ginger
1½ teaspoons ground cinnamon
¼ teaspoon salt
½ cup vegetable shortening
½ cup granulated sugar
1 large egg
1 cup molasses, warmed
1 teaspoon baking soda
1½ teaspoons warm water
Raisins for decorations

Ginger Cookies I

ROLLED COOKIES

YIELD: *5 to 6 dozen*
TOTAL TIME: *35 minutes*
CHILLING TIME: *24 hours*

1. Combine the flour, hazelnuts, and spices.

2. In a medium saucepan, melt the vegetable shortening with the molasses. Remove from the heat and beat in the powdered sugar. Transfer to a large bowl and let cool slightly.

3. One at a time, beat the eggs into the molasses mixture. Beat in the candied citron and orange peel. Gradually blend in all of the dry ingredients. Cover and chill overnight.

4. Preheat the oven to 350 degrees. Lightly grease 2 baking sheets.

5. On a floured surface, roll out the dough to a thickness of ¼ inch. Using a 1½-inch cookie cutter, cut out the cookies and place 1 inch apart on the prepared baking sheets.

6. Bake for 12 to 15 minutes, until lightly colored. Transfer to wire racks to cool.

4 cups all-purpose flour
⅓ cup hazelnuts, ground
1 tablespoon ground ginger
1 teaspoon ground cinnamon
1 teaspoon ground cardamom
½ teaspoon ground mace
1½ cups vegetable shortening
2 cups molasses
1 cup powdered sugar
2 large eggs
½ cup candied citron, chopped
½ cup candied orange peel, chopped

GINGER COOKIES II

ROLLED COOKIES

YIELD: 3 to 6 dozen
TOTAL TIME: 35 minutes
CHILLING TIME: 4 hours

2½ cups all-purpose flour
¾ teaspoon baking soda
1½ teaspoons ground ginger
*½ teaspoon ground
    cinnamon*
½ cup vegetable shortening
1 cup molasses
½ cup sour cream
⅓ cup granulated sugar
1 large egg

1. Combine the flour, baking soda, ginger, and cinnamon.

2. In a large saucepan, melt the vegetable shortening with the molasses. Beat in the sour cream. Remove from the heat and beat in the sugar. Beat in the egg. Gradually blend in the dry ingredients. Transfer the dough to a bowl, cover, and chill for at least 4 hours.

3. Preheat the oven to 350 degrees. Lightly grease 2 baking sheets.

4. On a floured surface, roll out the dough to a thickness of ¼ inch. Using a 1½-inch cookie cutter, cut out cookies and place 1 inch apart on the prepared baking sheets.

5. Bake for 10 to 12 minutes, until lightly colored. Transfer to wire racks to cool.

GINGER CRINKLES

FORMED COOKIES

YIELD: 4 to 5 dozen
TOTAL TIME: 40 minutes

2 cups all-purpose flour
2 teaspoons baking soda
*1 teaspoon ground
    cinnamon*
1 teaspoon ground ginger
¼ teaspoon salt
1 cup granulated sugar
⅔ cup canola oil
1 large egg
¼ cup molasses, warmed
*Granulated sugar for
    rolling.*

1. Preheat the oven to 350 degrees.

2. Combine the flour, baking soda, spices, and salt.

3. In a large bowl, beat the sugar and oil together. Beat in the egg. Beat in the molasses. Gradually blend in the dry ingredients.

4. Pinch off walnut-sized pieces of dough and roll into balls. Roll in granulated sugar until well coated and place the balls 3 inches apart on ungreased baking sheets.

5. Bake for 12 to 15 minutes, until lightly colored. Transfer to wire racks to cool.

Baking notes: The dough can also be dropped by spoonfuls into a bowl of sugar and then rolled into balls.

Ginger Shortbread

BAR COOKIES

YIELD: 3 dozen
TOTAL TIME: 45 minutes
CHILLING TIME: 4 hours

1½ cups all-purpose flour
1 teaspoon ground ginger
¼ teaspoon salt
½ cup vegetable shortening
½ cup granulated sugar
1 tablespoon heavy cream

1. Combine the flour, ginger, and salt.

2. In a large bowl, cream the vegetable shortening and sugar. Beat in the cream. Gradually blend in the dry ingredients. Cover and chill for 4 hours.

3. Preheat the oven to 350 degrees. Lightly grease a 9-inch square baking pan.

4. On a floured surface, roll out the dough to a 9-inch square. Fit it into the prepared baking pan and prick it all over with the tines of a fork.

5. Bake for 20 to 25 minutes, until lightly colored. Cool in the pan on a wire rack, then cut into 2 by 1-inch bars.

Gingersnaps

FORMED COOKIES

YIELD: 3 to 4 dozen
TOTAL TIME: 35 minutes

2¼ cups all-purpose flour
1 teaspoon ground ginger
1 teaspoon ground
   cinnamon
1 teaspoon ground cloves
1 teaspoon salt
¾ cup vegetable shortening
1 cup packed light brown
   sugar
1 large egg
¼ cup molasses
Granulated sugar for
   rolling

1. Preheat the oven to 375 degrees. Lightly grease 2 baking sheets.

2. Combine the flour, spices, and salt.

3. In a large bowl, cream the vegetable shortening and brown sugar. Beat in the egg. Beat in the molasses. Gradually blend in the dry ingredients.

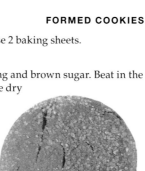

4. Pinch off walnut-sized pieces of dough and roll into balls. Roll in granulated sugar, and place 2 inches apart on the prepared baking sheets.

5. Bake for 10 to 12 minutes, until lightly colored. Transfer to wire racks to cool.

Glenda's Favorite Cookies

REFRIGERATOR COOKIES

YIELD: 7 to 8 dozen
TOTAL TIME: 30 minutes
CHILLING TIME: 4 hours

1 cup all-purpose flour
3 cups rolled oats
2 teaspoons baking powder
½ teaspoon salt
1 cup butter, melted
¼ cup boiling water
1 cup packed dark brown
   sugar
1 teaspoon vanilla extract

1. Combine the flour, oats, baking powder, and salt.

2. In a large bowl, whisk the melted butter and boiling water. Beat in the brown sugar. Beat in the vanilla extract. Gradually blend in the dry ingredients. Form the dough into a log 2 inches in diameter. Wrap in waxed paper and chill for at least 4 hours.

3. Preheat the oven to 350 degrees. Lightly grease 2 baking sheets.

4. Cut the log into 1/4-inch-thick slices and place 1 inch apart on the prepared baking sheets.

5. Bake for 10 to 12 minutes, until lightly colored. Transfer to wire racks to cool.

Baking notes: The longer you bake these cookies, the crisper they will be.

GOLDEN HONEY COOKIES

YIELD: 5 to 6 dozen
TOTAL TIME: 30 minutes

3 cups whole wheat flour
1 cup all-purpose flour
2 teaspoons baking soda
½ teaspoon salt
1 cup honey, warmed
½ cup vegetable shortening
3 large eggs
1 cup walnuts, chopped fine
1 cup golden raisins,
    plumped in brandy

1. Preheat the oven to 400 degrees. Lightly grease 2 baking sheets.

2. Combine the two flours, the baking soda, and salt.

3. In a large bowl, beat the honey and vegetable shortening until smooth. Beat in the eggs one at a time. Gradually blend in the dry ingredients. Fold in the walnuts and raisins.

4. Drop the dough by spoonfuls 1½ inches apart onto the prepared baking sheets. Flatten each cookie using the bottom of a glass dipped in flour.

5. Bake for 8 to 10 minutes, until lightly colored. Transfer to wire racks to cool.

GOOD-FOR-YOU PEANUT BUTTER COOKIES

YIELD: 3 to 4 dozen
TOTAL TIME: 30 minutes

1 cup whipped vegetable
    shortening
1 cup packed light brown
    sugar
½ cup peanut butter
3 large egg whites
2 cups all-purpose flour

1. Preheat the oven to 375 degrees. Lightly grease 2 baking sheets.

2. In a large bowl, cream the vegetable shortening and brown sugar. Beat in the peanut butter. Beat in the egg whites. Gradually blend in the flour.

3. Pinch off 1-inch pieces of dough and roll into balls. Place the balls 1½ inches apart on the prepared baking sheets. Using the tines of a fork, flatten the balls to ¼ inch thick.

4. Bake for 8 to 10 minutes, until lightly colored. Transfer to wire racks to cool.

GRAHAM CRACKER BROWNIES

YIELD: 1 to 2 dozen
TOTAL TIME: 25 minutes
CHILLING TIME: 2 hours

¾ cup vegetable shortening
¼ cup peanut butter
1 cup granulated sugar
2 large eggs
2½ cups graham crackers
    crumbs
2 cups miniature
    marshmallows
1 teaspoon vanilla extract

TOPPING

1 cup (6 ounces) semisweet
    chocolate chips
¼ cup peanuts, ground fine

1. Lightly grease a 9-inch square baking pan.

2. In the top of a double boiler, melt the vegetable shortening with the peanut butter. Beat in the sugar. Remove from the heat and beat in the eggs one at a time. Return to the heat and cook, stirring, until the mixture thickens. Remove from the heat and stir in the graham crackers, marshmallows, and vanilla extract.

3. Spread the mixture evenly into the prepared baking pan. Chill for 2 hours.

4. To make the topping, melt the chocolate chips in a double boiler over low heat, stirring until smooth. Remove from the heat and stir in the ground peanuts.

5. Spread the topping evenly over the chilled brownies. Chill for 1 hour before cutting into large or small bars.

Grandma's Refrigerator Cookies — REFRIGERATOR COOKIES

YIELD: *4 to 5 dozen*
TOTAL TIME: *35 minutes*
CHILLING TIME: *4 hours*

1 ounce semisweet chocolate, chopped
2 cups all-purpose flour
½ teaspoon baking soda
¼ teaspoon salt
1 cup butter, at room temperature
½ cup granulated sugar
½ cup packed light brown sugar
1 large egg
½ teaspoon vanilla extract
¼ cup raisins, chopped
¼ cup pecans, chopped
¼ cup shredded coconut
½ teaspoon ground nutmeg
½ teaspoon ground cinnamon

1. Melt the chocolate in a double boiler over low heat, stirring until smooth. Remove from the heat.

2. Combine the flour, baking soda, and salt.

3. In a large bowl, cream the butter and two sugars. Beat in the egg. Beat in the vanilla extract. Gradually blend in the dry ingredients.

4. Divide the dough into 6 equal parts. Add the melted chocolate to one piece and blend well. Shape the dough into a log and wrap in waxed paper. Add the chopped raisins to the second piece, the chopped pecans to the third, the shredded coconut to the fourth, the nutmeg to the fifth, and the ground cinnamon to the sixth piece, blending well. Shape each separate dough into a log and wrap in waxed paper. Chill for 4 hours.

5. Preheat the oven to 375 degrees.

6. Cut the logs into ⅛-inch-thick slices and place 1 inch apart on ungreased baking sheets.

7. Bake for 10 to 12 minutes, until lightly colored. Transfer to wire racks to cool.

Granny's Cookies — ROLLED COOKIES

YIELD: *7 to 8 dozen*
TOTAL TIME: *40 minutes*

4 cups all-purpose flour
1 tablespoon baking powder
¼ teaspoon ground nutmeg
¾ cup vegetable shortening
2 cups granulated sugar
2 large eggs
¼ cup milk
1 teaspoon vanilla extract

1. Preheat the oven to 400 degrees. Lightly grease 2 baking sheets.

2. Combine the flour, baking powder, and nutmeg.

3. In a large bowl, cream the vegetable shortening and sugar. Beat in the eggs one at a time. Beat in the milk and vanilla extract. Gradually blend in the dry ingredients.

4. On a floured surface, roll out the dough to a thickness of ¼ inch. Using cookie cutters, cut into shapes and place 1½ inches apart into the prepared baking sheets.

5. Bake for 10 to 12 minutes, until lightly colored. Transfer to wire racks to cool.

Baking notes: To decorate these cookies, sprinkle with colored sugar crystals or place a raisin or walnut half in the center of each one before baking.

Granola Bars

BAR COOKIES

YIELD: 3 to 4 dozen

TOTAL TIME: 50 minutes

6 cups (36 ounces) rolled
    oats
1 cup shredded coconut
1 cup wheat germ
1 cup golden raisins
½ cup sunflower seeds
¼ cup sesame seeds, toasted
1 teaspoon ground allspice
1 cup honey
¾ cup canola oil
⅓ cup water
1½ teaspoons vanilla
    extract

1. Preheat the oven to 350 degrees. Lightly grease a 13 by 9-inch baking pan.

2. Combine the oats, coconut, wheat germ, raisins, sunflower seeds, sesame seeds, and allspice in a large bowl.

3. In a saucepan, combine the honey, oil, and water and heat. Remove from the heat and stir in the vanilla extract. Add to the dry ingredients and stir to coat well. Spread the mixture evenly in the prepared baking pan.

4. Bake for 30 to 40 minutes, until firm to the touch and no longer sticky. Transfer to wire racks to cool before cutting into large or small bars.

5. To store, wrap the bars individually in waxed paper.

Granola Cookies

DROP COOKIES

YIELD: 3 to 5 dozen

TOTAL TIME: 30 minutes

2 cups all-purpose flour
½ teaspoon baking powder
1 teaspoon ground cinnamon
½ teaspoon ground nutmeg
2 cups granola
2 tablespoons canola oil
2 large eggs
1 cup unsweetened
    applesauce
2 tablespoons frozen apple
    juice concentrate, thawed

1. Preheat the oven to 350 degrees. Lightly grease 2 baking sheets.

2. Combine the flour, baking powder, and spices.

3. In a large bowl, beat the canola oil and eggs together. Beat in the applesauce and apple juice. Gradually blend in the dry ingredients. Stir in the granola.

4. Drop the mixture by spoonfuls 1½ inches apart onto the prepared baking sheets.

5. Bake for 8 to 10 minutes, until lightly colored and firm to the touch. Transfer to wire racks to cool.

Grape Bars

BAR COOKIES

YIELD: 1 to 3 dozen

TOTAL TIME: 45 minutes

CRUST
1½ cups all-purpose flour
½ teaspoon baking soda
½ teaspoon salt
¾ cup vegetable shortening
1 cup granulated sugar

TOPPING
1½ cups dried apricots,
    chopped fine
½ cup dates, pitted and
    chopped
½ cup grape jelly
¼ cup fresh orange juice
½ cup walnuts, grounds
1½ cups (9 ounces) rolled
    oats

1. Preheat the oven to 350 degrees. Lightly grease a 13 by 9-inch baking pan.

2. To make the crust, combine the flour, baking soda, and salt.

3. In a large bowl, cream the vegetable shortening and sugar. Gradually blend in the dry ingredients. Spread the mixture evenly in the prepared baking pan.

4. Bake for 20 minutes.

5. Meanwhile, make the topping: In a saucepan, combine the apricots, dates, grape jelly, orange juice, and walnuts and cook until soft. Remove from the heat.

6. Spread the topping over the hot crust. Sprinkle the oats evenly over the top and press down lightly.

7. Bake for 10 minutes longer, or until lightly colored. Transfer to wire racks to cool before cutting into large or small bars.

Grapefruit Bars

BAR COOKIES

1. Preheat the oven to 350 degrees. Lightly grease a 9-inch square baking pan.

2. Combine the flour, baking soda, cinnamon, and salt.

3. In a large bowl, cream the vegetable shortening and brown sugar. Beat in the eggs. Beat in the grapefruit juice and zest. Gradually blend in the dry ingredients. Spread the batter evenly into the prepared baking pan.

4. Bake for 25 to 30 minutes, until lightly colored on top. Cool in the pan on a wire rack before cutting into large or small bars.

Baking notes: You can substitute lemon or orange juice and zest for the grapefruit ingredients. An orange or lemon icing would go very well with these bars.

YIELD: *1 to 3 dozen*
TOTAL TIME: *35 minutes*

2 cups all-purpose flour
1 teaspoon baking soda
1 teaspoon ground
   cinnamon
½ teaspoon salt
¾ cup vegetable shortening
1½ cups packed light
   brown sugar
2 large eggs
3 tablespoons fresh
   grapefruit juice
3 tablespoons grated
   grapefruit zest

Greek Shortbread

ROLLED COOKIES

1. Combine the flour, baking powder, and baking soda.

2. In a large bowl, cream the vegetable shortening and sugar. Beat in the egg yolks. Beat in the brandy and rose water. Gradually blend in the dry ingredients. Cover and chill for 4 hours.

3. Preheat the oven to 325 degrees.

4. On a floured surface, roll out the dough to a thickness of ¼ inch. Using a 1½-inch round cookie cutter, cut out cookies. Dredge in the ground almonds and place 1 inch apart on ungreased baking sheets.

5. Bake for 25 to 30 minutes, until lightly colored. Transfer to wire racks to cool.

YIELD: *3 to 4 dozen*
TOTAL TIME: *45 minutes*
CHILLING TIME: *4 hours*

3½ cups all-purpose flour
½ teaspoon baking powder
½ teaspoon baking soda
1 cup vegetable shortening
¾ cup granulated sugar
2 large egg yolks
¼ teaspoon brandy
⅛ teaspoon rose water
½ cup almonds, ground

Green Wreaths

FORMED COOKIES

1. Line 2 baking sheets with waxed paper.

2. In the top of a double boiler, melt the vegetable shortening with the marshmallows. Add the vanilla and almond extracts. Stir in the food coloring. Remove from the heat and stir in the cornflakes. Replace over bottom half of double boiler to keep warm.

3. Drop the mix by tablespoonful 2 inches apart onto the prepared baking sheets. With well-oiled hands, form the batter into wreath shapes. Decorate with cinnamon candy and chill until set.

Baking notes: These are great cookies to let kids play with. You mix them and let the children form them. To give a more festive taste, use a few drops of peppermint in place of the vanilla and almond extracts.

YIELD: *2 to 3 dozen*
TOTAL TIME: *30 minutes*

6 tablespoons vegetable
   shortening
32 marshmallows
½ teaspoon vanilla extract
½ teaspoon almond extract
½ teaspoon green food
   coloring
4 cups cornflakes, crushed
Red cinnamon candy

Gumdrop Bars

BAR COOKIES

YIELD: *2 to 3 dozen*

TOTAL TIME: *35 minutes*

2 cups all-purpose flour
1 teaspoon ground
   cinnamon
¼ teaspoon salt
3 large eggs
2 cups packed light brown
   sugar
¼ cup evaporated milk
1 cup walnuts, chopped fine
1 cup gumdrops, chopped

1. Preheat the oven to 325 degrees. Lightly grease a 9-inch square baking pan.

2. Combine the flour, cinnamon, and salt.

3. In a large bowl, beat the eggs until thick and light-colored. Beat in the brown sugar. Beat in the milk. Gradually blend in the dry ingredients. Stir in the walnuts and gumdrops. Spread the dough evenly in the prepared baking pan.

4. Bake for 30 to 35 minutes, until lightly colored on top. Transfer to wire racks to cool.

Baking notes: For a whimsical look, frost the bars with Vanilla Icing and decorate with sliced gumdrops.

Gumdrop Cookies

FORMED COOKIES

YIELD: *5 to 6 dozen*

TOTAL TIME: *45 minutes*

1 cup all-purpose flour
¼ teaspoon salt
½ cup vegetable shortening
¼ cup packed light brown
   sugar
1 large egg yolk
1½ teaspoon vanilla extract
2 cups gumdrops, chopped
Gumdrops for decorating

1. Preheat the oven to 350 degrees.

2. Combine the flour and salt.

3. In a large bowl, cream the vegetable shortening and brown sugar. Beat in the egg yolk. Beat in the vanilla extract. Gradually blend in the dry ingredients. Fold in the gumdrops.

4. Pinch off walnut-sized pieces of dough and roll into balls. Place 1½ inches apart on ungreased baking sheets.

5. Bake for 5 minutes. Press a whole gumdrop into the center of each ball and bake for 8 to 10 minutes longer, until lightly colored. Transfer to wire racks to cool.

Halloween Cookies

1. Preheat the oven to 375 degrees. Lightly grease 2 baking sheets.

2. Combine the flour, baking soda, and salt.

3. In a large bowl, cream the vegetable shortening and sugar. Beat in the egg. Beat in the molasses and buttermilk. Gradually blend in the dry ingredients.

4. Drop the dough by spoonfuls 1½ inches apart onto the prepared baking sheets. Insert a popsicle stick into each cookie.

5. Bake for 12 to 15 minutes, until lightly colored. Transfer to wire racks to cool.

6. To decorate the cookies, put the powdered sugar in a small bowl and stir in enough milk to make a spreadable icing. Tint the icing with orange food coloring and spread the icing over the cookies. Or tint the icing another color, place it into a pastry bag fitted with a small plain tip, and pipe eyes, a nose, and a mouth on each cookie.

YIELD: 3 to 4 dozen
TOTAL TIME: 50 minutes

1 cup all-purpose flour
¼ teaspoon baking soda
¼ teaspoon salt
½ cup vegetable shortening
1 tablespoon granulated sugar
1 large egg
⅓ cup molasses, warmed
¼ cup buttermilk
¼ cup powdered sugar
A few drops of milk
Food coloring
Popsicle sticks

Hazelnut Bars

1. Preheat the oven to 350 degrees. Grease a 13 by 9-inch baking pan.

2. To make the crust, combine the flour and baking powder.

3. In a large bowl, cream the vegetable shortening and brown sugar. Gradually blend in the dry ingredients. Stir in the hazelnuts. Press the mixture evenly into the prepared baking pan.

4. Bake for 10 minutes.

5. Meanwhile, make the topping: In a medium bowl, beat the eggs until thick and light-colored. Beat in the brown sugar. Beat in the corn syrup and rum. Gradually blend in the flour and salt.

6. Spread the topping over the warm crust and sprinkle the hazelnuts on the top. Bake for 25 to 30 minutes longer, or until firm to the touch. Cool in the pan on a wire rack before cutting into large or small bars.

YIELD: 1 to 2 dozen
TOTAL TIME: 45 minutes

CRUST
1⅓ cups all-purpose flour
½ cup baking powder
⅓ cup vegetable shortening
½ cup packed light brown sugar
¼ cup hazelnuts, chopped

TOPPING
2 large eggs
¼ cup packed light brown sugar
½ teaspoon salt
¾ cup light corn syrup
1½ teaspoons rum
3 tablespoons all-purpose flour
¾ cup hazelnuts, ground fine

HAZELNUT COOKIES

REFRIGERATOR COOKIES

YIELD: *4 to 5 dozen*

TOTAL TIME: *30 minutes*

CHILLING TIME: *48 hours*

2½ cups all-purpose flour
½ teaspoon baking soda
¼ teaspoon salt
½ cup vegetable shortening
½ cup butter, at room temperature
1¼ cups packed light brown sugar
1 large egg
¼ teaspoon vanilla extract
½ cup hazelnuts, chopped fine
3 ounces semisweet chocolate, melted

1. Combine 1½ cups of the flour, the baking soda, and salt.

2. In a large bowl, beat the vegetable shortening, butter, and the remaining 1 cup of flour until smooth. Beat in the brown sugar. Beat in the egg. Beat in the vanilla extract. Gradually blend in the dry ingredients. Fold in ¼ cup of the hazelnuts.

3. Divide the dough into 2 logs 1 inch in diameter and roll in the remaining ¼ cup hazelnuts. Wrap in waxed paper and chill in the refrigerator for 48 hours.

4. Preheat the oven to 350 degrees.

5. Slice the logs into ¼-inch-thick slices and place 1 inch apart on ungreased baking sheets.

6. Bake for 8 to 10 minutes, until lightly colored. Transfer to wire racks to cool.

7. Dip half of each cookie into the melted chocolate and let cool until set.

HAZELNUT CRESCENTS

FORMED COOKIES

YIELD: *2 to 3 dozen*

TOTAL TIME: *40 minutes*

¾ cup butter, at room temperature
½ cup granulated sugar
½ teaspoon almond extract
½ teaspoon vanilla extract
2 cups all-purpose flour
½ cup hazelnuts, chopped fine
Powdered sugar for rolling

1. Preheat the oven to 300 degrees.

2. In a large bowl, cream the butter and sugar. Beat in the almond and vanilla extracts. Gradually blend in the flour. Fold in the hazelnuts. The dough will be stiff.

3. Pinch off walnut-sized pieces of dough and form each one into a crescent shape. Place 1½ inches apart on ungreased baking sheets.

4. Bake for 15 to 20 minutes, until lightly colored. Roll in powdered sugar and transfer to wire racks to cool.

HAZELNUT SHORTBREAD

FORMED COOKIES

YIELD: *4 to 5 dozen*

TOTAL TIME: *30 minutes*

4½ cups all-purpose flour
1 cup hazelnuts, ground
2 cups vegetable shortening
2½ cups packed light brown sugar
2 teaspoons vanilla extract

1. Preheat the oven to 350 degrees.

2. Combine the flour and hazelnuts.

3. In a large bowl, cream the vegetable shortening and brown sugar. Beat in the vanilla extract. Gradually blend in the dry ingredients.

4. Pinch off walnut-size pieces of dough and roll into balls. Place 2 inches apart on the ungreased baking sheets. Flatten the balls with the bottom of a glass dipped in flour.

5. Bake for 12 to 15 minutes, until lightly colored. Transfer to wire racks to cool.

HAZELNUT SQUARES

BAR COOKIES

YIELD: *1 to 2 dozen*

TOTAL TIME: *50 minutes*

1. Preheat the oven to 350 degrees. Lightly grease a 9-inch square baking pan.

2. To make the crust, combine the flour and salt in a medium bowl. Cut in the vegetable shortening until the mixture resembles coarse crumbs. Press evenly into the prepared baking pan.

3. Bake for 15 minutes.

4. Meanwhile, make the topping: Combine the flour and salt.

5. In a medium bowl, beat the eggs and sugar until thick. Beat in the rum. Gradually blend in the dry ingredients. Stir in the coconut and hazelnuts.

6. Spread the topping over the top of the hot crust. Bake for 15 minutes longer, or until firm to the touch. Cool in the pan on a wire rack before cutting into large or small bars.

CRUST
1 cup all-purpose flour
¼ teaspoon salt
¼ cup vegetable shortening

TOPPING
2 tablespoons all-purpose flour
¼ teaspoon salt
2 large eggs
¾ cup granulated sugar
1 teaspoon rum
2 cups flaked coconut
1 cup hazelnuts, chopped

HEALTH BARS

BAR COOKIES

YIELD: *2 to 3 dozen*

TOTAL TIME: *30 minutes*

SOAKING TIME: *1 hour*

CHILLING TIME: *3 hours*

1. In a medium bowl, combine the apple slices and banana chips. Add boiling water to cover and set aside for 1 hour.

2. Grease a 13 by 9-inch baking pan.

3. In a large bowl, combine the bran cereal, sesame seeds, walnuts, wheat germ, and cinnamon.

4. Drain the apples and bananas. Return to the medium bowl and mash together, then add to the bran mixture.

5. In a large saucepan, heat the honey until it registers 230 degrees on a candy thermometer. Stir in the peanut butter and vegetable shortening and cook, stirring constantly until the temperature returns to 230 degrees.

6. Add the honey mixture to the dry ingredients and stir to coat. Spread the mixture evenly in the prepared baking pan. Chill for at least 3 hours. Cut into large or small bars. Wrap individually in waxed paper and store in the refrigerator.

Baking notes: You can toast the bran cereal in a moderate overn before combining it with the other ingredients.

½ cup dried apple, sliced
½ cup banana chips
4 cups bran flakes
½ cup sesame seeds, toasted
½ cup walnuts, chopped
¼ cup wheat germ
1 teaspoon ground cinnamon
1 cup honey
1½ cups peanut butter
2 tablespoons vegetable shortening

Health Cookies

YIELD: *3 to 4 dozen*

TOTAL TIME: *30 minutes*

1 cup all-purpose flour
1 cup soy flour
¼ teaspoon salt
1 cup canola oil
1 cup packed dark brown sugar
2 large eggs
¼ cup skim milk
3 cups (18 ounces) rolled oats
1 cup dried apricots, chopped fine

1. Preheat the oven to 350 degrees. Lightly grease 2 baking sheets.

2. Combine the flour, soy flour, and salt.

3. In a large bowl, beat the oil and brown sugar together. Beat in the eggs. Beat in the skim milk. Gradually blend in the dry ingredients. Stir in the oats and apricots.

4. Drop the dough by spoonful 1½ inches apart onto the prepared baking sheets. Flatten each cookie with the bottom of a glass dipped in flour.

5. Bake for 10 to 12 minutes, until lightly colored. Transfer to wire racks to cool.

Health Sticks

YIELD: *4 to 5 dozen*

TOTAL TIME: *35 minutes*

1 cup all-purpose flour
1 cup whole wheat flour
½ teaspoon salt
¼ cup packed dark brown sugar
½ cup canola oil
⅔ cup skim milk
2 cups (12 ounces) rolled oats
2 cups dates, pitted and chopped fine
¾ cup almonds, chopped fine
½ cup sesame seeds, toasted
½ cup flaked coconut

1. Preheat the oven to 350 degrees. Lightly grease two 15 by 10-inch baking sheets.

2. Combine the two flours and the salt.

3. In a large bowl, beat the brown sugar, oil, and milk. Gradually blend in the dry ingredients. Stir in the oats, dates, almonds, sesame seeds, and coconut.

4. Divide the dough in half. Place each half on a prepared baking sheet and roll out to a thickness of ⅛ inch, leaving a 1-inch border all around. Prick the dough all over with the tines of a fork. Using a pastry cutter, cut into 3 by 1-inch strips.

5. Bake for 12 to 15 minutes, until lightly colored. Cool on the sheets on wire racks.

HELEN'S CHEESECAKE BARS

BAR COOKIES

1. Preheat the oven to 350 degrees. Lightly grease a 15 by 10-inch baking pan.

2. To make the crust, melt the chocolate chips and butter in a double boiler, stirring until smooth. Remove from the heat and blend in the graham cracker crumbs and almonds. Reserve 1½ cups of the mixture for topping, and press the remaining mixture evenly into the prepared baking pan.

3. Bake for 12 minutes.

4. Meanwhile, make the filling: In a medium bowl, beat the cream cheese and sugar. Beat in the eggs, lemon juice, and Amaretto. Beat in the flour.

5. Pour the filling over the hot crust. Sprinkle the reserved crust mixture over the top.

6. Bake for 20 to 25 minutes longer, until lightly colored on top and firm to the touch. Cool in the pan on a wire rack before cutting into large or small bars.

YIELD: 1 to 3 dozen
TOTAL TIME: 45 minutes

CRUST
2 cups (12 ounces) white chocolate chips
6 tablespoons butter, at room temperature
2 cups graham cracker crumbs
2 cups almonds, chopped

FILLING
1 pound cream cheese, at room temperature
½ cup granulated sugar
4 large eggs
1 tablespoon fresh lemon juice
1 tablespoon Amaretto
¼ cup all-purpose flour

HELLO DOLLY COOKIES

BAR COOKIES

1. Preheat the oven to 350 degrees. Lightly grease a 9-inch square baking pan.

2. Combine the graham crackers, chocolate chips, walnuts, and coconut in a medium bowl.

3. Pour the melted butter over the dry ingredients and stir. Press the mixture evenly into the prepared baking pan. Drizzle the condensed milk over the top.

4. Bake for 25 to 30 minutes, until lightly colored on top. Cool in the pan on a wire rack before cutting into large or small bars.

Baking notes: Other cookies, such as chocolate or vanilla wafers, can be substituted for graham cracker.

YIELD: 1 to 2 dozen
TOTAL TIME: 35 minutes

1 cup graham cracker crumbs
1 cup (6 ounces) semisweet chocolate chips
1 cup walnuts, chopped
1 cup shredded coconut
¼ cup butter, melted
One 14-ounce can sweetened condensed milk

HIKER'S TREATS

BAR COOKIES

1. Preheat the oven to 350 degrees. Lightly grease an 8-inch square baking pan.

2. Combine the flour, oats, wheat germ, brown sugar, and orange zest in a bowl. Cut in the vegetable shortening until the mixture resembles coarse crumbs. Press the dough, evenly into the prepared baking pan.

3. To make the topping, in a medium bowl, beat the eggs with the brown sugar until thick. Stir in the coconut. Pour over the dough and sprinkle the almonds over the top.

4. Bake for 30 to 35 minutes, until lighly colored on top and firm to the touch. Cool in the pan on wire rack before cutting into large or small bars.

Baking notes: To enhance the flavor of these bars, add ¼ teaspoon almond extract to the topping. Raisins may be added to the dough.

YIELD: 1 to 2 dozen
TOTAL TIME: 45 minutes

¾ cup all-purpose flour
½ cup rolled oats
¼ cup toasted wheat germ
6 tablespoons packed light brown sugar
1 tablespoon grated orange zest
½ cup vegetable shortening

TOPPING
2 large eggs
6 tablespoons packed light brown sugar
½ cup shredded coconut
⅔ cup slivered almonds

HOLIDAY COOKIES

YIELD: *1 to 2 dozen*

TOTAL TIME: *50 minutes*

CRUST
1 cup all-purpose flour
½ teaspoon ground ginger
¼ teaspoon ground cloves
¼ teaspoon ground nutmeg
½ cup vegetable shortening
½ cup packed light brown sugar

FILLING
½ teaspoon baking powder
¼ teaspoon ground mace
¼ teaspoon salt
1 cup packed light brown sugar
2 large eggs
1 teaspoon vanilla extract
1½ cups shredded coconut
1 cup almonds, chopped

1. Preheat the oven to 375 degrees. Lightly grease a 9-inch square baking pan.

2. To make the crust, combine the flour and spices.

3. In a large bowl, cream the vegetable shortening and brown sugar. Gradually blend in the dry ingredients. Spread the mixture evenly in the prepared baking pan.

4. Bake for 20 minutes.

5. Meanwhile, make the filling: Combine the baking powder, mace, and salt.

6. In a medium bowl, beat the brown sugar and eggs until thick. Beat in the vanilla extract. Beat in the dry ingredients. Fold in the coconuts and almonds.

7. Pour the over the hot crust. Bake for 20 to 25 minutes longer, until lightly colored on top. Cool in the pan on a wire rack before cutting into large or small bars.

Baking notes: Nutmeg may be used in place of the mace.

HOLIDAY WREATHS

YIELD: *3 to 4 dozen*

TOTAL TIME: *30 minutes*

1 cup vegetable shortening
½ cup granulated sugar
1 large egg
1 teaspoon vanilla extract
2½ tablespoons all-purpose flour
¼ cup maple syrup
1⅓ cup walnuts, chopped
Red and green glacé cherries, chopped, for decoration

1. Preheat the oven to 350 degrees. Lightly grease 2 baking sheets.

2. In a large bowl, cream the vegetable shortening and sugar. Beat in the egg. Beat in the vanilla extract. Gradually blend in the flour. Transfer one-third of the dough to a medium bowl.

3. Place the remaining dough in a cookie press or pastry bag fitted with a small plain tip, and press or pipe out rings onto the prepared baking sheets, spacing them 2 inches apart.

4. Stir the maple syrup into the reserved dough. Stir in the walnuts. Fill the centers of the rings with the maple syrup mix.

5. Bake for 12 to 15 minutes, until lightly colored. Transfer to wire racks and decorate with the glacé cherries. Let cool.

HONEY CHEWS

DROP COOKIES

YIELD: 3 to 5 dozen
TOTAL TIME: 35 minutes

1. Preheat the oven to 350 degrees. Lightly grease 2 baking sheets.

2. Combine the two flours, the oats, and salt.

3. In a large saucepan, combine the honey, oil, molasses, and orange juice and heat gently, stirring until well blended. Remove from the heat and stir in the coffee liqueur. Transfer to a large bowl, and gradually blend in the dry ingredients. Stir in the coconut.

4. Drop the dough by spoonfuls 1½ inches apart onto the prepared baking sheets.

5. Bake for 10 to 12 minutes, until lightly colored. Transfer to wire racks to cool.

2 cups whole wheat flour
1 cup soy flour
1 cup rolled oats
¼ teaspoon salt
1 cup honey
1 cup canola oil
½ cup molasses
1 tablespoon fresh orange juice
½ teaspoon coffee liqueur
1 cup flaked coconut

HONEY CHIPPERS

DROP COOKIES

YIELD: 4 to 5 dozen
TOTAL TIME: 35 minutes

1. Preheat the oven to 375 degrees. Lightly grease 2 baking sheets.

2. Combine the flour, baking soda, and salt.

3. In a large saucepan, melt the butter with the honey, stirring until smooth. Remove from the heat and beat in the egg. Beat in the brandy. Gradually blend in the dry ingredients. Stir in the chocolate chips and almonds.

4. Drop the dough by spoonfuls 2 inches apart onto the prepared baking sheets.

5. Bake for 10 to 12 minutes, until lightly colored. Transfer to wire racks to cool.

1¼ cups all-purpose flour
½ teaspoon baking soda
¼ teaspoon salt
⅓ cup butter, at room temperature
½ cup honey
1 large egg
1½ teaspoons apricot flavored brandy
1 cup (6 ounces) semisweet chocolate chips
½ cup almonds, chopped fine

HONEY CHOCOLATE-OATMEAL COOKIES

DROP COOKIES

YIELD: 4 to 5 dozen

TOTAL TIME: 30 minutes

2½ cups all-purpose flour
1 teaspoon baking powder
¼ teaspoon baking soda
1 teaspoon ground cinnamon
¼ teaspoon salt
1 cup vegetable shortening
2 ounces bittersweet chocolate, chopped
1¼ cups honey
2 large eggs
1½ cups (9 ounces) rolled oats
1 cup flaked coconut

1. Preheat the oven to 325 degrees. Lightly grease 2 baking sheets.

2. Combine the flour, baking powder, baking soda, cinnamon, and salt.

3. In a large saucepan, melt the vegetable shortening and chocolate with the honey, stirring until smooth. Remove from the heat and beat in the eggs one at a time. Gradually blend in the dry ingredients. Stir in the oats and the coconut.

4. Drop the dough by spoonfuls 1½ inches apart onto the prepared baking sheets.

5. Bake for 18 to 20 minutes, until lightly colored. Transfer to wire racks to cool.

HONEY DATE BARS

BAR COOKIES

YIELD: 1 to 3 dozen

TOTAL TIME: 40 minutes

¾ cup all-purpose flour
¾ teaspoon baking powder
¼ teaspoon salt
3 tablespoons vegetable shortening
¾ cup honey
2 large eggs
1 cup dates, pitted and chopped
⅔ cup walnuts, chopped fine
Powdered sugar for coating

1. Preheat the oven to 350 degrees. Lightly grease a 9-inch square baking pan.

2. Combine the flour, baking powder, and salt.

3. In a large saucepan, melt the vegetable shortening with the honey, stirring until smooth. Remove from the heat and beat in the eggs one at a time. Gradually blend in the dry ingredients. Stir in the dates and walnuts. Spread the mixture evenly in the prepared baking pan.

4. Bake for 25 to 30 minutes, until lightly colored on top. Cool in the pan on a wire rack.

5. Cut into large or small bars, and dip half of each bar in powdered sugar.

HONEY HERMITS — DROP COOKIES

YIELD: *4 to 5 dozen*
TOTAL TIME: *30 minutes*
CHILLING TIME: *4 hours*

1. Combine the flour, walnuts, baking soda, spices, and salt.

2. In a small saucepan, melt the vegetable shortening with the honey, stirring until smooth. Transfer to a large bowl and beat in the brown sugar. Beat in the eggs one at a time. Beat in the milk. Gradually blend in the dry ingredients. Stir in the raisins, currants, and dates. Cover and chill for at least 4 hours.

3. Preheat the oven to 400 degrees. Lightly grease 2 baking sheets.

4. Drop the dough by spoonfuls 1½ inches apart onto the prepared baking sheets.

5. Bake for 10 to 12 minutes, until lightly colored. Transfer to wire racks to cool.

2¼ cups all-purpose flour
½ teaspoon walnuts, ground fine
1 teaspoon baking soda
½ teaspoon ground allspice
½ teaspoon ground cinnamon
¼ teaspoon salt
½ cup vegetable shortening
1 cup honey
½ cup packed light brown sugar
2 large eggs
3 tablespoons milk
1 cup raisins
1 cup currants
1 cup dates, pitted and chopped fine

HONEY LACE WAFERS — DROP COOKIES

YIELD: *1 to 3 dozen*
TOTAL TIME: *30 minutes*

1. Preheat the oven to 400 degrees.

2. Combine the flour, baking powder, and baking soda.

3. In a large bowl, cream the vegetable shortening and sugar. Beat in the honey. Beat in the orange zest. Gradually blend in the dry ingredients. Fold in the coconut.

4. Drop the dough by spoonfuls at least 3 inches apart onto ungreased baking sheets.

5. Bake for 10 to 12 minutes, until lightly colored. Roll each warm cookie up around a thin dowel or a pencil to form a cylinder, remove from the round tool, and set on wire racks to cool. (If the cookies become too firm to shape, return them to the oven for a minute or so.)

Baking notes: These can be served plain or sprinkled with powdered sugar. For special occasions, fill them with whipped cream, using a pastry bag fitted with a small plain tip.

½ cup all-purpose flour
¼ teaspoon baking powder
⅛ teaspoon baking soda
¼ cup vegetable shortening
2 tablespoons granulated sugar
¼ cup honey
1¾ teaspoons grated orange zest
½ cup flaked coconut

HONEY SPICE COOKIES

YIELD: 3 to 4 dozen
TOTAL TIME: 30 minutes
CHILLING TIME: 2 hours

3¼ cups all-purpose flour
½ cup hazelnuts, ground
½ teaspoon baking soda
1 teaspoon ground ginger
½ teaspoon ground cinnamon
¼ teaspoon ground nutmeg
¼ teaspoon salt
⅔ cup packed light brown sugar
¼ cup vegetable shortening
2 large eggs
¾ cup honey
1 teaspoon grated lemon zest
½ cup grated orange zest

1. Combine the flour, hazelnuts, baking soda, spices, and salt.

2. In a large bowl, cream the vegetable shortening and brown sugar. Beat in the eggs. Beat in the honey. Beat in the lemon and orange zest. Gradually blend in the dry ingredients. Cover and chill in the refrigerator for 2 hours.

3. Preheat the oven to 350 degrees.

4. On a floured surface, roll out the dough to a thickness of ¼ inch. Using a 1½-inch round cookie cutter, cut into cookies. Place the round on ungreased baking sheets.

5. Bake for 10 to 12 minutes, until lightly colored. Transfer to wire racks to cool.

HUNGARIAN BUTTER COOKIES

YIELD: 2 to 4 dozen
TOTAL TIME: 30 minutes
CHILLING TIME: 2 hours

2¾ cups all-purpose flour
1 tablespoon baking soda
¼ teaspoon salt
1½ cups butter, at room temperature
¼ cup granulated sugar
4 large egg yolks
1 cup sour cream
1 large egg white, beaten
Granulated sugar for sprinkling

1. Combine the flour, baking soda, and salt.

2. In a large bowl, cream the butter and sugar. Beat in the egg yolks. Beat in the sour cream. Gradually blend in the dry ingredients. Cover and chill for 2 hours.

3. Preheat the oven to 350 degrees. Lightly grease 2 baking sheets.

4. On a floured surface, roll out the dough to a thickness of ¼ inch. Using a 1½-inch round cookie cutter, cut out cookies and place 1 inch apart on the prepared baking sheets.

5. Brush with the beaten egg white and sprinkle with granulated sugar.

6. Bake for 12 to 14 minutes, until lightly colored. Transfer to wire racks to cool.

IMPERIALS

DROP COOKIES

YIELD: *2 dozen*
TOTAL TIME: *30 minutes*
CHILLING TIME: *2 hours*

1. In a large bowl, cream the vegetable shortening and sugar. Beat in the egg yolks. Gradually blend in the flour. Cover and chill for 2 hours.

2. Preheat the oven to 350 degrees.

3. Drop the dough by spoonfuls 2½ inches apart onto ungreased baking sheets. Flatten with a glass dipped in water and then in granulated sugar.

4. Bake for 8 to 10 minutes, until lightly colored. Transfer to wire racks to cool.

5. Melt the chocolate in a double boiler over low heat, stirring until smooth. Remove from the heat. Spread a thin layer of chocolate over the bottoms of the cooled cookies and let cool until set.

¾ cup vegetable shortening
¾ cup granulated sugar
4 large egg yolks
1 cup all-purpose flour
Granulated sugar for flattening
3 ounces semisweet chocolate, chopped

ISCHL TARTLETS

ROLLED COOKIES

YIELD: *4 to 5 dozen*
TOTAL TIME: *45 minutes*
CHILLING TIME: *8 hours*

1. Combine the flour, almonds, and baking powder.

2. In a large bowl, cream the vegetable shortening and sugar. Beat in the egg. Beat in the cream cheese and lemon zest. Gradually blend in the dry ingredients. Divide the dough in half, wrap in waxed paper, and chill for 8 hours or overnight.

3. Preheat the oven to 350 degrees.

4. On a floured surface, roll out one-half of the dough to a thickness of ⅛ inch. Using a 3-inch round cookie cutter, cut into rounds. With a ½-inch round cutter, cut out the centers of the cookies. Place the rounds 1 inch apart on the prepared baking sheets. Roll out the remaining dough, cut into 3-inch rounds and place on the baking sheets.

5. Bake for 8 to 10 minutes, until lightly colored. Transfer to wire racks to cool.

6. To assemble, spread a thin layer of raspberry preserves over the plain rounds and top with the cut-out rounds. Dust the tops with powdered sugar.

Baking notes: For variety, try any one of the many fruit preserves available in grocery stores.

2¾ cups all-purpose flour
½ cup almonds, ground
½ teaspoon baking powder
1 cup vegetable shortening
1 cup granulated sugar
1 large egg
3 ounces cream cheese, softened
1 tablespoon grated lemon zest
½ cup raspberry preserves
Powdered sugar for dusting

ITALIAN ALMOND COOKIES

BAR COOKIES

YIELD: 1 to 3 dozen
TOTAL TIME: 75 minutes

2⅔ cups all-purpose flour
1 cup almonds, ground
Pinch of salt
1 cup vegetable shortening
1 cup granulated sugar
2 tablespoons fresh lemon juice
1 tablespoon brandy
1 teaspoon grated lemon zest

1. Preheat the oven to 350 degrees. Lightly grease a 9-inch square baking pan.

2. Combine the flour, almonds, and salt.

3. In a large bowl, cream the vegetable shortening and sugar. Beat in the lemon juice and brandy. Beat in the lemon zest. Gradually blend in the dry ingredients. Spread the mixture evenly in the prepared baking pan. (Do not press down on the mixture.)

4. Bake for 50 to 60 minutes, until lightly colored on top. Cool in the pan on a wire rack before cutting into large or small bars.

ITALIAN CHRISTMAS COOKIES

ROLLED COOKIES

YIELD: 2 to 4 dozen
TOTAL TIME: 30 minutes
CHILLING TIME: 4 hours

3 cups all-purpose flour
1 tablespoon baking powder
¼ teaspoon salt
1 cup vegetable shortening
1 cup granulated sugar
2 large eggs
1 teaspoon grated lemon zest
¼ cup pistachios, chopped
Lemon Glaze (see Pantry)
Chopped pistachios for sprinkling

1. Combine the flour, baking powder, and salt.

2. In a large bowl, cream the vegetable shortening and sugar. Beat in the eggs one at a time. Beat in the lemon zest. Gradually blend in the dry ingredients. Fold in the pistachios. Cover and chill for 4 hours.

3. Preheat the oven to 425 degrees. Lightly grease 2 baking sheets.

4. On a floured surface, roll out the dough to a thickness of ⅛ inch. Using a 1½-inch round cookie cutter, cut the cookies and place 1 inch apart on the prepared baking sheets.

5. Bake for 8 to 10 minutes, until lightly colored. Transfer to wire racks to cool.

6. Frost the cooled cookies with the lemon glaze and sprinkle with chopped pistachios.

Baking notes: Traditionally these cookies are made with pistachios, but any type of nut can be used. These cookies are being baked at a high temperature, so watch closely as they bake.

JAM SQUARES

BAR COOKIES

YIELD: *1 to 3 dozen*
TOTAL TIME: *50 minutes*

1. Preheat the oven to 400 degrees.

2. To make the crust, combine the flour and salt in a medium bowl. Cut in the butter until the mixture resembles coarse crumbs. Add just enough water to make a soft dough. Press the dough evenly into an ungreased 9-inch square baking pan.

3. Bake for 20 minutes.

4. Meanwhile, make the topping: In a medium bowl, beat the eggs until thick and light-colored. Beat in the powdered sugar. Stir in the coconut.

5. Spread the raspberry preserves over the hot crust. Spread the topping over the preserves.

6. Bake for 20 to 25 minutes longer, until lightly colored on top and firm to the touch. Cool in the pan on a wire rack before cutting into large or small bars.

CRUST
1½ cups all-purpose flour
¼ teaspoon salt
½ cup butter
2 to 2½ tablespoons ice water

TOPPING
2 large eggs
½ cup powdered sugar
2½ cups flaked coconut
⅓ cup raspberry preserves

JELLY COOKIES

FORMED COOKIES

YIELD: *3 to 4 dozen*
TOTAL TIME: *45 minutes*

1. Preheat the oven to 350 degrees. Lightly grease 2 baking sheets.

2. In a large bowl, cream the vegetable shortening and sugar. Beat in the egg. Beat in the vanilla extract and lemon juice. Gradually blend in the flour.

3. Pinch off walnut-sized pieces of the dough and roll into balls. Place 1 inch apart on the prepared baking sheets. Press your finger into the center of each cookie to make an indentation. Fill each cookie with a little jelly.

4. Bake for 20 to 25 minutes, until lightly colored. Transfer to wire racks to cool.

1 cup vegetable shortening
½ cup granulated sugar
1 large egg
1 teaspoon vanilla extract
½ teaspoon fresh lemon juice
2½ cups all-purpose flour
About ¼ to ½ cup grape jelly

Jewel Bars

BAR COOKIES

YIELD: *1 to 2 dozen*

TOTAL TIME: *45 minutes*

2¼ cups all-purpose flour
1½ teaspoons baking powder
1 teaspoon ground cinnamon
1 teaspoon ground nutmeg
1 teaspoon salt
½ cup vegetable shortening
1½ cups packed light brown sugar
8 ounces cream cheese, at room temperature
1 large egg
¼ cup honey
1 cup walnuts, chopped
1 cup mixed candied fruit, chopped fine
1 cup raisins
Lemon Icing (see Pantry)

1. Preheat the oven to 350 degrees. Lightly grease a 9-inch square baking pan.

2. Combine the flour, baking powder, cinnamon, nutmeg, and salt.

3. In a large bowl, cream the vegetable shortening and sugar. Beat in the cream cheese. Beat in the egg and honey. Gradually blend in the dry ingredients. Stir in the walnuts, mixed fruit, and raisins. Spread the mixture evenly in the prepared baking pan.

4. Bake for 30 to 35 minutes, until a toothpick inserted in the center comes out clean. Cool in the pan on a wire rack.

5. Spread the icing over the cooled cookies and cut into large or small bars.

Baking notes: If you prefer, use just one kind of candied fruit, such as cherries.

Jewish Cookies

ROLLED COOKIES

YIELD: *3 to 6 dozen*

TOTAL TIME: *40 minutes*

CHILLING TIME: *6 hours*

2 cups all-purpose flour
2 teaspoons bitter almonds, grated
1 teaspoon baking powder
3 teaspoons ground cardamom
½ cup butter, at room temperature
½ cup packed light brown sugar
1 large egg

TOPPING

1 large egg white
2 tablespoons granulated sugar
½ teaspoon ground cinnamon
½ cup butter, melted temperature

1. Combine the flour, almonds, baking powder, and cardamom.

2. In a large bowl, cream the butter and sugar. Beat in the egg. Gradually blend in the dry ingredients. Cover and chill in the refrigerator for 6 hours.

3. Preheat the oven to 375 degrees. Lightly grease 2 baking sheets.

4. To make the topping, beat the egg white in a small bowl until foamy. Beat in the sugar and cinnamon.

5. On a floured surface, roll out the dough to a thickness of ⅛ inch. Using a 1½-inch round cookie cutter, cut into rounds and place 1 inch apart on the prepared baking sheets. Brush each cookie with the melted butter and then with the egg white mixture.

6. Bake for 12 to 15 minutes, until lightly colored. Transfer to wire racks to cool.

JOE FROGGERS

ROLLED COOKIES

1. Combine the flour, baking powder, baking soda, ginger, cloves, and salt.

2. In a large bowl, cream the vegetable shortening and brown sugar. Beat in the molasses and water. Gradually blend in the dry ingredients. Cover and chill for 8 hours or overnight.

3. Preheat the oven to 350 degrees. Lightly grease 2 baking sheets.

4. On a floured surface, roll the dough out to a thickness of ¼ inch. Using a 3-inch round cookie cutter, cut into rounds and place 1 inch apart on the prepared baking sheets.

5. Bake for 10 to 12 minutes, until firm to the touch. Transfer to wire racks to cool.

Baking notes: This was one of the most popular cookies in my shop in New England.

YIELD: 5 to 6 dozen
TOTAL TIME: 35 minutes
CHILLING TIME: 8 hours

4½ cups all-purpose flour
1 teaspoon baking powder
1 teaspoon baking soda
1¼ teaspoons ground ginger
⅛ teaspoon ground cloves
1 teaspoon salt
¾ cup vegetable shortening
1 cup packed light brown sugar
1 cup molasses
½ cup water

JUBILEE WAFERS

REFRIGERATOR COOKIES

1. Combine the flour, baking powder, baking soda, and spices.

2. In a large bowl, cream the vegetable shortening and sugar. Beat in the corn syrup. Beat in the brandy. Gradually blend in the dry ingredients. Fold in the almonds and candied citrus peel.

3. Divide the dough in half. Form each half into a log 2 inches in diameter. Wrap in waxed paper and chill in the refrigerator for 24 hours.

4. Preheat the oven to 350 degrees. Lightly grease 2 baking sheets.

5. Cut the logs into ¼-inch-thick slices and place 1 inch apart on the prepared baking sheets.

6. Bake for 12 to 15 minutes, until lightly colored. Transfer to wire racks to cool.

YIELD: 5 to 6 dozen
TOTAL TIME: 35 minutes
CHILLING TIME: 24 hours

2½ cups all-purpose flour
1 teaspoon baking powder
½ teaspoon baking soda
1 teaspoon ground cinnamon
½ teaspoon ground cloves
¼ teaspoon ground mace
¼ teaspoon ground cardamom
½ cup vegetable shortening
1 cup granulated sugar
⅔ cup light corn syrup
½ cup brandy
1 cup almonds, chopped fine
½ cup candied citrus peel, chopped fine

JUMBLES

DROP COOKIES

1. Preheat the oven to 375 degrees. Lightly grease 2 baking sheets.

2. Combine the flour, baking powder, baking soda, and salt.

3. In a large bowl, cream the vegetable shortening and brown sugar. Beat in the egg. Beat in the milk and vanilla extract. Gradually blend in the dry ingredients. Fold in the dates, almonds, and walnuts.

4. Spread the cornflakes in a pie pan. Drop the dough by spoonfuls onto the cornflakes and roll in the cornflakes until well coated. Place them 3 inches apart on the prepared baking sheets.

5. Bake for 12 to 15 minutes, until lightly colored. Transfer to wire racks to cool.

YIELD: 3 to 4 dozen
TOTAL TIME: 45 minutes

1 cup all-purpose flour
½ teaspoon baking powder
¼ teaspoon baking soda
¼ teaspoon salt
⅓ cup vegetable shortening
½ cup packed light brown sugar
1 large egg
1½ tablespoons evaporated milk
1 teaspoon vanilla extract
½ cup dates, pitted and chopped
½ cup sliced almonds
½ cup walnuts, chopped
1½ cups cornflakes, crushed

KENTUCKY COCONUT DROPS

YIELD: 3 to 4 dozen
TOTAL TIME: 35 minutes

3 large egg whites
½ cup powdered sugar
1 cup grated fresh or
    packaged coconut

1. Preheat the oven to 325 degrees. Line 2 baking sheets with parchment paper.

2. In a large bowl, beat the egg whites until foamy. Beat in the powdered sugar and continue beating until stiff peaks form. Fold in the coconut.

3. Drop the mixture by spoonfuls 1 inch apart onto the prepared baking sheets.

4. Bake for 12 to 15 minutes, or until the edges start to color. Cool on the baking sheets on wire racks.

KENTUCKY PECAN BARS

YIELD: 1 to 2 dozen
TOTAL TIME: 45 minutes

CRUST
1⅓ cups all-purpose flour
1¼ cups packed light
    brown sugar
½ teaspoon baking soda
½ teaspoon salt
1 cup pecans, toasted and
    chopped
½ cup vegetable shortening

TOPPING
3 large eggs
⅓ cup granulated sugar
¼ cup butter, at room
    temperature
3 tablespoons bourbon
1 teaspoon vanilla extract

1. Preheat the oven to 350 degrees. Lightly grease an 8-inch square baking pan.

2. To make the crust, combine the flour, brown sugar, baking soda, salt, and pecans. Cut in the vegetable shortening until the mixture resembles coarse crumbs. Press the mixture evenly into the prepared baking pans.

3. Bake for 15 minutes.

4. Meanwhile, make the topping: In a medium bowl, beat the eggs until thick and light-colored. Beat in the sugar and butter. Beat in the bourbon and vanilla extract.

5. Spread the topping over the hot crust. Bake for 20 to 25 minutes longer, until lightly colored and firm to the touch. Cool in the pan on a wire rack before cutting into large or small bars.

Baking notes: You can decorate these bars by arranging pecan halves on the topping before baking.

KISSIES

FORMED COOKIES

YIELD: *3 to 4 dozen*
TOTAL TIME: *30 minutes*

1. Preheat the oven to 350 degrees.

2. Combine the flour, baking soda, and salt.

3. In a large bowl, cream the vegetable shortening and the two sugars. Beat in the peanut butter. Beat in the egg and vanilla extract. Gradually blend in the dry ingredients.

4. Pinch off walnut-sized pieces of the dough and roll into balls. Roll the balls in granulated sugar and place 1 inch apart on ungreased baking sheets.

5. Bake for 8 to 10 minutes, until just starting to color. Press a chocolate kiss into the center of each ball and return to the oven for 3 minutes. Transfer to wire racks to cool.

1⅓ cups all-purpose flour
1 teaspoon baking soda
½ teaspoon salt
½ cup vegetable shortening
½ cup granulated sugar
½ cup packed light brown sugar
½ cup peanut butter
1 large egg
1 teaspoon vanilla extract
Granulated sugar for rolling
Chocolate kisses for decoration

KRINGLES

FORMED COOKIES

YIELD: *2 to 3 dozen*
TOTAL TIME: *40 minutes*
CHILLING TIME: *24 hours*

1. Combine the flour and salt.

2. In a large bowl, cream the vegetable shortening and sugar. Beat in the egg and egg yolks. Beat in the vanilla extract. Gradually blend in the dry ingredients. Cover tightly and chill for 24 hours.

3. Preheat the oven to 350 degrees.

4. Pinch off pieces of dough and roll into pencil-thin ropes about 6 inches long. Form the ropes into pretzels on ungreased baking sheets, placing them 1 inch apart. Brush with the beaten egg white and sprinkle with granulated sugar.

5. Bake for 12 to 14 minutes, until lightly colored. Transfer to wire racks to cool.

Baking notes: Decorate the pretzels with white or Dark chocolate Frosting (see Pantry).

3 cups all-purpose flour
½ teaspoon salt
1 cup vegetable shortening
1 cup granulated sugar
1 large egg
2 hard-boiled large egg yolks, chopped
1 teaspoon vanilla extract
1 large egg white, beaten
Granulated sugar for sprinkling

KRISPIES

BAR COOKIES

YIELD: *1 to 2 dozen*
TOTAL TIME: *30 minutes*

1. Lightly grease a 13 by 9-inch baking pan. Chill in the freezer.

2. In a large saucepan, melt the chocolate and butter with the corn syrup, stirring until smooth. Remove from the heat and beat in the powdered sugar. Beat in the vanilla extract. Stir in the rice krispies. Press the mixture evenly into the prepared baking pan.

3. Chill in the refrigerator for 20 minutes or until set. Cut into large or small bars.

1½ ounces milk chocolate
½ cup butter
½ cup corn syrup
1 cup powdered sugar
2 teaspoons vanilla extract
4 cups rice krispies

LADYFINGERS

FORMED COOKIES

YIELD: *3 to 4 dozen*
TOTAL TIME: *35 minutes*

1¾ cups all-purpose flour
½ teaspoon ground cinnamon
¼ teaspoon ground cloves
4 large egg yolks
2 cups powdered sugar

1. Preheat the oven to 350 degrees. Line 2 baking sheets with parchment paper.

2. Combine the flour, cinnamon, and cloves.

3. In a large bowl, beat the egg yolks and powdered sugar until thick and light-colored. Gradually blend in the dry ingredients.

4. Fill a cookie press or a pastry bag fitted with a large plain tip and press or pipe out 3-inch-long strips 1 inch apart onto the prepared baking sheets.

5. Bake for 10 to 12 minutes, until lightly colored. Cool on the baking sheets on wire racks.

LEBKUCHEN

ROLLED COOKIES

YIELD: *3 to 5 dozen*
TOTAL TIME: *45 minutes*
CHILLING TIME: *24 hours*

3½ cups all-purpose flour
½ teaspoon baking soda
1 teaspoon ground cinnamon
1 teaspoon ground nutmeg
½ teaspoon ground allspice
½ teaspoon ground ginger
¼ teaspoon ground cloves
1 teaspoon salt
¾ cup honey
¾ cup packed light brown sugar
1 large egg
3 tablespoons fresh lemon juice
2 teaspoons grated lemon zest
1 cup candied citron, chopped
1 cup almonds, chopped
Glacé cherries, halved

1. Combine the flour, baking soda, spices, and salt.

2. In a large saucepan, bring the honey to a boil. Remove from the heat and beat in the brown sugar. Beat in the egg. Beat in the lemon juice and zest. Gradually blend in the dry ingredients. Fold in the candied citron and almonds. Transfer the dough to a bowl, cover, and chill for 24 hours.

3. Preheat the oven to 350 degrees.

4. On a floured surface, roll out the dough to a thickness of ¼ inch. Using a 2-inch round cookie cutter, cut out cookies and place 2 inches apart on ungreased baking sheets. Place the cherry halves on top of each cookie.

5. Bake for 10 to 12 minutes, until lightly colored. Transfer to wire racks to cool.

Baking Notes: Traditionally these are frosted with white icing and decorated with almonds and cherries.

LEMON BARS I BAR COOKIES

YIELD: *2 to 3 dozen*
TOTAL TIME: *40 minutes*

1. Preheat the oven to 350 degrees. Lightly grease a 13 by 9-inch baking pan.

2. Combine the flour, baking powder, baking soda, and allspice.

3. In a large bowl, cream the vegetable shortening until light and fluffy. Beat in the eggs. Beat in the lemon juice concentrate and lemon extract. Gradually blend in the dry ingredients. Fold in the raisins and walnuts. Spread the mixture evenly in the prepared baking pan. Sprinkle the coconut and pineapple over the top.

4. Bake for 20 to 25 minutes, until lightly colored on top and firm to the touch. Cool in the pan on a wire rack before cutting into large or small bars.

2½ cups all-purpose flour
2 teaspoons baking powder
1 teaspoon baking soda
½ teaspoon ground allspice
¼ cup vegetable shortening
2 large eggs
1½ cups frozen lemon juice
*   concentrate, thawed*
1 teaspoon lemon extract
1 cup golden raisins
1 cup walnuts, chopped
¾ cup flaked coconut
¾ cup canned crushed
*   pineapple, drained*

LEMON BARS II BAR COOKIES

YIELD: *1 to 3 dozen*
TOTAL TIME: *55 minutes*

1. Preheat the oven to 350 degrees. Lightly grease a 13 by 9-inch baking pan.

2. To make the crust, combine the two flours, the sugar, oats, and walnuts in a large bowl. Cut in the vegetable shortening until the mixture resembles coarse crumbs. Press the mixture evenly into the prepared baking pan.

3. Bake for 30 minutes.

4. Meanwhile, make the topping: In a large bowl, beat the eggs and sugar until thick and light-colored. Beat in the lemon juice and zest. Beat in the flour and baking powder.

5. Pour over the hot crust.

6. Bake for 15 to 18 minutes longer, until lightly colored on top and firm to the touch. Cool in the pan on a wire rack before cutting into large or small bars.

CRUST
1 cup all-purpose flour
1 cup soy flour
¼ cup granulated sugar
¼ cup (1½ ounces) rolled
*   oats*
¼ cup walnuts, ground
*   fine*
½ cup vegetable shortening

TOPPING
4 large eggs
2 cups granulated sugar
¼ cup frozen lemon juice
*   concentrate, thawed*
1 tablespoon grated lemon
*   zest*
¼ cup all-purpose flour
½ teaspoon baking powder

Lemon Caraway Cookies

ROLLED COOKIES

YIELD: 2 to 4 dozen
TOTAL TIME: 35 minutes
CHILLING TIME: 4 hours

3 cups all-purpose flour
½ teaspoon baking soda
½ teaspoon salt
½ cup vegetable shortening
1 cup granulated sugar
1 large egg
2 tablespoons fresh lemon
    juice
2 tablespoons caraway seeds

1. Combine the flour, baking soda, and salt.

2. In a large bowl, cream the vegetable shortening and sugar. Beat in the egg. Beat in the lemon juice. Gradually blend in the dry ingredients. Stir in the caraway seeds. Cover and chill for 4 hours.

3. Preheat the oven to 400 degrees.

4. On a floured surface, roll out the dough to a thickness of ¼ inch. Using a 1½-inch round cookie cutter, cut out cookies and place 1 inch apart on ungreased baking sheets.

5. Bake for 10 to 12 minutes, until lightly colored. Transfer to wire racks to cool.

Lemon-Cornmeal Cookies

DROP COOKIES

YIELD: 3 to 4 dozen
TOTAL TIME: 30 minutes
CHILLING TIME: 2 hours

2¾ cups all-purpose flour
½ cup yellow cornmeal
1 teaspoon baking soda
⅛ teaspoon salt
1 tablespoon grated lemon
    zest
1 cup packed light brown
    sugar
2 tablespoons canola oil
¾ cup unsweetened
    applesauce
1 tablespoon fresh lemon
    juice
1 large egg white

GLAZE
¾ cup powdered sugar
2 tablespoons fresh lemon
    juice

1. Combine the flour, cornmeal, baking soda, salt, and lemon zest.

2. In a large bowl, beat the brown sugar and oil. Beat in the applesauce and lemon juice. Fold the egg white into the applesauce mixture. Gradually blend in the dry ingredients: do not overmix. Cover and chill for at least 2 hours.

3. In a small bowl, beat the egg white stiff but not dry.

4. Preheat the oven to 350 degrees. Line 2 baking sheets with parchment paper.

5. Drop the dough by spoonfuls 1½ inches apart on the prepared baking sheets.

6. Bake for 8 to 10 minutes, until lightly colored. Transfer to wire racks to cool.

7. Meanwhile, make the glaze: Combine the powdered sugar and lemon juice in a small bowl and stir until smooth.

8. Drizzle the white glaze over the top of the cooled cookies.

Lemon-Glazed Apple Squares

BAR COOKIES

1. Preheat the oven to 350 degrees. Lightly grease a 15 by 10-inch baking pan.

2. To make the crust, combine the flour and sugar in a large bowl. Cut in the vegetable shortening until the mixture resembles coarse crumbs. Work in the egg yolks one at a time until a smooth dough forms. Press the dough evenly into the prepared baking pan.

3. Combine the granola, almonds, sugar, and cinnamon. Stir in the lemon juice.

4. Layer the sliced apples on top of the crust. Sprinkle the granola mixture over the apples.

5. Bake for 55 to 60 minutes, until the top is lightly colored and the apples are soft.

6. Meanwhile, make the glaze: Combine the powdered sugar and lemon juice in a small bowl and stir until smooth.

7. Drizzle the glaze over the top of the warm bars. Cool in the pan on a wire rack before cutting into large or small bars.

YIELD: 2 to 3 dozen
TOTAL TIME: 70 minutes

CRUST
2 cups all-purpose flour
¼ cup granulated sugar
¾ cup vegetable shortening
2 large egg yolks

FILLING
1½ cups granola cereal
½ cup almonds, chopped fine
½ cup granulated sugar
1 teaspoon ground cinnamon
3 tablespoons fresh lemon juice
6 medium apples, peeled, cored, and sliced

GLAZE
¾ cup powdered sugar
2 tablespoons fresh lemon juice

Lemon Sugar Rounds

ROLLED COOKIES

1. Combine the flour, baking powder, and salt.

2. In a large bowl, cream the vegetable shortening and sugar. Beat in the eggs. Beat in the lemon extract and zest. Gradually blend in the dry ingredients.

3. Divide the dough in half. Form each half into a log 2 inches in diameter. Wrap in waxed paper and chill for 4 hours.

4. Preheat the oven to 400 degrees. Lightly grease 2 baking sheets.

5. On a floured surface, roll out the dough to a thickness of ¼ inch. Using a 3-inch round cookie cutter, cut into rounds and place 1 inch apart on the prepared baking sheets. Sprinkle with granulated sugar.

6. Bake for 6 to 8 minutes, until lightly colored. Transfer to wire racks to cool.

Baking notes: You can substitute orange extract and zest for the lemon.

YIELD: 1 to 2 dozen
TOTAL TIME: 30 minutes
CHILLING TIME: 4 hours

2¼ cups all-purpose flour
2 teaspoons baking powder
1 teaspoon salt
¾ cup vegetable shortening
1 cup granulated sugar
2 large eggs
1 tablespoon lemon extract
1 tablespoon grated lemon zest
Granulated sugar for sprinkling

LITHUANIAN PRESKUCHIAI

ROLLED COOKIES

YIELD: 4 to 5 dozen
TOTAL TIME: 30 minutes

2½ cups whole wheat flour
1½ tablespoons brewer's yeast
1 tablespoon honey
1 teaspoon salt
¼ cup warm water
¾ cup nonfat dry milk

1. Preheat the oven to 400 degrees. Lightly grease 2 baking sheets.

2. Combine the flour and yeast.

3. In a saucepan, stir in the honey, salt, water, and milk. Gradually blend in the dry ingredients.

4. Form the dough into a rectangle ½ inch thick. Cut lengthwise into ½-inch-wide strips, then cut the strips into ½-inch cubes. Place 1½ inches apart on the prepared baking sheets.

5. Bake for 8 to 10 minutes, until lightly colored. Transfer to wire racks to cool.

LOVE LETTERS

FORMED COOKIES

YIELD: 4 to 5 dozen
TOTAL TIME: 40 minutes

FILLING
2 large egg whites
¼ cup granulated sugar
½ teaspoon ground cinnamon
1 cup almonds, ground fine
1 teaspoon grated lemon zest

CRUST
2 cups all-purpose flour
¼ teaspoon salt
¾ cup vegetable shortening
2 tablespoons granulated sugar
4 large egg yolks

1. Preheat the oven to 350 degrees.

2. To make the filling, in a medium bowl, beat the egg whites until stiff but not dry. Beat in the sugar and cinnamon. Fold in the almonds and lemon zest. Set aside.

3. Combine the flour and salt.

4. In a large bowl, cream the vegetable shortening and sugar. Beat in the egg yolks. Gradually blend in the dry ingredients.

5. On a floured surface, roll out the dough to a thickness of ¼ inch. Using a sharp knife, cut into 3-inch squares. Place 1 inch apart on ungreased baking sheets. Drop a teaspoonful of the filling into the center of each square and fold the corners into the center like an envelope. Lightly seal the seams.

6. Bake for 18 to 20 minutes, until lightly colored. Transfer to wire racks to cool.

Macadamia Nut Cookies

DROP COOKIES

YIELD: 2 to 3 dozen
TOTAL TIME: 35 minutes
CHILLING TIME: 4 hours

1. Combine the flour, baking soda, and salt.

2. In a large bowl, cream the vegetable shortening and two sugars. Beat in the eggs one at a time, beating well after each addition. Beat in the vanilla extract and lemon juice. Gradually blend in the dry ingredients. Fold in the macadamia nuts and oats. Cover and chill for 4 hours.

3. Preheat the oven to 325 degrees. Lightly grease 2 baking sheets.

4. Drop the dough by spoonfuls 1½ inches apart onto the prepared baking sheets.

5. Bake for 15 to 18 minutes, until lightly colored. Transfer to wire racks to cool.

3 cups all-purpose flour
2 teaspoons baking soda
1 teaspoon salt
1½ cups vegetable shortening
1½ cups packed light brown sugar
⅔ cup granulated sugar
4 large eggs
1 teaspoon vanilla extract
1 teaspoon fresh lemon juice
2 cups macadamia nuts, chopped
½ cup (3 ounces) rolled oats

Macaroon Nut Wafers

DROP COOKIES

YIELD: 1 to 2 dozen
TOTAL TIME: 35 minutes.

1. Preheat the oven to 350 degrees. Line 2 baking sheets with parchment paper.

2. In a medium bowl, beat the egg whites with the salt until they form stiff peaks. Fold in the powdered sugar. Fold in the Amaretto. Fold in the almonds.

3. Drop the dough by spoonfuls 1½ inches apart onto the prepared baking sheets.

4. Bake for 15 to 20 minutes, until lightly colored. Cool slightly on the pans, then transfer to wire racks to cool completely.

2 large egg whites
¼ teaspoon salt
½ cup powdered sugar
1 teaspoon Amaretto
1 cup almonds, ground fine

Macaroons

DROP COOKIES

YIELD: 3 to 4 dozen
TOTAL TIME: 35 minutes

1. Preheat the oven to 350 degrees. Line 2 baking sheets with parchment paper.

2. In a large bowl, beat the egg whites with the salt until they hold stiff peaks. Fold in the sugar. Fold in the almond extract. Fold in the coconut and almonds. Fold in the cornflakes.

3. Drop the dough by spoonfuls 1½ inches apart onto the prepared baking sheets.

4. Bake for 12 to 15 minutes, until lightly colored. Cool slightly on the pans on wire racks before removing from the paper.

4 large egg whites
¼ teaspoon salt
1½ cups granulated sugar
1 teaspoon almond extract
1 cup shredded coconut
½ cup almonds, ground fine
3 cups cornflakes

M

MAGIC BARS

BAR COOKIES

YIELD: 1 to 3 dozen
TOTAL TIME: 45 minutes

1½ cups graham cracker
    crumbs
½ cup butter, melted
1 cup flaked coconut
1 cup (6 ounces)
    butterscotch chips
1 cup pecans, chopped

1. Preheat the oven to 350 degrees. Lightly grease a 13 by 9-inch baking pan.

2. Put the graham cracker crumbs in a large bowl and stir in the butter. Press the mixture into the prepared baking pan.

3. Combine the coconut, butterscotch chips, and pecans in a medium bowl and toss to mix. Spread this mixture evenly over the graham cracker mixture.

4. Bake for 25 to 30 minutes, until lightly colored on top. Cool in the pan on a wire rack before cutting into large or small bars.

MANDELBROT

FORMED COOKIES

YIELD: 3 to 4 dozen
TOTAL TIME: 50 minutes

3 cups all-purpose flour
1 teaspoon baking powder
¼ teaspoon salt
½ cup honey, warmed
6 tablespoons butter, at
    room temperature
3 large eggs
½ teaspoon grated lemon
    zest
½ cup pistachio nuts,
    chopped
1 teaspoon anise seeds,
    crushed

1. Preheat the oven to 350 degrees.

2. Combine the flour, baking powder, and salt.

3. In a large bowl, beat the honey and butter together. Beat in the eggs one at a time, beating well after each addition. Beat in the lemon zest. Gradually blend in the dry ingredients. Stir in the pistachio nuts and anise seeds.

4. Divide the dough in half. Shape each half into a loaf 12 inches long, 3 inches wide, and 1½–2 inches high. Place the logs on an ungreased baking sheet, leaving 1½ inches between them.

5. Bake for 25 to 30 minutes, until lightly colored and firm to the touch.

6. Transfer the loaves to a cutting board and cut into ½-inch-thick slices. Place 1 inch apart on the baking sheets and bake for 5 to 7 minutes longer, or until the slices are lightly toasted. Transfer to wire racks to cool.

Manu's Best

DROP COOKIES

YIELD: 4 to 5 dozen

TOTAL TIME: 35 minutes

1. Preheat the oven to 350 degrees. Lightly grease 2 baking sheets

2. Combine the flour, cocoa, baking powder, and salt.

3. In a large bowl, cream the vegetable shortening and two sugars. Beat in the egg. Beat in the water, butter flavoring, crème de menthe, and coffee liqueur. Gradually blend in the dry ingredients. Fold in the chocolate chips.

4. Drop the dough by spoonfuls 1½ inches apart onto the prepared baking sheets.

5. Bake for 12 to 15 minutes, until the tops look dry. Transfer to wire racks to cool.

2 cups all-purpose flour
⅓ cup unsweetened cocoa
   powder
1 teaspoon baking powder
½ teaspoon salt
1 cup vegetable shortening
¾ cup packed dark brown
   sugar
½ cup granulated sugar
1 large egg
⅓ cup water
2 tablespoons butter
   flavoring
2 tablespoons white crème
   de menthe
1 tablespoon coffee liqueur
1⅓ cups (8 ounces) white
   chocolate chips

Maple Sugar Cookies

ROLLED COOKIES

YIELD: 3 to 4 dozen

TOTAL TIME: 35 minutes

CHILLING TIME: 1 hour

1. Combine the flour, baking powder, and salt.

2. In a large bowl, cream the butter and maple sugar. Beat in the eggs. Beat in the milk and lemon extract. Gradually blend in the dry ingredients. Cover and chill for 1 hour

3. Preheat the oven to 350 degrees. Lightly grease 2 baking sheets.

4. On a floured surface, roll out the dough to a thickness of ¼ inch. Using a 2-inch round cookie cutter, cut out the cookies and place on the prepared baking sheets. Dust with sifted light brown sugar.

5. Bake for 12 to 15 minutes, until lightly colored. Transfer to wire racks to cool.

2½ cups all-purpose flour
2½ teaspoons baking
   powder
1 teaspoon salt
½ cup butter, at room
   temperature
1 cup maple sugar
2 large eggs
1 tablespoon milk
½ teaspoon lemon extract
Sifted light brown sugar for
   sprinkling

M

Marbled Cream Cheese Brownies

YIELD: 1 to 3 dozen
TOTAL TIME: 45 minutes

4 ounces cream cheese, at
    room temperature
5 tablespoons vegetable
    shortening
1 cup granulated sugar
1 tablespoon cornstarch
3 large eggs
1½ teaspoons vanilla
    extract
½ teaspoon fresh lemon
    juice
½ cup all-purpose flour
½ teaspoon baking powder
½ teaspoon salt
⅔ cup (4 ounces) semisweet
    chocolate chips

1. Preheat the oven to 350 degrees. Lightly grease a 9-inch square baking pan.

2. In a medium bowl, combine the cream cheese, 2 tablespoons of the vegetable shortening, ¼ cup of the sugar, and the cornstarch and beat until smooth. Beat in 1 of the eggs. Beat in the ½ teaspoon of the vanilla extract and lemon juice. Set aside.

3. Combine the flour, baking powder, and salt.

4. In the top of a double boiler, melt the chocolate and the remaining 3 tablespoons vegetable shortening, stirring until smooth. Remove from the heat and stir in the remaining 1 teaspoon vanilla extract.

5. In a large bowl, beat the remaining 2 eggs and ¾ cup sugar. Beat in the cooled chocolate. Beat in the dry ingredients.

6. Spread the batter evenly in the prepared baking pan. Pour the cream cheese mixture over the top and swirl a knife back and forth a few times through the mixture to marble it.

7. Bake for 25 to 30 minutes, until a toothpick inserted in the center comes out clean. Cool in the pan on a wire rack before cutting into large or small bars.

Meringue Pecan Bars

BAR COOKIES

YIELD: 4 to 5 dozen
TOTAL TIME: 50 minutes

CRUST
1 cup vegetable shortening
⅓ cup granulated sugar
5 large egg yolks
1 teaspoon rum
2½ cups all-purpose flour

TOPPING
5 large egg whites
1 cup sugar
3 cups pecans, chopped fine
2 tablespoons Amaretto
About ½ cup black currant
    jam

1. Preheat the oven to 350 degrees. Lightly grease a 15 by 10-inch baking pan.

2. To make the crust, cream the vegetable shortening and sugar. Beat in the egg yolks one at a time, beating thoroughly after each addition. Beat in the rum. Gradually blend in the flour.

3. Press the dough evenly into the prepared baking pan. Spread the black currant jam over the crust.

4. To make the topping, beat the egg whites in a large bowl until they form soft peaks. Beat in the sugar and beat until the whites hold stiff peaks. Fold in the chopped pecans. Fold in the Amaretto. Carefully spread the topping over the jam.

5. Bake for 35 to 40 minutes, until firm to the touch. Cool in the pan on a wire rack before cutting into large or small bars.

MERINGUE-TOPPED BROWNIES

BAR COOKIES

1. Preheat the oven to 375 degrees. Lightly grease a 13 by 9-inch baking pan.

2. Combine the flour, baking powder, baking soda, and salt.

3. In a large bowl, cream the vegetable shortening, butter, and two sugars. Beat in the egg yolks. Beat in the coffee and crème de cacao. Gradually blend in the dry ingredients.

4. Spread the batter evenly in the prepared baking pan. Sprinkle the chocolate chips over the top.

5. To make the topping, in a bowl, beat the egg whites until foamy. Gradually beat in the sugar and beat until the whites form stiff peaks. Spread the topping over the chocolate chips.

6. Bake for 20 to 25 minutes, until lightly colored and firm to the touch. Cool in the pan on a wire rack before cutting into large or small bars.

YIELD: 1 to 3 dozen
TOTAL TIME: 45 minutes

2 cups all-purpose flour
1 teaspoon baking powder
¼ teaspoon baking soda
¼ teaspoon salt
¼ cup vegetable shortening
¼ cup butter, at room temperature
½ cup granulated sugar
½ cup packed light brown sugar
2 large egg yolks
1 tablespoon strong brewed coffee
1½ teaspoons crème de cacao
1½ cups (9 ounces) semisweet chocolate chips

TOPPING
2 large egg whites
1 cup granulated sugar

MEXICAN WEDDING CAKES

FORMED COOKIES

1. Preheat the oven to 350 degrees.

2. In a large bowl, cream the vegetable shortening and powdered sugar. Beat in the tequila. Gradually blend in the flour. Fold in the pecans.

3. Pinch off walnut-sized pieces of dough and roll into balls. Place 1 inch apart on ungreased baking sheets.

4. Bake for 12 to 15 minutes, or until golden brown. Roll in powdered sugar and transfer to wire racks to cool.

YIELD: 4 to 5 dozen
TOTAL TIME: 30 minutes

1 cup vegetable shortening
6 tablespoons powdered sugar
1 teaspoon tequila
2 cups all-purpose flour
1 cup pecans, chopped
Powdered sugar for rolling

MICROWAVE FUDGE BROWNIES

**BAR COOKIES
(MICROWAVE RECIPE)**

1. Lightly grease an 8-inch square microwave-proof baking pan.

2. Combine the flour, baking powder, and salt.

3. In the top of a double boiler, melt the chocolate chips and vegetable, stirring until smooth. Remove from the heat and beat in the sugar. Beat in the eggs. Beat in the vanilla extract. Gradually blend in the dry ingredients. Stir in the walnuts. Spread the batter evenly in the prepared baking pan.

4. Cook on high for 7 minutes, stopping to turn the pan a quarter-turn every 2 minutes until the center is set. Cool in the pan on a wire rack before cutting into large or small bars.

YIELD: 1 to 2 dozen
TOTAL TIME: 20 minutes

⅔ cup all-purpose flour
¼ teaspoon baking powder
¼ teaspoon salt
1 cup (6 ounces) semisweet chocolate chips
¼ cup vegetable shortening
¾ cup granulated sugar
2 large eggs
½ teaspoon vanilla extract
½ cup walnuts, chopped

Mincemeat Cookie Bars

BAR COOKIES

YIELD: 2 to 3 dozen
TOTAL TIME: 35 minutes

1½ cups all-purpose flour
1¾ cups (10½ ounces)
*   rolled oats*
2 teaspoons baking powder
¼ teaspoon salt
½ cup butter, at room
*   temperature*
1 cup packed light brown
*   sugar*
1 teaspoon vanilla extract
1 cup prepared mincemeat

1. Preheat the oven to 325 degrees. Lightly grease a 13 by 9-inch baking pan.

2. Combine the flour, oats, baking powder, and salt.

3. In a large bowl, cream the butter and brown sugar. Beat in the vanilla extract. Gradually blend in the dry ingredients.

4. Spread half of the dough evenly in the bottom of the prepared baking pan. Spread the mincemeat over the top, and spread the remaining dough over the mincemeat. Press down lightly.

5. Bake for 20 to 25 minutes, until a toothpick inserted in the center comes out clean. Cool slightly, then cut into large or small bars and transfer to wire racks to cool.

Mincemeat Goodies

DROP COOKIES

YIELD: 5 to 6 dozen
TOTAL TIME: 30 minutes

4 cups all-purpose flour
½ cup walnuts, ground
1 teaspoon baking soda
1 teaspoon ground cloves
1 teaspoon ground nutmeg
¼ teaspoon ground ginger
½ teaspoon salt
1 cup vegetable shortening
2 cups granulated sugar
3 large eggs
1 cup prepared mincemeat

1. Preheat the oven to 375 degrees.

2. Combine the flour, walnuts, baking soda, spices, and salt.

3. In a large bowl, cream the vegetable shortening and sugar. Beat in the eggs. Gradually blend in the dry ingredients. Stir in the mincemeat.

4. Drop the dough by spoonfuls 1½ inches apart onto an ungreased baking sheets.

5. Bake for 10 to 12 minutes, until lightly colored. Transfer to wire racks to cool.

MINCEMEAT SQUARES

ROLLED COOKIES

YIELD: 4 to 5 dozen
TOTAL TIME: 35 minutes

1. Preheat the oven to 375 degrees. Lightly grease 2 baking sheets.

2. In a large bowl, combine the flour, sugar, and salt. Cut in the vegetable shortening.

3. Put the yeast in a medium bowl. In a small saucepan, heat the milk until tepid. Pour the milk over the yeast and stir to dissolve it. Beat in the eggs.

4. Add the yeast mix to the flour mixture and work to a soft dough. Knead for 3 to 5 minutes.

5. On a floured surface roll out the dough to a thickness of ¼ inch. Using a sharp knife, cut into 2-inch squares. Place a spoonful of mincemeat in the center of half the squares.

4 cups all-purpose flour
6 tablespoons granulated sugar
Pinch of salt
6 tablespoons vegetable shortening
2 teaspoons active dry yeast
1 cup milk
2 large eggs
6 tablespoons prepared mincemeat
2 large egg yolks, beaten
½ cup almonds, ground fine
Granulated sugar for sprinkling

6. Cover with the remaining squares, pinch to seal the edges. Place 1½ inches apart on the prepared baking sheets, brush with the beaten egg yolks, and sprinkle with the ground almonds.

7. Bake for 18 to 20 minutes, until golden brown. Sprinkle the tops with granulated sugar. Transfer to wire racks to cool.

MINT BARS

BAR COOKIES

YIELD: 1 to 3 dozen
TOTAL TIME: 35 minutes
CHILLING TIME: 2 hours

1. Preheat the oven to 350 degrees. Lightly grease a 13 by 9-inch baking pan.

2. Combine the flour and baking powder.

3. In a large bowl, cream the vegetable shortening and sugar. Beat in the eggs. Beat in the chocolate syrup. Gradually blend in the dry ingredients. Spread the dough evenly in the prepared baking pan.

4. Bake for 20 to 25 minutes, until the top is lightly colored. Let cool in the pan on a wire rack, then refrigerate for 1 hour or until chilled.

1 cup all-purpose flour
½ teaspoon baking powder
½ cup vegetable shortening
1 cup granulated sugar
4 large eggs
2 cups chocolate syrup

TOPPING
½ cup margerine
2 cups powdered sugar
2 tablespoons fresh milk
1 teaspoon crème de menthe
3 drops green food coloring
6 ounces (1 cup) semisweet chocolate chips
½ cup butter

5. To make the topping, cream the butter and powdered sugar in a large bowl. Beat in the milk and crème de menthe. Beat in the food coloring. Spread evenly over the chilled bars. Chill for 1 hour longer.

6. In the top of a double boiler, melt the chocolate chips and butter, stirring until smooth. Carefully spread this mixture over the chilled cookies and cut into large or small bars.

MINT CHOCOLATE COOKIES

YIELD: 3 to 4 dozen
TOTAL TIME: 35 minutes
CHILLING TIME: 4 hours

3 cups all-purpose flour
1½ cups walnuts, ground
½ teaspoon baking soda
½ teaspoon salt
1 cup vegetable shortening
1 cup granulated sugar
½ cup packed light brown
  sugar
2 large eggs
1 teaspoon vanilla extract
14 ounces mint-chocolate
  wafer candies, such as
  After Eights or Andies,
  chopped

1. Combine the flour, walnuts, baking soda, and salt.

2. In a large bowl, cream the vegetable shortening and two sugars. Beat in the eggs. Beat in the vanilla extract. Gradually blend in the dry ingredients. Fold in the mint wafers. Cover and chill for 4 hours.

3. Preheat the oven to 350 degrees.

4. Drop the dough by spoonfuls 1½ inches apart onto ungreased baking sheets.

5. Bake for 10 to 12 minutes, until lightly colored. Transfer to wire racks to cool.

Baking notes: For a stronger mint flavor, add 2 drops of peppermint oil. Instead of chocolate mint wafers, you can use mint-flavored chocolate chips, or grated chocolate and a teaspoon of mint extract.

MOCHA-COFFEE BROWNIES

YIELD: 1 to 2 dozen
TOTAL TIME: 35 minutes

2 ounces semisweet
  chocolate, chopped
⅓ cup vegetable shortening
¾ cup all-purpose flour
½ teaspoon baking powder
¼ teaspoon salt
2 large eggs
1 cup granulated sugar
1 teaspoon vanilla extract
2½ tablespoons instant
  mocha coffee crystals
½ cup walnuts, chopped

1. Preheat the oven to 375 degrees. Lightly grease an 8-inch square baking pan.

2. In a double boiler, melt the chocolate and vegetable shortening, stirring until smooth. Remove from the heat.

3. Combine the flour, baking powder, and salt.

4. In a large bowl, beat the eggs until thick and light-colored. Beat in the sugar. Beat in the melted chocolate mixture and vanilla extract. Gradually blend in the dry ingredients. Stir in the coffee crystals. Spread the mixture evenly in the prepared baking pan. Sprinkle the walnuts on top.

5. Bake for 20 to 25 minutes, until a toothpick inserted into the center comes out clean. Cool in the pan on a wire rack before cutting into large or small bars.

Mohn Cookies

ROLLED COOKIES

1. Combine the flour, baking powder, and salt.

2. In a medium bowl, beat one egg white until foamy.

3. In a large bowl, cream the butter and sugar. Beat in the egg yolk and liqueur. Beat in the egg whites. Gradually blend in the dry ingredients. Stir in the poppy seeds. Cover and chill for 6 hours.

4. Preheat the oven to 375 degrees. Lightly grease 2 baking sheets.

5. On a floured surface, roll out the dough to a thickness of ⅛ inch. Using a cookie cutter, cut into diamond shapes and place the diamonds 1 inch apart on the prepared baking sheets.

6. Bake for 7 to 9 minutes, until lightly colored. Transfer to wire racks to cool.

Baking notes: For variation, leave the poppy seeds out of the dough; then brush the cut-out cookies with milk and sprinkle with the poppy seeds before baking.

YIELD: 8 to 10 dozen
TOTAL TIME: 40 minutes
CHILLING TIME: 6 hours

3¼ cups all-purpose flour
2½ teaspoons baking powder
½ teaspoon salt
1 large egg, separated
½ cup butter, at room temperature
¾ cup granulated sugar
3 tablespoons orange liqueur
2 large egg whites
¼ cup poppy seeds

Molasses Balls

FORMED COOKIES

1. Combine the flour, baking soda, and spices.

2. In a large saucepan, heat the vegetable oil and molasses until warm. Remove from the heat and stir in the sugar. Gradually blend in the dry ingredients. Cover and chill for 24 hours.

3. Preheat the oven to 350 degrees. Lightly grease 2 baking sheets.

4. Pinch off walnut-sized pieces of dough and roll into balls. Roll the balls in the granulated sugar and place 1 inch apart on the prepared baking sheets.

5. Bake for 10 to 14 minutes, until lightly colored. Transfer to wire racks to cool.

Baking notes: Any cookies containing ground ginger will be more flavorful if the dough is allowed to chill before forming the cookies. For a tip on measuring molasses, see Hint 14 in Baking Hints.

YIELD: 3 to 4 dozen
TOTAL TIME: 30 minutes
CHILLING TIME: 24 hours

2¾ cups all-purpose flour
1½ teaspoons baking soda
1 teaspoon ground cinnamon
1 teaspoon ground ginger
¼ teaspoon ground cloves
¾ cup vegetable oil
¼ cup molasses
1 cup granulated sugar
Granulated sugar for rolling

M

YIELD: 3 to 4 dozen

TOTAL TIME: 35 minutes

CHILLING TIME: 24 hours

3 cups all-purpose flour
2 teaspoons baking powder
1 teaspoon baking soda
2 teaspoons ground ginger
1 teaspoon ground
*   cinnamon*
1 teaspoon ground nutmeg
1 cup molasses
1 cup vegetable shortening
1 large egg
1 cup sour milk
1 teaspoon vanilla extract

MOLASSES COOKIES

ROLLED COOKIES

1. Combine the flour, baking powder, baking soda, and spices.

2. In a large bowl, beat the molasses and vegetable shortening until smooth. Beat in the egg. Beat in the sour milk and vanilla extract. Gradually blend in the dry ingredients. Cover and chill for 24 hours.

3. Preheat the oven to 375 degrees. Lightly grease 2 baking sheets.

4. On a floured surface, roll out the dough to a thickness of ⅛ inch. Using a 2-inch round cookie cutter, cut into cookies and place 1 inch apart on the prepared baking sheets.

5. Bake for 10 to 12 minutes, until lightly colored. Transfer to wire racks to cool. Store in an airtight container.

YIELD: 4 to 5 dozen

TOTAL TIME: 35 minutes

CHILLING TIME: 4 hours

2 cups all-purpose flour
2 teaspoons baking soda
2 teaspoons ground ginger
1 teaspoon ground
*   cinnamon*
1 teaspoon ground cloves
½ teaspoon ground nutmeg
¼ cup vegetable shortening
¼ cup molasses
⅔ cup granulated sugar
1 large egg
1 large egg white, beaten
Granulated sugar for
*   coating*

MOLASSES GINGER COOKIES

FORMED COOKIES

1. Combine the flour, baking soda, and spices.

2. In a large bowl, cream the vegetable shortening, molasses, and sugar. Beat in the egg. Gradually blend in the dry ingredients. Cover and chill for 4 hours.

3. Preheat the oven to 350 degrees. Lightly grease 2 baking sheets.

4. Pinch off walnut-sized pieces of dough and roll into balls. Dip half of each ball first in the beaten egg white and then in the granulated sugar and place 2 inches apart, the sugar sides up, on the prepared baking sheets.

5. Bake for 10 to 12 minutes, until lightly colored. Transfer to wire racks to cool.

MOLASSES JUMBLES

ROLLED COOKIES

1. Combine the flour, baking powder, baking soda, and spices.

2. In a large bowl, cream together the vegetable shortening and brown sugar. Beat in the egg. Beat in the molasses. Gradually blend in the dry ingredients. Cover and chill for 24 hours.

3. Preheat the oven to 350 degrees. Lightly grease 2 baking sheets.

4. On a floured surface, roll out the dough to a thickness of ¼ inch. Using cookie cutters, cut into shapes and place 1 inch apart on the prepared baking sheets. Sprinkle with any combination of the toppings.

5. Bake for 8 to 10 minutes, until lightly colored. Transfer to wire racks to cool.

YIELD: 8 to 9 dozen
TOTAL TIME: 45 minutes
CHILLING TIME: 24 hours

3¼ cups all-purpose flour
2 teaspoons baking powder
½ teaspoon baking soda
1 teaspoon ground ginger
½ teaspoon ground cloves
½ teaspoon ground nutmeg
¾ cup vegetable shortening
1 cup packed light brown sugar
1 large egg
¼ cup molasses

TOPPING
Colored sugar crystals, walnuts, chopped, flaked coconut, and/or gumdrops, diced fine

MOON PIES

DROP COOKIES

1. Preheat the oven to 350 degrees. Lightly grease 2 baking sheets.

2. Combine the flour, cocoa powder, baking powder, and salt.

3. In a large bowl, cream the vegetable shortening and sugar. Beat in the egg. Beat in the sour milk and vanilla extract. Gradually blend in the dry ingredients.

4. Drop the dough by heaping tablespoonfuls 3 inches apart onto the prepared baking sheets.

5. Bake for 7 to 10 minutes, or until a toothpick inserted in a cookie comes out clean. Transfer to wire racks to cool.

6. To make the filling, beat the vegetable shortening and powdered sugar in a medium bowl. Beat in the vanilla extract. Beat in the marshmallow topping.

7. To assemble, cut the cookies horizontally in half. Spread a generous layer of the topping over the bottom halves, replace the top halves, and press lightly together.

Baking notes: Metal crumpet or English muffin rings are perfect for making these; it takes 2 heaping full tablespoons of the batter to fill each ring.

YIELD: 3 to 4 dozen
TOTAL TIME: 30 minutes

2 cups all-purpose flour
6 tablespoons unsweetened cocoa powder
2½ teaspoons baking powder
½ teaspoon salt
⅓ cup vegetable shortening
1 cup granulated sugar
1 large egg
1 cup sour milk
1 teaspoon vanilla extract

FILLING
¾ cup vegetable shortening
1 cup powdered sugar
1 teaspoon vanilla extract
½ cup store-bought marshmallow topping

NEW ENGLAND MOLASSES COOKIES

DROP COOKIES

YIELD: 4 to 5 dozen
TOTAL TIME: 35 minutes

3 cups all-purpose flour
½ teaspoon baking soda
½ cup vegetable shortening
½ cup granulated sugar
2 large eggs
½ cup molasses
¼ cup hot water

1. Preheat the oven to 350 degrees.

2. Combine the flour and baking soda.

3. In a large bowl, cream the vegetable shortening and sugar. Beat in the eggs. Beat in the molasses and hot water. Gradually blend in the dry ingredients.

4. Drop the dough by spoonfuls 1½ inches apart onto ungreased baking sheets.

5. Bake for 12 to 15 minutes, until firm to the touch. Transfer to wire racks to cool.

NEW HAMPSHIRE FRUIT COOKIES

DROP COOKIES

YIELD: 3 to 4 dozen
TOTAL TIME: 30 minutes

3¼ cups all-purpose flour
½ teaspoon ground
    cinnamon
¼ teaspoon salt
1 cup vegetable shortening
1½ cups granulated sugar
3 large eggs
1 teaspoon baking soda
1½ tablespoons warm
    water
1 cup chestnuts, chopped
½ cup raisins, chopped
½ cup currants, chopped

1. Preheat the oven to 350 degrees. Lightly grease 2 baking sheets.

2. Combine the flour, cinnamon, and salt.

3. In a large bowl, cream the vegetable shortening and sugar. Beat in the eggs one at a time, beating well after each addition.

4. Dissolve the baking soda in the warm water and add to the egg mixture, beating until smooth. Gradually blend in the dry ingredients. Stir in the chestnuts, raisins, and currants.

5. Drop the dough by spoonfuls 1½ inches apart onto the prepared baking sheets.

6. Bake for 12 to 15 minutes, until lightly colored. Transfer to wire racks to cool.

NEW YEAR'S EVE BISCUITS

ROLLED COOKIES

YIELD: 3 to 5 dozen
TOTAL TIME: 35 minutes

3 cups all-purpose flour
1 teaspoon baking powder
¾ cup butter, at room
    temperature
1 cup granulated sugar
1 cup warm water

1. Preheat the oven to 375 degrees. Lightly grease 2 baking sheets.

2. Combine the flour and baking powder.

3. In a large bowl, cream the butter and sugar. Gradually blend in the dry ingredients. Add just enough water to form a smooth dough.

4. On a floured surface, roll the dough out to a thickness of ½ inch. Using cookie cutters, cut into shapes and place the cookies 1 inch apart on the prepared baking sheets.

5. Bake for 12 to 15 minutes, until lightly colored. Transfer to wire racks to cool.

Baking notes: This is a very English recipe. These cookies are like sweet baking powder biscuits and are usually cut into rounds. They can be served for breakfast in place of sweet rolls.

No-Bake Brownies

BAR COOKIES

YIELD: 1 to 2 dozen
TOTAL TIME: 75 minutes

1. Lightly grease a 9-inch square baking pan.

2. In a double boiler, melt the chocolate chips with the milk, stirring until smooth. Stir in the sugar to dissolve. Remove from the heat.

3. In a large bowl, combine the vanilla wafers, marshmallows, walnuts, and salt. Transfer ½ cup of this mixture to a small bowl. Add 2 teaspoons of the warm chocolate mixture and stir to blend.

4. Add the remaining chocolate mixture to the vanilla wafer mixture and stir to blend. Press the dough evenly into the prepared baking pan, pressing down hard to pack the mixture into the pan. Spread the reserved chocolate mixture on top.

5. Refrigerate until thoroughly chilled and set. Cut into large or small bars.

Baking notes: Graham crackers or chocolate wafers can be used in place of the vanilla wafers.

2 cups (12 ounces) semisweet chocolate chips
1 cup evaporated milk
1 cup granulated sugar
3 cups crushed vanilla wafers
2 cups miniature marshmallows
1 cup walnuts, chopped
½ teaspoon salt

No-Bake Chocolate Cookies

BAR COOKIES

YIELD: 2 to 3 dozen
TOTAL TIME: 15 minutes
CHILLING TIME: 4 hours

1. Lightly grease a 13 by 9-inch baking pan.

2. Combine the cereal, walnuts, coconut, and salt.

3. Melt the shortening in a large saucepan. Remove from the heat and beat in the powdered sugar. Beat in the corn syrup. Blend in the cocoa. Gradually blend in the dry ingredients, coating well. Press the mixture evenly into the prepared baking pan.

4. Refrigerate for 4 hours, or until thoroughly chilled, then cut into large or small bars.

4½ cups puffed wheat cereal
1 cup walnuts, ground
⅔ cup flaked coconut
Pinch of salt
¼ cup vegetable shortening
1 cup powdered sugar
½ cup light corn syrup
⅔ cup unsweetened cocoa powder

No-Bake Cookie Balls

FORMED COOKIES

YIELD: 3 to 5 dozen
TOTAL TIME: 35 minutes
STORING TIME: 2 days

2 teaspoons instant coffee
  powder
½ cup hot water
1 cup (6 ounces) semisweet
  chocolate chips
3 tablespoons light corn
  syrup
3 cups powdered sugar
1¾ cups graham cracker
  crumbs
1 cup walnuts, chopped fine
Powdered sugar for rolling

1. Dissolve the coffee in the hot water.

2. In the top of a double boiler, melt the chocolate over low heat, stirring until smooth. Stir in the corn syrup. Stir in the coffee. Remove from the heat and beat in the powdered sugar. Gradually blend in the graham crackers and walnuts.

3. Pinch off 1-inch pieces of dough and roll into balls. Roll each ball in powdered sugar. Store in an airtight container for at least 2 days before serving.

Baking notes: For cookies with more of a kick, use ½ cup of coffee liqueur in place of the water and coffee.

No-Bake Oatmeal Bars

BAR COOKIES

YIELD: 2 to 3 dozen
TOTAL TIME: 20 minutes
CHILLING TIME: 2 hours

3 tablespoons vegetable
  shortening
3 cups miniature
  marshmallows
¼ cup honey
½ cup peanut butter
1 cup raisins
¼ cup (1½ ounces) rolled
  oats
½ cup peanuts, chopped

1. Lightly grease a 9-inch square baking pan.

2. In a large saucepan, combine the vegetable shortening, marshmallows, honey, and peanut butter and heat, stirring, until smooth. Remove from the heat and gradually blend in the raisins, oats, and peanuts.

3. Spread the mixture evenly in the prepared baking pan. Chill for at least 2 hours.

4. Cut into large or small bars and wrap individually in waxed paper.

Baking notes: You can spread this mixture in a larger pan to make make thinner bars. For a different version, plump the raisins in boiling water while heating the marshmallow mixture. Spread half of the mixture in the prepared pan. Drain the raisins, pat dry, and sprinkle over the marshmallow mixture. Then sprinkle with finely chopped peanuts, and spread the remaining marshmallow mixture on top.

NO-BAKE PEANUT COOKIES

DROP COOKIES

YIELD: 2 to 3 dozen
TOTAL TIME: 30 minutes

1. Line 2 baking sheets with waxed paper.

2. In a saucepan, combine the sugar, vegetable shortening, milk, and cocoa powder and bring to a simmer over low heat, stirring until smooth. Simmer for 2 minutes. Remove from the heat and beat in the peanut butter and vanilla extract. Gradually blend in the oats and peanuts.

3. Drop the dough by spoonfuls 1 inch apart onto the prepared baking sheets. Flatten the cookies with the bottom of a glass dipped in water and then in granulated sugar. Let cool.

2 cups granulated sugar
¼ cup vegetable shortening
½ cup milk
3 tablespoons unsweetened cocoa powder
⅓ cup peanut butter
1 teaspoon vanilla extract
3 cups (18 ounces) rolled oats
1 cup peanuts, chopped fine

NORWEGIAN CHRISTMAS COOKIES

ROLLED COOKIES

YIELD: 4 to 5 dozen
TOTAL TIME: 35 minutes
CHILLING TIME: 8 hours

1. In a large bowl, beat the egg yolks and hard-cooked eggs until smooth. Beat in the powdered sugar. Beat in the butter. Gradually blend in the flour. Cover and chill for 8 hours or overnight.

2. Preheat the oven to 350 degrees. Lightly grease 2 baking sheets.

3. In a small bowl, beat the egg whites until stiff but not dry.

4. On a floured surface, roll out the dough to a thickness of ½ inch. Cut the dough into pencil-thin strips about 8 inches long. For each cookie, braid 3 strips together and form into a wreath, placing them 1 inch apart on the prepared baking sheets. Brush the egg whites over the wreaths and sprinkle with powdered sugar.

5. Bake for 12 to 15 minutes, until golden brown. Transfer to wire racks to cool.

Baking notes: It is important to let the dough mix sit for 8 hours or overnight. For added taste and texture, combine finely chopped hazelnuts with the powdered sugar for sprinkling.

2 large eggs, separated
2 hard-boiled large eggs, chopped fine
1½ cups powdered sugar
¾ cup butter, at room temperature
2 cups all-purpose flour
Powdered sugar for sprinkling

NUGGETS

DROP COOKIES

YIELD: 3 to 4 dozen
TOTAL TIME: 30 minutes
CHILLING TIME: 6 hours

2 cups all-purpose flour
½ teaspoons baking soda
½ teaspoons salt
⅔ cup vegetable shortening
1 cup granulated sugar
⅔ cup peanut butter
3 large eggs
⅓ cup milk
2 cups (12 ounces) rolled
 oats
1 cup raisins
1 cup walnuts, chopped
 (optional)
1 cup dates, pitted and
 chopped (optional)

1. Combine the flour, baking soda, and salt.

2. In a large bowl, cream the vegetable shortening and sugar. Beat in the peanut butter. Beat in the eggs. Beat in the milk. Gradually blend in the dry ingredients. Fold in the oats, raisins, and the optional walnuts and dates. Cover and chill for 6 hours.

3. Preheat the oven to 375 degrees.

4. Drop the dough by spoonfuls 1½ inches apart onto ungreased baking sheets.

5. Bake for 12 to 15 minutes, or until lightly colored. Transfer to wire racks to cool.

Baking notes: Two cups of chopped dried fruit may be used in place of the raisins and dates; instead of adding the chopped nuts to the dough, sprinkle them over the tops of the cookies before baking.

NÜRNBERGERS

DROP COOKIES

YIELD: 5 to 6 dozen
TOTAL TIME: 30 minutes
CHILLING TIME: 24 hours

5½ cups all-purpose flour
1 teaspoon baking soda
¼ teaspoon baking powder
2 teaspoons ground
 cinnamon
½ teaspoon ground nutmeg
¼ teaspoon ground cloves
1½ cups packed light
 brown sugar
4 large eggs
2 cups honey
1 tablespoon plus 1
 teaspoon vanilla extract
⅔ cup orange peel, zested
 and chopped
1 cup walnuts, chopped fine

1. Combine the flour, baking soda, baking powder, and spices.

2. In a large bowl, beat together the brown sugar and eggs until thick. Beat in the honey and vanilla extract. Beat in the orange zest. Gradually blend in the dry ingredients. Stir in the walnuts. Cover and chill for 24 hours.

3. Preheat the oven to 350 degrees.

4. Drop the dough by spoonfuls 1½ inches apart onto ungreased baking sheets.

5. Bake for 8 to 10 minutes, or until lightly colored. Transfer to wire racks to cool.

Baking notes: In place of the citrus zest, mixed candied fruit can be used.

Nut Cookies I

DROP COOKIES

YIELD: 1 to 2 dozen
TOTAL TIME: 35 minutes

1. Preheat the oven to 350 degrees.

2. Combine the flour and baking powder.

3. In a large bowl, cream the butter, vegetable shortening, and sugar. Beat in the eggs. Beat in the vanilla extract. Gradually blend in the dry ingredients.

4. Drop the dough by spoonfuls 1½ inches apart onto ungreased baking sheets. Sprinkle with chopped nuts.

5. Bake for 10 to 12 minutes, until lightly colored. Transfer to wire racks to cool.

¾ cup all-purpose flour
1 teaspoon baking powder
¼ cup butter, at room temperature
¼ cup vegetable shortening
½ cup granulated sugar
2 large eggs
1 teaspoon vanilla extract
¾ cup walnuts, chopped

Nut Cookies II

FORMED COOKIES

YIELD: 3 to 4 dozen
TOTAL TIME: 30 minutes

1. Preheat the oven to 350 degrees. Lightly grease 2 baking sheets.

2. In a large bowl, cream the vegetable shortening, butter, and sugar. Beat in the vanilla extract. Gradually blend in the flour.

3. Spread the pecans in a shallow bowl or pie plate.

4. Pinch off walnut-sized pieces of dough and roll into pencil-thin ropes about 8 inches long. Fold the ropes in half and twist them, roll in the pecans, and place 1 inch apart on the prepared baking sheets.

5. Bake for 12 to 15 minutes, until lightly colored. Transfer to wire racks to cool.

Baking notes: This dough can be formed into crescents, rolled in the pecans, and baked.

¾ cup vegetable shortening
¼ cup butter, at room temperature
½ cup powdered sugar
½ teaspoons vanilla extract
2 cups all-purpose flour
1¼ cups pecans, ground

Nutmeg Cookies

ROLLED COOKIES

YIELD: 3 to 4 dozen
TOTAL TIME: 35 minutes
CHILLING TIME: 4 hours

4 cups all-purpose flour
2 teaspoons baking powder
¼ teaspoon ground nutmeg
¾ cup vegetable shortening
2 cups granulated sugar
2 large eggs
¼ cup milk
1½ teaspoons vanilla extract
1 teaspoon grated lemon zest

1. Combine the flour, baking powder, and nutmeg.

2. In a large bowl, cream the vegetable shortening and sugar. Beat in the eggs. Beat in the milk and vanilla extract. Beat in the lemon zest. Gradually blend in the dry ingredients. Cover and chill for 4 hours.

3. Preheat the oven to 375 degrees. Lightly grease 2 baking sheets.

4. On a floured surface, roll out the dough to a thickness of ⅛ inch. Using a 2-inch round cookie cutter, cut into rounds and place 1 inch apart on the prepared baking sheets.

5. Bake for 10 to 12 minutes, or until lightly colored. Transfer to wire racks to cool.

Nutty Sugar Cookies

ROLLED COOKIES

YIELD: 5 to 6 dozen
TOTAL TIME: 35 minutes

3¾ cups all-purpose flour
1½ teaspoons baking powder
¼ teaspoon salt
1 cup vegetable shortening
1½ cups granulated sugar
2 large eggs
2 teaspoons vanilla extract
1 cup pecans, chopped fine
Colored sugar crystals for sprinkling

1. Preheat the oven to 375 degrees. Lightly grease 2 baking sheets.

2. Combine the flour, baking powder, and salt.

3. In a large bowl, cream the vegetable shortening and sugar. Beat in the eggs one at a time. Beat in the vanilla extract. Gradually blend in the dry ingredients. Fold in the pecans.

4. On a floured surface, roll out the dough to a thickness of ⅛ inch. Using cookie cutters, cut into shapes and place 1 inch apart on the prepared baking sheets.

5. Bake for 8 to 10 minutes, until lightly colored. Sprinkle with sugar crystals and transfer to wire racks to cool.

Baking notes: For softer cookies, roll the dough out to a thickness of ¼ inch; increase the baking time to 10 to 12 minutes.

Oasis Cookies

ROLLED COOKIES

YIELD: 5 to 6 dozen
TOTAL TIME: 35 minutes

1. Preheat the oven to 350 degrees. Lightly grease 2 baking sheets.

2. Combine the flour, baking powder, and baking soda.

3. In a large bowl, cream the vegetable shortening, butter, and brown sugar. Beat in the eggs. Beat in the lemon juice. Gradually blend in the dry ingredients. Fold in the raisins, walnuts, candied citron, prunes, and coconut.

4. On a floured surface, roll out the dough to a thickness of ⅛ inch. Using a 1½-inch round cookie cutter, cut out cookies and place 1½ inches apart on the prepared baking sheets.

5. Bake for 12 to 15 minutes, until lightly colored. Transfer to wire racks to cool.

Baking notes: This is an English recipe; candied citron is particularly popular in England, but mixed candied fruit can be substituted if preferred. Frost the cookies with lemon icing if you like.

4 cups all-purpose flour
1 teaspoon baking powder
1 teaspoon baking soda
1 cup vegetable shortening
½ cup butter, at room temperature
1 cup packed light brown sugar
2 large eggs
1 teaspoon fresh lemon juice
1 cup raisins
1 cup walnuts, chopped
1 cup candied citron, chopped
1 cup prunes, pitted and chopped
½ cup flaked coconut

Oatmeal Brownies

BAR COOKIES

YIELD: 1 to 2 dozen
TOTAL TIME: 35 minutes

1. Preheat the oven to 325 degrees. Lightly grease a 13 by 9-inch baking pan.

2. Melt the chocolate in a double boiler over low heat, stirring until smooth. Remove from the heat.

3. Combine the flour and salt.

4. In a large bowl, cream the vegetable shortening and two sugars. Beat in the eggs one at a time, beating well after each addition. Beat in the vanilla extract. Beat in the melted chocolate. Gradually blend in the dry ingredients. Fold in the oats and walnuts. Spread the mixture evenly in the prepared baking pan.

5. Bake for 25 to 30 minutes, or until a toothpick inserted in the center comes out clean; don't overbake. Cool in the pan on a wire rack before cutting into large or small bars.

Baking notes: Raisins can be added to this batter.

3 ounces semisweet chocolate, chopped
1 cup all-purpose flour
½ teaspoon salt
⅔ cup vegetable shortening
1 cup packed light brown sugar
½ cup granulated sugar
4 large eggs
2 teaspoons vanilla extract
1 cup (6 ounces) rolled oats
1 cup walnuts, chopped

YIELD: 4 to 5 dozen
TOTAL TIME: 30 minutes

1 cup all-purpose flour
1 teaspoon baking powder
½ teaspoon baking soda
¼ teaspoon salt
¾ cup vegetable shortening
1⅔ cups granulated sugar
2 large eggs
1½ teaspoons vanilla
  extract
2½ cups (15 ounces) rolled
  oats
1 cup flaked coconut

Oatmeal-Coconut Crisps

DROP COOKIES

1. Preheat the oven to 375 degrees. Lightly grease 2 baking sheets.

2. Combine the flour, baking powder, baking soda, and salt.

3. In a large bowl, cream the vegetable shortening and sugar. Beat in the eggs. Beat in the vanilla. Gradually blend in the dry ingredients. Fold in the oats and coconut.

4. Drop the dough by spoonfuls 3 inches apart onto the prepared baking sheets.

5. Bake for 12 to 14 minutes, until golden brown. Transfer to wire racks to cool.

YIELD: 3 to 4 dozen
TOTAL TIME: 30 minutes

2 cups all-purpose flour
1 teaspoon baking soda
1 teaspoon ground
  cinnamon
1 teaspoon salt
¾ cup vegetable shortening
1 cup granulated sugar
2 large eggs
1 cup (6 ounces) rolled oats
1 cup raisins

Oatmeal Cookies I

DROP COOKIES

1. Preheat the oven to 350 degrees.

2. Combine the flour, baking soda, cinnamon, and salt.

3. In a large bowl, cream the vegetable shortening and sugar. Beat in the eggs. Gradually blend in the dry ingredients. Fold in the oats and raisins.

4. Drop the dough by spoonfuls 1½ inches apart onto ungreased baking sheets.

5. Bake for 10 to 12 minutes, until lightly colored. Transfer to wire racks to cool.

Baking notes: You can add vanilla extract or almond extract to the dough to enhance the flavor of these cookies.

Oatmeal Cookies II

FORMED COOKIES

1. Combine the flour, wheat germ, baking soda, cinnamon, and salt.

2. In a large bowl, cream the vegetable shortening and two sugars. Beat in the eggs. Beat in the almond extract. Gradually blend in the dry ingredients. Fold in the oats and almonds. Cover and chill for 6 hours.

3. Preheat the oven to 350 degrees. Lightly grease 2 baking sheets.

4. Pinch off walnut-sized pieces of dough and roll into balls. Place 1½ inches apart on the prepared baking sheets. Flatten each ball with the bottom of a glass dipped in water and then in granulated sugar.

5. Bake for 8 to 10 minutes, until golden. Transfer to wire racks to cool.

YIELD: 3 to 4 dozen
TOTAL TIME: 30 minutes
CHILLING TIME: 6 hours

1 cup whole wheat flour
½ cup wheat germ
1 teaspoon baking soda
1 teaspoon ground cinnamon
½ teaspoon salt
1 cup vegetable shortening
1 cup packed light brown sugar
½ cup granulated sugar
2 large eggs
1 teaspoon almond extract
1½ cups (9 ounces) rolled oats
1 cup almonds, chopped
Granulated sugar

Oatmeal Crisps

DROP COOKIES

1. Preheat the oven to 350 degrees.

2. Combine the flour, baking powder, baking soda, and salt.

3. In a large bowl, cream the vegetable shortening and two sugars. Beat in the eggs. Beat in the milk and vanilla extract. Gradually blend in the dry ingredients. Fold in the oats and chocolate chips.

4. Drop the dough by spoonfuls 1½ inches apart onto ungreased baking sheets.

5. Bake for 10 to 12 minutes, until lightly colored. Transfer to wire racks to cool.

Baking notes: You can use semisweet chocolate, milk chocolate, or butterscotch chips. If making these for kids, omit the chips and press several M&Ms into the top of each cookie.

YIELD: 2 to 3 dozen
TOTAL TIME: 30 minutes

1¼ cups all-purpose flour
½ teaspoon baking powder
½ teaspoon baking soda
½ teaspoon salt
1 cup vegetable shortening
¼ cup granulated sugar
1 cup packed light brown sugar
2 large eggs
¼ teaspoon milk
1 teaspoon vanilla extract
3 cups (18 ounces) rolled oats
1 cup (6 ounces) chocolate chips (see Baking notes)

O

OATMEAL HEALTH COOKIES

DROP COOKIES

YIELD: 3 to 5 dozen

TOTAL TIME: 30 minutes

1¼ cups all-purpose flour
¼ teaspoon baking soda
¼ cup carob powder
⅓ cup canola oil
2 large eggs
¼ cup skim milk
½ cup mashed bananas
¼ teaspoon fresh lemon
    juice
1 cup pecans, chopped
⅔ cup rolled oats

1. Preheat the oven to 350 degrees. Lightly grease 2 baking sheets.
2. Combine the flour, baking soda, and, carob powder.
3. In a large bowl, beat the oil and eggs. Beat in the skim milk. Beat in the bananas and lemon juice. Gradually blend in the dry ingredients. Stir in the pecans and oats.
4. Drop the dough by spoonfuls 1½ inches apart onto the prepared baking sheets.
5. Bake for 8 to 10 minutes, until golden. Transfer to wire racks to cool.

OATMEAL LEMONADE BARS

BAR COOKIES

YIELD: 1 to 2 dozen

TOTAL TIME: 50 minutes

FILLING

12 ounces prunes, pitted
¾ cup water
¾ cup frozen lemon juice
    concentrate, thawed
⅓ cup granulated sugar
¼ cup all-purpose flour
¼ teaspoon salt

CRUST

1 cup all-purpose flour
1 cup (6 ounces) rolled oats
¼ teaspoon baking soda
½ cup vegetable shortening
1 cup packed light brown
    sugar

1. Preheat the oven to 400 degrees. Lightly grease a 13 by 9-inch baking pan.
2. To make the filling, combine the prunes, water and lemon juice concentrate in a saucepan and bring to a boil. Cook for 15 minutes, or until the prunes are a puree. Remove from the heat and stir in the sugar, flour, and salt.
3. To make the crust, combine the flour, oats, and baking soda.
4. In a large bowl, cream the vegetable shortening and brown sugar. Gradually blend in the dry ingredients.
5. Spread half of the crust mixture evenly in the bottom of the prepared baking pan. Spread the filling over the crust, leaving a ½-inch border all around. Spread the remaining crust mixture over the filling and press down lightly.
6. Bake for 18 to 20 minutes, until golden brown on top. Cool in the pan on a wire rack before cutting into large or small bars.

OLD-FASHIONED COOKIES

ROLLED COOKIES

YIELD: 5 to 6 dozen

TOTAL TIME: 30 minutes

3½ cups all-purpose flour
2½ teaspoons baking
    powder
½ teaspoon salt
1 cup vegetable shortening
1½ cups granulated sugar
2 large eggs
1 tablespoon rum
Vanilla Icing (see Pantry)

1. Preheat the oven to 350 degrees.
2. Combine the flour, baking powder, and salt.
3. In a large bowl, cream the vegetable shortening and sugar. Beat in the eggs. Beat in the rum. Gradually blend in the dry ingredients.
4. On a floured surface, roll out the dough to a thickness of ¼ inch. Using a 2-inch round cookie cutter, cut out cookies and place 1 inch apart on ungreased baking sheets.
5. Bake for 10 to 12 minutes, until lightly colored and firm to the touch. Transfer to wire racks to cool.
6. Drizzle the icing over the cooled cookies.

Baking notes: You can decorate these cookies with gum drops or small candies—be creative.

OLD-FASHIONED SOFT GINGER COOKIES   ROLLED COOKIES

1. Combine the flour, baking soda, ginger, and salt.

2. In a large bowl, cream the vegetable shortening and brown sugar. Add in the molasses and boiling water, beating until smooth. Gradually blend in the dry ingredients. Cover and chill for at least 6 hours.

3. Preheat the oven to 350 degrees. Lightly grease 2 baking sheets.

4. On a floured surface, roll out the dough to a thickness of ¼ inch. Using a 2-inch round cookie cutter, cut the cookies and place 1 inch apart on the prepared baking sheets.

5. Bake for 18 to 20 minutes, until lightly colored. Transfer to wire racks to cool.

Baking notes: These cookies may be iced once cool. Store tightly covered to retain their flavor and softness; should the cookies become hard, place half an apple in the cookie container for 8 hours to soften them.

YIELD: 4 to 5 dozen
TOTAL TIME: 35 minutes
CHILLING TIME: 6 hours

4 cups all-purpose flour
2 teaspoons baking soda
1 tablespoon ground ginger
1 teaspoon salt
¾ cups vegetable shortening
2 cups packed light brown
*   sugar*
⅔ cup molasses
⅔ cup boiling water

ORANGE BARS I   BAR COOKIES

1. Preheat the oven to 350 degrees. Lightly grease a 13 by 9-inch baking pan.

2. Combine the flour, baking powder, baking soda, and cardamom.

3. In a large bowl, beat together the eggs, vegetable shortening, orange juice concentrate, and orange liqueur until smooth. Gradually blend in the dry ingredients. Stir in the cranberries and almonds. Spread the mixture evenly in the prepared baking pan and sprinkle the coconut over the top.

4. Bake for 20 to 25 minutes, until the top is lightly colored. Cool in the pan on a wire rack before cutting into large or small bars.

YIELD: 2 to 3 dozen
TOTAL TIME: 35 minutes

2½ cups all-purpose flour
2 teaspoons baking powder
1 teaspoon baking soda
1 teaspoon ground
*   cardamom*
2 large eggs
¼ cup vegetable shortening,
*   melted*
1½ cups frozen orange juice
*   concentrate, thawed*
1 teaspoon orange liqueur
1 cup cranberries, chopped
1 cup almonds, chopped
¾ cup shredded coconut

ORANGE BARS II

BAR COOKIES

YIELD: *1 to 3 dozen*
TOTAL TIME: *35 minutes*

2 cups all-purpose flour
1 teaspoon baking soda
1 teaspoon ground cinnamon
½ teaspoon ground cloves
½ teaspoon salt
¾ cup vegetable shortening
1½ cups packed light
   brown sugar
2 large eggs
3 tablespoons fresh orange
   juice
3 tablespoons grated orange
   zest
1 cup raisins
1 cup walnuts, chopped

1. Preheat the oven to 350 degrees. Lightly grease a 9-inch square baking pan.

2. Combine the flour, baking soda, spices, and salt.

3. In a large bowl, cream the vegetable shortening and brown sugar. Beat in the eggs. Beat in the orange juice and zest. Gradually blend in the dry ingredients. Fold in the raisins and walnuts. Spread the mixture evenly in the prepared baking pan.

4. Bake for 25 to 30 minutes, until lightly colored on top. Cool in the pan on a wire rack before cutting into large or small bars.

Baking notes: Frost if desired when cooled; orange or lemon icing is good with these bars.

ORANGE-CRANBERRY BARS

BAR COOKIES

YIELD: *2 to 3 dozen*
TOTAL TIME: *30 minutes*

2 cups all-purpose flour
1 teaspoon baking powder
½ teaspoon baking soda
1 teaspoon ground cinnamon
¼ cup vegetable shortening
3 large eggs
⅔ cup fresh orange juice
½ teaspoon orange extract
1 cup cranberries, minced

TOPPING
⅓ cup almonds, ground
   fine
¼ teaspoon ground nutmeg

1. Preheat the oven to 350 degrees. Lightly grease an 8-inch square baking pan.

2. Combine the flour, baking powder, baking soda, and cinnamon.

3. In a large bowl, beat the vegetable shortening, eggs, orange juice, and orange extract until smooth. Gradually blend in the dry ingredients. Stir in the cranberries. Spread the mixture evenly in the prepared baking pan.

4. Combine the almonds and nutmeg and sprinkle over the top.

5. Bake for 20 to 25 minutes, until golden brown on top. Cool in the pan on a wire rack before cutting into large or small bars.

ORANGE DROPS

DROP COOKIES

YIELD: *3 to 5 dozen*
TOTAL TIME: *30 minutes*

1½ cups all-purpose flour
½ cup whole wheat flour
½ teaspoon baking powder
½ cup canola oil
4 large eggs
½ cup frozen orange juice
   concentrate, thawed
¼ cup orange-flavored
   brandy
1 tablespoon grated orange
   zest

1. Preheat the oven to 375 degrees. Lightly grease 2 baking sheets.

2. Combine the two flours and the baking powder.

3. In a large bowl, beat the oil and eggs until thick and light-colored. Beat in the orange juice concentrate and brandy. Beat in the orange zest. Gradually blend in the dry ingredients.

4. Drop the dough by spoonfuls 1½ inches apart onto the prepared baking sheets.

5. Bake for 6 to 8 minutes, until lightly colored. Transfer to wire racks to cool.

Orange-Pecan Cookies

DROP COOKIES

IELD: 3 to 5 dozen
TOTAL TIME: 35 minutes

1. Preheat the oven to 375 degrees. Lightly grease 2 baking sheets.

2. Combine the flour, baking powder, and salt.

3. In a large bowl, cream the vegetable shortening and sugar. Beat in the egg. Beat in the orange juice and orange liqueur. Gradually blend in the dry ingredients. Stir in the pecans.

4. Drop the dough by spoonfuls 1½ inches apart onto the prepared baking sheets.

5. Bake for 12 to 15 minutes, until lightly colored. Transfer to wire racks to cool.

1 cup all-purpose flour
¼ teaspoon baking powder
¼ teaspoon salt
¼ cup vegetable shortening
1 cup granulated sugar
1 large egg
6 tablespoons fresh orange juice
2 tablespoons orange liqueur
¼ cup pecans, chopped fine

Orange Sugar Rounds

ROLLED COOKIES

YIELD: 1 to 2 dozen
TOTAL TIME: 30 minutes
CHILLING TIME: 4 hours

1. Combine the flour, baking powder, and salt.

2. In a large bowl, cream the vegetable shortening and sugar. Beat in the eggs. Beat in the orange extract and zest. Gradually blend in the dry ingredients. Cover and chill for 4 hours.

3. Preheat the oven to 400 degrees. Lightly grease 2 baking sheets.

4. On a floured surface, roll out the dough to a thickness of ¼ inch. Using a 3-inch round cookie cutter, cut out cookies and place 1 inch apart on the prepared baking sheets. Sprinkle with the granulated sugar.

5. Bake for 6 to 8 minutes, until lightly colored. Transfer to wire racks to cool.

Baking notes: Add a few drops of orange coloring to give an orange tint to these cookies if you like.

2¼ cups all-purpose flour
2 teaspoons baking powder
1 teaspoon salt
¾ cup vegetable shortening
1 cup granulated sugar
2 large eggs
1 tablespoon orange extract
1 tablespoon grated orange zest
Granulated sugar for sprinkling

PASTEL COOKIES

YIELD: 3 to 5 dozen
TOTAL TIME: 30 minutes
CHILLING TIME: 2 hours

3¼ cups all-purpose flour
1 teaspoon baking powder
¼ teaspoon salt
1 cup granulated sugar
1 cup vegetable shortening
2 large egg yolks
6 tablespoons milk

1. Combine the flour, baking powder, and salt.

2. In a large bowl, cream the vegetable shortening and sugar. Beat in the egg yolks. Beat in the milk. Gradually blend in the dry ingredients. Cover and chill for 2 hours.

3. Form the cookies using any of the variations below. Bake in a 350-degree oven for 7 to 10 minutes, until lightly colored. Transfer to wire racks to cool.

Checkerboard: Divide the dough in half and work a few drops of food coloring into one half. Divide each half in three pieces and form each piece into a log. Flatten each log into a ½-inch-thick strip. Stack the strips, alternating the colors and brushing each strip lightly with water. Cut the stack lengthwise into ½-inch-wide strips. Lay these strips on their sides and stack them, reversing every other strip to alternate the pattern and lightly moistening each layer as you stack. Slice, place 1 inch apart on ungreased baking sheets, and bake as directed.

Pinwheels: Divide the dough into 4 pieces and color 2 of them. Form each piece into a log. On a floured surface, roll out each log to a ¼-inch-thick rectangle. Stack the rectangles, alternating the colors and moistening each layer. Starting at a long edge, roll up jelly-roll fashion. Wrap in waxed paper and chill for 2 hours. Cut into ¼-inch-thick slices, place 1 inch apart on ungreased baking sheets, and bake as directed.

Ribbons: Divide the dough into at least 3 pieces. Color each piece of the dough with a different food coloring. Form each piece into a log. On a floured surface, roll each piece into a 2-inch-wide strip ½-inch-thick. Stack the stips 2 to 3 inches high, alternating the colors and moistening each strip. Trim the edges and chill for 2 hours. Cut into ¼-inch-thick slices, lay 1 inch apart on ungreased baking sheets, and bake as directed.

Pumpkins: Color about ⅛ of the dough green for the stems and leaves. Color the remaining dough orange. Roll out the orange dough and use a cookie cutter to cut out 3-inch circles. Place 1 inch apart on ungreased baking sheets and cut a small V in the top of each cookie. Roll out the green dough and cut out freehand stems and leaves. Moisten the Vs and attach the stems and leaves. Decorate with chocolate chips and/or raisins for the eyes and mouthuse your imagination. Bake as directed.

Pastiniai Natale

ROLLED COOKIES

YIELD: 2 to 4 dozen
TOTAL TIME: 30 minutes
CHILLING TIME: 4 hours

1. Combine the flour, baking powder, and salt.

2. In a large bowl, cream the vegetable shortening and sugar. Beat in the eggs. Gradually blend in the dry ingredients. Fold in the lemon zest. Fold in the pistachio nuts. Cover and chill for 4 hours.

3. Preheat the oven to 325 degrees. Lightly grease 2 baking sheets.

4. On a floured surface, roll out the dough to a thickness of ¼ inch. Using a 2-inch round cookie cutter, cut out the cookies and place 1 inch apart on the prepared baking sheets.

5. Bake for 8 to 10 minutes, until lightly colored. Transfer to wire racks to cool.

6. Ice the cooled cookies with the lemon glaze and sprinkle chopped pistachio nuts over the tops.

3 cups all-purpose flour
1 tablespoon baking powder
¼ teaspoon salt
1 tablespoon lemon zest, grated
1 cup vegetable shortening
1 cup granulated sugar
2 large eggs
¼ cup pistachio nuts, chopped
Lemon Glaze (see Pantry)
Chopped pistachio nuts for sprinkling

Peanut Blondies

BAR COOKIES

YIELD: 2 to 3 dozen
TOTAL TIME: 40 minutes

1. Preheat the oven to 350 degrees. Lightly grease a 9-inch square baking pan.

2. In a large bowl, cream the vegetable shortening and brown sugar. Beat in the peanut butter. Beat in the eggs. Beat in the vanilla extract. Gradually blend in the flour. Spread the mixture evenly in the prepared baking pan and sprinkle the chopped nuts over the top.

3. Bake for 30 to 35 minutes, until a knife inserted in the center comes out clean. Cool in the pan on a wire rack before cutting into large or small bars.

Baking notes: Chunky peanut butter makes an even nuttier bar.

½ cup vegetable shortening
2 cups packed light brown sugar
1 cup peanut butter
4 large eggs
2 teaspoons vanilla extract
1 cup all-purpose flour
2 cups peanuts, chopped

Peanut Butter-Banana Squares

BAR COOKIES

YIELD: 2 to 3 dozen
TOTAL TIME: 30 minutes

1. Preheat the oven to 350 degrees. Lightly grease an 8-inch square baking pan.

2. Combine the flour, baking powder, and baking soda.

3. In a large bowl, beat the peanut butter, bananas, and yogurt until smooth. Beat in the egg. Gradually blend in the dry ingredients. Fold in the peanuts. Spread the mixture evenly in the prepared baking pan.

4. Bake for 18 to 20 minutes, until lightly colored on top and firm to the touch. Cool in the pan on a wire rack before cutting into large or small bars.

1 cup all-purpose flour
1 teaspoon baking powder
1 teaspoon baking soda
¼ cup peanut butter
1 cup mashed bananas
¼ cup banana-flavored yogurt
1 large egg
½ cup peanuts, chopped

Peanut Butter Bars

YIELD: 3 to 4 dozen
TOTAL TIME: 45 minutes

1 cup all-purpose flour
½ cup (3 ounces) rolled oats
1 teaspoon baking powder
½ teaspoon salt
½ cup vegetable shortening
¾ cup packed light brown sugar
1 cup peanut butter
3 large eggs
½ cup milk
1 teaspoon vanilla extract
1 cup (6 ounces) semisweet chocolate chips

1. Preheat the oven to 350 degrees.

2. Combine the flour, oats, baking powder, and salt.

3. In a large bowl, cream the vegetable shortening and brown sugar. Beat in the peanut butter. Beat in the eggs. Beat in the milk and vanilla extract. Gradually blend in the dry ingredients. Spread the mixture evenly into an ungreased 8-inch square baking pan.

4. Bake for 25 to 30 minutes, until lightly colored on top. Sprinkle the chocolate chips over the hot crust. Let sit for 1 to 2 minutes to melt the chocolate, then spread it evenly over the top with a spatula. Cool in the pan on a wire rack before cutting into large or small bars.

Baking notes: Use peanut butter chips for the topping to add even more peanut butter flavor. Raisins may be added to the dough if desired.

Peanut Butter Cookies

YIELD: 3 to 4 dozen
TOTAL TIME: 30 minutes
CHILLING TIME: 4 hours

2½ cups all-purpose flour
1 teaspoon baking powder
1 teaspoon baking soda
½ teaspoon ground ginger
½ teaspoon ground cinnamon
¼ teaspoon ground cloves
1 cup packed light brown sugar
2 large eggs
½ cup peanut butter
2 tablespoons sour milk

1. Combine the flour, baking powder, baking soda, and spices.

2. In a large bowl, beat together the brown sugar and eggs. Beat in the peanut butter. Beat in the sour milk. Gradually blend in the dry ingredients. Cover and chill for at least 4 hours.

3. Preheat the oven to 350 degrees. Lightly grease 2 baking sheets.

4. Drop the dough by spoonfuls 1½ inches apart onto the prepared baking sheets. Use a fork dipped in flour to flatten the cookies, making a crisscross pattern.

5. Bake for 8 to 10 minutes, until golden brown. Transfer to wire racks to cool.

Peanut Butter Jumbo Cookies DROP COOKIES

YIELD: *2 to 3 dozen*
TOTAL TIME: *30 minutes*

1. Preheat the oven to 350 degrees. Lightly grease 2 baking sheets.

2. Combine the flour, baking powder, and baking soda.

3. In a large bowl, beat together the brown sugar, vegetable shortening, peanut butter, and eggs. Gradually blend in the dry ingredients. The dough will be very soft.

4. Using a serving spoon, drop the dough by spoonfuls 3 inches apart onto the prepared baking sheets. Using the back of a spoon dipped in flour, spread the cookies into large rounds.

5. Bake for 10 to 12 minutes, until golden brown. Cool on the baking sheets on wire racks.

Baking notes: Chunky peanut butter can be used for more crunch.

2½ cups all-purpose flour
1 teaspoon baking powder
1½ teaspoons baking soda
2 cups packed light brown sugar
1 cup vegetable shortening
1 cup peanut butter
2 large eggs

Peanut Butter Refrigerator Cookies REFRIGERATOR COOKIES

YIELD: *4 to 5 dozen*
TOTAL TIME: *30 minutes*
CHILLING TIME: *8 hours*

1. Combine the flour, baking soda, and salt.

2. In a large bowl, cream the vegetable shortening and sugar. Beat in the peanut butter. Beat in the egg and vanilla extract. Beat in the lemon zest. Gradually blend in the dry ingredients.

3. Divide the dough in half. Shape each half into a log 2 inches in diameter. Wrap in waxed paper and chill for 8 hours or overnight.

4. Preheat the oven to 350 degrees.

5. Cut the logs into ¼-inch-thick slices and place 1 inch apart on ungreased baking sheets. With a fork dipped in flour, flatten each cookie, pressing a crisscross pattern into the top.

6. Bake for 7 to 10 minutes, until lightly colored. Transfer to wire racks to cool.

Baking notes: The logs can be rolled in chopped peanuts before chilling.

1¾ cups all-purpose flour
2 teaspoons baking soda
¼ teaspoon salt
½ cup vegetable shortening
1 cup granulated sugar
½ cup chunky peanut butter
1 large egg
1 teaspoon vanilla extract
½ teaspoon grated lemon zest

Peanut Butter Shortbread

BAR COOKIES

YIELD: 3 to 4 dozen
TOTAL TIME: 40 minutes

1⅓ cups all-purpose flour
1 cup (6 ounces) rolled oats
1 cup packed light brown sugar
1 cup vegetable shortening
¼ cup peanut butter
1 large egg, separated
1 teaspoon vanilla extract
1 cup peanuts, ground fine

1. Preheat the oven to 300 degrees. Lightly grease a 15 by 10-inch baking pan.

2. Combine the flour and oats.

3. In a large bowl, beat the brown sugar, vegetable shortening, and peanut butter together until smooth and creamy. Beat in the egg yolk and vanilla extract. Gradually blend in the dry ingredients. Spread the mixture evenly in the prepared baking pan.

4. In a small bowl, beat the egg white until frothy. Spread over the dough and sprinkle the ground peanuts over the top.

5. Bake for 25 to 30 minutes, until lightly colored on top and firm to the touch. Cut into large or small bars and cool in the pan on a wire rack.

Pear Bars

BAR COOKIES

YIELD: 2 to 3 dozen
TOTAL TIME: 40 minutes

½ cup dates, pitted and chopped fine
1½ cups all-purpose flour
2 teaspoons baking powder
¼ teaspoon ground nutmeg
⅓ cup canola oil
2 large eggs
1½ to 2 pears, peeled, chopped and pureed
1 cup (6 ounces) rolled oats

1. Preheat the oven to 350 degrees. Lightly grease an 8-inch square baking pan.

2. To make the filling, place the dates in a blender and process to a puree adding just enough water to reach the desired consistency.

3. Combine the flour, baking powder, and nutmeg.

4. In a large bowl, beat the oil and eggs until thick and light-colored. Beat in the pureed pears. Gradually blend in the dry ingredients. Stir in the oats.

5. Spread half of the pear mixture evenly in the bottom of the prepared baking pan. Spread the date filling on top of the batter. Spread the remaining batter over the dates.

6. Bake for 20 to 25 minutes, until lightly browned on the top. Cool in the pan on a wire rack before cutting into large or small bars.

Pecan Bars

BAR COOKIES

YIELD: *1 to 2 dozen*

TOTAL TIME: *45 minutes*

1. Preheat the oven to 350 degrees. Lightly grease a 13 by 9-inch baking pan.

2. To make the crust, combine the flour, brown sugar, baking powder, and pecans in a large bowl. Cut in the vegetable shortening until the mixture resembles coarse crumbs. Press the dough evenly into the prepared baking pan.

3. Bake for 10 minutes.

4. To make the filling, combine the flour and salt.

5. In a medium bowl, beat the brown sugar and eggs until thick. Beat in the corn syrup and vanilla extract. Gradually blend in the dry ingredients.

6. Pour the filling over the hot crust and sprinkle the pecans over the top. Bake for 25 to 30 minutes longer, until lightly colored and firm to the touch. Cool in the pan on a wire rack before cutting into large or small bars.

CRUST
1⅓ cups all-purpose flour
½ cup packed light brown
    sugar
½ teaspoon baking powder
¼ cup pecans, chopped
⅓ cup vegetable shortening

FILLING
3 tablespoons all-purpose
    flour
½ teaspoon salt
¼ cup packed light brown
    sugar
2 large eggs
¾ cup light corn syrup
1½ teaspoons vanilla
    extract
¾ cup pecans, ground fine

Pecan Crispies

FORMED COOKIES

YIELD: *2 to 3 dozen*

TOTAL TIME: *30 minutes*

CHILLING TIME: *4 hours*

1. Combine the flour, baking powder, and salt.

2. In a large bowl, cream the vegetable shortening and sugar. Beat in the eggs. Beat in the vanilla extract. Gradually blend in the dry ingredients. If the dough seems too dry, add a little water ½ teaspoonful at a time. Cover and chill for 4 hours.

3. Preheat the oven to 350 degrees.

4. Pinch off walnut-sized pieces of the dough and roll into balls. Roll in the chopped pecans and place 1½ inches apart on ungreased baking sheets. Flatten each ball with the bottom of a glass dipped in powdered sugar.

5. Bake for 6 to 8 minutes, until lightly colored. Cool slightly on the baking sheets, then transfer to wire racks to cool completely.

2 cups all-purpose flour
2 teaspoons baking powder
½ teaspoon salt
1½ cups vegetable
    shortening
1 cup granulated sugar
2 large eggs
1 teaspoon vanilla extract
¾ cup pecans, chopped
Powdered sugar

Pecan Health Cookies

DROP COOKIES

YIELD: 3 to 4 dozen
TOTAL TIME: 30 minutes

½ cup golden raisins
¼ cup currants
1 cup whole wheat flour
1½ cups (9 ounces) rolled oats
¼ cup wheat germ
¼ teaspoon baking powder
½ teaspoon ground nutmeg
½ teaspoon salt
¾ cup vegetable shortening
1¼ cups raw sugar
1 large egg
¼ cup skim milk
¼ cup fresh orange juice
1 cup pecans, chopped

1. Preheat the oven to 350 degrees.

2. Combine the raisins and currants in a small bowl and add just enough water to cover them. Set aside to soak.

3. Combine the flour, oats, wheat germ, baking powder, nutmeg, and salt.

4. In a large bowl, cream the vegetable shortening and sugar. Beat in the egg. Beat in the milk and orange juice. Gradually blend in the dry ingredients. Stir in the pecans. Drain the raisins and currants thoroughly and fold into the dough.

5. Drop the dough by spoonfuls 1½ inches apart onto ungreased baking sheets. Flatten each cookie with the back of a spoon dipped in flour.

6. Bake for 12 to 15 minutes, until golden brown. Transfer to wire racks to cool.

Baking notes: For even more texture, sprinkle the cookies with sesame seeds before you flatten them.

Pecan Shortbread

FORMED COOKIES

YIELD: 4 to 5 dozen
TOTAL TIME: 30 minutes

4½ cups all-purpose flour
1 cup pecans, ground
2 cups (1 pound) butter, at room temperature
2½ cups packed light brown sugar
2 teaspoons vanilla extract

1. Preheat the oven to 350 degrees.

2. Combine the flour and pecans.

3. In a large bowl, cream the butter and brown sugar. Beat in the vanilla extract. Gradually stir in the dry ingredients. The dough will be stiff.

4. Pinch off walnut-sized pieces of dough and roll into small balls. Place the balls 1½ inches apart on ungreased baking sheets and flatten the cookies with the back of a spoon dipped in flour.

5. Bake for 10 to 12 minutes, until lightly colored. Transfer to wire racks to cool.

Pecan Squares

BAR COOKIES

YIELD: 1 to 2 dozen
TOTAL TIME: 50 minutes

CRUST
1 cup all-purpose flour
¼ teaspoon salt
¼ cup vegetable shortening

FILLING
2 tablespoons all-purpose flour
¼ teaspoon salt
¾ cup granulated sugar
2 large eggs
2 teaspoons bourbon
2 cups flaked coconut
1 cup pecans, chopped

1. Preheat the oven to 350 degrees. Lightly grease a 9-inch square baking pan.

2. To make the crust, combine the flour and salt in a medium bowl. Cut in the shortening until the mixture resembles coarse crumbs. Press the dough evenly into the prepared baking pan.

3. Bake for 15 minutes.

4. To make the filling, combine the flour and salt.

5. In a large bowl, beat the sugar and eggs. Beat in the bourbon. Gradually blend in the dry ingredients. Stir in the coconut and pecans.

6. Spread the filling over the hot crust. Bake for 12 to 15 minutes longer, or until lightly colored on top and firm to the touch. Cool in the pan on a wire rack before cutting into large or small bars.

Pennsylvania Dutch Christmas Cookies

DROP COOKIES

YIELD: 7 to 8 dozen
TOTAL TIME: 30 minutes
CHILLING TIME: 4 hours

1. Combine the flour and salt.

2. In a large bowl, cream the vegetable shortening and sugar. Beat in the eggs. Beat in the lemon juice and zest. Gradually blend in the dry ingredients. Fold in the currants. Cover and chill for 4 hours.

3. Preheat the oven to 350 degrees.

4. Drop the dough by spoonfuls 1½ inches apart onto ungreased baking sheets.

5. Bake for 8 to 10 minutes, until lightly colored. Transfer to wire racks to cool.

6. Drizzle the sugar icing over the tops of the cooled cookies.

3½ cups all-purpose flour
¼ teaspoon salt
2 cups vegetable shortening
2¼ cups granulated sugar
6 large eggs
2 tablespoons fresh lemon juice
2 teaspoons grated lemon zest
1½ cups currants
Vanilla Icing (see Pantry)

Pepparkakor

ROLLED COOKIES

YIELD: 6 to 7 dozen
TOTAL TIME: 30 minutes
CHILLING TIME: 24 hours

1. Combine the flour, baking soda, spices, and salt.

2. In a large bowl, cream the butter and sugar. Beat in the molasses. Beat in the orange zest. Gradually blend in the dry ingredients. Fold in the almonds. Cover and chill for 24 hours.

3. Preheat the oven to 350 degrees. Lightly grease 2 baking sheets.

4. On a floured surface, roll out the dough to a thickness of ⅛ inch. Using cookie cutters, cut into shapes and place the cookies 1 inch apart on the prepared baking sheets.

5. Bake for 5 to 7 minutes, until lightly colored. Transfer to wire racks to cool.

Baking notes: These can be decorated with Vanilla Icing (see Pantry).

1⅔ cups all-purpose flour
½ teaspoon baking soda
¾ teaspoon ground ginger
½ teaspoon ground cinnamon
¼ teaspoon ground cloves
¼ teaspoon ground cardamom
½ teaspoon salt
6 tablespoons butter, at room temperature
⅓ cup granulated sugar
¼ cup molasses
1 teaspoon grated orange zest
¼ cup almonds, chopped

PEPPERMINT MERINGUES

FORMED COOKIES

YIELD: *2 to 3 dozen*
TOTAL TIME: *45 minutes*

3 large egg whites
¾ cup granulated sugar
¾ teaspoon cider vinegar
6 drops peppermint oil
*Green food coloring
    (optional)*

1. Preheat the oven to 200 degrees. Line 2 baking sheets with parchment paper.

2. In a large bowl, beat the egg whites until foamy. Gradually beat in the sugar and beat until the whites hold stiff peaks. Fold in the vinegar and peppermint oil. Fold in the optional food coloring and beat for 5 minutes longer.

3. Place the mixture in a cookie press or a pastry bag fitted with a star tip and press or pipe out 1-inch mounds onto the prepared baking sheets, spacing them 1 inch apart.

4. Bake for 30 to 35 minutes, until firm to the touch. Cool on the baking pans on a wire racks.

PERSIMMON COOKIES

DROP COOKIES

YIELD: *4 to 5 dozen*
TOTAL TIME: *30 minutes*

2 cups all-purpose flour
1 cup almonds, ground
1 teaspoon baking soda
*1 teaspoon ground
    cinnamon*
1 teaspoon ground cloves
1 teaspoon ground nutmeg
⅛ teaspoon salt
½ cup vegetable shortening
1 cup granulated sugar
1 large egg
*1 persimmon, peeled and
    pureed*
1 cup raisins (optional)

1. Preheat the oven to 350 degrees.

2. Combine the flour, almonds, baking soda, spices, and salt.

3. In a large bowl, cream the vegetable shortening and sugar. Beat in the egg. Beat in the persimmon puree. Gradually blend in the dry ingredients. Stir in the optional raisins.

4. Drop the dough by spoonfuls 1½ inches apart onto ungreased baking sheets.

5. Bake for 10 to 12 minutes, until lightly colored. Transfer to wire racks to cool.

Baking notes: Use overripe persimmons for these intensely flavorful cookies. These cookies are delicious but perishable; store in the refrigerator.

Pfeffernüsse

ROLLED COOKIES

YIELD: *4 to 5 dozen*
TOTAL TIME: *30 minutes*
CHILLING TIME: *4 hours*
RESTING TIME: *4 hours*

1. Combine the flour, baking powder, spices, and salt.

2. In a large bowl, beat the sugar and eggs until thick and light-colored. Beat in the lemon juice and hazelnut syrup. Beat in the lemon zest. Gradually blend in the dry ingredients. Stir in the hazelnuts. Cover and chill for 4 hours.

3. Lightly grease 2 baking sheets.

4. On a floured surface, roll out the dough to a thickness of ½ inch. Using a 1½-inch round cookie cutter, cut out cookies and place 1 inch apart on the prepared baking sheets. Cover the baking sheets with clean towels and leave undisturbed for 4 hours.

5. Preheat the oven to 350 degrees.

6. Turn the cookies over and place a drop of brandy in the center of each cookie. Bake for 8 to 10 minutes, until lightly colored. Transfer to wire racks to cool.

3 cups all-purpose flour
1 teaspoon baking powder
½ teaspoon ground cinnamon
¼ teaspoon ground nutmeg
¼ teaspoon ground cloves
¼ teaspoon salt
1 cup granulated sugar
3 large eggs
1½ tablespoons fresh lemon juice
1 teaspoon hazelnut syrup (optional)
½ teaspoon grated lemon zest
¼ cup hazelnuts, chopped
About 1 teaspoon brandy

Pineapple-Coconut Bars

BAR COOKIES

YIELD: *2 to 3 dozen*
TOTAL TIME: *40 minutes*

1. Preheat the oven to 350 degrees. Lightly grease a 9-inch square baking pan.

2. Combine the flour, baking powder, and salt.

3. In a large bowl, cream the vegetable shortening and brown sugar. Beat in the eggs. Beat in the pineapple and rum. Gradually blend in the dry ingredients. Stir in the coconut. Spread the mixture evenly in the prepared baking pan.

4. Bake for 25 to 30 minutes, until lightly colored on top. Cool in the pan on a wire rack before cutting into large or small bars.

¾ cup all-purpose flour
¾ teaspoon baking powder
½ teaspoon salt
½ cup vegetable shortening
1 cup packed light brown sugar
2 large eggs
One 8-ounce can crushed pineapple, drained
½ teaspoon rum
¾ cup flaked coconut

PINE NUT COOKIES

FORMED COOKIES

YIELD: 3 to 4 dozen

TOTAL TIME: 30 minutes

½ cup vegetable shortening
2 tablespoons granulated
sugar
2 tablespoons honey
2 tablespoons brandy
1 cup all-purpose flour
¼ cup pine nuts

1. Preheat the oven to 375 degrees. Lightly grease 2 baking sheets.

2. In a large bowl, cream the shortening and sugar. Beat in the honey and brandy. Gradually blend in the flour. Stir in the pine nuts.

3. Pinch off walnut-sized pieces of dough and roll into balls. Place 1 inch apart on the prepared baking sheets.

4. Bake for 8 to 10 minutes, until lightly colored. Transfer to wire racks to cool.

PLAY CLAY

NONEDIBLE COOKIES

YIELD: 1½ pounds dough

2 cups cornstarch
4 cups baking soda
2½ cups water

1. In a saucepan, combine all of the ingredients and stir until smooth. Turn the mixture out onto a flat surface and cover with a damp cloth until cool.

2. Knead until the dough is smooth and elastic. Store in a tightly closed container when not in use.

Baking notes: Food coloring can be added if desired.

P-NUTTIES

FORMED COOKIES

YIELD: 4 to 5 dozen

TOTAL TIME: 30 minutes

1 cup all-purpose flour
2 cups rice flour
¼ cup unsweetened cocoa
powder
1 teaspoon baking powder
¾ cup vegetable shortening
1 cup granulated sugar
1 teaspoon vanilla extract
1 cup raisins, chopped
1 cup peanuts, chopped

1. Preheat the oven to 350 degrees. Lightly grease 2 baking sheets.

2. Combine the two flours, cocoa, and baking powder.

3. In a large bowl, cream the vegetable shortening and sugar. Beat in the vanilla extract. Gradually blend in the dry ingredients. Fold in the raisins. If the dough is not binding, add 1 teaspoon of water at a time to achieve the right consistency.

4. Pinch off walnut-sized pieces of dough and roll into balls. Roll each ball in the chopped peanuts and place 3 inches apart on the prepared baking sheets. Flatten each ball to a thickness of ¼ inch with the bottom of a glass dipped in flour.

5. Bake for 10 to 12 minutes, until golden. Transfer to wire racks to cool.

Baking notes: Decorate with chocolate icing: Combine 1 cup powdered sugar, 2 teaspoons unsweetened cocoa, and 1 teaspoon of water and stir until smooth. Add a drop or so more water if necessary.

Poppy Seed Cookies

REFRIGERATOR COOKIES

YIELD: *3 to 4 dozen*
TOTAL TIME: *25 minutes*
CHILLING TIME: *8 hours*

1. Combine the flour, nutmeg, and salt.

2. In a large bowl, cream the vegetable shortening and sugar. Beat in the egg yolks. Beat in the orange zest. Gradually blend in the dry ingredients. Fold in the poppy seeds.

3. Divide the dough in half. Form each half into a log 2 inches in diameter. Wrap in waxed paper and chill for 8 hours or overnight.

4. Preheat the oven to 350 degrees.

5. Cut the logs into ¼-inch-thick slices and place 1 inch apart on ungreased baking sheets.

6. Bake for 6 to 9 minutes, until lightly colored. Transfer to wire racks to cool.

2¼ cups all-purpose flour
½ teaspoon ground nutmeg
¼ teaspoon salt
1 cup vegetable shortening
1 cup granulated sugar
2 large egg yolks
2 tablespoons grated orange zest
2 tablespoons poppy seeds

Portsmouth Cookies

DROP COOKIES

YIELD: *4 to 5 dozen*
TOTAL TIME: *30 minutes*
CHILLING TIME: *4 hours*

1. Combine the flour, cocoa powder, baking powder, allspice, and salt.

2. In a large bowl, cream together the vegetable shortening and two sugars. Beat in the eggs. Beat in the vanilla extract. Gradually blend in the dry ingredients. Fold in the chocolate chips. Cover and chill for 4 hours.

3. Preheat the oven to 350 degrees. Lightly grease 2 baking sheets.

4. Drop the dough by spoonfuls 1½ inches apart onto the prepared baking sheets.

5. Bake for 10 to 12 minutes, until lightly colored. Transfer to wire racks to cool.

Baking notes: I created this recipe in 1980 in honor of the city of Portsmouth, New Hampshire. For a different flavor variation, substitute coffee liqueur for the vanilla extract.

2½ cups all-purpose flour
1½ teaspoons unsweetened cocoa powder
1 teaspoon baking powder
1 teaspoon ground allspice
Pinch of salt
1 cup vegetable shortening
1 cup granulated sugar
1 cup packed light brown sugar
2 large eggs
1 teaspoon vanilla extract
1½ cups (9 ounces) semisweet chocolate chips

Potato Chip Cookies

DROP COOKIES

YIELD: 3 to 5 dozen

TOTAL TIME: 30 minutes

1 cup vegetable shortening
1 cup powdered sugar
1½ cups all-purpose flour
1 teaspoon vanilla extract
1½ cups potato chips, crushed
Powdered sugar for sprinkling

1. Preheat the oven to 350 degrees.

2. In a large bowl, cream the vegetable shortening and powdered sugar. Stir in the flour. Beat in the vanilla extract. Fold in the potato chips.

3. Drop the dough by spoonfuls 1½ inches apart onto ungreased baking sheets.

4. Bake for 15 to 18 minutes, until lightly colored. Sprinkle with powdered sugar and transfer to wire racks to cool.

Baking notes: It is best to use "lite" potato chips because they are less oily. This is a good cookie for children to make. For an after-school snack rather than a sweet treat, substitute water for the vanilla extract and use one of the many flavored potato chips available. Sprinkle with onion powder instead of powdered sugar.

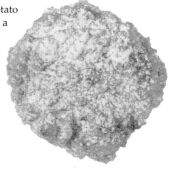

Power Crunch Cookies

DROP COOKIES

YIELD: 2 to 3 dozen

TOTAL TIME: 30 minutes

½ cup all-purpose flour
¼ cup whole wheat flour
½ teaspoon baking soda
¼ teaspoon salt
⅓ cup vegetable shortening
½ cup packed light brown sugar
1 large egg
1 tablespoon warm water
1 teaspoon vanilla extract
1 cup (6 ounces) rolled oats
¾ cup bran cereal
½ cup mixed dried fruit, chopped fine

1. Preheat the oven to 375 degrees.

2. Combine the two flours, the baking soda, and salt.

3. In a large bowl, cream the vegetable shortening and brown sugar. Beat in the egg. Beat in the water and vanilla extract. Gradually blend in the dry ingredients. Fold in the oats, cereal, and dried fruit.

4. Drop the dough by spoonfuls 2 inches apart onto ungreased baking sheets.

5. Bake for 4 to 6 minutes, until lightly colored. Transfer to wire racks to cool.

PRIDE COOKIES

DROP COOKIES

YIELD: 2 to 3 dozen
TOTAL TIME: 30 minutes

1. Preheat the oven to 350 degrees. Lightly grease 2 baking sheets.

2. Combine the flour, baking powder, baking soda, and salt.

3. In a large bowl, cream the butter and two sugars. Beat in the eggs one at a time, beating vigorously after each addition. Beat in the almond extract. Gradually blend in the dry ingredients. Fold in the oats, coconut, almonds, and raisins.

4. Drop the dough by spoonfuls 1½ inches apart onto the prepared baking sheets.

5. Bake for 8 to 10 minutes, until lightly colored. Transfer to wire racks to cool.

2 cups all-purpose flour
1 teaspoon baking powder
1 teaspoon baking soda
¼ teaspoon salt
1 cup butter, at room
*   temperature*
1 cup granulated sugar
1 cup packed light brown
*   sugar*
2 large eggs
2 teaspoons almond extract
3 cups (18 ounces) rolled
*   oats*
1 cup flaked coconut
1 cup almonds, chopped
*   fine*
½ cup golden raisins

PUMPKIN BARS

BAR COOKIES

YIELD: 1 to 2 dozen
TOTAL TIME: 45 minutes

1. Preheat the oven to 350 degrees. Lightly grease a 13 by 9-inch baking pan.

2. Combine the flour, baking powder, baking soda, spices, and salt.

3. In a large bowl, beat the eggs and sugar until thick and light-colored. Beat in the oil. Beat in the pumpkin. Gradually blend in the dry ingredients. Scrape the mixture into the prepared baking pan.

4. Bake for 30 to 35 minutes, until the edges pull away from the sides and the top springs back when lightly touched. Cool in the pan on a wire rack.

5. Frost the cooled cookies with the icing and cut into large or small bars.

2 cups all-purpose flour
2 teaspoons baking powder
1 teaspoon baking soda
2 teaspoons ground
*   cinnamon*
½ teaspoon ground ginger
½ teaspoon ground cloves
½ teaspoon ground nutmeg
¾ teaspoon salt
4 large eggs
2 cups granulated sugar
¾ cup vegetable oil
One 16-ounce can solid-
*   pack pumpkin*
Vanilla Icing (see Pantry)

Pumpkin Cookies

DROP COOKIES

YIELD: 3 to 5 dozen

TOTAL TIME: 30 minutes

1 cup golden raisins
1½ cups (or enough to cover raisins) brandy
2 cups all-purpose flour
1 teaspoon baking powder
½ teaspoon baking soda
1 teaspoon ground cinnamon
½ teaspoon ground nutmeg
¼ teaspoon ground allspice
1 large egg
1 cup vegetable shortening
1 cup solid-pack pumpkin
1 teaspoon brandy from the raisin bowl
½ cup walnuts, chopped

1. Place the raisins in a small bowl and add enough brandy to just cover. Let soak for 15 minutes. Drain thoroughly, reserving the brandy.

2. Preheat the oven to 350 degrees. Lightly grease 2 baking sheets.

3. Combine the flour, baking powder, baking soda, and spices.

4. In a large bowl, beat the egg until thick and light-colored. Beat in the vegetable shortening and pumpkin. Beat in the 1 teaspoon of the reserved brandy. Gradually blend in the dry ingredients. Fold in the walnuts and raisins.

5. Drop the dough by spoonfuls 1½ inches apart onto the prepared baking sheets. Flatten each cookie with the back of a spoon dipped in flour.

6. Bake for 10 to 12 minutes, until lightly colored. Transfer to wire racks to cool.

Pure Fruit Cookies

DROP COOKIES

YIELD: 2 to 3 dozen

TOTAL TIME: 35 minutes

1½ cups (9 ounces) rolled oats
½ cup oat bran cereal
¼ teaspoon salt
⅓ cup canola oil
3 mashed bananas
1 teaspoon vanilla extract
1½ cups dried apricots, chopped
½ cup almonds, chopped fine

1. Preheat the oven to 350 degrees. Lightly grease 2 baking sheets.

2. Combine the oats, oat bran cereal, and salt.

3. In a large bowl, beat the oil, bananas, and vanilla extract until smooth. Gradually blend in the dry ingredients. Stir in the apricots and almonds.

4. Drop the dough by spoonfuls 1½ inches apart onto the prepared baking sheets.

5. Bake for 20 to 25 minutes, or until lightly colored. Transfer to wire racks to cool.

Raisin Bars

BAR COOKIES

1. Preheat the oven to 350 degrees. Lightly grease a 15 by 10-inch baking pan.

2. Combine the flour, baking soda, spices, and salt.

3. In a large bowl, cream the vegetable shortening and two sugars. Beat in the eggs. Beat in the orange juice. Gradually blend in the dry ingredients. Fold in the raisins and coconut. Spread the mixture evenly in the prepared baking pan.

4. Bake for 20 to 25 minutes, until lightly colored on top and firm to the touch.

5. Meanwhile, make the glaze: Combine the sugar, orange juice, and orange zest in a small bowl and stir until smooth.

6. Drizzle the glaze over the hot crust. Cool in the pan on a wire rack before cutting into large or small bars.

YIELD: 3 to 4 dozen
TOTAL TIME: 35 minutes

3 cups all-purpose flour
½ teaspoon baking soda
½ teaspoon ground
  cinnamon
¼ teaspoon ground cloves
½ teaspoon salt
1 cup vegetable shortening
¾ cup granulated sugar
¾ cup packed light brown
  sugar
2 large eggs, lightly beaten
¼ cup fresh orange juice
1 cup raisins
1 cup flaked coconut

GLAZE
¾ cup powdered sugar
1 tablespoon plus 1
  teaspoon fresh orange
  juice
1 teaspoon orange zest,
  chopped

Raisin Bran Cookies

DROP COOKIES

1. Preheat the oven to 350 degrees. Lightly grease 2 baking sheets.

2. In a large bowl, combine the raisin bran, sugar, and apple. Stir in the milk and vanilla extract and mix well.

3. Drop the dough by spoonfuls 1 inch apart onto the prepared baking sheets.

4. Bake for 12 to 15 minutes, until lightly colored. Transfer to wire racks to cool.

YIELD: 3 to 5 dozen
TOTAL TIME: 30 minutes

1 cup raisin bran
½ cup granulated sugar
1 apple, peeled, cored, and
  grated
½ cup milk
1 teaspoon vanilla extract

R

Raisin Sandwich Cookies

ROLLED COOKIES

YIELD: 4 to 5 dozen
TOTAL TIME: 30 minutes
CHILLING TIME: 4 hours

3½ cups all-purpose flour
2 teaspoons baking powder
¼ teaspoon salt
½ cup vegetable shortening
1 cup granulated sugar
2 large eggs
½ cup milk

FILLING
¼ cup butter
½ cup granulated sugar
½ cup raisins
½ teaspoon grated orange zest
1 tablespoon all-purpose flour

1. Combine the flour, baking powder, and salt.

2. In a large bowl, cream the vegetable shortening and sugar. Beat in the eggs. Beat in the milk. Gradually blend in the dry ingredients. Cover and chill for 4 hours.

3. Meanwhile, make the filling: In a medium saucepan melt the butter with the sugar. Add the raisins and orange zest. Sprinkle in the flour and continue stirring until the mixture thickens.

4. Preheat the oven to 350 degrees. Lightly grease 2 baking sheets.

5. On a floured surface, roll out the dough to a thickness of ⅛ inch. Using a 1½-inch round cookie cutter, cut out an even number of rounds. Place half the rounds 1 inch apart on the prepared baking sheets and spread each one with a small spoonful of the filling. Place the remaining rounds on top.

6. Bake for 10 to 12 minutes, until golden brown. Transfer to wire racks to cool.

Raspberry Meringue Bars

BAR COOKIES

YIELD: 1 to 4 dozen
TOTAL TIME: 45 minutes

CRUST
¾ cup vegetable shortening
¼ cup granulated sugar
2 large eggs, yolks
1½ cups all-purpose flour

TOPPING
2 large egg whites
½ cup granulated sugar
1 cup almonds, chopped fine
1 cup raspberry puree
1 cup flaked coconut

1. Preheat the oven to 350 degrees. Lightly grease a 13 by 9-inch baking pan.

2. To make the crust, cream the vegetable shortening and sugar in a large bowl. Beat in the egg yolks. Gradually blend in the flour. Spread the dough evenly in the prepared baking pan.

3. Bake for 15 minutes.

4. Meanwhile, make the topping: In a large bowl, beat the egg whites until foamy. Gradually beat in the sugar and beat until the whites hold stiff peaks. Fold in the chopped nuts.

5. Spread the raspberry puree over the hot crust and sprinkle with the coconut. Spread the topping over the coconut.

6. Bake for 20 to 25 minutes longer, or until lightly colored on top and firm to the touch. Cool in the pan on a wire rack before cutting into large or small bars.

Refrigerator Cookies

REFRIGERATOR COOKIES

1. Combine the flour, baking powder, and salt.

2. In a large bowl, cream the vegetable shortening and sugar. Beat in the eggs and lemon extract. Gradually blend in the dry ingredients.

3. Divide the dough into 4 pieces. Form each piece into a log 2 inches in diameter. Wrap in waxed paper and chill for 2 hours.

4. Preheat the oven to 350 degrees.

5. Cut the logs into ¼-inch-thick slices and place 1 inch apart on ungreased baking sheets.

6. Bake for 10 to 12 minutes, until lightly colored. Transfer to wire racks to cool.

Baking notes: These are just some of the possible variations using this basic dough.

Black-and-White Cookies: Add in 1 tablespoon of unsweetened cocoa powder or melted chocolate to half the dough and ½ teaspoon of mint extract to the other half. Chill, roll out and cut into rounds. Sandwich the cooled cookies with a creamy fudge frosting (see Pantry), using one of each type for each sandwich.

Pecan Cookies: Add ¼ to ½ cup finely chopped pecans to the dough. Press a pecan half into each cookie before baking.

Filled Cookies: Place the cookies on the baking sheets and make a shallow indentation in the centers with your finger. Fill with a filling of your choice.

Banana Cookies: Use banana extract in place of the lemon extract.

Peppermint Cookies: Substitute 3 drops of peppermint oil for the lemon extract.

Almond Cookies: Substitute almond extract for the lemon extract and add ½ cup finely ground almonds to the dough.

YIELD: will vary
TOTAL TIME: 30 minutes
CHILLING TIME: 2 hours

3½ cups all-purpose flour
2 teaspoons baking powder
½ teaspoon salt
1 cup vegetable shortening
2 cups granulated sugar
2 large eggs
2 teaspoons lemon extract

Refrigerator Spice Cookies

FORMED COOKIES

1. Combine the flour, baking soda, and spices.

2. In a large bowl, cream the vegetable shortening and two sugars. Beat in the egg. Gradually blend in the dry ingredients.

3. Divide the dough in half. Form each half into a log 1½ inches in diameter. Wrap in waxed paper and chill for 8 hours.

4. Preheat the oven to 375 degrees. Lightly grease 2 baking sheets.

5. Cut the logs into ¼-inch-thick slices. Place 1 inch apart on the prepared baking sheets.

6. Bake for 10 to 15 minutes, until lightly colored. Transfer to wire racks to cool.

YIELD: 3 to 6 dozen
TOTAL TIME: 30 minutes
CHILLING TIME: 8 hours

2¾ cups all-purpose flour
1 teaspoon baking soda
1 teaspoon ground cinnamon
1 teaspoon ground nutmeg
½ teaspoon ground cloves
1 cup vegetable shortening
½ cup granulated sugar
½ cup packed light brown sugar
1 large egg

Rocky Road Bars

YIELD: 1 to 3 dozen
TOTAL TIME: 40 minutes

¼ cup all-purpose flour
½ cup walnuts, ground fine
¼ teaspoon baking powder
⅛ teaspoon salt
1 tablespoon vegetable shortening
⅓ cup packed light brown sugar
½ teaspoon vanilla extract

TOPPING
1 cup miniature marshmallows
1 cup (6 ounces) semisweet chocolate chips
½ cup walnuts, chopped

1. Preheat the oven to 350 degrees. Lightly grease an 8-inch square baking pan.

2. Combine the flour, walnuts, baking powder, and salt.

3. In a large bowl, cream the vegetable shortening and brown sugar. Beat in the vanilla extract. Gradually blend in the dry ingredients. Spread the mixture evenly in the prepared baking pan.

4. Bake for 15 minutes.

5. Meanwhile, to make the topping: In a small bowl, combine the marshmallows, chocolate chips, and walnuts and toss to blend.

6. Spread the topping mixture evenly over the hot crust. Bake for 15 to 18 minutes longer, until the topping is melted and lightly colored. Cool in the pan on a wire rack before cutting into large or small bars.

Rugelach

YIELD: 2 to 3 dozen
TOTAL TIME: 40 minutes
CHILLING TIME: 4 hours

1 cup butter, at room temperature
8 ounces cream cheese, at room temperature
6 tablespoons powdered sugar
1 tablespoon raspberry-flavored brandy
2¾ cups all-purpose flour

FILLING
¾ cup packed light brown sugar
½ cup almonds, chopped
½ cup raisins, plumped in warm water and drained
1 teaspoon ground cinnamon

1. Combine the butter, cream cheese, and powdered sugar in a large bowl and beat until smooth and creamy. Beat in the brandy. Gradually blend in the flour. Divide the dough into 4 pieces. Wrap the dough in waxed paper and chill for 4 hours.

2. Preheat the oven to 350 degrees. Lightly grease 2 baking sheets.

3. To make the filling, combine all the ingredients in a small bowl and toss to mix.

4. On a floured surface, roll out each piece of dough into a 9-inch circle. Spread one-quarter of the filling over each round. Cut each round into 8 wedges. Starting at the wide end, roll up each wedge. Place 1 inch apart on the prepared baking sheets, curving the ends to form crescents.

5. Bake for 20 to 25 minutes, until lightly colored. Transfer to wire racks to cool.

RUM BALLS

FORMED COOKIES

1. In a large bowl, combine all of the ingredients and stir to form a sticky dough. Pinch off small pieces of dough and roll into balls. Roll each ball in powdered sugar.

2. Store in an airtight container for at least 1 week before serving. Before serving, roll the balls a second time in powdered sugar.

Baking notes: These cookies are not for children.

YIELD: 3 to 5 dozen
TOTAL TIME: 30 minutes
AGING TIME: 1 week

2½ cups crushed
    gingersnaps
½ cup honey
6 tablespoons rum
1½ cups pecans, ground
    fine
Powdered sugar for rolling

RUM COOKIES

DROP COOKIES

1. Combine the flour, baking powder, and salt.

2. In a large bowl, cream the butter and sugar. Beat in the eggs. Beat in the rum and almond extract. Gradually blend in the dry ingredients. Cover and chill for 4 hours.

3. Preheat the oven to 400 degrees.

4. Drop the dough by spoonfuls 1½ inches apart onto the prepared baking sheets.

5. Bake for 6 to 8 minutes, until lightly colored. Transfer to wire racks to cool.

YIELD: 6 to 8 dozen
TOTAL TIME: 30 minutes
CHILLING TIME: 4 hours

2 cups all-purpose flour
2 teaspoons baking powder
½ teaspoon salt
1 cup butter, at room
    temperature
1 cup packed light brown
    sugar
3 large eggs
½ cup rum
1 teaspoon almond extract

RUM-TOPPED GINGER COOKIES

ROLLED COOKIES

YIELD: 3 to 4 dozen
TOTAL TIME: 45 minutes
CHILLING TIME: 30 minutes

2 cups all-purpose flour
⅔ cup granulated sugar
2 teaspoons ground ginger
Pinch of salt
½ cup butter, chilled and cut into small pieces
½ cup large-curd cottage cheese
1 large egg white, beaten with 2 teaspoons water for egg glaze
Colored sugar crystals

TOPPING
1½ cups butter, at room temperature
3 cups powdered sugar
1 tablespoon minced crystallized ginger
3 tablespoons rum

1. Preheat oven to 350 degrees. Lightly grease 2 baking sheets.

2. In a large bowl, combine the flour, sugar, ginger, and salt. Cut in the butter until the mixture resembles coarse crumbs. Blend in the cottage cheese. The dough will be stiff. If the dough is too dry, add a little water 1 teaspoon at a time. Cover and chill for 30 minutes.

3. On a floured surface, roll out dough to a thickness of ⅛ inch. Using a 2-inch round or 2-inch scalloped cookie cutter, cut out cookies. Place 1 inch apart on the prepared baking sheets and brush with egg glaze. Sprinkle with the sugar crystals.

4. Bake for 10 to 12 minutes, or until browned around the edges. Transfer to wire racks to cool.

5. To make the topping, cream the butter and sugar in a small bowl. Beat in the ginger and rum. Spread over the top of the cooled cookies.

RUSSIAN TEA BISCUITS

FORMED COOKIES

YIELD: 3 to 6 dozen
TOTAL TIME: 35 minutes

2¼ cups all-purpose flour
¼ teaspoon salt
1 cup butter, at room temperature
¾ cup powdered sugar
1 teaspoon vodka
¾ cup hazelnuts, chopped fine
Powdered sugar for sprinkling

1. Preheat the oven to 325 degrees.

2. Combine the flour and salt.

3. In a large bowl, cream the butter and powdered sugar. Beat in the vodka. Gradually blend in the dry ingredients. Fold in the hazelnuts.

4. Pinch off walnut-sized pieces of dough and roll into balls. Place 1½ inches apart on ungreased baking sheets. Flatten each ball with the bottom of a glass dipped in flour.

5. Bake for 12 to 15 minutes, until lightly colored. Sprinkle with powdered sugar and transfer to wire racks to cool

SAND TARTS

ROLLED COOKIES

1. Combine the flour and baking powder.

2. In a large bowl, cream the butter and sugar. Beat in the egg. Gradually blend in the dry ingredients. Cover and chill for 2 hours.

3. Preheat the oven to 375 degrees. Lightly grease 2 baking sheets.

4. In a cup, combine the sugar and cinnamon for the topping.

5. On a floured surface, roll out the dough to a thickness of ⅛ inch. Using a 2-inch round cookie cutter, cut out cookies and place 1 inch apart on the prepared baking sheets. Brush the rounds with the beaten egg white and sprinkle the cinnamon sugar over the top. Press a whole almond into the center of each round.

6. Bake for 8 to 10 minutes, until lightly colored. Transfer to wire racks to cool.

YIELD: 4 to 5 dozen
TOTAL TIME: 30 minutes
CHILLING TIME: 2 hours

2 cups all-purpose flour
1½ teaspoons baking powder
½ cup butter, at room temperature
1 cup granulated sugar
1 large egg

TOPPING
1 tablespoon granulated sugar
½ teaspoon ground cinnamon
1 large egg white, beaten
About 1 cup whole almonds

SCOTCH SHORTBREAD

ROLLED COOKIES

1. In a large bowl, cream the butter and powdered sugar. Gradually blend in the flour to make a smooth dough. Divide the dough into quarters. Wrap in waxed paper and chill for 2 hours.

2. Preheat the oven to 350 degrees.

3. Work with one piece of dough at a time, keeping the remaining dough in the refrigerator. On a floured surface, roll out each piece of dough to a 6-inch round. Place the rounds 1 inch apart on ungreased baking sheets and prick all over with a fork. Score each round into wedges.

4. Bake for 12 to 15 minutes, until very dry and lightly colored. Transfer to wire racks to cool, then cut into wedges.

Baking notes: Be sure to use unsalted butter. This dough can also be rolled out to a thickness of ½ inch and cut into small rounds. Or it can be pressed into a 13 by-9 inch baking pan, pricked all over with a fork, and scored into bite-sized pieces.

YIELD: 2 to 3 dozen
TOTAL TIME: 30 minutes
CHILLING TIME: 2 hours

2 cups (1 pound) butter, at room temperature
1 cup powdered sugar
4 cups all-purpose flour

Scottish Oatcakes

ROLLED COOKIES

YIELD: 1 to 3 dozen
TOTAL TIME: 30 minutes

1 tablespoon vegetable oil
1 teaspoon baking soda
½ teaspoon salt
2 cups rolled oats
Boiling water

1. In a large bowl, combine the vegetable oil, baking soda, and salt. Gradually blend in the oats. Add enough boiling water ½ teaspoonful at a time to make a soft dough.

2. Scatter additional oatmeal on a board and knead the dough. Roll out the dough to a thickness of ½ inch. With a sharp knife, cut into 2½- by 3-inch small triangles.

3. Heat a griddle or nonstick frying pan. Cook the triangles turning only once, until golden brown. Transfer to a plate and cover with a clean towel.

Baking notes: The recipe for these oatcakes was created before there were ovens as we know them today. These are Scottish biscuits served warm with preserves or marmalade.

Sesame Cheese Wafers

REFRIGERATOR COOKIES

YIELD: 2 to 3 dozen
TOTAL TIME: 30 minutes
CHILLING TIME: 24 hours

1 cup soft cheese, such as brie
¼ cup vegetable shortening
⅔ cup all-purpose flour
3 tablespoons sesame seeds

1. In a large bowl, beat the cheese and vegetable shortening until smooth. Gradually blend in the flour. If the dough seems a little dry, add water a teaspoonful at a time. If it seems very soft, add a little all-purpose flour a tablespoonful at a time. Shape the dough into a log and roll the log in the sesame seeds. Wrap in waxed paper and chill for 24 hours.

2. Preheat the oven to 375 degrees. Lightly grease 2 baking sheets.

3. Cut the log into ¼-inch-thick slices and place 1 inch apart on the prepared baking sheets.

4. Bake for 10 to 12 minutes, until lightly colored. Transfer to wire racks to cool.

Sesame Chips

FORMED COOKIES

YIELD: 2 to 3 dozen
TOTAL TIME: 30 minutes

3 cups whole wheat flour
1 cup all-purpose flour
½ teaspoon baking soda
½ teaspoon salt
1 cup vegetable shortening
1 cup granulated sugar
1 large egg
1 teaspoon vanilla extract
2 cups sesame seeds

1. Preheat the oven to 375 degrees. Lightly grease 2 baking sheets.

2. Combine the two flours, the baking soda, and salt.

3. In a large bowl, cream the vegetable shortening and sugar. Beat in the egg. Beat in the vanilla extract. Gradually blend in the dry ingredients.

4. Pinch off walnut-sized pieces of dough and roll into balls, flouring your hands if the dough is sticky. Roll the balls in the sesame seeds and place 1½ inches apart on the prepared baking sheets. Flatten the balls with the bottom of a glass dipped in flour.

5. Bake for 8 to 10 minutes, until lightly colored. Transfer to wire racks to cool.

Baking notes: Use coarse-ground whole wheat flour for these cookies. If a product called Wheat-a-lax is available in your area, use it.

Seven-Layer Cookies

BAR COOKIES

YIELD: 2 to 3 dozen
TOTAL TIME: 35 minutes

1 cup vegetable shortening
1 cup cookie crumbs, such as vanilla wafers or Oreos
1 cup (6 ounces) semisweet chocolate chips
1 cup coconut
1 cup almonds, chopped
1 cup (6 ounces) butterscotch chips
One 14-ounce can sweetened condensed milk

1. Preheat the oven to 350 degrees.

2. Melt the vegetable shortening in a small saucepan and pour into a 13 by 9-inch baking pan. Sprinkle the cookie crumbs over the shortening. Sprinkle the chocolate chips over the crumbs, then sprinkle the coconut over the chocolate chips. Sprinkle the almonds over the coconut and the butterscotch chips over the almonds. Drizzle the condensed milk over the top.

3. Bake for 20 to 30 minutes, until firm to the touch. Cool in the pan on a wire rack before cutting into large or small bars.

SIMPLE CREAM CHEESE COOKIES

ROLLED COOKIES

YIELD: 3 to 4 dozen
TOTAL TIME: 30 minutes

8 ounces cream cheese, at
    room temperature
¼ cup butter, at room
    temperature
3 tablespoons powdered
    sugar
½ teaspoon vanilla extract
2 cups all-purpose flour
About ¼ cup fruit preserves
    (optional)
Powdered sugar for
    sprinkling

1. Preheat the oven to 350 degrees. Lightly grease 2 baking sheets.

2. In a large bowl, beat the cream cheese, butter, and powdered sugar until smooth and creamy. Beat in the vanilla extract. Gradually blend in the flour.

3. On a floured surface roll the dough out to a thickness of ¼ inch. Using a 2-inch round cookie cutter, cut into rounds and place 1 inch apart on the prepared baking sheets. If desired, place a dab of fruit preserves in the center of each cookie.

4. Bake for 12 to 15 minutes, until lightly colored. Sprinkle with powdered sugar and transfer to wire racks to cool.

SNICKER DOODLES

FORMED COOKIES

YIELD: 3 to 4 dozen
TOTAL TIME: 30 minutes

3 cups all-purpose flour
2 teaspoons baking powder
¼ teaspoon salt
1 cup vegetable shortening
1⅓ cups granulated sugar
2 large eggs
1 teaspoon vanilla extract
3 tablespoons granulated
    sugar
2 teaspoons ground
    cinnamon

1. Preheat the oven to 350 degrees. Lightly grease 2 baking sheets.

2. Combine the flour, baking powder, and salt.

3. In a large bowl, cream the vegetable shortening and sugar. Beat in the eggs. Beat in the vanilla extract. Gradually blend in the dry ingredients.

4. In a small bowl, combine the sugar and cinnamon.

5. Pinch off 1-inch pieces of dough and roll into balls. Roll each ball in the cinnamon sugar and place 1 inch apart on the prepared baking sheets.

6. Bake for 10 to 12 minutes, until lightly colored. Transfer to wire racks to cool.

SODA CRACKER COOKIES

BAR COOKIES

YIELD: 3 to 4 dozen
TOTAL TIME: 20 minutes

18 double-packed soda
   crackers
1 cup butter
1 cup packed light brown
   sugar
1 cup (6 ounces) semisweet
   chocolate chips
¾ cup walnuts, chopped
   fine

1. Preheat the oven to 375 degrees. Line a 15 by 10-inch baking pan with aluminum foil and grease it well. Line the pan with soda crackers.

2. In a medium saucepan, melt the butter. Add the brown sugar and cook, stirring until it dissolves. Bring to a boil and cook for about 3 minutes, stirring constantly. Immediately pour the mixture over the soda crackers.

3. Bake for 3 to 5 minutes, or until the mixture starts to bubble.

4. Spread the chocolate chips over the hot cookies. Let sit for a minute or so to melt the chocolate, then use a knife or spatula to spread the chocolate evenly over the top. Sprinkle with chopped walnuts. Let cool, then cut into large or small bars.

Baking notes: These are an instant favorite of everyone who tries them.

SOME-MORE BARS

BAR COOKIES

YIELD: 1 to 2 dozen
TOTAL TIME: 30 minutes

¾ cup vegetable shortening
⅓ cup granulated sugar
3 cups graham cracker
   crumbs
2 cups miniature
   marshmallows
1 cup (6 ounces) semisweet
   chocolate chips

1. Preheat the oven to 350 degrees. Lightly grease a 13 by 9-inch baking pan.

2. In a large bowl, cream the vegetable shortening and sugar. Gradually blend in the cookie crumbs. Press half of this mixture firmly into the prepared baking pan. Sprinkle the marshmallows and chocolate chips over the top. Crumble over the remaining crumb mix.

3. Bake for 8 to 10 minutes, until firm to the touch. Cool in the pan on a wire rack before cutting into large or small bars.

SOUR CREAM AND SPICE COOKIES

ROLLED COOKIES

YIELD: 4 to 5 dozen
TOTAL TIME: 30 minutes
CHILLING TIME: 4 hours

3 cups all-purpose flour
1½ teaspoons baking
   powder
½ teaspoon baking soda
½ teaspoon ground
   coriander
½ teaspoon salt
½ cup vegetable shortening
1 cup granulated sugar
1 large egg
½ cup sour cream
½ teaspoon vanilla extract
½ teaspoon almond extract

1. Combine the flour, baking powder, baking soda, coriander, and salt.

2. In a large bowl, cream the vegetable shortening and sugar. Beat in the egg. Beat in the sour cream. Beat in the vanilla and almond extracts. Gradually blend in the dry ingredients. Cover and chill for 4 hours.

3. Preheat the oven to 350 degrees. Lightly grease 2 baking sheets.

4. On a floured surface, roll out the dough to a thickness of ¼ inch. Using a 2-inch round cookie cutter, cut into rounds and place 1 inch apart on the prepared baking sheets.

5. Bake for 10 to 12 minutes, until lightly colored. Transfer to wire racks to cool

SPANISH CHRISTMAS COOKIES

ROLLED COOKIES

YIELD: 3 to 5 dozen
TOTAL TIME: 30 minutes
CHILLING TIME: 2 hours

1½ cups all-purpose flour
¼ teaspoon ground
    cinnamon
¼ teaspoon ground allspice
6 tablespoons butter, at
    room temperature
¼ cup granulated sugar
1 large egg
2 tablespoons canola oil
1½ teaspoons white port
½ teaspoon grated orange
    zest
¼ teaspoon grated lemon
    zest

1. Combine the flour and spices.

2. In a large bowl, cream the butter and sugar. Beat in the egg and oil. Beat in the port. Beat in the orange and lemon zest. Gradually blend in the dry ingredients. Cover and chill for 2 hours.

3. Preheat the oven to 350 degrees.

4. On a floured surface, roll out the dough to a thickness of ¼ inch. Using 2-inch round cookie cutter, cut into rounds and place 1 inch apart on ungreased baking sheets.

5. Bake for 12 to 15 minutes, until lightly colored. Transfer to wire racks to cool.

6. Sprinkle the cooled cookies with powdered sugar.

SPICE BARS

BAR COOKIES

YIELD: 2 to 3 dozen
TOTAL TIME: 35 minutes

1 cup all-purpose flour
¼ cup unsweetened cocoa
    powder
1 teaspoon baking powder
1 teaspoon ground
    cinnamon
½ teaspoon ground cloves
½ teaspoon ground allspice
Pinch of salt
¼ cup vegetable shortening
1 cup granulated sugar
3 large eggs
1 teaspoon vanilla extract
½ cup raisins
½ cup walnuts, chopped

1. Preheat the oven to 350 degrees. Lightly grease a 13 by 9-inch baking pan.

2. Combine the flour, cocoa powder, baking powder, spices, and salt.

3. In a large bowl, cream the vegetable shortening and sugar. Beat in the eggs. Beat in the vanilla extract. Gradually blend in the dry ingredients. Fold in the raisins and walnuts. Spread the dough evenly in the prepared baking pan.

4. Bake for 20 to 30 minutes, until the tip of a knife inserted in the center comes out clean. Cool in the pan on a wire rack before cutting into large or small bars.

Baking notes: If you want to frost these bars, do so while they are still warm.

Spice Cones

DROP COOKIES

1. Preheat the oven to 350 degrees.

2. Combine the flour and spices.

3. In a large bowl, cream the vegetable shortening and sugar. Beat in the molasses and brandy. Gradually blend in the dry ingredients.

4. Drop the dough by spoonfuls 2½ inches apart onto ungreased baking sheets.

5. Bake for 5 to 6 minutes, until golden brown. As soon as the cookies are cool enough to handle, remove them from the baking sheet and roll up around metal cone shapes. Place seam side down on wire racks to cool.

Baking notes: You will need metal cone forms for this recipe; they are available in specialty cookware shops. If the cookies harden before you are able to form them, reheat them for about 30 seconds in the oven. These cones can be filled with many types of dessert topping or ice cream. If you are filling them with ice cream, chill the cones in the freezer for at least 30 minutes before filling them. If you fill the cookies too soon, they will soften before they are served.

YIELD: 5 to 6 dozen
TOTAL TIME: 30 minutes

¾ cups all-purpose flour
1½ teaspoons ground ginger
1½ teaspoons ground nutmeg
6 tablespoons vegetable shortening
½ cup packed light brown sugar
¼ cup molasses
1 tablespoon brandy

Spice Cookies

ROLLED COOKIES

1. Combine the flour, baking powder, spices, and salt.

2. In a large bowl, beat the sugar and eggs until thick and light-colored. Beat in the orange juice concentrate and orange zest. Gradually blend in the dry ingredients. Stir in the hazelnuts. Cover and chill for 4 hours.

3. Lightly grease 2 baking sheets.

4. On a floured surface, roll the dough out to a thickness of ½ inch. Using a 1½-inch round cookie cutter, cut out the cookies and place 1 inch apart on the prepared baking sheets. Cover with clean towels and set aside for 8 hours.

5. Preheat the oven to 350 degrees.

6. Turn the cookies over and place a drop of amaretto in the center of each one. Bake for 8 to 10 minutes, until lightly colored. Transfer to wire racks to cool.

YIELD: 4 to 5 dozen
TOTAL TIME: 30 minutes
CHILLING TIME: 4 hours
RESTING TIME: 8 hours

3 cups all-purpose flour
1 teaspoon baking powder
½ teaspoon ground cinnamon
¼ teaspoon ground nutmeg
¼ teaspoon ground cloves
¼ teaspoon salt
1 cup granulated sugar
3 large eggs
1½ tablespoons frozen orange juice concentrate, thawed
½ teaspoon grated orange zest
¼ cup hazelnuts, chopped

Spritz Cookies

YIELD: 3 to 4 dozen
TOTAL TIME: 30 minutes

2 cups all-purpose flour
⅓ cup almonds, ground fine
1 cup vegetable shortening
½ cup powdered sugar
1 large egg yolk
1 teaspoon almond extract

1. Preheat the oven to 350 degrees. Lightly grease 2 baking sheets.

2. Combine the flour and almonds.

3. In a large bowl, cream the vegtable shortening and powdered sugar. Beat in the egg yolk and almond extract. Gradually blend in the dry ingredients.

4. Place the dough in a cookie press or a pastry bag fitted with a star tip and press or pipe out into small rings onto the prepared baking sheets, spacing them 1 inch apart.

5. Bake for 8 to 10 minutes, until lightly colored. Transfer to wire racks to cool.

Baking notes: If you do not have a cookie press or pastry bag, roll out the dough on a floured surface. Using a round cutter, cut out cookies, then cut out the centers with a smaller cutter. In Sweden, where the recipe originated, the rings are traditional, but S-shaped cookies are often made from the same basic Spritz Cookie dough.

Stained Glass Cutouts

YIELD: 3 to 4 dozen
TOTAL TIME: 60 minutes
CHILLING TIME: 24 hours

3¾ cups all-purpose flour
½ teaspoon baking soda
1 teaspoon ground nutmeg
½ teaspoon salt
½ cup vegetable shortening
1½ cups powdered sugar
1 large egg
½ cup plain yogurt
1 teaspoon almond extract

FILLING
2 cups granulated sugar
1 cup light corn syrup
½ cup water
2 drops flavoring of choice, such as mint or vanilla extract
A few drops of food coloring

1. Combine the flour, baking soda, nutmeg, and salt.

2. In a large bowl, cream the vegetable shortening, powdered sugar, and egg. Beat in the yogurt. Beat in the almond extract. Gradually blend in the dry ingredients. Divide the dough into 4 equal pieces. Wrap in waxed paper and chill for 24 hours.

3. Lightly grease 2 baking sheets.

4. Work with one piece of dough at a time, keeping the remaining dough refrigerated. On a floured surface, roll out the dough to a thickness of ¼ inch. Using cookie cutters, cut into fancy shapes. Using small cookie cutters, of different shapes, or a knife, cut out the centers of the cookies. Place 1 inch apart on the prepared baking sheets and chill for 1 hour.

5. Preheat the oven to 350 degrees.

6. Bake the cookies for 10 to 12 minutes, until lightly colored. Transfer to wire racks to cool.

7. To make the filling, combine all of the ingredients in a saucepan and cook over medium heat, stirring, until the sugar dissolves. Bring to a boil and cook until the syrup registers 250 to 265 degrees (hard-ball state) on a candy thermometer. Remove from the heat.

8. Carefully spoon the syrup into the center cut-outs of each cookie. Refrigerate until chilled and set. When cool, carefully twist the cookies to release them and slide them off the baking sheets.

Baking notes: These cookies are designed to be displayed so that "stained glass" can be seen against the light. They can be used as ornaments on a Christmas tree or to decorate presents. In fact, they can be made for almost any holiday of the year. If you wish to make nonedible cookies that will last for several years, use only ½ cup granulated sugar in the dough and add 1 cup of salt. To store, lay them flat in a box so the "stained glass" will not crack.

Strawberry Meringue Bars

BAR COOKIES

YIELD: 3 to 4 dozen

TOTAL TIME: 45 minutes

CRUST
¾ cup vegetable shortening
¼ cup granulated sugar
2 large egg yolks
1½ cups all-purpose flour

FILLING
2 large egg whites
½ cup granulated sugar
1 cup almonds, chopped
1 cup strawberry puree
1 cup flaked coconut

1. Preheat the oven to 350 degrees. Lightly grease a 13 by 9-inch square baking pan.

2. To make the crust, cream the vegetable shortening and sugar in a large bowl. Beat in the egg yolks. Gradually blend in the flour. Spread the dough evenly in the bottom of the prepared baking pan.

3. Bake for 15 minutes.

4. Meanwhile, make the topping: In a large bowl, beat the egg whites until foamy. Gradually beat in the sugar and beat in until the whites hold stiff peaks. Fold in the chopped nuts.

5. Spread the strawberry puree over the hot crust and sprinkle with the coconut. Spread the topping over the coconut.

6. Bake for 20 to 25 minutes longer, or until the topping is firm to the touch. Cool in the pan on a wire rack before cutting into large or small bars.

Sugar Cookies

FORMED COOKIES

YIELD: 3 to 4 dozen

TOTAL TIME: 30 minutes

2 cups all-purpose flour
1 teaspoon baking powder
1 teaspoon salt
½ cup vegetable shortening
1 cup granulated sugar
¼ cup milk
1 teaspoon vanilla extract
Granulated sugar for
*   rolling*

1. Preheat the oven to 350 degrees. Lightly grease 2 baking sheets.

2. Combine the flour, baking powder, and salt.

3. In a large bowl, cream the vegetable shortening and sugar. Beat in the milk and vanilla extract. Gradually blend in the dry ingredients.

4. Pinch off walnut-sized pieces of dough and roll into balls. Roll the balls in granulated sugar and place 1½ inches apart on the prepared baking sheets. Flatten each ball with the bottom of a glass dipped in water and then in granulated sugar.

5. Bake for 10 to 12 minutes, until lightly colored. Transfer to wire racks to cool.

Sugar-Plum Drops

FORMED COOKIES

YIELD: *2 to 3 dozen*
TOTAL TIME: *30 minutes*

2 cups all-purpose flour
1 teaspoon baking soda
1 teaspoon salt
1 cup vegetable shortening
1 cup granulated sugar
1 cup packed light brown
  sugar
2 large eggs
1 teaspoon vanilla extract
2 cups (12 ounces) rolled
  oats
1 cup shredded coconut
1 cup gumdrops, chopped
Granulated sugar for
  rolling

1. Preheat the oven to 350 degrees. Lightly grease 2 baking sheets.

2. Combine the flour, baking soda, and salt.

3. In a large bowl, cream the vegetable shortening and two sugars. Beat in the eggs. Beat in the vanilla extract. Gradually blend in the dry ingredients. Fold in the oats, coconut, and gum drops.

4. Pinch off 1-inch pieces of the dough and roll into balls. Place 1 inch apart on the prepared baking sheets.

5. Bake for 10 to 12 minutes, until lightly colored. Transfer to wire racks to cool.

6. Roll the cooled cookies in granulated sugar.

Baking notes: These can be made as balls or flattened with the bottom of a glass dipped in flour.

Swedish Butter Cookies

DROP COOKIES

YIELD: *3 to 4 dozen*
TOTAL TIME: *30 minutes*

2 cups all-purpose flour
1 teaspoon baking powder
½ teaspoon salt
¾ cup butter, at room
  temperature
¾ cup granulated sugar
¼ cup powdered sugar
1 teaspoon vanilla extract
1 cup (6 ounces) semisweet
  chocolate chips
½ cup hazelnuts, chopped

1. Preheat the oven to 350 degrees. Lightly grease 2 baking sheets.

2. Combine the flour, baking powder, and salt.

3. In a large bowl, cream butter and two sugars. Beat in the vanilla extract. Gradually blend in the dry ingredients. Fold in the chocolate chips and hazelnuts.

4. Drop the dough by spoonfuls 1½ inches apart onto the prepared baking sheets.

5. Bake for 12 to 14 minutes, until lightly colored. Transfer to wire racks to cool.

Swedish Pinwheels

ROLLED COOKIES

YIELD: *2 to 3 dozen*
TOTAL TIME: *60 minutes*
CHILLING TIME: *90 minutes*

2 cups all-purpose flour
1 cup cold butter
¼ cup ice water
About ½ cup fruit preserves
1 large egg, beaten
Sugar crystals for sprinkling

1. Put the flour in a large bowl and cut in the butter. Add just enough ice water to make a soft dough. Cover and chill for 1 hour.

2. On a floured surface, roll out the dough to a 14-inch square. Trim the edges. Fold the dough in half and roll to a 21 by 7-inch rectangle. Fold in thirds like a business letter. Roll out to a rectangle and fold up 2 more times. Wrap in waxed paper and chill for 30 minutes.

3. Preheat the oven to 400 degrees.

4. On a floured surface, roll out the dough to a 14-inch squares. Trim the edges. Cut into 25 squares. Cut diagonally corner to corner with a pastry wheel. Place 1 inch apart on ungreased baking sheets and put a small spoonful of the preserves in the center of each diagonal. Brush with the beaten egg and sprinkle with crystal sugar.

5. Bake for 10 to 12 minutes, until lightly colored. Transfer to wire racks to cool.

Baking notes: For best results, keep the dough thoroughly chilled at all times.

TEATIME COOKIES

FORMED COOKIES

1. Preheat the oven to 375 degrees. Lightly grease 2 baking sheets.

2. In a small saucepan, melt the 3 tablespoons vegetable shortening. Remove from the heat and blend in the cocoa, and powdered sugar, stirring until smooth. Set aside.

3. Combine the flour, baking powder, and salt.

4. In a large bowl, cream the remaining ¾ cup vegetable shortening and granulated sugar. Beat in the egg. Beat in the vanilla extract and almond extract.

5. Transfer half the dough to another bowl. Add the cocoa mixture and blend well.

6. Drop the dough by spoonfuls 3 inches apart onto the prepared baking sheets. Spread into rounds with the back of a spoon dipped in flour. Drop spoonfuls of the chocolate dough on top of the rounds and use the back of a spoon dipped in flour to spread the chocolate dough to the edges.

7. Bake for 8 to 10 minutes, until firm to touch. Transfer to wire racks to cool.

Baking notes: A whole nut (or half a large nut) can be pushed into the top of each cookie before baking.

¾ cup plus 3 tablespoons vegetable shortening
½ cup unsweetened cocoa powder
3 tablespoons powdered sugar
1¾ cups all-purpose flour
1 teaspoon baking powder
½ teaspoon salt
½ cup granulated sugar
1 large egg
1 teaspoon vanilla extract
½ teaspoon almond extract

TEATIME FAVORITES

BAR COOKIES

1. Preheat the oven to 350 degrees. Lightly grease a 9-inch square baking pan.

2. Combine the flour and almonds.

3. In the top of a double boiler, melt the chocolate and vegetable shortening, stirring until smooth. Remove from the heat and beat in the sugar. Beat in the eggs one at a time, beating vigorously after each addition. Beat in the almond extract. Gradually blend in the dry ingredients. Spread the mixture evenly in the prepared baking pan.

4. Bake for 35 to 40 minutes, or until a toothpick inserted in the center comes out clean. Cool in the pan on a wire rack.

5. Frost the cooled cookies with Vanilla Icing (see Pantry) and cut into large or small bars.

Baking notes: To make a different version of these cookies, bake in a 13 by 9-inch baking pan for 25 to 30 minutes. Let cool in the pan on a wire rack, then use cookie cutters to cut into fancy shapes and frost.

½ cup all-purpose flour
1 cup almonds, ground
2 ounces semisweet chocolate, chopped
½ cup vegetable shortening
1 cup granulated sugar
2 large eggs
½ teaspoon almond extract

THIMBLES

FORMED COOKIES

YIELD: 3 to 4 dozen
TOTAL TIME: 30 minutes

1 cup vegetable shortening
½ cup packed light brown sugar
2 large eggs, separated
1½ teaspoons vanilla extract
2¼ cups all-purpose flour
1½ cups almonds, ground
About ¼ cup fruit preserves

1. Preheat the oven to 350 degrees. Lightly grease 2 baking sheets.

2. In a large bowl, cream the vegetable shortening and brown sugar. Beat in the egg yolks and vanilla extract. Gradually blend in the flour.

3. In a small bowl, beat the egg whites stiff until stiff but not dry.

4. Pinch off small pieces of dough and roll into balls. Roll the balls in the beaten egg white, then in the ground almonds, and place 1 inch apart on the prepared baking sheets. With your finger, press an indentation into the center of each ball.

5. Bake for 12 to 15 minutes, until lightly colored. Fill each cookie with a dab of fruit preserves, then transfer to wire racks to cool.

Baking notes: These are good filled with preserves; but for a real treat, fill them with a lemon custard or banana custard. Even Jell-O can be used: Chill the cookies, then spoon the Jell-O into the cookies just before it sets.

THUMBPRINT COOKIES

ROLLED COOKIES

YIELD:: 5 to 7 dozen
TOTAL TIME: 40 minutes

3½ cups all-purpose flour
3 tablespoons baking powder
¼ teaspoon salt
¾ cup vegetable shortening
1 cup granulated sugar
2 large eggs
⅓ cup milk
½ teaspoon vanilla extract
Filling (see Baking notes)

1. Preheat oven to 400 degrees. Lightly grease 2 baking sheets.

2. Combine the flour, baking powder, and salt.

3. In a large bowl, cream the vegetable shortening and sugar. Beat in the eggs. Beat in the milk and vanilla extract. Gradually blend in the dry ingredients.

4. On a floured surface, roll out the dough to a thickness of about ½ inch. Using a 1½-inch round cookie cutter, cut out the cookies and place 1 inch apart on the prepared baking sheets. Press your fingertip into the center of each cookie to make a shallow depression and fill with the desired filling.

5. Bake for 12 to 15 minutes, until lightly colored. Transfer to wire racks to cool.

Baking notes: The filling for these cookies can range from fruit preserves or jams or jelly to mini-marshmallows or melted chocolate. Be creative.

Tortas de la Boda del Mexicano

FORMED COOKIES

YIELD: 3 to 4 dozen
TOTAL TIME: 40 minutes

1. Preheat the oven to 200 degrees. Lightly grease 2 baking sheets.

2. In a large bowl, cream the vegetable shortening and sugar. Beat in the vanilla extract. Gradually blend in the flour. Fold in the walnuts.

3. Pinch off walnut-sized pieces of dough and roll into small balls. Place 1 inch apart on the prepared baking sheets.

4. Bake for 25 to 35 minutes, until golden brown. Transfer to wire racks to cool.

5. Roll the cooled cookies in powdered sugar.

¾ cup vegetable shortening
¼ cup granulated sugar
1 teaspoon vanilla extract
2 cups all-purpose flour
½ cup walnuts, chopped
Powdered sugar for rolling

Tosca Cookies

DROP COOKIES

YIELD: 3 to 4 dozen
TOTAL TIME: 30 minutes
CHILLING TIME: 2 hours

1. Combine the flour, almonds, farina, and baking powder.

2. In a large bowl, cream the vegetable shortening and sugar. Beat in the egg. Gradually blend in the dry ingredients. Cover and chill for 2 hours.

3. Preheat the oven to 350 degrees. Lightly grease 2 baking sheets.

4. To make the glaze, combine the butter, sugar, and corn syrup in a small bowl and beat until smooth.

5. Drop the dough by spoonfuls 1½ inches apart onto the prepared baking sheets.

6. Bake for 10 to 12 minutes, just until lightly colored. Brush the cookies with the glaze, sprinkle with the slivered almonds, and bake for 5 minutes longer. Transfer to wire racks to cool.

1 cup all-purpose flour
⅓ cup almonds, ground
⅓ cup farina ceral, such as Cream of Wheat
½ teaspoon baking powder
1 cup vegetable shortening
⅔ cup granulated sugar
1 large egg

GLAZE
4 tablespoons butter, melted
6 tablespoons granulated sugar
1 teaspoon corn syrup
⅓ cup slivered almonds

T

TRAIL MIX COOKIES

DROP COOKIES

YIELD: 3 to 4 dozen
TOTAL TIME: 30 minutes

¾ cup all-purpose flour
½ teaspoon baking soda
½ cup vegetable shortening
1 cup packed light brown sugar
½ cup peanut butter
1 large egg
1 teaspoon vanilla extract
1 cup (6 ounces) semisweet chocolate chips
1 cup raisins
⅔ cup peanuts, chopped

1. Preheat the oven to 375 degrees. Lightly grease 2 baking sheets.

2. Combine the flour and baking soda.

3. In a large bowl, cream the vegetable shortening and brown sugar. Beat in the peanut butter. Beat in the egg and vanilla extract. Gradually blend in the dry ingredients. Fold in the chocolate chips, raisins, and peanuts.

4. Drop the dough by spoonfuls 1½ inches apart onto the prepared baking sheets.

5. Bake for 10 to 12 minutes, until lightly colored. Transfer to wire racks to cool.

6. When the cookies are cool, wrap individually and store in an airtight container.

TROPICAL BARS

BAR COOKIES

YIELD: 2 to 3 dozen
TOTAL TIME: 35 minutes

¾ cup all-purpose flour
¾ teaspoon baking powder
½ teaspoon salt
½ cup vegetable shortening
1 cup packed light brown sugar
2 large eggs
½ teaspoon rum
8 ounces canned crushed pineapple, drained
¾ cup flaked coconut

1. Preheat the oven to 350 degrees. Lightly grease a 9-inch square baking pan.

2. Combine the flour, baking powder, and salt.

3. In a large bowl, cream the vegetable shortening and brown sugar. Beat in the eggs and rum. Gradually blend in the dry ingredients. Fold in the pineapple and coconut. Spread the batter evenly in the prepared baking pan.

4. Bake for 25 to 30 minutes, until colored on top. Cool in the pan on a wire rack before cutting into large or small bars.

Vanilla Daisies

ROLLED COOKIES

YIELD: 3 to 4 dozen
TOTAL TIME: 30 minutes

1. Preheat the oven to 350 degrees.

2. Combine the flour, baking powder, and salt.

3. In a large bowl, cream the vegetable shortening and sugar. Beat in the egg and vanilla extract. Beat in the lemon zest. Gradually blend in the dry ingredients.

4. On a floured surface, roll the dough out to a thickness of ¼ inch. Using a flower-shaped cookie cutter, cut out cookies and place 1 inch apart on ungreased baking sheets. Press a half-cherry into the center of each cookie.

5. Bake for 10 to 12 minutes, until lightly colored. Transfer to wire racks to cool.

2⅓ cups all-purpose flour
½ teaspoon baking powder
¼ teaspoon salt
1 cup vegetable shortening
⅔ cup granulated sugar
1 large egg
1 teaspoon vanilla extract
1 teaspoon grated lemon zest
About ¼ cup glacé cherries, cut in half

Vanilla Sour Cream Rosettes

FORMED COOKIES

YIELD: 3 to 4 dozen
TOTAL TIME: 30 minutes

1. Preheat the oven to 350 degrees.

2. Combine the flour, baking powder, baking soda, and salt.

3. In a large bowl, cream the butter and sugar. Beat in the egg. Beat in the sour cream. Beat in the vanilla extract. Gradually blend in the dry ingredients.

4. Place the dough in a cookie press or a pastry bag fitted with a star tip and press or pipe out small rosettes 1 inch apart onto ungreased baking sheets.

5. Bake for 10 to 12 minutes, until lightly colored. Transfer to wire racks to cool.

1½ cups all-purpose flour
½ teaspoon baking powder
⅛ teaspoon baking soda
¼ teaspoon salt
¼ cup butter, at room temperature
½ cup granulated sugar
1 large egg
¼ cup sour cream
1 teaspoon vanilla extract

YIELD: *3 to 4 dozen*

TOTAL TIME: *30 minutes*

CHILLING TIME: *2 hours*

2 cups all-purpose flour
2 tablespoons corn flour
1¾ cups vegetable shortening
1 cup powdered sugar
1 tablespoon plus 1 teaspoon grated orange zest

FILLING

2 tablespoons butter, at room temperature
½ cup powdered sugar
1 teaspoon fresh orange juice

VIENNESE SHORTCAKES   REFRIGERATOR COOKIES

1. Combine the two flours.

2. In a large bowl, cream the vegetable shortening and powdered sugar. Beat in the orange zest. Gradually blend in the dry ingredients. Form the dough into a log 1½ inches in diameter. Wrap in waxed paper and chill for 2 hours.

3. Preheat the oven to 350 degrees.

4. To make the filling, combine the butter, powdered sugar, and orange juice in a small bowl and beat until smooth.

5. Cut the log into ¼-inch-thick slices and place 1 inch apart on ungreased baking sheets.

6. Bake for 10 to 12 minutes, until lightly colored. Transfer to wire racks to cool.

7. To assemble, spread the filling over the bottom half of the cookies and place the remaining cookies on top.

Baking notes: For a different filling, beat 2 ounces of softened cream cheese and 1 tablespoon soft butter together.

YIELD: *3 to 4 dozen*

TOTAL TIME: *30 minutes*

1 cup all-purpose flour
6 tablespoons unsweetened cocoa powder
½ teaspoon baking soda
½ teaspoon salt
1¼ cups vegetable shortening
1½ cups granulated sugar
1 large egg
¼ cup water
½ teaspoon whiskey
3 cups rolled oats

VIRGINIA REBELS   DROP COOKIES

1. Preheat the oven to 350 degrees.

2. Combine the flour, cocoa powder, baking soda, and salt.

3. In a large bowl, cream the vegetable shortening and sugar. Beat in the egg. Beat in the water and whiskey. Gradually blend in the dry ingredients. Stir in the oats.

4. Drop the dough by spoonfuls 1½ inches apart onto ungreased baking sheets.

5. Bake for 10 to 12 minutes, or until lightly colored. Transfer to wire racks to cool.

Walnut Bars

BAR COOKIES

YIELD: *3 to 4 dozen*
TOTAL TIME: *45 minutes*

1. Preheat the oven to 350 degrees. Grease a 13 by 9-inch baking pan.

2. To make the crust, combine the flour, baking powder, and brown sugar in a large bowl. Cut in the vegetable shortening until the mixture resembles coarse crumbs. Stir in the walnuts. Spread the mixture evenly in the prepared baking pan.

3. Bake for 10 minutes.

4. Meanwhile, make the filling: Combine the flour and salt.

5. In a medium bowl, beat the brown sugar and eggs until thick and light-colored. Beat in the corn syrup. Beat in the vanilla extract. Gradually blend in the dry ingredients. Pour the filling over the hot crust. Sprinkle the walnuts over the top. Bake for 25 to 30 minutes longer, until the top is firm to the touch. Cool in the pan on a wire rack before cutting into large or small bars.

CRUST
1⅓ cups all-purpose flour
½ teaspoon baking powder
½ cup packed light brown sugar
⅓ cup vegetable shortening
¼ cup walnuts, chopped

FILLING
3 tablespoons all-purpose flour
½ teaspoon salt
¼ cup packed light brown sugar
2 large eggs
¾ cup dark corn syrup
1 teaspoon vanilla extract
¾ cup walnuts, ground fine

Walnut Shortbread

FORMED COOKIES

YIELD: *4 to 5 dozen*
TOTAL TIME: *30 minutes*

1. Preheat the oven to 350 degrees.

2. Combine the flour and walnuts.

3. In a large bowl, cream the vegetable shortening and brown sugar. Beat in the vanilla extract. Gradually blend in the dry ingredients.

4. Pinch off walnut-sized pieces of dough and roll into balls. Place 1½ inches apart on ungreased baking sheets. Flatten with the back of a spoon dipped in flour.

5. Bake for 10 to 15 minutes, until lightly colored. Transfer to wire racks to cool.

4½ cups all-purpose flour
1 cup walnuts, ground fine
2 cups vegetable shortening
2½ cups packed light brown sugar
2 teaspoons vanilla extract

Walnut Squares

BAR COOKIES

YIELD: 2 to 3 dozen
TOTAL TIME: 40 minutes

CRUST
1 cup all-purpose flour
¼ teaspoon salt
¼ cup vegetable shortening

FILLING
2 tablespoons all-purpose
flour
¼ teaspoon salt
¾ cup granulated sugar
2 large eggs
1 teaspoon vanilla extract
2 cups flaked coconut
1 cup walnuts, chopped
Granulated sugar for
sprinkling

1. Preheat the oven to 350 degrees. Lightly grease a 9-inch square baking pan.

2. To make the crust, combine the flour and salt in a medium bowl. Cut in the vegetable shortening until the mixture resembles coarse crumbs. Press the mixture evenly into the prepared baking pan.

3. Bake for 12 minutes.

4. Meanwhile, make the topping: Combine the flour and salt.

5. In a medium bowl, beat the sugar and eggs together until thick and light-colored. Beat in the vanilla extract. Gradually blend in the dry ingredients. Stir in the coconut and walnuts.

6. Pour the filling over the hot crust. Bake for 15 minutes longer, or until the topping is set. Sprinkle with granulated sugar and cool in the pan on a wire rack before cutting into large or small bars.

Wheat Flake Jumbles

DROP COOKIES

YIELD: 3 to 4 dozen
TOTAL TIME: 30 minutes

1 cup all-purpose flour
½ teaspoon baking powder
¼ teaspoon baking soda
¼ teaspoon salt
⅓ cup vegetable shortening
½ cup packed light brown
sugar
1 large egg
1½ tablespoons sour milk
1 teaspoon vanilla extract
½ cup dates, pitted and
chopped fine
½ cup walnuts, chopped
1½ cups cornflakes

1. Preheat the oven to 375 degrees. Lightly grease 2 baking sheets.

2. Combine the flour, baking powder, baking soda, and salt.

3. In a large bowl, cream the vegetable shortening and brown sugar. Beat in the egg. Beat in the sour milk and vanilla extract. Gradually blend in the dry ingredients. Fold in the dates and walnuts.

4. Spread the cornflakes in a pie plate.

5. Drop the dough by spoonfuls onto the cornflakes and roll in the cornflakes until completely coated. Place 3 inches apart on the prepared baking sheets.

6. Bake for 12 to 15 minutes, until golden brown. Transfer to wire racks to cool.

WHOLE WHEAT SUGAR COOKIES   **DROP COOKIES**

YIELD: 3 to 4 dozen
TOTAL TIME: 30 minutes

1. Preheat the oven to 350 degrees.

2. Combine the two flours, the baking powder, baking soda, nutmeg, and salt.

3. In a large bowl, cream the vegetable shortening and sugar. Beat in the eggs. Beat in the sour milk. Gradually blend in the dry ingredients.

4. Combine the sugar and cinnamon in a saucer.

5. Drop the dough by spoonfuls 1½ inches apart onto ungreased baking sheets. Flatten each cookie with the bottom of a glass dipped in the cinnamon sugar.

6. Bake for 10 to 12 minutes, until lightly colored. Transfer to wire racks to cool.

3½ cups whole wheat flour
½ cup all-purpose flour
2 teaspoons baking powder
1 teaspoon baking soda
1 teaspoon ground nutmeg
1 teaspoon salt
1 cup vegetable shortening
2 cups granulated sugar
2 large eggs
2 teaspoons sour milk
2 tablespoons granulated sugar
2 teaspoons ground cinnamon

WHOOPIE PIES   **DROP COOKIES**

YIELD: 3 to 4 dozen
TOTAL TIME: 30 minutes

1. Preheat the oven to 375 degrees. Lightly grease 2 baking sheets.

2. Combine the flour, carob powder, baking powder, and salt.

3. In a large bowl, cream the vegetable shortening and powdered sugar. Beat in the egg. Beat in the milk and crème de cacao. Gradually blend in the dry ingredients. Fold in the chocolate chips.

4. Drop the dough by heaping tablespoonfuls 3 inches apart onto the prepared baking sheets.

5. Bake for 7 to 10 minutes, until a toothpick inserted in the center comes out clean. Transfer to wire racks to cool.

6. To make the filling, beat the vegetable shortening and powdered sugar in a medium bowl. Beat in the coffee liqueur. Beat in the marshmallow topping.

7. To assemble, cut the cookies horizontally in half. Spread the filling liberally over the bottoms and sandwich with the tops.

Baking notes: To make more uniform cookies, you can use crumpet or muffin rings to form the pies.

2 cups all-purpose flour
6 tablespoons carob powder
2 teaspoons baking powder
½ teaspoon salt
⅓ cup vegetable shortening
1 cup powdered sugar
1 large egg
1 cup skim milk
1 teaspoon crème de cacao
½ cup white chocolate chips

FILLING
¾ cup vegetable shortening
1 cup powdered sugar
1 teaspoon coffee liqueur
½ cup store-bought marshmallow topping

Zucchini Bars

BAR COOKIES

YIELD: 2 to 3 dozen
TOTAL TIME: 45 minutes

2½ cups all-purpose flour
1 teaspoon ground
   cinnamon
½ cup granulated sugar
½ cup vegetable oil
2 large eggs
¾ cup finely chopped
   zucchini
½ cup mashed cooked
   carrots
1 cup pecans, chopped
⅓ cup raisins

1. Preheat the oven to 350 degrees. Lightly grease and flour a 13 by 9-inch baking pan.

2. Combine the flour and cinnamon.

3. In a large bowl, beat the sugar and vegetable oil together. Beat in the eggs one at a time. Beat in the zucchini and carrots. Gradually blend in the dry ingredients. Stir in the pecans and raisins. Spread the batter evenly in the prepared baking pan.

4. Bake for 20 to 25 minutes, until a toothpick inserted in the center comes out clean. Cool in the pan on a wire rack before cutting into large or small bars.

Zwieback

FORMED COOKIES

YIELD: 2 to 3 dozen
TOTAL TIME: 50 minutes

1½ cups all-purpose flour
½ cup almonds, ground
1½ teaspoons baking
   powder
½ cup vegetable shortening
½ cup granulated sugar
2 large eggs
2 teaspoons amaretto

1 Preheat the oven to 325 degrees.

2. Combine the flour, almonds, and baking powder.

3. In a large bowl, cream the vegetable shortening and sugar. Beat in the eggs one at a time. Beat in amaretto. Gradually blend in the dry ingredients.

4. Shape the dough into a loaf 13 inches long and 2½ inches wide and place on an ungreased baking sheet.

5. Bake for 18 minutes, or until firm to the touch.

6. Transfer the loaf to a cutting boards and cut into ½-inch-thick slices. Cut each slice in half diagonally. Place the slices on the baking sheets and bake for 20 minutes. Turn off the oven and leave the cookies in the oven 20 minutes longer; do not open the oven door. Transfer to wire racks to cool.

Weight

¼ oz.	07 g
½ oz.	17 g
1 oz.	28 g
2 oz.	57 g
5 oz.	142 g
8 oz.	227 g
12 oz.	340 g
16 oz.	454 g
32 oz.	907 g
64 oz.	1.8 kg

Volume

¼ tsp.	1.25 ml
½ tsp.	2.5 ml
1 tsp.	5 ml
1 tbl.	15 ml
¼ cup	59 ml
⅓ cup	79 ml
½ cup	119 ml
¾ cup	177 ml
1 cup	237 ml
1 pint (2 cups)	473 ml
1 quart (4 cups)	946 ml
1 gallon (4 quarts)	3.78 litres

Length

¼ in.	5 mm
½ in.	1 cm
¾ in.	2 cm
1 in.	2.5 cm
2 in.	5 cm
4 in.	10 cm
1 foot (12 in.)	30 cm

Heat

very cool	250–275 F	130–140 C
cool	300 F	150 C
warm	325 F	170 C
moderate	350 F	180 C
moderate hot	375–400 F	190–200 C
hot	425 F	220 C
very hot	450–475 F	230–250 C

Dash = 2 to 3 drops (less than ⅛ teaspoon)

1 teaspoon = 5 milliliters

1 tablespoon = 3 teaspoons = 15 milliliters

⅛ cup = 2 tablespoons = 1 fluid ounce = 30 milliliters

¼ cup = 4 tablespoons = 2 fluid ounces = 60 milliliters

½ cup = 8 tablespoons = 4 fluid ounces = 120 milliliters

1 cup = 16 tablespoons = 8 fluid ounces = 240 milliliters

1 pint = 2 cups = 16 fluid ounces = 480 milliliters

1 quart = 4 cups = 32 fluid ounces = 960 milliliters (.96 liter)

1 gallon = 4 quarts = 16 cups = 128 fluid ounces = 3.84 liters

1 ounce = 28 grams

¼ pound = 4 punces = 114 grams

1 pound = 16 ounces = 454 grams

2.2 pounds = 1,000 grams = 1 kilogram

NUTS

1 pound almonds in shell	1 to 1¼ cups shelled nuts
1 pound shelled almonds	3 cups
1 pound almonds slivered	5⅔ cups nutmeat
1 pound brazil nuts in the shell	1½ cups shelled nuts
1 pound brazil nuts shelled	3¼ cups
1½ cups unshelled chestnuts	1 pound shelled chestnuts
1 pound hazelnuts in the shell	1½ cups shelled nuts
1 pound shelled hazelnuts	3½ cups
1 pound peanuts in the shell	2 to 2½ cups shelled nuts
1 pound shelled peanuts	3 cups
1 pound pecans in the shell	2¼ cups shelled nuts
1 pound shelled pecans	4 cups
1 pound walnuts in the shell	2 cups shelled nuts
1 pound shelled walnuts	4 cups

SUGAR

1 cup white granulated sugar	1 cup raw sugar
1 cup white granulated sugar	1 cup brown sugar
1 cup white granulated sugar	1 cup powdered sugar

1 cup white granulated sugar	1¾ cups confectioner's sugar
1 pound granulated sugar	2¼ cups sugar
1 pound brown sugar	2¼ cups brown sugar
1 pound powdered sugar	4 cups powdered sugar
1 tablespoon maple sugar	1 tablespoon granulated sugar

EGGS

1 egg	2 egg yolks
1 cup egg yolks	yolks of 12 to 14 large eggs
1 cup egg whites	whites of 8 large eggs

MILK & DAIRY

1 cup heavy cream	2 cups whipped cream
⅓ cup evaporated milk	⅓ cup dry milk plus 6 tablespoon water
One 14-oz can evaporated milk	1⅔ cups
8 ounces sour cream	1 cup
1 pound cheese	4 cup grated cheese
8 ounces cream cheese	6 tablespoons

FATS

1 stick butter or margarine	½ cup
1 stick butter or margarine	8 tablaespoons
2 sticks butter or margarine	1 cup
4 sticks butter or margarine	2 cups
1 cup butter or margarine	⅞ cup lard
1 cup hydrogentated fat	6⅔ ounces

FRUIT

4 medium apples	4 cups sliced apples
1 pound apples (2 medium)	3 cups sliced apples
1 pound dried apricots	3 cups dried apricots
1 pound banana (3 medium)	2 cups mashed

1 pint of berries	1¾ cups
3½ ounces flaked coconut	1⅓ cup 4 ounces shredded coconut
1⅓ cup 1 pound candied cherries	3 cups
1 pound dates, pitted	2–2½ cups chopped
1 pound figs	2⅔ cups chopped
1 medium lemon	1½ teaspoon grated lemon zest
1 medium lemon	2 tablespoons juice
1 medium orange	3 teaspoons grated orange peel
1 pound prunes	2¼ cups pitted prunes
1 pound raisins	3 cups

CHOCOLATE

1 square baking chocolate	1 ounce
1 ounce unsweeted chocolate	4 tablespoon grated
6 ounces chocolate chips	1 cup chocolate chips
1 pound cocoa powder	4 cups cocoa powder

SPICES & HERBS

2 teaspoons crystallized ginger	1 teaspoon chopped fresh ginger
¼ teaspoon ground ginger	1 teaspoon chopped fresh ginger
¼ teaspoon ground ginger	2 teaspoons chopped crystallized ginger

GRAINS

1 cup rolled oats	5 ounces
1 cup rice	7½ ounces
1 cup uncooked rice	2 cups cooked rice

MISCELLANEOUS

1 inch-piece vanilla bean	1 teaspoon vanilla extract
13 ounces molasses	3 cups
7 coarsly crumbled crackers	approximately 1 cup
30 vanilla wafers	1 cup

GLOSSARY

All-Purpose Flour "The everything flour" for the home kitchen. It is a white wheat flour, bleached or unbleached, enriched with various vitamins and minerals.

Almond Extract An extract of almonds.

Almond Paste A creamy mixture of ground almonds, sugar, and egg whites, used in some recipes to give an enhanced almond flavor. (See Marzipan.)

Amaretto A liqueur with a nutty flavor, which can be used as a flavoring in baking.

Anise Extract An extract of anise seeds, used in company with the seeds in breads and cookies.

Anise Seeds Also called aniseed. An aromatic spice used in baking.

Apricot Butter A flavorful blend of apricot puree and butter.

Arrowroot A starch used in many older European recipes; it is not in wide use today. Usually interchangeable with cornstarch and in some cases wheat flour.

Bake To cook food in an oven using air.

Baking Powder A leavening agent assed to abtters and doughs to cause them to rise during baking. Baking powder is a combination of baking soda and cream of tartar. It is usually added to mixtures that contain acids, and reacts with the liquids in the batter or dough, producing gas-bubbles. Double-acting baking powder, the most common type, will produce the bubbling effect, first during mixing and then in the heat of the oven.

Baking soda Baking soda, or bicarbonate of soda, is a leavening agent used alone or in combination with baking powder. Doughs or batters containing baking soda should be baked as soon as they are mixed because the soda starts reacting as soon as it comes into contact with a liquid. Dissolving the soda in a small amount of water before adding it to the other ingredients ensures that it dissolves completely.

Banana Chips Dried thin banana slices.

Batter A thin combination of flour, liquid, and other ingredients, such as eggs and flavorings.

Beat To make a mixture smooth and uniform by combining the ingredients with a rapid motion, using an implement or utensil such as a wire whisk, a spoon, an egg beater, or an electric mixer.

Beaten egg whites, stages of: Frothy means the mass of eggs whites in the bowl has formed small bubbles. **Soft peaks** means the peaks of the beaten whites fall back on themselves when the beater is removed from the bowl. **Stiff peaks** means the peaks hold their shape when the beater is removed, and there is a uniform consistency.

Blend To thoroughly mix ingredients together.

Boil To heat liquid so bubbles rise from the bottom of the cooking vessel and break on the surface.

Bread In baking or cooking, to coat ingredients with a thin layer of flour, cracker crumbs, cookie crumbs or bread crumbs, or another such ingredient.

Brown Sugar is a refined sugar that is a combination of molasses and granulated sugar. The amount of molasses determines whether the sugar will be light or dark brown; dark brown sugar has a stronger flavor.

Brush To spread liquid mixture or coating over the surface of a solid food. It also refers to brushing on and coating over an ingredient with a (pastry) brush.

Butter A dairy by-product made from sweet or sour cream. Butter contains not less than 80 percent butter-fat. It can be purchased salted and unsalted, also called sweet butter. Most butter is artificially colored. Whipped butter should never be substituted for regular butter in a recipe. Unlike vegetable shortening all its own to the baked goods. To butter means to spread a thin layer of butter over a surface in preparation for baking.

Buttermilk Originally the liquid left over after making butter. Today it is commercially produced. It is used in many baking recipes.

Cake Flour A superfine flour milled from a soft wheat. It is too soft for general use, but it produces fine-grained cakes.

Candied Fruit Candied fruit, has been dried and coated with sugar syrup.

Canned Milk See Evaporated milk.

Caramelize To cook sugar until it melts and turns golden brown.

Carob Also called St. John's Bread. Often used as a chocolate substitute. The pod of the carob tree is available toasted and untoasted. Unlike chocolate it is water-soluble.

Chill To place food in a refrigerator or other cold place, or in a bowl of ice or in ice water, until cold.

Chocolate A processed product derived from the cocoa bean.

Chop To cut an ingredient into smaller pieces.

Chutney A relish made from fruits, herbs, and/or spices. In some cookie recipes, it can be a good substitute for jam or jelly.

Citron A citrus fruit larger, than a lemon, it is also less acidic with a thicker peel. The fruit is not usually considered edible, but the rind is made into jam or preserves or candied, to decorate baked goods.

Coat To sprinkle, dredge, roll, or cover with or dip into flour or other dry or liquid ingredients.

Cocoa The powdered, unsweetened form of the cocoa bean. It is a by-product of chocolate liquor.

Coconut The fruit of the tropical coconut palm. The meat is sold in shredded, flaked, or sometimes chunk form. Some recipes also call for Coconut. Milk: The liquid from a coconut that also comes sweetened and canned.

Combine To mix ingredients together.

Cookie Press A device for dropping or otherwise placing cookie dough onto a baking sheet.

Cooking Oil (See Vegetable Oil.)

Cool To let food stand at room temperature until it is no longer warm to the touch.

GLOSSARY

Cornmeal Coarsely ground corn kernels. Cornmeal contributes a crumbly texture to baked good.

Cornstarch A thickener made from corn that can sometimes be used in place of flour.

Corn Syrup A thick liquid sweetener available in light and dark forms. (The difference in color has no effect on the taste of the cookie.) Corn syrup is considered by some cooks and bakers to be interchangeable with honey and molasses.

Cream To make an ingredient such as butter, or a mixture such as butter and sugar, soft, smooth, and creamy by pressing on it with the back of a spoon or beating it with an electric mixer.

Cream of Tartar A water-soluble powder that is mixed with baking soda to make baking powder.

Cube To cut an ingredient into small cubes, usually ½ inch in size.

Currants A small dark seedless fruit similar to raisins. Dried currants are actually raisins.

Cut in To distribute a solid fat throughout flour or a flour mixture by using a pastry blender, two knives, or the back of a fork. Usually the resulting mixture looks crumbly. An electric hand mixer can also do the job, but overmixing is more likely.

Dates The sweet fruit of a palm tree.

Dice To cut something into very small cubes, V4 inch in size or less.

Dissolve To liquefy a solid, by adding it to a liquid ingredient, or to melt a solid ingredient.

Drop Cookies Cookies made from a dough that is dropped, usually from the end of a spoon onto the baking sheet.

Dust To sprinkle an ingredient with a light coating of, for example, flour or sugar.

Enriched Refers to a food product which has been resupplied with vitamins and minerals lost during processing.

Evaporated Milk Milk that has been processed to remove a percentage of its water, then sterilized and canned.

Fat Butter, margarine, shortening, lard, and oil of any kind.

Flake To shave or break into small thin pieces.

Flour One of the primary ingredients in baking; In this book "flour" refers to enriched all-purpose flour unless otherwise specified in the recipe.

Flute To make a decorative edge on a pie tart or other pastry product before baking, usually using your fingers.

Fold in To combine delicate mixtures such as whipped cream or beaten egg whites and other ingredients. Using a gentle circular motion, cut down through the mixture near the side of the mixing bowl with a spatula or other such utensil, then across the bottom of the bowl and up the other side, to bring some of the mixture up and over the surface.

Formed Cookies Cookies that are shaped by hand; also cookies made using a cookie press or a pastry bag. (See also Molded Cookies.)

Frost To spread icing or frosting over a baked good.

Frosting A coating, usually sugar-based, that is spread over the tops of cookies, either as a decoration or flavor-enhancer. Frosting is generally spread in a thicker layer then icing. (See Icing.)

Fry To cook food in a small amount of fat over high heat. To deep-fry is to fry or boil by completely immersing food in a large quantity of fat.

Garnish To decorate, add color, etc. to a finished dish with fruits or other foods.

Glaze To coat a baked good or other food with a sugarbased mixture or liquid.

Grate To rub an ingredient across a food grater or chop in a blender or food processor to produce fine, medium, or coarse particles. Often refers to the process of shaving small amounts of zest from citrus fruit.

Grease To rub the surface of a dish, pan, or other cooking or baking utensil with a fat such as butter or vegetable shortening to keep food from sticking to it.

Grind To reduce an ingredient, such as nuts, to smaller particles, usually using a food grinder or blender.

Honey A natural sweetener "produced by bees" sold in comb form or, usually, as an extracted liquid. In some recipes, honey can be used as a substitute for sugar.

Icing A sugar-based mixture that is spread over the surface of a cookie. Icing is generally spread in a thinner layer than frosting, which is creamier. (See Frosting.)

Knead To use your hand(s) to work a mixture (such as a dough), using a "press, fold over, and press" motion to make it smooth.

Lard White pork fat that has been rendered down to 'a solid fat. Lard was used in many baked goods that now use butter or vegetable shortening in its place.

Liqueur A sweet alcoholic beverage, usually distilled from fruit and/or flavored with spices.

Liquor An alcoholic beverage such as rum, brandy, bourbon, or vodka.

Madeira A fortified wine from the island of Madeira; it resembles well-matured, full-bodied sherry.

Maple Sugar A sugar made by evaporating maple syrup.

Margarine A solid cooking fat made from vegetable oil.

Marrons The French word for chestnut. Marrons glackes are chestnuts preserved in syrup or candied.

Marzipan A sweetened almond paste often made into confections; it is also used as an ingredient in baking and sometimes is spread over a baked good, such as a cake, instead frosting. (See Almond Paste.)

Melt To liquefy by heating

Meringue A mixture of stiffly beaten egg whites and sugar.

Mocha A coffee flavoring; chocolate is often added.

Molasses A thick, dark syrup produced in the processing of sugar.

Molded Cookies Cookies formed into a particular shape by using a mold of some kind.

Nuts Edible seeds of various trees.

Pastry Bag A cone-shaped bag that can be fitted with metal tips, through which frosting and decorative icing can be pressed onto cookies or other baked goods. (See Pipe.)

Patty Shell An edible container made from puff pastry, used to hold creamed mixtures, fruit, or ice cream.

Pipe To force a mixture such as frosting through a pastry tube or the end of a pastry bag, to decorate cookies.

Peel The skin of a citrus fruit.

Port Wine A fortified wine from Portugal.

Preheat To heat an oven to a desired temperature in preparation for baking.

Phyllo Paper-thin pastry sheets used to make rich pastries and cookies.

Powdered Sugar: Sugar that is ground to a fine powder and mixed with a small amount of corn starch to keep it from caking. In many and powdered sugar are used interchangeably. The difference between the two is in how finely they are ground.

Raw Sugar Sugar that has not been processed.

Reduce To decrease the volume of a liquid by rapid boiling in an uncovered pan.

Rice Flour Flour made from ground rice, with a sweeter taste than wheat flour. In most cookie recipes, rice flour can be substituted for about one quarter of the wheat flour.

Roll To roll dough out thin using a rolling pin (on a floured board) or similar utensil.

Rolled Cookies Cookies formed by the rolling out dough and cutting it into desired shapes.

Rolled Oats Oats that have been hulled, steamed, and flattened. Rolled oats add a moist, sweet, chewy texture to baked goods. When toasted, they add a crunchy texture.

Rose Water A liquid made from the extracted oil of rose petals. It can usually be purchased at many drugstores.

Scald To heat a liquid to just below the boiling point.

Score To cut or press shallow lines in the surface of a food for decoration or for easy division after baking.

Sesame Seeds Also called benne seeds, used as a flavorful garnish in cookies and breads.

Shortening A fat produced from bleached refined hydrogenated vegetable oil or animal fat. High-quality shortening is a solid fat that is a very good substitute for butter in baking.

Sherry A dry wine often used in cooking.

Simmer To heat a liquid to a low boil, so that a few bubbles come to the surface.

Sliver To cut or shred an 'ingredient into thin lengths.

Stir To blend ingredients with a spoon, using a circular motion.

Sugar A sweetener available in many forms; granulated sugar is most commonly used in cooking.

Sultanas Small green seedless raisins.

Sweetened Condensed Milk Processed milk that has a greater concentration of sugar because water has been removed and sugar added. The milk has the consistency of thick honey.

Toast To brown an ingredient in an oven or by means of direct heat.

Vanilla Extract A flavoring extracted from the vanilla bean.

Vanilla Bean The pod of a vanilla orchid plant.

Vegetable Oil A cooking oil extracted from corn.

Vinegar An acid liquid used for flavoring and preserving. It can be

INGREDIENTS AND FLAVORINGS

NUTS Most nuts are available in a variety of forms, including unshelled or shelled, blanched (peeled or skinned) or unblanched, chopped, halved, sliced, or slivered. Cashew nuts are unique in that they are not sold in the shell. Although walnuts, almonds, and pecans are the nuts most commonly used in baking, many other types can result in delicious cookies and baked goods-hazelnuts and hickory nuts, to name just two. The most inexpensive way to purchase any nuts is in the shell. As a general rule of thumb, one pound of unshelled nuts will equal half a pound of shelled. However, for ease and convenience, many home bakers prefer to buy shelled nuts. Although nuts in the shell stay fresh for a long time, keeping them in the lower part of the refrigerator will prolong their shelf life. Shelled nuts turn rancid quickly and are best kept in airtight containers in the freezer. The recipes in this book use sliced, slivered, chopped, and ground nuts as well as whole nuts. Chopped means that the nuts are in small corn kernelsize chunks. Ground is when the nut has been reduced to a very coarse, almost powder

Almond The fruit of the almond tree can be purchased shelled or unshelled, blanched, or unblanched, slivered, sliced, and chopped. The shell is soft and easy to crack open. Unblanched almonds have a soft brown color; blanched nuts are a pale ivory color.

Black Walnuts Black walnuts were once used extensively in baking recipes, but more widely available English walnuts have replaced them in popularity. Black Walnuts are still preferred by many cooks and bakers; if you come across them, you will want to try baking with these flavorful nuts.

Brazil Nut Although brazil nuts were once available only during the Christmas holiday season, now they are available all year long. They are large nuts most effectively used ground or chopped in cookie recipes.

Cashew This is one of the most popular eating nuts in the world. For baking purposes they are considered a soft nut.

Chestnuts Chestnuts are available fresh in the winter and canned all year around. The best way to prepare fresh chestnuts for cookie recipes is to score them on the bottom and toast them in the oven to loosen their outer shells and skins.

English Walnuts In the United States this is the most Popular nut for cooking purposes (See Black Walnuts.)

Filbert (See Hazelnuts.)

Hazelnuts The hazelnut, also called filbert, is one of the most flavorful of all nuts. Hazelnuts are far more popular in Europe than in the United States, which is unfortunate in light of the nut's rich taste.

Macadamia Nuts The macadamia nut is one of the most expensive nuts in the world, partly, no doubt, because it takes up to five years before the macadamia tree can start to bear fruit. In addition, macadamia nut trees have never been successfully transplanted to mainland United States. Macadamia nuts have a rich, buttery flavor and are usually toasted in coconut oil.

Peanut This small slick nut (actually a legume), is the most popular eating nut in the United States. Half of the peanut crop is blended into peanut butter, but peanuts turn up in a variety of baked goods, including peanut butter cookies, a perennial favorite.

Pecans Many cooks and bakers prefer the pecan to any other nut; pecans are especially popular in the southern regions of the United States, where they grow profusely.

Pine Nuts Known as piñon in Spanish and pignola in Italian, the pine nut is usually considthan a baking nut, but it works very well in a variety of cookies because of its rich, full flavor.

Pistachio Nuts These nuts, when shelled and toasted work extremely well in cookies because of their complex flavor that melds so well with a variety of spices.

FRUITS Hundreds of cookie recipes that include fruit in various states-fresh, dried, or frozen. Dried fruit should be rehydrated before use. The process of rehydration is simply nothing more than soaking the dried fruit in boiling water or another liquid.

Apples Although apples are available throughout the year, they are at their peak in the fall. Cored and sliced dried apples should usually be hydrated before they are used. Applesauce is added to many recipes both to make the cookies softer and to give them a fresh apple taste. Canned apples are not suitable for cookies.

Apricots Fresh apricots are generally available only in season, from May through July. But dried apricots are delicious. Canned apricots tend to be flavorless if used for baking.

Bananas Bananas are available every day of the year. There are two varieties: One is for eating and drying, the its dark skin color, is for cooking. The cooking banana is also smaller than the eating banana. Most home bakers use the eating variety for cooking. Dried banana chips are also available.

Berries Fresh berries including strawberries, blackberries, blueberries, boysenberries, raspberries, black raspberries, are available only in season. We are fortunate that they are always available in the form 'of jams and preserves which are used in many cookie recipes.

Cherries Fresh cherries are seldom used in cookie baking. They are seldom used as an additive in cookies. (See Glace/Candied Cherries.)

Dates The fruit of the date palm tree has been used for centuries, as far back as ancient Egypt, as a means of sweetening dishes. Most of the recipes here call for pitted dates.

Figs It is surprising that so few cookie recipes use figs. Fig Newtons are one of this country's most popular cookies.

Lemon Zest Zest and juice of the lemon rind is seldom used in any state other than grated. This adds a pleasing lemon flavor to the cookies in which it is used.

Orange Zest Only the zest and the juice of the orange may be used in baking. The cookies using this zest may have subtle or strong flavor, depending upon the amounts used.

Peaches Only dried peaches are appropriate for cookies; canned peaches do not hold up under the heat of cooking and become mushy. Fresh peaches may be sliced and layered in bar cookies. Peach puree can be used as a flavor in cookie recipes.

Persimmons A seasonal fruit with a sweet flavor, the persimmon really isn't edible until it is overripe. When the skin starts to turn brown and the pulp inside becomes almost mushy, it is ready to eat or use.

Pineapple Pineapples are readily available all year round, but for baking the canned fruit is most popular because of ease of preparation. It should be well drained before using. Candied pineapple is also good in cookies. Prunes Dried prunes are used pitted, sliced, or diced in recipes.

SPICES AND HERBS

Allspice These berries, the seeds of the allspice tree, are harvested and sun-dried until they are a deep reddish brown. They are made available whole and ground. Their flavor resembles a soft blend of cloves, cinnamon, and nutmeg (hence the name). Allspice is used to flavor cakes, vies, cookies, and breads. It is especially good in pastries made with fruit.

Anise Anise seeds, or aniseed, are greenish brown with a strong licorice flavor. They are available whole or crushed. Anise seeds are used extensively in cookies and fruit pies, especially in holiday specialties.

Apple pie spice This is a commercial blend of cinnamon, cloves, nutmeg, and some other sweet-type spices. It is used mainly for pies, but in baking,

it can be substituted in any recipe that calls for cinnamon or nutmeg.

Caraway seeds Small greenish brown crescent-shaped seeds. Although caraway seeds are perhaps most associated with rye bread, they can be very flavorful in cookies and cakes. The seeds are always sold whole.

Cardamom A member of the ginger family, has a long history; its use has been documented as early as the fourth century B.C. It is available whole or ground. Its sweet flavor makes it a favorite spice in Danish pastries, and it is also used in cakes of all kinds and many cookies. Cardamom is the third most expensive spice in the world.

Cinnamon The bark of a laurel tree; it and its cousin cassia are the two oldest spices known. Both are available in reddish brown rolled sticks or ground. Its sweet pungent taste makes cinnamon one of our most popular spices, used in cakes, pies, cookies, breads, puddings, and other baked goods.

Cloves Cloves are the dried bud of a tropical tree. They have a strong, pungent flavor. Cloves are available both whole and ground; the ground form is used in many cakes, cookies, pies, and fruit desserts; whole cloves are occasionally used in sweets, such as baklava.

Coriander The seed of the coriander, or cilantro plant; it is available whole or ground. The ground seeds are used in cookies, cakes, pies, candies, and other sweets.

Cumin An aromatic seed very similar to caraway seeds in flavor. It is available as seeds or ground.

English spice Commercial blend of several spices with a predominately cinnamon allspice flavor. It can be used on its own or as a substitute in any baked good that calls for cinnamon, allspice, nutmeg, and cloves.

Fennel seeds These have a mild licorice flavor. They are used in breads and breakfast baked goods.

Ginger Fresh ginger, or ginger root, and the powdered, or dried spice have a hot sweet-spicy flavor. Ginger, both fresh and dried, is used in cakes, breads, cookies, and fruit desserts. Crystallized, or candied, ginger is preserved fresh zinger that has been rolled in sugar.

Mace The lacy outer rnembrane-like covering of the shell of the nutmeg. Its flavor is sweet, warm, and highly spicy. Mace is usually seen as a powder, but it is also available in flakes or blades.

Mint A perennial herb; peppermint and spearmint are the most popular varieties for flavorings. The dried leaves are available whole, crushed, and powdered.

Nutmeg The seed of the nutmeg tree. It has a sweet-hot taste and a pungent aroma. Available whole or ground, it is used in cakes, pies and cookies. (See Mace.)

Poppy seeds These have a sweet nut-like taste. The tiny black seeds are used extensively to garnish breads, rolls, and cookies.

Sesame seeds Known as benne seeds in the South, these are used to garnish breads, rolls, and cookies. When toasted, the seeds have a very nutty flavor.

Vanilla bean The seed capsule of the vanilla orchid. From this bean is

derived the flavoring used to make vanilla extract. The bean itself is used in the preparation of vanilla sugar.

Vanilla extract A liquid derived from the vanilla bean and used extensively as a flavoring in baking and cooking. Synthetic vanillas are available for a lesser price.

CHOCOLATE For our purposes, cocoa powder, unsweetened chocolate, semisweet or bittersweet chocolate, chocolate syrup, and chocolate chips are the foundations of the world of the chocolate cookie.

Unsweetened chocolate means baker's-style chocolate. Baker's-style chocolate is bitter chocolate and is the base for most other chocolate products. It can be found in the supermarket in the baking section in 14- to 16-ounce packages. The chocolate is divided into small squares, and each square weighs one ounce.

Semisweet chocolate, sometimes called bittersweet, is packaged the same way, too, but there is a wide variety of imported bittersweet or semisweet chocolate available as well.

Cocoa is the powdered form of chocolate. For baking, use unsweetened cocoa powder, not the sweet cocoa for drinking.

Milk chocolate has long been a favorite of the candy-loving public. But milk chocolate can't be used interchangeably with other types of chocolate in most recipes.

White chocolate has gained in popularity in recent years. White chocolate is not actually chocolate, because it contains no chocolate liquor. It is cocoa butter with sugar and milk added.

Many of the recipes in this book call for melting chocolate. It isn't difficult if you follow a few separate rules. Chocolate should always be melted over low heat in an absolutely dry pan. Dry is the key word. When you are melting chocolate by itself, the slightest drop of liquid or moisture can cause the chocolate to seize, or to become stiff and lumpy. (If you are adding other ingredients, the general rule of thumb is one tablespoon of liquid to one ounce of chocolate. It is the minute amounts of liquid that cause the trouble.) For this reason, the pan melting the chocolate in should never be covered because condensation may form on the lid and drip into the chocolate. If chocolate should seize, you often can save it by stirring in one teaspoon per ounce of chocolate of vegetable shortening. (Do not use butter or margarine.)

Chocolate burns easily, so using a double boiler is recommended. If you don't have one, you can put the chocolate in a heatproof cup and place it in a saucepan partially filled with water, over very low heat. (Milk chocolate should be melted at a lower temperature than unsweetened or semisweet chocolate.) Then stir the chocolate occasionally, until it is smooth

A microwave oven also works well for melting. Consult your owner's manual for instructions with your particular microwave.

MISCELLANEOUS

Candied Beads (Silver or Gold Balls) Candied beads or balls have been around for many years. They are used more for decoration, especially for holiday cookies.

Candied Citron The citron is rarely available in the United States. At a time when oranges and lemons were not readily available its peel was used in place of other members of the citrus family.

Chocolate Candies Usually the chocolate candies used in cookies are of the wafer type, such as mints or pralines.

Chocolate Chips In the early 1900s Ruth Wakefield, who worked at the The Tollhouse Inn in Massachusetts, chopped a baker's style bar of chocolate and added the pieces to a batch of cookie dough, making the first chocolate chip cookies. Because of that woman's inventiveness, a whole industry developed. In addition to semisweet chocolate chips, there are now butterscotch, peanut butter, and white chocolate used in baking.

Glacé/Candied Cherries This form of dried cherries sweetened with sugar are used diced up in cookie recipes, and as decorative toppings on cookies.

Jelly Candies Like other candies, they are used more for a decoration than for flavor. Jelly candies and gumdrops are used whole, or are chopped and added to the dough.

Jimmies These candies come in chocolate or rainbow colors, and are a great addition to many cookies.

Sugar Crystals These are sprinkled on the cookies after they have been formed and or baked. Like candy beads, they are added to a cookie strictly for decoration. They come colored or white.

FLAVORINGS Using liqueur or brandy in cookie recipes opens up a whole new world of flavoring possibilities, while keeping your costs at a minimum. Each liqueur or brandy listed below is as economical as a small 1- or 2-ounce bottle of vanilla extract. If the products are kept well-corked or capped, there is little chance of them going bad before you have time to use them. Also, most of the imitation flavoring products have

PANTRY

FROSTINGS AND ICING

Butter Cream

YIELD: 2 to 2½ cups

3½ cups powdered sugar
½ cup butter, at room temperature
⅛ teaspoon salt
1 each large egg yolk
1 tablespoon sweet milk

1. Cream the butter fluffy. Beat in the sugar, salt and egg yolk until the mixture is thick and creamy. 2. Use the milk only if needed to thin the mixture. 3. Flavor this with anyone of the following. Note: Butter cream frostings have a tendency to soften during hot weather. If this happens whip in a little cornstarch to bring the mixture back to consistency.

Vanilla Butter Cream

Add 1 teaspoon vanilla extract

Almond Butter Cream

Add 1 teaspoon almond extract or add 1 teaspoon Amaretto liqueur

Orange Butter Cream

Add 1 teaspoon orange liqueur

Lemon Butter Cream

Add 1 teaspoon lemon extract

Rum Butter Cream

Add 1 teaspoon rum

Brandy Butter Cream

Add 1 teaspoon brandy or

add 1 teaspoon cognac

Cocoa Butter Cream

Add 1 teaspoon creme de cocoa

Raspberry Butter Cream

Add 1 teaspoon raspberry liqueur

Coffee Butter Cream

Add 1 teaspoon strong coffee

Apricot Butter Cream

Add 1 teaspoon apricot brandy.

Note: For other varieties of this mixture see the section on flavorings.

Decorating Butter Cream

YIELD: 4 to 4½ cups

4 cups powdered sugar
2 cups vegetable shortening
1 to 2 large egg whites
Pinch salt
Flavoring

1. Cream the shortening until light and fluffy. 2. Slowly add the powdered sugar, salt and your choice of flavoring to taste. (Remember that a little flavoring goes a long way. Think in terms of drops, not spoonfuls.) In hot weather consider adding a little cornstarch to keep the shortening from getting to soft.

Chocolate Frosting I

YIELD: 2 to 2½ cups

½ cup Dutch process unsweetened cocoa powder

1½ cups powdered sugar

5⅓ tablespoons butter, at room temperature

3 tablespoons boiling water

Pinch salt

1. Heat the butter and beat the chocolate into it. 2. Add the salt and boiling water. 3. Beat in the cocoa powder until you have a smooth paste. 4. Continue beating and add the powdered sugar. Beat until you have the desired consistency. If it is a little thick add a few drops of water. If it is too thin add a little more powdered sugar.

Chocolate Frosting II

YIELD: 1 to 1½ cups

1½ ounces unsweetened chocolate, chopped

1 tablespoon butter, at room temperature

¼ cup sour cream

½ teaspoon vanilla extract

1½ cups powdered sugar

1. Melt the unsweetened chocolate. 2. Beat the butter and sour cream into the chocolate. 3. Add the vanilla extract. 4. Continue to beat and add the powdered sugar a little at a time. If the mixture is too thin for your needs add a little more powdered sugar. If too thick add a little water a few drops at a time.

Chocolate Frosting III

YIELD: 1 to 1¼ cups

1 cup semi-sweet chocolate chips

2 tablespoons light corn syrup

2 teaspoons strong coffee

2 teaspoons boiling water

1. Place the chocolate chips in a small bowl and pour the boiling water over the top of them. 2. Start beating and add the light corn syrup and coffee. If the mix is a little thick add a little more boiling water, a few drops at a time. If a little thin add a little powdered sugar.

Dark Chocolate Icing

YIELD: 1 to 1½ cups

2 cups powdered sugar

6 ounces unsweetened chocolate, grated

2 tablespoons butter, at room temperature

1 teaspoon vanilla extract

⅛ teaspoon salt

⅓ cup sweet milk

1. Melt the chocolate in the top of a double boiler. 2. Add the butter, vanilla and salt. 3. Beat in the sugar using a wooden spoon. 4. Add only enough milk to make a spreadable frosting.

Vanilla Icing

YIELD: about ½ cup

½ cup powdered sugar

1 tablespoon water

Put the powdered sugar in a bowl. Beat in the water and continue beating until the icing reaches the desired consistency. If the icing is too think, add more water, if too thin, add more powdered sugar.

Vanilla Frosting

also known as white sugar icing

YIELD: 2 to 2¼ cups

3 cups powdered sugar

1½ teaspoons vanilla extract

5 tablespoons evaporated milk

1. Place the milk and vanilla extract in a bowl with 1 cup of powdered sugar. 2. Start to beat vigorously. 3. Add the remaining powdered sugar a little at a time until you get to the desired consistency.

Green Crème de Menthe Icing

YIELD: 2 to 2¼ cups

Use the same ingredients as in Vanilla Frosting, except replace the vanilla extract with 1½ teaspoons green crème de menthe liqueur, and follow the same instructions.

Lemon Sugar Icing

YIELD: about ½ cup

½ cup powdered sugar

1 teaspoon fresh lemon juice

1 tablespoon water

Put the powdered sugar in a small bowl. Beat in the lemon juice and water and continue beating until the icing reaches the desired consistency. If the icing is too thick, add more water, if it is too thin add more powdered sugar.

Baking notes: For a tarter lemon taste, use lemon extract in place of the lemon juice.

FILLINGS

Almond Cream Filling: Boil together 1½ cups of heavy cream, 1 cup powdered sugar, and 1 cup finely ground almonds. Stir constantly until the mixture is reduced to about 2 cups. Off the heat add 2 tablespoons of Amaretto liqueur.

Chocolate Cheesecake Filling: Blend together 16 ounces of cream cheese, 3/4 cup cocoa powder, ½ cup white granulated sugar, 4 large whole eggs, and 2 tablespoons of chocolate syrup.

Chopped Apple Filling: Peel, core and slice 5 apples. Place them in a saucepan with just enough water to cover them completely. Boil until they are soft. Drain and mash by hand. (Do not use a food processor or blender.) Add 1 tablespoon grated lemon peel, 1 tablespoon lemon juice, ⅛ teaspoon nutmeg, ½ cup powdered sugar and 2 tablespoons Amaretto liqueur. Work all of this together until well blended.

Coconut Pecan Filling: Combine 1 cup evaporated milk, 3 large egg yolks, ½ cup vegetable shortening, 1 cup white granulated sugar and 1 teaspoon coconut flavoring together. Heat this mixture slowly until the mixture thickens, 10 to 12 minutes usually. Remove from the heat and add 1 cup flaked coconut and 1 cup finely chopped pecans.

Lemon Filling: Beat 4 eggs. Add 2 cups white granulated sugar and beat until thick and light colored. Add 1 teaspoon grated lemon rind, 6 tablespoon of lemon juice concentrate and ⅓ cup of all purpose flour. (This mixture is to be poured over a baked crust and then baked until set and firm to the touch.)

Pumpkin Cheesecake Filling: Blend together 11 ounces of cream cheese, 16 ounces of pumpkin, 3 large whole eggs, ⅔ cup of white granulated sugar, 1½ teaspoon ground cinnamon, 1 teaspoon ground ginger and 1 teaspoon of your favorite flavoring.

Vanilla Sugar: Rinse the vanilla bean in cold water. Dry thoroughly between two sheets of paper towels. Place it in a pint jar with 1½ to 2 cups of white granulated sugar. Let stand a few day, shaking several times during the down period.

BAR COOKIE CRUSTS

Here are twenty-one ideas for bar cookie crusts. (These are to be spread or patted into the bottom of a baking pan and partially baked before a topping or filling is spread over the crust and baked until done.) But, in fact, these will provide you with ideas for dozens of crusts. Any of these combinations can be varied according to your personal taste. For example, in a recipe that calls for all-purpose flour, you could substitute whole wheat flour, rice flour, or even buckwheat flour for some (usually no ore than about a quarter) of the white flour. Or use vegetable shortening in place of butter in a crust. Or replace granulated sugar with brown sugar or raw sugar. Use your favorite nuts in any nut crust, or your favorite cookies in a crumb crust. And of course you can also change the flavoring, substituting another extract for vanilla, and adding a liqueur for example.

Use your imagination, but do keep one guideline in mind. If you are changing the crust in a favorite recipe, be sure to replace it with a similar crust, one that "matches" the filling or topping as in the original recipe. A filling that is very runny before it is baked needs the right kind of crust to support the unbaked filling. A crust that takes a long time to bake will not be cooked through if it is combined with a topping that takes only minutes to bake. Keep baking times in mind when you are experimenting. And have fun!

See Bar Cookies in the text for basic procedures for combining particular ingredients to make a crust.

1

1 cup all-purpose flour
½ cup powdered sugar
6 tablespoons butter
1 tablespoon heavy cream

2

3 cups all-purpose flour
1 cup white granulated sugar
1 cup butter
4 large whole egg yolks
2 large whole egg whites
½ teaspoon salt

3

16 graham crackers, crushed
½ cup white granulated sugar
¼ cup butter

4

1 cup all-purpose flour
¾ cup white granulated sugar
½ cup butter
⅓ cup fresh milk
1 large whole egg
¾ teaspoon Amaretto

5

1 cup all-purpose flour
¼ teaspoon salt
½ cup butter

6

24 gingersnap cookies, crushed
¼ cup powdered sugar
½ cup canola oil

7

2 cups all-purpose flour
¼ cup white granulated sugar
½ cup butter
¼ cup walnuts, ground fine

8

1½ cups whole wheat flour
¾ teaspoon butter
2 tablespoons white granulated sugar

9

1¼ cups all-purpose flour
½ cup vegetable shortening
¼ teaspoon salt
3 tablespoons ice cold water

10

1 cup all-purpose flour
½ cup powdered sugar
½ cup butter
½ cup coconut, shredded
¼ teaspoon salt

11

1½ cups all-purpose flour
⅔ cup white granulated sugar
½ cup butter
3 large whole egg yolks
2 tablespoons fresh milk

12

1⅓ cups all-purpose flour
½ cup light brown sugar
⅓ cup butter
½ teaspoon baking powder
½ cup almonds, chopped

13

2 cups all-purpose flour
3 tablespoons powdered sugar
2 large whole egg yolks
1 teaspoon instant coffee crystals
1 tablespoon water

14

1⅓ cup gingersnap cookies, crushed
¼ cup light brown sugar
2 tablespoons butter
3½ ounces macadamia nuts, ground fine
1½ teaspoon ginger, crystallized, chopped

15

1 cup all-purpose flour
¼ cup light brown sugar
6 tablespoons butter
½ cup pecans, chopped fine
¼ teaspoon salt

16

1⅓ cup all-purpose flour
½ cup light brown sugar
⅓ cup butter
½ teaspoon baking powder
¼ cup hazelnuts, ground fine

17

1 cup all-purpose flour
½ cup light brown sugar
½ cup butter
¼ teaspoon ground cloves
½ teaspoon ground ginger
¼ teaspoon ground nutmeg

18

1½ cups all-purpose flour
½ cup butter
¼ teaspoon salt
2½ tablespoon warm water

19

2 cups all-purpose flour
¼ cup white granulated sugar
½ cup butter
½ cup walnuts, ground fine

20

2 cups all-purpose flour
2 cups light brown sugar
1 cup butter